A Culture of Justice

SUNY series in American Philosophy and Cultural Thought

———————

Randall E. Auxier and John R. Shook, editors

A Culture of Justice

Eric Thomas Weber

EU GPSR Authorised Representative:
Logos Europe, 9 rue Nicolas Poussin, 17000, La Rochelle, France
contact@logoseurope.eu

For information, contact State University of New York Press, Albany, NY
www.sunypress.edu

Library of Congress Cataloging-in-Publication Data

Name: Weber, Eric Thomas, author.
Title: A culture of justice / Eric Thomas Weber.
Description: Albany : State University of New York Press, [2026]. | Series: SUNY series in American philosophy and cultural thought | Includes bibliographical references and index.
Identifiers: LCCN 2025023488 | ISBN 9798855805291 (hardcover : alk. paper) | ISBN 9798855805314 (epub) | ISBN 9798855806878 (PDF) | ISBN 9798855805307 (pbk. : alk. paper)
Subjects: LCSH: Dewey, John, 1859–1952. | Rawls, John, 1921–2002. | Justice (Philosophy). | Political culture. | Political science—Philosophy.
Classification: LCC B105.J87 W43 2025
LC record available at https://lccn.loc.gov/2025023488

Contents

Acknowledgments

Since I began working on this book more than ten years ago, I have many people to thank for their encouragement, support, and insight.

My students and colleagues at the University of Kentucky are a constant source of intellectual stimulation and inspiration for me. I am especially grateful to John Thelin, my senior mentor in the department of Educational Policy Studies and Evaluation, for his invigorating collaborations, the example he embodies as a publicly engaged scholar, and his encouragement upon reading chapters of this book.

John Dewey saw formal education as the intelligent transmission of culture, and given the importance of his thought for my work, I could not be more fortunate to have as a mentor the great Dewey scholar and philosopher of technology Larry A. Hickman. When I struggled with a key consideration for chapter 7, on the freedom of speech, Larry and Tom Alexander, another of my former professors and a top authority on Dewey's work, guided me. Each of them took the time to consider my questions carefully and offered confirming and mutually supportive indications that were pivotal to my understanding and ultimate argument.

It is a blessing to have a mentor in life, but I have been fortunate enough to have two. John Lachs's work features prominently in several chapters of this book. John was an example for me since my undergraduate days. When I had the opportunity to comment on his work in 2015, I jumped at the chance and found deep inspiration about how to keep one's head while fighting for justice and encountering only slow or modest progress. I know few people who have been as lucky as I have been to be able to talk with a deeply caring and irrepressibly funny friend and mentor on a monthly basis for years. John is missed profoundly, but his ideas remain and inspire me and others. I can think of no greater honor in John's own estimation than to engage with his ideas and to think about how philosophy can make life better.

Along the way as I worked on this project, a number of friends and colleagues taught me a great deal. Among them, for example, was Leonard Harris at Purdue University, who kindly attended my talk there on the essay that became chapter 5. Leonard recommended I build on Alain Locke, an excellent resource and underappreciated philosophical Pragmatist. Nicholas Tampio of Fordham University has been a great inspiration as a publicly engaged scholar and critic of the Common Core curriculum development in American schools. He has encouraged my applications of Deweyan insights and has contributed richly to increasing access to Dewey's work.

Few friends and colleagues have opened my eyes as widely as has Tommy Curry of the University of Edinburgh. In addition to being another terrific example of a prolific and publicly engaged scholar, Tommy introduced me to many resources and scholars who have not historically been included in standard curricular instruction of the history of philosophy. Tommy's insights have been invaluable in teaching me about Derrick Bell, legal scholarship on the First Amendment, and his own powerful scholarship that challenges unquestioned assumptions about gender and race.

Before I moved to the University of Kentucky, colleagues at the University of Mississippi had already taught me a great deal and supported my work on this book. Among them, Bob Haws was the ideal department chair who could not have done more to support me. In addition to all of his encouragement, Bob inspired me in questions about the University of Mississippi Creed, questioning whether or not a public university should have such a statement. While I have come to value such statements, Bob raised the important questions that got my mind racing at the time.

Also at the University of Mississippi at the time, Jack Nowlin engaged with me and colleagues around the university to establish collaborations, which included making me an affiliated faculty member in the School of Law. Jack also taught me about the idea important in chapter 7 concerning the difference between seditious speech that is persuasive versus that which is not, a concept that turns out to be important to my claim in that chapter.

Over the past decade, I have presented papers that were turned into chapters of this book at a number of conferences, where feedback for me was invaluable. For a number of engaging experiences giving talks and receiving enormously helpful feedback, I am grateful to Tommy Curry, who was at Texas A&M University at the time; Andrea Christelle, who was at Northern Arizona University at the time; Kyle Whyte who was at Michigan State University at the time; John Stuhr of Emory University and the American Philosophies Forum; and Ed Halper at the University of Georgia. I am grateful to the Southeastern Conference (S.E.C.) for a travel grant they awarded me to support collaborations between S.E.C. institutions. Chris Skowronski of the Berlin Practical Philosophy International Forum was also instrumental for me in inviting me to reflect on John Lachs's work, for which purpose I drafted one of the essays that became part of chapter 4.

Next, I was deeply fortunate to be selected to give the Ron Messerich Distinguished Lecture at Eastern Kentucky University in 2019, where I first presented my essay on "Correcting Political Correctness," which became chapter 8 of this book. Then Dina Mendonça of the Universidad Nova de Lisboa, Portugal, was a wonderful host and commentator on my talk in 2022 for IFILNOVA, the Nova Institute of Philosophy in Lisbon. Attendees offered rich thoughts and insights for me to consider regarding the essay that became chapter 7, on the freedom of speech.

Randy Auxier and John Shook deserve my thanks also both as teachers and mentors and as scholars who have created a much-needed forum for thought about American philosophy and culture, as evident in this book series and in the American Institute of Philosophical and Cultural Thought.

At the University of Kentucky, one of the "research priority areas" that the institution established is titled "United in True Racial Equity." I am most grateful to that initiative and to the university for awarding me a grant in support of the publication of this work, given my aim of rendering the book as affordable and accessible as I can. I am also grateful to the department of Educational Policy Studies and Evaluation and to doctoral candidate Brett Wolff, whom the department awarded a Martin Fellowship for the creation of the index for this book.

The Pew Research Center deserves my thanks also for permission to republish the chart that I include in the introduction, on political typology. In addition, I am grateful to the editors and publishers of several journals and an edited book for their permission to republish essays and material that were converted into chapters of this book. An earlier version of chapter 1, "Justice as an Evolving Regulative Ideal," was originally published in *Pragmatism Today* 6, no. 2 (2015): 105–16, http://www.pragmatismtoday.eu/winter2015/10%20Weber.pdf. An earlier version of chapter 2, "Converging on Culture," was originally published as "Converging on Culture: Rawls, Rorty, and Dewey on Culture's Role in Justice," *Essays in the Philosophy of Humanism* 22, no. 2 (2014): 231–61. Chapter 4 was originally published as two separate essays, which were revised and edited into the one chapter together. They were first published as Eric Thomas Weber, "Self-Respect, Positive Power, and Stoic Pragmatism: Rawls, Dewey, and Lachs on Justice and Happiness," in *John Lachs's Practical Philosophy: Critical Essays on His Thought with Replies and Bibliography*, ed. Krzysztof Piotr Skowroski (Netherlands: Brill Publishers, 2018), 182–96, and Eric Thomas Weber, "Self-Respect and a Sense of Positive Power: On Protection, Self-Affirmation, and Harm in the Charge of 'Acting White,'" *Journal of Speculative Philosophy* 30, no. 1 (2016): 45–63. Last, chapter 8, "Correcting Political Correctness," was drawn from a short essay first published in *The Philosopher's Magazine* in 2016. I am grateful to all of the publishers of these previous versions of the chapters for their permission to use the work in various forms in this volume.

For all of my projects, I owe gratitude to my parents, Collin and Dominique Weber, who have encouraged me and offered unwavering support at every step of my career. And finally, this work and others I have released have been improved profoundly with the help and careful, critical eye of Tibor Solymosi, a terrific colleague and friend, who offered tough yet encouraging feedback on drafts of this project.

Altogether, I have been enormously fortunate to have had a great deal of support as I have worked in a rewarding and joyous profession. Given that, I believe I and others have an obligation to make use of these many resources and good fortunes to call attention to and advocate for a wiser and more humane world. In this respect, I owe John Lachs perhaps most for embodying such aims and for offering himself as an example for others to follow.

I therefore dedicate this book to John, who is sorely missed, though he continues to inspire me every day.

Introduction

In February 2014, on a friend's recommendation, a young African American undergraduate student at the University of Mississippi came to my office to talk. She began to cry as we sat down. She told me that she did not know if she could stay at the university after the recent incident, in which freshman Graeme Phillip Harris and two of his friends had hung a noose and an old Georgia flag, two-thirds of which feature the Confederate battle flag emblem, on the statue of James Meredith.[1] Meredith was the first African American student to integrate the university. The young woman said that she didn't feel safe, that she didn't know if it was the right thing for her to stay.

We discussed her situation and some ways of thinking about her future and options. Harris's and his friends' actions made her feel threatened. She was afraid. A noose around the symbol of a man who integrated the university appeared to her to be a threat to her and people like her.

The day after her visit, I read an op-ed in the *Huffington Post* by Geoffrey R. Stone of the University of Chicago Law School, author of *Perilous Times: Free Speech in Wartime*.[2] Stone argued that the act, while "deeply disrespectful and hateful," did "not *quite* fit the conventional definition of a 'threat.'" Threats, he explained, "must not just put people in fear, but must (a) be directed at specific individuals and (b) be unambiguous."[3]

My sense was that either Stone was wrong or the law is.[4] The language of "specific individuals" fails to account for the idea that threats can be made to groups. The criterion that threats be unambiguous, furthermore, appeared to me to be met with the implication that persons of said target groups would be hanged, killed. If the past precedents failed to appreciate how reasonable it is for black students to feel their lives are in danger of threats of racial violence when a noose is draped over a symbol of the man who integrated the university, then something is profoundly wrong with the policy or its interpreters are tone-deaf. Just three years earlier, white twenty-one-year-old Deryl Dedmon murdered African American James Craig Anderson in Jackson, Mississippi, by driving over the victim with the assailant's truck on a late-night spree of racial harassment that followed a pattern of racially motivated attacks on African Americans.[5]

It was some relief for me to learn that Harris "pleaded guilty," albeit to a misdemeanor charge[6] of "using a threat of force to intimidate African-American students and employees."[7] A scholar I spoke with on the matter who works for an organization that offers grants for research on free speech issues told me that in his view Harris "just had a bad lawyer." Harris's friend, Austin Reed Edenfield, also pleaded guilty to the same charge, however, and admitted "that he knew the rope and flag would be threatening and intimidating to black students," according to the *New York Times*.[8] Defenses of Harris's and Edenfield's speech rights felt to me tragically unappreciative of the palpability of real threats to others' safety.

A racially motivated threat like the one Harris and his friends presented is an extreme and stark example of the kind of problem I aim to address in this book. Far subtler concerns about culture show the range of problem that I would refer to as cultural, which can impede justice. The opposite extreme is evident in the less obviously defensible calls for "political correctness," in which a demand for cultural sensitivity might be thought to be unrealistic. James Taranto raised criticisms of the University of New Hampshire's "Bias-Free Language Guide," for example, which was said to have called terms like "American," "homosexual," and "foreigners" "problematic."[9] Famed historian of education Diane Ravitch has argued in her book *The Language Police* that "an elaborate, well-established protocol of beneficent censorship [has been] quietly endorsed and broadly implemented by textbook publishers, testing agencies, professional associations, states, and the federal government."[10] The harshest critic of this trend has perhaps been former presidential candidate Ben Carson, who has argued that "political correctness" is "going to destroy our nation."[11] He continued on to say that "I think this whole concept of political correctness—you can say this, you can't say that, you can't repeat what someone said—it's total foolishness, and it's going to destroy our nation and we need to be more mature than that."[12]

In these two examples we see the range of worries about culture. Of course, if one thinks that Carson is unconcerned about the role of culture in justice, I would argue that in fact he is attentive to the need for freedom of expression and for a kind of reaction to cultural differences. In calling for less emphasis placed on things like word choice or the value or weight of symbols, he is in fact advocating for a kind of culture too. In that sense, then, the first and overarching premise of this book is broadly accepted, namely that culture can inhibit or enable the pursuit of justice. Andrew Kernohan defended this view, furthermore, as well as some additional claims with which I agree and on which I draw in this project, in his book *Liberalism, Equality, and Cultural Oppression*.[13]

In between the direct and palpable cases of threats and the subtler matters of language, offensiveness, and word choice in textbooks, we can find troubling cases in which flags have been matters of debate.

In Louisiana, the American Civil Liberties Union (ACLU) argued in 2011 that a black defendant in a capital case could not expect a fair trial in a courthouse over which the Confederate battle flag was flying.[14] Denny LeBoeuf, director of the ACLU Capital Punishment Project, argued that "Flying the flag outside the courthouse only risks diminishing the trust of African-Americans[15] in the criminal justice system and priming white jurors to view African-American defendants and victims as second-class citizens. Removing the flag brings us one step closer to justice." According to a November 2011 press release by the ACLU, "Caddo Parish commissioners voted 11-1 . . . to take down the flag, which was raised outside the Caddo Parish Courthouse in 1951 as an act of resistance to the civic and civil rights advances of African-Americans."[16] The argument that defendants in a death penalty case could not expect a fair trial in a courthouse over which the Confederate Battle flag was flying proved motivating for all but Commissioner Doug Dominick, the "sole vote against the resolution."[17]

At the time, news on the matter only vaguely referenced supporters' motivations for keeping the flag. According to reporter Jeff Ferrell, "Supporters argue the flag became a symbol of southern heritage and a monument to all those who died in the Civil War."[18] While the Louisiana Supreme Court did not compel the parish to take down the flag, in its opinion the court wrote that "It is not an irrational inference that one who displays the Confederate Flag may harbor racist bias against African Americans."[19] Commissioner Dominick was more vocal about his reasoning later, as the same parish voted to remove also the Confederate monument outside the courthouse. He explained his belief in 2017 that the matter should be put to a public vote in the then-forthcoming special election,[20] a way of defending the monument on democratic grounds of popularity rather than on any kind of denial that it does harm. The move is a common red herring against progressive or anti-racist causes, especially in the South,[21] as it ignores the claim of harm or wrongdoing or assumes the matter in question to be defensible if popular. Democratic popularity is a value, to be sure, but within the limits of the protection of minority rights. According to the *Shreveport Times*, Dominick also argued that the United Daughters of the Confederacy "probably will sue if the commission votes for removal. He said he's concerned about the cost of litigation."[22] Defenders of Confederate monuments and symbols often appeal to democratic reasoning in their defense, despite the radically undemocratic meanings the artifacts in question communicate. Fortunately, in Louisiana's 2011 flag conflict eleven of the remaining commissioners were persuaded, and, for the sake of justice, a flag was taken down.

A few years later, Dylann Roof murdered nine members of the African Methodist Episcopal (AME) Church in Charleston, South Carolina.[23] Photos of him burning an American flag and waving a Confederate battle flag in pride emerged.[24] Soon after, in cities around the South protests erupted, calling for taking down such flags from public grounds.[25] In July 2015, South Carolina Governor Nikki Haley signed a bill removing the Confederate flag from the state capitol.[26] Alabama Governor Robert Bentley similarly ordered the Confederate flag to be taken down from the capitol building in Montgomery, Alabama.[27] I wrote an op-ed at the time calling for the state of Mississippi to change its flag, which featured an emblem of the Confederate battle flag in its canton.[28] Leaders of the Black Student Union at the University of Mississippi called the university to take down the state flag, a complicated matter, as the school is a state institution and such institutions are expected to fly the state flag. Changing the state flag requires a vote of the legislature, furthermore, and many people told me the state would never change the flag. Students in my classes asked me why a flag matters. What is the big deal about a piece of cloth? These concerns appeared to echo the kinds of worries that Ben Carson has been voicing for some time.

That July, I published an op-ed on "What a Flag Has to Do with Justice," as I had begun research and sketches for this book the year before.[29] Over the course of a remarkable semester, in which student leaders organized a variety of efforts to change the culture, including a strangely riveting meeting of the Associated Student Body,[30] the university was convinced to take down the flag.[31] Some students in my classroom continued to struggle to appreciate why the flag removal mattered, until the Ku Klux Klan organized a protest of the flag removal.[32] In response to the Klan's protest, students organized a counterprotest called "Turn Your Back on Hate." Every one of my most skeptical students participated in the counterprotest and felt quite confident of the importance of taking down the state flag. The governor of Mississippi at the time said that "college students react a lot emotionally," to which I responded in *The Clarion Ledger* that the "Students' Flag Request Was 'Emotional' but Courageous."[33] After all, Plato understood courage to be a matter of fearing the right things and not the wrong things, and as such, that virtue is indeed a matter of emotion, intelligently guided by wisdom, moderation, and justice.[34]

Some people, including me, take the Caddo Parish's and the University of Mississippi's decisions to lower their flags as important steps toward justice. It is not only a number of white Southerners who question such a judgment, however. My eyes were opened by a thoughtful and kind African American friend in Mississippi, Joanna Henderson,[35] when the students at the university called for the state flag to be taken down. My friend surprised me at the time when we talked about the state flag. "I don't care if you take down the flag but don't change what's in people's hearts," she said to me. I was taken aback, because she was absolutely right, yet taking down the flags and moving Confederate monuments were clearly to my mind the right things to do. Mike Williams of the Sons of Confederate Veterans made the same argument about Alabama's move to take down the flag. Regarding Alabama Governor Bentley's order to take down Confederate battle flags from the capitol following Roof's 2015 mass murders in Charleston, Williams argued that "If you don't change people's hearts, changing a flag won't do anything toward racism."[36]

Serious court battles can be fought, and victories sometimes won with great effort, yet they can also at times reasonably seem only cosmetic, superficial. My friend was not wrong, but the weight of her point was both right and devastating. It is conceivable to take a flag down or move a statue to a museum. Metaphorically, one can understand the idea of a person's heart changing, but how to make it happen, and not just for one person but for a whole community and culture seems so heavy a task as to be impossible. Just because a symbol is removed or disallowed forcefully does not mean that people have changed. If flags are removed begrudgingly, furthermore, resentment grows and so do its consequences. What matters is what is in people's hearts, she pointed out to me, not merely what symbol adorns a flagpole or building.

Even while appreciating my friend's point, it is also true that cultures change a step at a time. When students express cynicism about the potential for progress, I find that they see value in looking to analogous examples of profound cultural change. In my lifetime, American culture has shifted radically with regard to respect for persons in same-sex relationships.[37] In the 1980s, Eddie Murphy made audiences laugh uproariously at humor about homosexuals, using the epithet "faggot."[38] Such language seems striking to people today, and is referred to as "the f-slur."[39] In 1998, Matthew Shepard's murder raised calls for hate crimes legislation, which resulted eleven years later in the passage of the Matthew Shepard and James Byrd Jr. Hate Crimes Prevention Act of 2009.[40] In addition to hate crimes legislation, change has come for marriage equality, partner benefits, and so much more.[41] I can think of few other examples of so dramatic a cultural shift as the one I have been witness to in one generation, yet it suggests the potential for progress in other areas with effort and persistence. It is worth noting, however, that the march of progress includes periods of backstepping, as well as question raising, such as in US Supreme Court reversals,[42] in the potential for them,[43] and in questions for and concerning transgendered persons.[44]

I recall countless times being told that Mississippi will never change its flag. It was put to a vote in 2001, at which point more than 64 percent of voters chose to keep the Confederate battle flag emblem in the state flag's canton.[45] Nevertheless, in 2020, a few months after the police murder of George Floyd, the Mississippi legislature voted to change the state flag[46] and put a referendum to the people for the approval of the new Magnolia flag, which has been flying since 2021.[47]

For a time, George Floyd's murder[48] moved Americans, and people sought solutions to the nation's racial problems through education.[49] Unsurprisingly, a countermovement has emerged swiftly,[50] in which more than seventy bills were advanced in state legislatures calling for a ban on the incorporation of critical race theory in public school curricula and higher education.[51] There are countless spheres in which culture is a matter of debate and challenge, but few are as intense as in education. As I explain in the pages that follow, culture, which I understand as the set of symbols, languages, beliefs, practices, and institutions passed down from one generation to the next,[52] is of especially great importance in education. The great philosopher of education John Dewey saw education essentially as the transmission of culture, and good, democratic education as its empowering, intelligent, and humane transmission.[53] The transmission of culture must not be superficial, yet in countless ways we see, debate, and champion the need for the right symbols, language, beliefs, and practices for the sake of more just institutions and a more just society.

My friend was right that what matters ultimately is what is in people's hearts, but the places of pride in society should be reserved for messages and symbols that are the right ones to champion. People may be upset or change reluctantly, but our public spaces speak[54] and can be forces for progress or regress. All people should be enabled to feel that they can have a fair trial in court and that their institutions of higher education see them as equal citizens and students. These matters can be addressed, furthermore, while at the same time we work to address the further and related structures attached to inequalities and injustices, such that our practices, policies, and institutions live up to our words, expectations, and ideals.

These examples and challenges presented so far illustrate the form of the problem at the heart of this book, rooted in the first premise mentioned above. It is that culture can enable or inhibit the pursuit of justice. As such, the fundamental argument of this book is a call for the right kind of culture necessary for justice. The next section presents the scholarly philosophical context in which my argument is situated, and then presents the argument of the book.

Philosophical Context and the Argument

As a philosopher, I am indebted especially to the work of John Dewey, from whom I derive the central value of starting one's philosophical thinking with real-life problems, and of drawing on one's own experience. That explains my emphasis on matters of race and Confederate symbols in the opening of this chapter and in the book as a whole. I grew up in the North and then the South, and later moved to teach at the University of Mississippi, a hub of conflict between efforts for racial progress and corresponding resistance. I have also grown concerned about how the democratizing power of social media tools, developed during my lifetime, can be manipulated in dangerous ways to influence culture, especially in a nation that has decided that "money is speech."[55] Social media tools have empowered some people to grow their communities, but they have also enabled others bent on spreading distrust and hatred, rendering questions of culture all the more important.

Differences in culture have felt palpable at a number of times in my life, and when I studied Dewey, I found a thinker attentive to the power of such forces. Dewey thought it important to cut through the complexity of one's culture, to get at the roots of problems, and to apply philosophical clarity and insight. In his 1947 essay on "The Future of Philosophy," he writes that

> My standpoint is that philosophy deals with cultural problems. The principal task of philosophy is to get below the turmoil that is particularly conspicuous in times of rapid cultural change, to get behind what appears on the surface, to get to the soil in which a given culture has its roots. The business of philosophy is the relation that [people have] to the world in which [they live,] as far as both [people] and the world are affected by culture, which is very much more than is usually thought.[56]

In the context of Dewey's outlook here, it is sensible to begin with an important distinction when talking about culture. For one version of the term considers a certain sense of the word as found in the idea of "high culture," as being elevated. Being cultured in that sense refers to a kind of development, perhaps of enlightenment, or of empowerment to appreciate finer aspects of art and beauty. This sense of culture may sound especially European or colonialist, but is not meant in that way in the works of the African American fellow pragmatist Alain Locke.

In his essay "The Ethics of Culture," Locke argues, "In my judgment, the highest intellectual duty is the duty to be cultured." He continues, "Quite unfortunately, it seems, duty toward the beautiful and the cultural is very generally ignored, and certainly, beauty as a motive has been taken out of morality, so that we confront beautiless duty and dutiless beauty. In an issue like this, it behooves education to try to restore the lapsing ideals of humanism, and to center more vitally in education the duty to be cultured."[57] The sense Locke gives here to culture is one that philosophers call normative, virtuous, or prescriptive, the sort of thing that is the right target of human aspirations. Locke's understanding, at least in this passage,[58] is to be contrasted with a conception of culture that is merely descriptive, the sense of the term that sees culture in societies as something inevitable, but which can take forms that could be morally better or worse, oppressive and harmful versus freeing and empowering.

On the one hand, the general sense of the term "culture" with which I begin this project is the descriptive sense; nevertheless, my point overall is to argue for a certain aim for culture, one that enables justice. My thesis is aspirational, therefore, in the way that Locke understands culture to be. In addition, Locke's thought was influential in the development of the Harlem Renaissance movement, which itself provides a rich and important point of emphasis for the discussion about self-respect that I develop in the argument of this book. For Locke's point of view did not call black Americans to accept and adopt European values and colonialist tropes about culture. Rather, the Harlem Renaissance was about appreciating the beauty and originality of black culture in America and its power to effect a cultural revolution.[59] In short, while many political philosophers think about oppressed, disadvantaged, and impoverished people as victims, thinkers like Locke show the ways in which self-culture is possible and desirable, even when presented differently from the norms to which dominant groups are accustomed. This point is important for understanding and explaining how and why the argument of this book differs from past contributions that have attended to the force of culture in justice.

Perhaps the most important consonance here between Locke and Dewey on the issue of culture is how thoroughly central both took the importance of education to be in its development. In the essay, Locke continues:

> I speak to a group that has already chosen to be educated. I congratulate you upon that choice. Though you have so chosen for many motives and with very diverse reasons and purposes, I fear that education for most of you means, in last practical analysis, the necessary hardship that is involved in preparing to earn a better living, perhaps an easier living. It is just such narrowing and truncating of the conception of education, that the ideals and motives of culture are effective to remove or prevent. Education should not be so narrowly construed, for in the best sense, and indeed in the most practical sense, it means not only the fitting of the man to earn his living, but to live and to live well. It is just this latter and higher function of education, the art of living well, or, if I may so express it, of living up to the best, that the word *culture* connotes and represents.[60]

For reasons such as these, Locke and Dewey both saw education to be of supreme social and personal importance, in contrast with later liberal philosophers, who believe that the state should intrude minimally on culture for the sake of noninterference in people's lives.

Much political philosophy of the last seventy years has avoided talk about education. Indeed, among the most influential liberal philosophers of the last half-century was John Rawls, and he had surprisingly little to say about education. Inattention to education appears strange, furthermore, given how powerfully important he took matters of culture to be. To his credit, in *A Theory of Justice*, he wrote that "the value of education should not be assessed solely in terms of economic efficiency and social welfare. Equally if not more important is the role of education in enabling a person to enjoy the culture of his [their[61]] society and to take part in its affairs, and in this way to provide for each individual a secure sense of his or her [or their] own worth."[62] We see consonance here in this passing moment of Rawls's argument. And the sense of a person's worth is seen to be of profound importance, perhaps of the greatest importance for justice. He continues, arguing that

> perhaps the most important primary good is that of self-respect . . . We may define self-respect (or self-esteem) as having two aspects. First of all, as we noted earlier, it includes a person's sense of his [sic] own value, his secure conviction that his conception of his good, his plan of life, is worth carrying out. And second, self-respect implies a confidence in one's ability, so far as it is within one's power, to fulfill one's intentions. When we feel that our plans are of little value, we cannot pursue them with pleasure or take delight in their execution. Nor plagued by failure and self-doubt can we continue in our endeavors. It is clear, then, why self-respect is a primary good. Without it nothing may seem worth doing, or if some things have value for us, we lack the will to strive for them. All desire and activity become empty and vain, and we sink into apathy and cynicism. . . . *[Thus, we must] avoid at almost any cost the social conditions that undermine self-respect.*[63]

It is important to ask oneself at this point what kinds of conditions can undermine self-respect, if not some that we might call cultural. Consider the case of the person who is said to be unable to expect a fair trial in a courthouse over which the Confederate battle flag is flying.

Rawls's claim about the vital role of self-respect for justice as I am discussing it is drawn from his early work *A Theory of Justice*, before his next major contribution, *Political Liberalism*.[64] In that later book, he argued it is a fact that there can be many cultures that are different and reasonable, such that people can freely live in different ways that meet expectations of justice. Given that, freedom to embody one's culture can lead to disagreements and clashes with others' cultures, but such freedom should be protected so long as the exercise of one's cultural norms does not harm other people, a central norm of traditional liberalism. There can be as a result various moral and religious doctrines that are irreconcilable yet each reasonable on its own account, according to Rawls. For that reason, Rawls's later work sought to focus only on a political conception of justice, rather than one rooted in any specific culture within a broader whole. "For Rawls," as Joshua Forstenzer clarifies, "the fact of reasonable pluralism entails that the only legitimate ideal for settling debates about constitutional arrangements and matters of basic justice is a political conception of justice which can be the object of an overlapping consensus among all reasonable citizens."[65]

Over the course of writing this book, one reviewer claimed that one cannot call for a certain kind of culture in the way that this book does precisely because of the "fact of reasonable pluralism." I disagree for two reasons. The first reason for disagreement is the presumption in the language and theory of "the fact of reasonable pluralism"—that conflicts cannot be reconciled even though the different beliefs and persons in question are reasonable. If philosophers seek to avoid unnecessary assumptions, as is a common expectation, then we must not assume that differences are irreconcilable when persons and beliefs are reasonable. Religious doctrines, among others, change or are reinterpreted, and it should not be assumed in advance that reconciliation is impossible.[66]

The second reason I disagree about the potential challenge is that cultures together create a larger culture in, with, and through which they all transact and influence each other. That larger, shared context is the sphere of culture with which I am concerned. Rawls's claim that the justifications must be political does not change the fact that the enveloping unity to which such arguments apply is nevertheless an overarching culture, transacting with the many cultures within it. An apt metaphor here is the tapestry, in which many different threads make up the whole. There is no limit to the number of layers of culture, yet they make up a unity, which itself can be the locus of demands for justice.[67] The tapestry metaphor suggests that the process of addressing conflicts of culture is akin to sorting out the tensions in the different threads that make up the tapestry. In addition, the incorporation of different threads enriches the tapestry, and the combination of strings in balance yields greater strength as a whole than any individual strand on its own. Given these considerations, it is vital for people to theorize about how and why there are or should be limitations to what is acceptable for justice in the various cultural interactions of diverse societies. The complexity of the topic here calls for clarification of the numerous premises that together lead to the central claim of this work, a task to which I turn now.

The first premise of the argument of this book has been mentioned already, but is repeated here, where I highlight each moving forward, one at a time.

Premise 1: Culture can enable or inhibit the pursuit of justice.

The literature has attended too little to Rawls's distinction about what he calls the two facets of self-respect. One aspect of his point concerns a sense of a person's own value, but the other concerns their confidence that one's plan of life is within one's power to pursue. That aspect of Rawls's concerns is lumped into the term "self-respect," but could not a person who is perfectly self-respecting live in an unjust society in which they are given little cause to believe that their plan of life is within their ability to pursue? When I see a four-ton boulder, I know from experience that it would be absurd for me to consider lifting it up straight with my arms, legs, and back alone. I know from my interactions with the world that something of that weight is not worth my time. What if a reasonable plan of life is made impossible by the immense weight of poverty and racism? What about hopes for a fair trial in a courthouse over which the Confederate battle flag is flying? Returning to the boulder analogy, what we do when we wish to move a boulder is to employ tools and techniques that amplify one's power, such as levers and artifacts like gas-fueled construction machines. Culturally speaking, one can confront time and again reason to doubt that society will be sufficiently fair to make one's plan of life possible. Or one can lack the education and tools needed to move impediments to one's aims. When we cannot move the boulder, we figure out how to cope with it, go around it, or otherwise ignore it. It is important to note, furthermore, that lacking in education is not a fault of one's own, particularly when the wider public intentionally narrows the scope and power of public education.[68] Sadly, liberal philosophers, including Rawls, advocate for a narrow public education[69] to avoid conflicts with people's different backgrounds, prioritizing noninterference over democratic empowerment.

Rawls is understood to be a philosopher in the liberal tradition. Liberalism centers on liberty of the individual, rooted in the idea that people should be maximally free to pursue their aims in a way consistent with like liberty for others. Both in *A Theory of Justice* and then even further in his follow-up book, *Political Liberalism,* Rawls inclines toward the argument that the dominant political tradition of the Western world hinges upon an outlook that calls for minimal interference in people's lives so that people may be maximally free. It is in this context that I identify the second premise of the argument of this book, namely:

Premise 2: The liberal norm of equal citizenship and its implications for a culture of justice conflict in many ways with liberalism's further norm of minimalist interference in people's lives and culture.

After all, if each person is to be maximally free, then it is perfectly plausible that a dominant majority will see as natural and to its own benefit to make up and sustain a culture in which its dominance and supremacy are supported culturally and embedded in the social fabric of society. Books for children can teach kids to count with humor at the expense of the less fortunate children, such as in examples like "Ten Little Nigger Boys," in which a young boy is eliminated from the story one at a time, often in developments that involve the death of the child.[70] The text of the book was even put to music.[71] In other contexts, young people learned of "Ten Little Indians."[72] Today, parents teach children about "Five Little Monkeys Jumping on the Bed." In short, what parents read to their children to teach them how to count could have substantial consequences on how people think about others. I return to this subject especially in chapter 4. At bottom, however, it is important to note that what people choose to do with their liberty can have an effect on the ways in which disadvantaged groups interact with the world and do or do not experience the conditions that give them confidence that they can expect a fair chance in any number of life's tests and trials.

A significant body of research has weighed in on the subject of self-respect. To be sure and as I have noted, there are matters on which I agree with Andrew Kernohan's book *Liberalism, Equality, and Cultural Oppression.* Kernohan recognizes that culture can be a force for oppression and injustice. Steven Young, in his extended review of Kernohan's book in the *University of Toronto Law Journal,* notes that "Kernohan's conception of the manner in which culture shapes individual preferences is a major advance over the accounts of most of his liberal contemporaries."[73] I support Kernohan's claim that culture is an important force and target for efforts to pursue justice, but with Young, I agree that "Kernohan focuses almost exclusively on the knowledge that individuals possess, rather than the process by which individuals come to know their own interests."[74] In other words, Kernohan and most in the liberal tradition tend to underestimate the importance of education and of those forces that can get in the way not only of a person's self-respect, but of that second part of Rawls's conception that he strangely calls self-respect, namely people's confidence in their ability to pursue meaningful life plans. That confidence is affected by others. For these reasons, I turn to Dewey for insight. First, Dewey is a strong advocate for the advancement of democratic values in education. Second, he calls for a term more appropriate than "self-respect" for the second aspect of Rawls's meaning, namely "a sense of one's positive power."

When I have a sense of my positive power, I do not lack self-respect if I fail to believe that I can lift the four-ton rock with only my bare arms, legs, and back. Rather, I have experience of the world that gives me a sense of what powers I have or lack, given the facts of the world and its repeated reactions to my efforts. If we accept the importance of Rawls's directive, however, as I do, if not thinking his terminology is ideal, then we must aim for both the development of self-respect in all people as well as a sense of their own positive power. Thus, the third premise of my argument runs as follows:

Premise 3: A culture of justice involves the conditions necessary for the development of self-respect and a sense of positive power in all people.

A further and important feature of my argument about self-respect and the need for a new term for what Rawls calls its second aspect is the matter of whose burden is at work. For it is commonly thought that persons should have self-respect, as a matter of individual responsibility. Thomas E. Hill, for example, argues that persons have individual duties to themselves to be self-respecting, even in the face of oppression.[75] Alain Locke's notion of the ethics of culture appears to suggest that all people could make the decision to aspire to be cultured, furthermore. At the same time, the idea of how a person's confidence is developed or could be impeded through experience with one's society and the world can clearly be beyond one's control, as Polycarp Ikuenobe argues in "Culture of Racism, Self-Respect, and Blameworthiness."[76] The point here, and it appears in the passage above that Rawls acknowledged as much, is that responsibility for self-respect and a sense of one's own positive power in the world is shared, not merely a matter of an individual's choice or responsibility. In sum:

Premise 4: Self-respect and a sense of one's own positive power are not merely individual matters of character, but require conditions for their development for which other people are partly responsible, such as with respect to education, food, healthcare, and enabling opportunities for employment.

When one accepts the importance of external forces in conditioning a person's confidence in their ability to pursue meaningful life plans, that does not necessarily deny the importance of considering the ways in which a person has some responsibility for self-examination and analysis of their experiences. In other words, what makes sense is not some foolish confidence that a person can be anything they want to be, even if that attitude has benefited some people. Barbara Ehrenreich's *Brightsided* argues that the "relentless promotion of positive thinking has undermined America."[77] At the same time, approaching one's possibilities with no belief in the potential for one's success is also troubling and self-defeating. A significant number of my African American students when I taught at the University of Mississippi told me that they had a relative who urged them not to go to school there. "You'll get killed!" they were warned. On the one hand, it is foolish not to be concerned about the dangers of racism in America and in Mississippi. On the other hand, when the kids visited the university and believed it to be the right place for them, they had to combat the social and familial pressures that may have nudged them away from some of their life plans achievable only through attendance at that university. For example, there is no other public school of pharmacy in Mississippi than the one at the University of Mississippi, the graduates of whose program are at the time of writing said to earn starting salaries more than $105,000 today.[78] Thus, while forces external to ourselves condition our confidence in whether our life plans can reasonably be pursued to fruition, there are ideal attitudes for examining such conditions, involving some amount of openness or optimism to be balanced by a degree of stoicism. This explains, in brief, the next premise:

Premise 5: A sense of positive power is not simply a mindset or a kind of naive confidence, but instead must be informed by realistic feelings and experiences, a kind of stoic pragmatism[79] or optimism conditioned by the exercise of one's own powers and the experience of others' reactions and responses to such exercise.

Efforts to address the need for public or social contributions to help people are commonly met with worries and criticisms of so-called "social entitlements," which politicians like former US Representative Paul Ryan have said lead to a culture of dependency.[80] In response, Anna Maria Santiago has argued that the war on poverty shifted into a war on the poor.[81] In the United States, there are stark differences in points of view concerning whether the lives of the poor are hard or easy. The Pew Research Center, for instance, found that 86 percent of "steadfast conservatives" believed that "the poor have it easy because they can get government benefits without doing anything." And, in stark yet strikingly balanced contrast, 86 percent of "solid liberals" believe that "the poor have hard lives because government benefits don't go far enough to help them live decently" (see fig. I.1).

Wherever one falls on the political spectrum, it is generally agreed on that dependency on hard drugs can be dangerous, such as with regard

Figure I.1. Pew Research Center poll showing how political leaning affects perceptions of the causes of poverty. *Source*: "Beyond Red vs. Blue: The Political Typology," Pew Research Center, Washington DC (June 2014), https://www.pewresearch.org/politics/wp-content/uploads/sites/4/2014/06/6-26-14-Political-Typology-release1.pdf, 44.

Wide Differences Between Right and Left Over Why Some People are Poor

% who say...

Poor people have hard lives because government benefits don't go far enough to help them live decently, or poor people have it easy because they can get government benefits without doing anything?

	Poor have hard lives	Poor have it easy
Total	47	44
Steadfast Conservs	7	86
Business Conservs	9	77
Young Outsiders	10	81
Hard-Pressed Skeptics	71	21
Next Generation Left	54	32
Faith and Family Left	62	29
Solid Liberals	86	6

Which is generally more often to blame if a person is poor?

	Lack of effort on his or her part	Circumstances beyond his or her control
Total	39	50
Steadfast Conservs	61	29
Business Conservs	58	26
Young Outsiders	56	30
Hard-Pressed Skeptics	22	66
Next Generation Left	42	47
Faith and Family Left	32	58
Solid Liberals	9	83

2014 Political Typology. Q25c & Q53.

PEW RESEARCH CENTER

to powerful pain medicines, yet other forms of dependency are normal to live with for life. People come to need glasses, medicines, breathing machines, and more as part of the necessities of life, yet we do not think of such needs as vices. My thinking is further framed by the notion that "No Man Is an Island,"[82] and the self-made person is, in my view, a pernicious, atomistic myth.[83] Thus, while in some narrow senses we know that some forms of dependency are dangerous, we must nevertheless consider the ways in which people have needs that the public must fill. John Dewey was a frequent advocate not merely for negative liberty, sweeping away impediments to freedom, but also for enabling people to exercise and grow their powers. We attend to such needs in small ways already when we provide "free and reduced" breakfast and lunch programs in American schools through the US Department of Agriculture.[84] While it is true that some stigma can be attached to kids receiving free and reduced lunch, contrary to the expectations of critics of entitlement programs, spending more and providing all schoolchildren with free breakfast and lunch can avoid the stigmatizing feeling and cultural differentiations at work.[85] I summarize this step of the argument for a culture of justice as follows:

Premise 6: While dependency on others can in some cases become a vice, it is not one inherently. As such, mechanisms that enable the development of self-respect and a sense of positive power should avoid stigmatizing dependency, as all people are in various ways dependent on others.

One of the challenges to the argument I make in this book takes the form of Robert Nozick's rebuttal to claims about patterns of injustice.[86] Nozick's argument can be captured by a strange experience I had at a conference. An architect gave a presentation at a meeting on "Space and Place," in which he criticized the skyline of Philadelphia. He mocked the city for the juxtaposition of new, modern, and stark buildings next to what he took to be more beautiful and older ones. He bemoaned the ugliness of the skyline. I found his talk strange. No one in particular had intended a certain look to the city's skyline. No one was to blame for how it looked. In effect, the odd arrangement of the city's skyline appeared to me to be a consequence of freedom, the freedom of individuals or of groups to pursue their interests in proximity to one another. The skyline that resulted could accidentally turn out to be beautiful, but if it did not, who could be blamed for its appearance?

In retrospect and in fairness to that architect, one can notice that as cities develop, it could make sense for people to decide to care about what their towns and skylines look like. Of course, to do so would be to prioritize one set of values over the freedom of individuals and groups to do as they please. In Charleston, South Carolina, for example, Rainbow Row is a beautiful lane of homes, and a historic one at that. There are great restrictions on freedoms for those who wish to sell or purchase homes there. An aesthetic decision made in the community determined the fact. Similarly, when a city wishes to have a certain look or to prioritize some things over others, it might decide that no building can be built above a given height. Washington, DC, for instance, is regulated by the Height of Buildings Act of 1910, creating "an unmistakable skyline and unobstructed views to civic symbols," according to the US National Capital Planning Commission.[87] Homeowners' associations abound, furthermore, creating rules that are to be followed regarding landscaping, home maintenance, appearance, and waste removal practices, among other matters.

The thing to note here is that while at one point in time the resulting pattern of free individuals' activities may be no one's fault, once people band together and make decisions collaboratively, they certainly can and often do decide to choose some patterns over others, some regulations over others. As such, just because some matters are the results of individual actions does not mean that what is everyone's responsibility is thereby no one's. Similarly, when it comes to culture, we can see that the patterns that emerge from individual action can be matters of public and shared responsibility. Hence, the next premise runs as follows:

Premise 7: The powers that establish, maintain, and change culture are shared among individuals and institutions. Correspondingly, responsibility for culture is also public and shared. In short, it is false to say that what is everyone's responsibility is therefore no one's responsibility in particular.

The final premise of this book concerns one of the most difficult areas to address for those who fervently wish for a culture of justice, and it hearkens back to the second premise, concerning the tensions inherent within liberalism. In particular, in the United States, a central and founding value of the Constitution is the protection of the freedom of speech. It is so foundational because if people are not free to express their ideas, how can a society be said to truly consider all perspectives on how to think and what to do? There are many reasons why the United States profoundly protects the freedom of speech, yet by means of the exercise of that freedom, individuals can purposefully aim to express ideas that undercut a culture of justice. The point here is to acknowledge and consider again the challenge that is not new, yet is always vital, namely concerning the question of how a tolerant society is to treat and react to intolerant people and actions. Dewey, the philosopher of democracy, was a profound and vocal defender of the freedom of expression, yet he argued in 1941 that "There are still many, too many, persons who feel free to cultivate and express racial prejudices as if they were within their personal rights, not recognizing how the attitude of intolerance infects, perhaps fatally as the example of Germany so surely proves, the basic humanities without which democracy is but a name."[88] Prejudices that can be viciously dangerous for democracy are not limited to matters of race, of course, but also are troubling on many other fronts, too many to name briefly here. Key examples in the United States have taken the form of hate speech and religious attacks on others. These areas are important to address in this project to show that while expression is defensible, when such acts become a kind of cultivation of hatred, concerns are warranted. Similar arguments have been made regarding sedition, on which Geoffrey Stone has concentrated,[89] a thinker to whose arguments I return in chapter 7. In addition, there are, I argue, areas in which previously protected forms of speech have yet to be sufficiently appreciated as the dangerous threats they are. These areas of consideration about the need for a culture of justice must be most carefully considered both because they involve something of profound importance, as in the freedom of thought and expression, as well as in the freedom of religion, and because they represent areas of powerful resistance to the effort to strive for justice. Hence, the final premise of the book is summarized as follows:

Premise 8: The remaining tensions inherent in liberalism impeding a culture of justice must be overcome, especially with regard to the protection of hateful speech, religious attacks on self-respect, and resistance to social norms of cultural respectfulness.

Together these premises support the thesis of this book, which I present in detailed and abbreviated forms:

Conclusion: There is a shared, public obligation to establish and maintain a culture that maximally fosters self-respect in all people and a sense of their own positive power to pursue meaningful life plans.

Abbreviated thesis: There is a shared, public obligation to establish and maintain a culture of justice.

I have gathered the premises and conclusion in the following summary.

Premise 1: Culture can enable or inhibit the pursuit of justice.

Premise 2: The liberal norm of equal citizenship and its implications for a culture of justice conflict in many ways with liberalism's further norm of minimalist interference in people's lives and culture.

Premise 3: A culture of justice involves the conditions necessary for the development of self-respect and a sense of positive power in all people.

Premise 4: Self-respect and a sense of one's own positive power are not merely individual matters of character, but require conditions for their development for which other people are partly responsible, such as with respect to education, food, healthcare, and enabling opportunities for employment.

Premise 5: A sense of positive power is not simply a mindset or a kind of naive confidence, but instead must be informed by realistic feelings and experiences, a kind of stoic pragmatism or optimism conditioned by the exercise of one's own powers and the experience of others' reactions and responses to such exercise.

Premise 6: While dependency on others can in some cases become a vice, it is not one inherently. As such, mechanisms that enable the development of self-respect and a sense of positive power should avoid stigmatizing dependency, as all people are in various ways dependent on others.

Premise 7: The powers that establish, maintain, and change culture are shared among individuals and institutions. Correspondingly, responsibility for culture is also public and shared. In short, it is false to say that what is everyone's responsibility is therefore no one's responsibility in particular.

Premise 8: The remaining tensions inherent in liberalism impeding a culture of justice must be overcome, especially with regard to the protection of hateful speech, religious attacks on self-respect, and resistance to social norms of cultural respectfulness.

Conclusion: There is a shared, public obligation to establish and maintain a culture that maximally fosters self-respect in all people and a sense of their own positive power to pursue meaningful life plans.

Abbreviated thesis: There is a shared, public obligation to establish and maintain a culture of justice.

The Plan

To argue for a culture of justice, I begin with a chapter considering the ideal of justice. For, while I draw on resources from the philosophical pragmatist John Dewey, ideals are nevertheless important, practical tools for living better in the real world. To be sure, ideals will never be achieved in full, but that does not keep them from being valuable guides for how to get closer to goals that we aim to achieve. In addition, what appears to be the ideal today nevertheless can be refined, and the goal for tomorrow will continue to remain on the moral horizon. The recognition of these characterizations of justice is important for keeping in mind that progress will always and only ever be partial, that justice will be ever evolving, yet nevertheless that ideals can be meaningful. In a nod to a concept drawn from fellow pragmatist Charles Sanders Peirce's philosophy, an inspiration for Dewey, I call chapter 1 "Justice as an Evolving Regulative Ideal."

Next, it is important to appreciate how a set of theories has come to converge on the importance of culture for justice. In fact, Peirce's philosophy of science included an appreciation for the convergence of theories on the truth. When different theories, approached from various directions, come to converge on a conclusion, that is at any given time taken to be a strong indication that there lies the truth. This chapter considers the convergence of the social and political theories of John Dewey, John Rawls, and Richard Rorty on the vital importance of culture for the sake of justice. Hence, chapter 2 is titled "Convergence on Culture."

After that, the next chapter examines the set of impediments to a culture of justice, taken as an overview attended to in greater detail than I could offer in this introduction. Chapter 3 is therefore titled "Impediments to a Culture of Justice." The chapter begins with further examination of some background tensions that lead Rawls to attend to the matter of culture in justice. Then, I categorize two forms of challenge, the first of which are theoretical and the second of which are difficulties for implementation. Responses to these challenges are addressed throughout the course of the book, but this chapter revisits several introduced here and adds more that must be considered in a robust defense of the need for and efforts to establish and maintain a culture of justice.

Chapter 4 centers on the distinction between the concept of self-respect and a sense of a person's own positive power. Both conceptions are taken to be important much in the way that Rawls notes in *A Theory of Justice*. The distinction is emphasized both for its rhetorical force and its consequences for concepts of responsibility, respect for oppressed groups, and appreciation for people's self-respect even when they have reason to doubt that their unjust society will truly give them a fair chance in life and in court trials. As I have noted, an ideal and guiding attitude for testing one's own potential for positive power is captured in the concept of stoic pragmatism, a term I borrow from philosopher John Lachs.[90] Hence, chapter 4 is titled "Self-Respect, Positive Power, and Stoic Pragmatism."

Chapter 5 examines an application of the test of the distinction between self-respect and positive power in the case of poverty. Titled "Culture, Poverty, and Positive Empowerment," the chapter aims to consider the ways in which challenging economic conditions can get in the way of people's development of a sense of their positive powers to pursue meaningful life plans. In the United States, people have often presumed that there is equality of opportunity for all, that anyone can become president, yet there are compelling reasons to believe that the path of upward mobility has been on a downward spiral.[91] The purpose here is to consider the various ways in which people's aims and purposes can be empowered, both through the removal of barriers and through the positive support of the growth of their powers to pursue meaningful life plans. And, as much as possible, policy ought to eliminate stigmatizing forces that get in the way of people's participation in the channels of opportunity.

Next, I focus chapter 6 on the libertarian challenge to patterns, considering how and why we should think that the obligation to establish a culture of justice is both public and shared. Chapter 6, on "Obligations for Culture as Public and Shared," considers education in the broad sense as the transmission of culture. Here, I note the ways in which liberal political philosophers have tended not to appreciate Dewey's claim that "democracy is a way of life."[92] The implications of this chapter are not limited to the power and need for democratic schools, but also for related practices in news media and social media engagement. Supporting democracy and the needs for justice is a public obligation and is shared, even if and when people fail or purposefully resist such expectations. The point is to note that, like in a fish tank, the cultural environment of the water is one in which we all swim. There is therefore a need for the cultivation of a culture of justice, much in the way that scholars in the field of education have studied the question of "what kind of citizen" schools should be working to cultivate.[93] My version of the question to ask and my thesis to answer: What kind of culture? A culture of justice.

Chapter 7 then turns to the deeply difficult matter of the freedom of speech, especially as concerns cases of hate speech and the need to revisit questions about the nature of threats. Titled "Free Speech and the Cultivation of Hatred," chapter 7 centers on the distinction very briefly introduced in this chapter between mere expression of ideas for their consideration versus the cultivation of hatred and other forms of threats on self-respect and people's senses of their own positive power to pursue meaningful life plans.

Finally, chapter 8 returns to the subtler matters of culture, those about which Ben Carson thought people are threatening to "destroy our nation." Titled "Correcting Political Correctness," the chapter examines the popular term and reasons why its very language seems imperfectly suited to address the concerns that prompt its use. At the same time, the need for a kind of care and concern for respecting people's cultures seems both called for and reasonable to expect and ask of people. Where conflicts between cultures exist, compromises can be sought and at least conflicts minimized with respect for differences. At the same time, those problems about which "political correctness" is invoked are matters on a spectrum that raise more or fewer concerns for people on both sides of the political aisle, though usually about different things and values. Relabeling the need for what political correctness might better refer to could be of some help, while we both aim to appreciate the need for cultural respectfulness, yet with some understanding that matters of culture take time to change. Public consciousness can be changed gradually and with occasional revolutionary moments and phases. Nevertheless, whether on matters large or small, the aim ultimately can be to establish and maintain a culture that maximally fosters self-respect for all people and a sense of their own positive power to pursue meaningful life plans.

1

Justice as an Evolving Regulative Ideal

In 1829, David Walker argued that emancipation from slavery would not be enough for justice and the moral uplift of former slaves.[1] More recently, Derrick Bell argued that *Brown v. Board of Education* was no success at all[2] and that racism was and would remain a permanent force in American society.[3] Walker and Bell both give reason to believe that emancipation from slavery and past forms of oppression were incomplete or false victories yielding little more than negative liberty. The moral development of individuality and positive liberty take not only intelligence and goodwill, but also material means to accomplish. The question that arises in both instances is whether we can call such changes progress. In the case of slavery, abolition is thought of as one of the clearest steps toward greater justice. The *Brown* case is generally thought to be a success over some past problems, yet a failure with regard to the underlying problem.[4]

In this book, I examine the cultural forces that can undermine or enable justice. Cultural influence can be large or small, such as in hyperincarceration on the one hand, or in subtle uses of language that demean groups of people on the other. My overarching concern throughout this project centers on democratic justice and its demands for equality of citizenship. Consequently, ways of understanding the pursuit of justice are important, since even grand moments in history can reasonably be found wanting. From the start of such a project, then, two frustrating paradigmatic responses present themselves and raise difficulties for the pursuit of justice.

The first response takes the form of a dismissive cynicism. The question is whether a just culture is in fact possible or realistic. The cynical attitude rejects the idea that an ideal of justice is meaningful, since the world we live in is not ideal. Such an outlook gives up on the goal of pursuing justice and accepts inequality of citizenship as insuperable. The cynic gives up on the goal of making large-scale changes to culture and would find petty those calls for justice that concern people's use of language or the norms referred to as "political correctness."

At the other end of the spectrum, the second problematic response is absolutist. The absolutist response to the challenges for equality of citizenship rejects claims that progress has been made. It says that unless we reach the kind of justice that our ideals require, anything short of revolution is complacency and complicity, a reinforcement of injustice. Such an outlook has two worrisome outlets. The first is to give in to the cynical view, disbelieving in the meaningfulness of justice.[5] The second is to pursue radical action. If only ideal justice is acceptable, and if civil, political means of pursuing justice can only end in frustration, one can feel that no recourse is left for change except violence. Misguided though they are, racist white secessionists fall into this absolute camp. People with democratic, non-racist outlooks on justice can also be absolutists, of course.

When people in democratic societies fight for equality of citizenship, it is important at the same time to appreciate the critics of partial progress yet to welcome steps toward justice, even if soberly. In this chapter, I argue that a just culture is an elusive and evolving ideal, yet one that can nevertheless serve valuably to regulate behavior and policy for the better.

In what follows, I first address the elusive quality of justice as an ideal always on the horizon, yet nevertheless meaningful. Next, I explain the ways in which it is useful to see justice as evolving rather than fixed. When interracial marriage was controversial, the United States was entirely unready or unwilling to consider homosexual marriage. With time and considerable effort to fight outmoded prejudices against homosexuality, a new culture and more inclusive sense of justice came into view. In this sense, justice evolves. Finally, I look to Charles Sanders Peirce's concept of a regulative ideal to show how a pragmatist outlook can at the same time appreciate ideals yet let go of outmoded understandings of their metaphysical status. Ideals thus are best understood to be tools for regulating behavior.

Justice as an Ideal

Though the arc of the moral universe is long, it bends towards justice.

Justice too long delayed is justice denied.

—Dr. Martin Luther King Jr.[6,7]

For sailors on long trips, the horizon hides and then reveals their destination. Such is our experience in pursuing justice. What we conceive of as justice at any given moment may sound idyllic and final yet is akin to the horizon. Once the merchant sailor arrives at a destination, further destinations and horizons present themselves. The horizonal quality of justice also contributes to the sense in which justice appears to evolve. Past generations thought that shaking hips on television were a moral threat. White Americans at one time resisted the desegregation of restaurants and schools. It is easy to find examples today that suggest that ours is a more just society than those of past generations, even if in many other ways justice appears far away.

Issues of race in the United States offer examples of continuing injustice—of inequality of democratic citizenship—falling short of an ideal. People often tire of talking about race.[8] Nevertheless, back in 2013 the Sentencing Project revealed that if trends were to continue, one in three African American men could expect to be imprisoned in his lifetime.[9] Ten years later, the Sentencing Project released an update noting change for the better, given that since 2000, the "imprisonment rate of black men has fallen by nearly 50%."[10] Such a change is welcome news, yet even with updated numbers, the new findings show that "one in five Black men born in 2001 is likely to experience imprisonment within their lifetime."[11]

Understanding that there appears always to be more work to do with respect to justice, we can appreciate disagreements between Martin Luther King Jr. and Malcolm X. Malcolm's famous and often repeated line was that "If you stick a knife nine inches into my back and pull it out three inches, that is not progress. Even if you pull it all the way out, that is not progress. Progress is healing the wound, and America hasn't even begun to pull out the knife."[12] King was an advocate for moderate, peaceful means to social change, while Malcolm asked him how and why he could advocate for nonviolence in response to violence inflicted. King was inspired by the work and philosophy of Mahatma Gandhi,[13] but Malcolm was right to wonder how King knew that he was not simply bringing sheep to the slaughter when he led protests. There is reason to believe that Gandhi's tactics would have failed utterly against the Nazis in Germany. In the American South, black men and women were lynched. Churches were bombed. Protesters were murdered. Malcolm had cause to doubt King's methods. The desegregation of schools and the protection of the right to vote, to figures like Malcolm, were partial measures for progress, pulling out the knife only symbolically, not substantively. Appreciating Malcolm's worries, consider that even with desegregation as law, some school districts have been described as still today not having desegregated.[14] In 2012, it was argued that schools had become more segregated than they were in the late 1960s.[15]

Contrast these conditions with the fact that the United States has elected and reelected its first African American president. On the one hand, the United States appears to have made some unmistakable progress, racially speaking, given that years ago President Obama's candidacy would have been thought so unrealistic as to be impossible. Even in what some have called the "age of Obama,"[16] however, conditions for African Americans in the United States have reasonably inspired Michelle Alexander to call today's prison conditions a "New Jim Crow."[17] What are we to say about progress toward justice when it is partial? Have there been victories in the pursuit of justice? One response to partial measures for progress or to progress accompanied by apparent regress is to say that not much has changed. If we see justice as an ideal, however, any changes could only ever be partial progress, at best. Therefore, if change is desired, leaders must recognize that it will never be totally fulfilled.

In the tradition of American Pragmatism, we find in John Dewey's work an approach to progress more sympathetic with King's nonviolent philosophy. In "Democracy Is Radical," Dewey argues that you cannot achieve democratic ends with undemocratic means.[18] In other words, if we are to pursue democratic aims of equality and social cooperation, violence will frustrate rather than enable our ends. Of course, there is cause to appreciate the rebuttal. When one's people are murdered, hanged, and bombed, not welcomed to the same table for discussion or to the same schools or voting booths, there is a foundational threat to overcome that makes the aim of cooperation seem unrealistic.

The three possible responses to the frustrated pursuit of an ideal of justice presented in the introduction to this chapter—namely the cynic, the absolutist, and the pragmatist—represent different outlooks on the disagreements between King and X. On the one hand, seeing justice as an ideal that so thoroughly fails to match up with the real world can inspire cynicism. Justice is not meaningful on this view, as it is imaginary, not realistic. The cynic will not aim to achieve greater justice, as it is a foolish dream anyway, on his or her view. King and X both believed that action was necessary, rejecting the cynic's view. In fact, cynicism reinforces unjust social structures, King argued. He wrote, "He who passively accepts evil is as much involved in it as he who helps to perpetrate it."[19]

The second response sees the ideal of justice as necessary, real, and wholly frustrated in today's world. This view becomes absolutist and possibly violent. To say this is not to deny that people should have the right of self-defense. This reasonable aspect of X's argument is typically omitted when people think of him as extreme or as an advocate for violence in contrast with the King. The worry for King was that even violence in self-defense can be spun in public perception as aggressive violence. In addition, the violent actor undermines his or her own ends, as Dewey suggested, if one is looking to bring about peaceful results. To appreciate King's challenge for X, consider that the American South remained in the union only by force. Even to this day, Southerners continue to express their pride in the region's resistance to the federal government with defenses of the Confederate Battle flag, as well as occasional outbursts of terrible violence.[20] King believed that if the aim was transformation into a community, violence would frustrate the end, not speed its arrival.

Finally, the third possibility is that an ideal can be an inspiration. It can be the star in whose direction we travel, always elusive, yet helpful for guiding our efforts. This last approach is the outlook inspired by lines like King's, which explain, "Though the arc of the moral universe is long, it bends towards justice."[21] In this sense, an ideal is aspirational. It is imagined in real life, as we recognize a spectrum of better and worse conditions than those that exist presently. Dewey had something like this in mind when he spoke of the divine in *A Common Faith*.[22] It is an idealized moral extension of our experience of the world, which we value as better and worse, envisioned as a matter of degree. The ideal, the perfect, is a vision of the progress of present conditions carried infinitely toward what would be better.

There are practical reasons why we must not follow the cynic's course, as well as conceptual ones. Things will only stay the same or get worse without effort, given the cynic's outlook. Beyond that, the fact that a goal is unattainable is in no way evidence of the meaninglessness of its pursuit. This argument can best be understood with reference to the idea that "ought implies can." One's moral obligations cannot reasonably include things impossible for one to do. While David Hume's insight may be true—that one cannot derive an "ought" from an "is"—we might say with Gideon Yaffe that "sometimes the way things ought to be does indeed tell us how they are."[23] We do not blame a person for a condition that they could not avoid. When a person is drugged without his consent, for instance, we do not blame him for his intoxicated state. On such grounds, we might say that if a society could never achieve ideal conditions of justice, it cannot be that we ought to achieve them. That interpretation is only half right. If all one can be morally required to do is that which is within one's power, the question is whether or not striving for an ideal could not help one to come closer to it. If an ideal is impossible to achieve in one's lifetime, it may nevertheless be considered a limit toward which infinite effort can progress infinitely over time. Understanding the concepts of the ideal perfect circle may mean that a person could never draw a perfect circle by hand. It is unreasonable to say that they ought to draw a perfect circle and is a failure when they inevitably fall short of that perfection. Nevertheless, the idea of a perfect circle is meaningful, as it is instructive of the kind of aim one is striving for as well as the sorts of steps one ought to take in working toward that perfection. Thus, the pursuit of perfection, the effort to come as close to justice as a society can in a generation's lifetime is within that generation's power. The ideal can be meaningful in that sense, despite the inevitability of falling short of it as a goal.

An ideal of justice can only obligate a person to do what is in his or her power to control. This does not mean that one gives up when things cannot be changed en masse immediately. When enough people make a small change, great change can occur. A change of this sort appears to be the mechanism by which gay marriage laws were changed. First there were activists calling for change. Then scholars and entertainers discussed the issue and combated unconsidered sensibilities. Next, the general public resisted traditional prejudices against homosexual behavior. Finally, individuals adapted and saw that criticisms of homosexual behavior were discriminatory and unacceptable. Past criticisms came to look like the unfair arguments against interracial marriage. Such changes are slow and reveal the extent to which all people participate in the transmission, acceptance, and modification of culture. Examples such as these also demonstrate reason for what John Lachs has dubbed "stoic pragmatism," a stoicism spirited by a pragmatic optimism to try, while not despairing when particular individuals cannot alone change all that needs to be changed.[24]

Given these approaches to the nature of an ideal, it is important to tie them to the modern democratic norms of equal citizenship and justice. In Plato's day, it seemed necessary to the great philosopher to divide up people into classes and castes. It is one thing to see and divide the needs for agriculture, civil defense, and political work. We still follow much of Plato's advice when it comes to the benefits of a broad education in general, accompanied by specialized education and focus in one's trade. The further step Plato takes, however, of calling certain social roles or castes bronze, silver, and gold today clashes with the democratic ethos.

We have the sobering advantage of having witnessed in the early twentieth century some of the most grotesque forms of dehumanization and devaluation of people.[25]

The gross atrocities of the last century undermined any assuredness people might have felt in trusting powerful groups to treat those whom they command with their best interests at heart. The modern world has seen the results of classifying people into castes, valuing some far more than others. It has come to signal one of the greatest sources of injustice, even while today many have argued that the United States is an oligarchy, not a democracy.[26] Such claims make the news because nations like the United States call themselves democracies and allegedly aspire to the values of democratic justice. The democratic pursuit of justice fundamentally must reject hierarchies of citizenship, yet they persist.

Plato's optimism about the trustworthiness of unchecked rulers[27] has been thoroughly tested and failed. While no person is perfect, it is worth considering that had General George Washington wanted a monarchy, or to have remained president until his death, he may have been able to do so. He also could have rendered the United States far less democratic than it has become. We reify figures like him because they are so unusual for not clutching to power. Washington made present democratic developments possible in many ways. Of course, he owned many slaves and was known to have sold some to separate them from their families as a form of punishment.[28] Washington had his troubling flaws as well. Had Washington not acted in such ways, we still would have reason to doubt that leaders could be trusted to the extent that Plato's Socrates called for. The division of powers and checks and balances of modern democratic states ensure that no individual can single-handedly wield all governmental power. The clumsy government that results from such divisions is necessary because of the long history of abuses on the part of powerful classes.

Today, the democratic era takes the opposite view on Plato's mistake. While we still speak of classes and oligarchy,[29] hierarchies of citizenship are denounced. John Dewey and James Tufts distilled one of the central democratic values of the modern era, explaining that

> the worth and dignity of every human being of moral capacity is fundamental in nearly every moral system of modern times. It is implicit in the Christian doctrine of the worth of the soul, in the Kantian doctrine of personality, in the Benthamic dictum, "every man to count as one." It is embedded

> in our democratic theory and institutions. With the leveling
> and equalizing of physical and mental power brought about
> by modern inventions and the spread of intelligence, no State
> is permanently safe except on a foundation of justice. And
> justice cannot be fundamentally in contradiction with the
> essence of democracy.[30]

This democratic ideal, of having each person count as one, rejects hierarchical citizenship. Of course, it does not capture all that justice instructs. Nor does it address every concern for democracy. But it offers invaluable insight into ways in which today American and other societies can be more just. There is reason why we must not expect a complete and final definition of the full meaning of justice, however. The reason is that justice grows and evolves with changing human conditions and potential, the subject of the next section of this chapter.

Given my sense that justice is an ideal and one that evolves, my own understanding of that ideal can only at best be provisional and emphasize some aspects of the matter, subject to future refinement and within the limits of my purposes here. And, like Dewey, I believe that philosophy should proceed from experience, not start from abstractions. Thus, as I present my outlook on the ideal of justice here briefly, I will at each step explain the problem motivating the aspect of the ideal at issue.

1) Dehumanization is rampant today. People who are deserving of equal moral consideration as citizens are not afforded circumstances necessary for healthy growth. As I have argued elsewhere,[31] many Americans are channeled into poverty and prison, in what the US Justice Department has called a "school-to-prison pipeline."[32] In addition, the proliferation of for-profit prisons has created powerful undemocratic economic incentives for criminalizing groups of people and underfunding public schools in preparation for that criminalization. Hierarchies of citizenship remain today, though they should end and all people should be treated with the dignity and respect that moral agents deserve. In addition, non-citizens and immigrants have long and routinely been dehumanized as well. Nations must design policies for many reasons regarding processes of immigration, yet none must dehumanize non-citizens. Democracy matters because all people matter. And moral consideration is reasonably extended to other beings and subjects. The history of moral progress has involved growth in appreciation of the moral value of more kinds of life that can suffer or thrive.

2) Many people suffer today because of ignorance and public neglect of the economic, social, environmental, and cultural conditions necessary for the kind of education that democracy needs to flourish. Outbreaks of diseases for which there are available vaccines are unnecessary sources of harm. Ignorance of the most effective means to be safe, sexually speaking, leads many young people unnecessarily to unintended pregnancy and to contracting sexually transmitted diseases. Anti-science attitudes rooted in economic interests and purposefully spread falsehoods affect budgetary decision-making about climate science and other sciences. Each person has moral value, but not every opinion deserves attention and promotion. Even more importantly, some intentionally or unintentionally falsified messages do great harm in steering people away from greater health and happiness. Given that, it is essential, as John Dewey argued many times, to cultivate in all people the scientific attitudes and habits of mind necessary to appreciate wisdom and to put it to use. Education is essential for democracy, Dewey argued, and is an end in itself as well. With respect to justice, what is vital is its empowerment of people with the wisdom to pursue chosen, meaningful lives.

3) When people are poorly educated, many often blame schools, even though parents are influential and can be impoverished or undereducated, television and other media abound and affect people all day long, and kids go hungry or sick from economic need. Educational empowerment takes more than a classroom. A person's life, community, and environment are together in contributing to his or her education. The approach to liberty and justice that many take in merely thinking about avoiding harm to others fails to appreciate that inaction can kill a child from neglect. Orphans are the obvious examples to demonstrate the public obligation to enact positive liberty, but there is no reason to believe that such obligations end when children have a parent or guardian. People struggle. Poverty is deep and consequential. And a just culture is one in which people feel an obligation toward all of society's children and members, not just those without assigned guardians. Thus, if an education is essential to appreciate wisdom, live a healthy life, and allay the threats of poverty and prison, then the empowerment of people must be positive, active, and supportive of the development of each person's humanity. In short, positive social support is essential to ensure the cultivation of each person's potential and powers.

Given these considerations, I would say that the ideal of justice is widely inclusive of moral consideration and respect, and positively supports the environments and conditions necessary for personal growth and positive power. In this sense, the ideal of justice must be democratic. It must be expansive of our understanding of the demos, the people or group of moral agents deserving of respect. It must also maximally and positively empower people. In briefest terms, I would say that the ideal of justice is respectful empowerment.

The next step for the present chapter is to consider the ways in which justice evolves and can nevertheless ultimately serve as a regulative ideal.

Justice as an Evolving Ideal

Perhaps the key figure with whom I disagree on the issue of the evolution of ideals is Plato. While I believe that there is much to learn still today from Plato, there is also much that must be rejected. The Platonic view that there is a realm of unchanging forms, which are perfect in part because they are unchanging, has had many critics. I will be brief in explaining my rejection of his view, which can be associated with a kind of absolutism.

One way of thinking suggests that there is a perfect sense of justice, that it is unchanging, and that the world changes, progressing or regressing in reference to it. That perfect form of justice is one that we will never achieve. The ideal of a just person, as unchanging and perfect, is difficult to reconcile with the contingent development of human beings. Plato's Socrates did not hesitate to suggest the appropriateness of infanticide for the children of "inferior parents" or for "deformed" offspring.[33] Such outlooks today sound barbaric and unthinkable, even if a very small set of narrow exceptions has been considered in highly controversial debates about the most extreme and unusual cases.[34] If permanent truths are most important to Plato, it is remarkable just how profoundly at odds his view of the infanticide of many healthy children is today. One way of considering the vast changes from the ancient period to today would be to suggest that we are at a step in the process toward that greater perfection, which always was. To the pragmatist, the question at this point is about the meaning of ideas. What conceivable practical consequence can there be in the different beliefs—between thinking that there is a perfect ideal of humanity that is unchanging and always has been, versus the belief that human beings evolve?

One conceivable consequence comes from thinking one knows the nature of that human perfection and can thereby judge others according to that standard. For instance, if one were to believe that human bodies have a purpose, related to procreation, then they might think that the homosexual use of reproductive organs is a misuse, and correspondingly a moral failure on grounds of violating one's nature. Michael Levin's argument in "Why Homosexuality Is Abnormal" depends on beliefs about the nature of the human body and the purpose of our parts in this way.[35] In contrast with the absolutist or fixed form theorist, the view that sees ideals as evolving with human beings sees variation as a natural part of humanity. Such a view inclines one toward greater toleration of and respect for people's differences. In a democratic society, in which variety and freedom are key, such toleration is the wiser course. Given this understanding, the danger involved comes more from a lack of humility about the nature of ideals than from the belief that they are unchanging versus evolving. At the same time, John Lachs has offered another reason to reject the absolutist picture—namely that it is singular. He has argued that we ought to consider there to be not one, but many human natures.[36] Lachs's view considers the vastness of human variety and also appreciates or is supported by the facts of evolutionary sciences, which see divergences of branches and strains of animals in the genus *Homo*. Animals' conditions influence the success of their offspring, and hence the generations that continue over time change. To pragmatists like Dewey, ideas are some of the most powerful tools we have for managing our environmental challenges. Tools must be modified as conditions change, and their nature adapts with the needs for which we must use them.

As circumstances change, another consequence of absolutism arises. If one believes adamantly in a value, thought to be unchanging, and if one thinks that society is departing ever more from it, the absolutist might be inclined toward drastic action. For example, if one believes in white supremacy, when non-white persons thrive at work or in public life, one might become angry to the point of taking drastic action. Dylann Roof, the mass murderer in Charleston, South Carolina, spoke of the threat of non-white people, for example. He was incapable of accepting the consequences of increasing social equality.[37]

One final point is worth noting. Some historians like to point to the Declaration of Independence as an example of one of the great, enduring moral documents, which remains as true today in the rightness of its aspirations as it was in its own day. President Lincoln was said to have called it a lodestar, a guiding principle for his life and work. Lewis Lehrman sees in the important document evidence of something that captured the unchanging truth about humanity and our values.[38]

While I agree about the moral importance of the Declaration of Independence, I see it as a significant step in the evolution of human ideals, not as something of perfection that is unchanging. Not the least reason for this is the fact that at the time, the founders referred to "men" while not considering non-whites relevant. Even when people such as Lincoln eventually came around on that point, it was *men*, not women, referred to, and the idea that the term "man" captures also women was not in fact accepted. Women had to wait until the twentieth century to get the right to vote in the United States. Therefore, the Declaration of Independence is a useful example of my point about the evolution of ideals.[39]

Justice as a Regulative Ideal

Ideals can sound otherworldly, impractical, or unrealistic. In the pragmatist tradition, Charles Peirce has shown why and how ideals can be practical, such as in relation to truth as an ideal or to other ideals that can regulate behavior. An explanation of Peirce's understanding of truth can by analogy illustrate the way in which we can see justice as an evolving, regulative ideal. I end this section with some applications of this outlook to democratic ideals of equal citizenship.

Peirce has, with justification, been called an American genius.[40] Robert Neville has explained that Peirce "invented pragmatism, much modern symbolic logic, and semiotics."[41] While his father, Benjamin Peirce, himself a great Harvard mathematician and scientist, reinforced his son's tendencies toward snobbishness and hubris,[42] C. S. Peirce's philosophy of inquiry pointed to the importance of community and of varied points of view. In both philosophy and the sciences, Peirce thought that "philosophy ought to imitate the successful sciences in its methods, so far as to proceed only from tangible premisses [sic] which can be subjected to careful scrutiny, and to trust rather to the multitude and variety of its arguments than to the conclusiveness of any one. Its reasoning should not form a chain which is no stronger than its weakest link, but a cable whose fibers may be ever so slender, provided they are sufficiently numerous and intimately connected."[43] While it takes specialists to interpret data and conduct studies, Peirce recognized that inquiry needs community, volume, and time. Peirce referred in a number of passages to the work of Pierre Simon Laplace,[44] the French mathematician known for *Théorie Analytique des Probabilités*,[45] a foundational contribution leading up to what we now call the central limit theorem. In simplest terms, that theorem, which is the basis of modern probability theory and statistics, says that when multiple samples of a population are taken over and over and plotted on a graph, they will form a normal curve. That curve's mean value is the true population mean. We can appreciate the lesson here with an analogy. If one inquirer were to check the height of 100 Americans selected without any effort at randomization, the mean value of his or her sample would not be generalizable to all Americans. When 100 inquirers from different parts of the country check the height of 100 Americans with efforts at randomization, the central limit theorem says that the means of the various samples will come to form a normal (bell) curve. The more samples that are taken, even of a modest number, like 100, the closer and closer the plotted means will fill in the shape of the bell curve, which points to the true mean of the whole distribution.

While some of the mathematical developments relevant for contemporary statistics came after Peirce's death, he is known as "one of the founders of statistics."[46] He was among the key figures who illustrated how mathematical ideals help us to arrive at truth. They teach us how to design studies and how to control maximally for error and to sharpen our conclusions, rendering them more and more likely to be true. In addition, he showed that the community of inquiry, carrying out studies together, generates insights that converge on an ideal limit that we call the truth.

Peirce illustrates the power of the ideal of truth and of the corresponding process of inquiry leading to it. In his famous essay "The Fixation of Belief," he writes, "The trial of this method of experience in natural science for these three centuries . . . encourages us to hope that we are approaching nearer and nearer to an opinion which is not destined to be broken down—though we cannot expect ever quite to reach that ideal goal."[47] As a mathematician and, among other things, a philosopher of science, Peirce famously explained "How to Make Our Ideas Clear." In that essay, he wrote,

> [A]ll the followers of science are animated by a cheerful hope that the processes of investigation, if only pushed far enough, will give one certain solution to each question to which they apply it. One man may investigate the velocity of light by studying the transits of Venus and the aberration of the stars; another by the oppositions of Mars and the eclipses of Jupiter's satellites; a third by the method of Fizeau; a fourth by that of

Foucault; a fifth by the motions of the curves of Lissajoux; a sixth, a seventh, an eighth, and a ninth, may follow the different methods of comparing the measures of statical and dynamical electricity. They may at first obtain different results, but, as each perfects his method and his processes, the results are found to move steadily together toward a destined centre. So with all scientific research. Different minds may set out with the most antagonistic views, but the progress of investigation carries them by a force outside of themselves to one and the same conclusion. This activity of thought by which we are carried, not where we wish, but to a fore-ordained goal, is like the operation of destiny. No modification of the point of view taken, no selection of other facts for study, no natural bent of mind even, can enable a man to escape the predestinate opinion. This great hope is embodied in the conception of truth and reality. *The opinion which is fated*[48] *to be ultimately agreed to by all who investigate, is what we mean by the truth,* and the object represented in this opinion is the real. That is the way I would explain reality.[49]

We often think of the realm of ideals in terms of morals. Pragmatists tend not to make hard distinctions between matters of fact and value, but in everyday experience, it is common to think that ideals are reserved for the social realm, not for understanding the way matter functions. Peirce shows that mundane distinction as wrongheaded, revealing that the pursuit of truth is at bottom a process guided by hope and an ideal of inquiry.

Peirce's Pragmatism grew out of his reaction to Kant, seeing the power of reason to direct practice, even if ideals are not somehow ever fully known. He wrote,

Truth is a character which attaches to an abstract proposition, such as a person might utter. It essentially depends upon that proposition's not professing to be exactly true. But we hope that in the progress of science its error will indefinitely diminish, just as the error of 3.14159, the value given for π, will indefinitely diminish as the calculation is carried to more and more places of decimals. What we call π is an ideal limit to which no numerical expression can be perfectly true.[50]

When we consider π as an example, we see that a mathematical idea, which we realize is not fully known to us, is in fact enormously powerful for directing human behavior. Likewise, we can think of justice as the target of progressive refinement of understanding. It is also an ideal that helps us to carry out social functions.

While Peirce's general focus was on the sciences and mathematics, he recognized that these insights apply to the moral realm. He continued,

> In the above we have considered positive scientific truth. But the same definitions equally hold in the normative sciences. If a moralist describes an ideal as the *summum bonum*, in the first place, the perfect truth of his statement requires that it should involve the confession that the perfect doctrine can neither be stated nor conceived. If, with that allowance, the future development of man's moral nature will only lead to a firmer satisfaction with the described ideal, the doctrine is true.[51]

We can appreciate what Peirce has in mind here through an example. The concept of consent, such as what we find in social contract theory or in bioethics, is an ideal notion when considered complete or perfect. Citizens rarely have moments in which they consent explicitly to their participation in a society. Immigrants are an exception, as they choose to enter and live in a country. Most citizens do not have many, if any, such moments. Nevertheless, in the twentieth century, the concept of consent has come to be of paramount importance in bioethics. We understand the value and importance of consent, such as of the human subjects of scientific research. Because of the terrible mistakes that past scientists have made, harming people, like in the Tuskegee syphilis experiments, we now carefully regulate studies involving human subjects.[52] At the same time, we still have much to learn and decide about the future of consent as a moral tool for justice. When doctors offer explanations to patients, they get the patients to sign forms for consent, yet a person without a high school degree might reasonably claim that he or she did not understand a doctor's explanation. When consent is needed, new mechanisms and understandings of the ideal can be developed and refined to address limitations in our past practices. How we might in the future ensure that a patient or patient's representative has clearly and fully consented to a risky operation is under debate and development.[53] This example helps to explain the extent to which ideals are never actually achieved or met in real life, yet can be behavior-directing concepts that enable people to approach more carefully what the culture's aims and values intend.

Peirce's understanding of ideals is also at work in his sense of inquiry, which he took to be regulated by them. In his essay "Some Consequences of Four Incapacities," he wrote, "We individually cannot reasonably hope to attain the ultimate philosophy which we pursue; we can only seek it, therefore, for the *community* of philosophers. Hence, if disciplined and candid minds carefully examine a theory and refuse to accept it, this ought to create doubts in the mind of the author of the theory."[54] The community of inquirers, as Peirce explained it, is regulated by ideals. Those ideals concretely instruct us on how to pursue truth together. The lesson here is that early pioneers in the fight for an underrepresented group or for a cause that society has yet to take seriously are likely to move few people in their lifetime. Nevertheless, the larger aim must be to shift the culture over time, something that courageous individuals can motivate, but to which the masses must eventually contribute, even if in small ways. Peirce shows us how to see an ideal as something that evolves, is pursued in community, and is at the same time elusive, always beyond our full understanding. Such regulative ideals are nevertheless powerful in directing behavior to success in more proximal fulfillment of their aims.

In the United States today, many have celebrated the election twice over of an African American president. People have used language like "post-racial" or the "age of Obama." At the same time, record numbers of African Americans drop out of school in places like the impoverished regions of Mississippi. Vast numbers of Americans are incarcerated, including disproportionate numbers of African Americans. While in the country some doors have opened to higher positions of power and opportunity, a small minority of historically disadvantaged people is afforded such widened opportunities. Meanwhile, public officials are found to take money, selling African American young men to private prisons for profit.[55] As a country, we have a long way to go in the fight against inequalities of citizenship. At the same time, exposure of apparent oligarchy makes the news. Some corrupt judges get caught and are incarcerated. We are far from having achieved an ideally just society, yet we have more tools today than ever before to record and spread messages and videos, such as in recordings of police brutality and unfairness. Despite these developments, select top-level officials have managed to avoid accountability time and again for their misdeeds. This is understood to be scandalous and troubling, as well as not yet over.[56] Peirce's insights reveal the need to cultivate a community of accountability, a culture of democratic justice that can more closely watch and more severely punish those officials who frustrate the movement to approach greater equity. We can use the ideals of objectivity, fairness, and due process, even if never achieving them perfectly, to better advance the aims of justice. If we avoid the dangers of cynicism and of absolutist overreach, we can do the best we can to achieve a maximally just culture.

Conclusion

While it is not new to call justice an ideal, there is reason to make the point. When a family loses a child at the hands of someone charged with their protection, that family calls for justice. What they want is for the relevant person to be punished. In that sense, when a killer does end up in jail, sometimes family members or journalists say that "justice was done."[57] There is a sense, then, that in certain circumstances, an injustice can be partially redressed. At the cultural level, the focus of my overarching project, injustice is not something quickly or simply addressed in a trial. Even if reparations were granted for past harms done,[58] we would not say that we finally have a just culture. When it comes to culture, we have in mind many layers of historically entrenched power and influence, embedded in our very uses of language, the beliefs people harbor, the practices we engage in, and our consequent institutions, all of which we pass along from one generation to the next. The fact that it took mass murder in Charleston, South Carolina, to finally, in 2015, prompt people to take down the Confederate Battle flag from state buildings illustrates how entrenched power structures can be.[59] The cause of justice is so important, however, that we must neither be cynical nor despair, nor hold unflinchingly to some absolute, unwilling to open our minds to new evidence or problems. Instead, we should see justice as an evolving, regulative ideal toward which we can progress, with an engaged democratic community and true and unrelenting good faith effort.

2

Converging on Culture

Poets are the unacknowledged legislators of the world.

—Percy Shelley[1]

When thinkers from different traditions agree, readers can often find various contributions to scholarship mutually supportive. John Rawls and Richard Rorty, two highly influential political thinkers of the twentieth century, bear some overlap in their backgrounds in the tradition of analytic philosophy, but in ethics and political philosophy, their favored intellectual resources differ. Rorty was a big fan of Rawls's work and appreciated how it sought common ground across philosophical difference,[2] especially with attention to the role of culture in philosophy and vice versa.

Rawls drew on or conversed with thinkers from the traditions of analytic, Continental, and American philosophy to varying degrees. Among his important contributions was the recognition of the crucial role of psychological and cultural conditions and forces in shaping the potential for justice. Critics from the libertarian tradition, whom I address in chapter 6, argue that the level of patterns, such as culture, is not a sphere in which one should look for justice or injustice, instead pointing to the level of individual, free transactions.[3] Others, such as former presidential candidate and later US Secretary of Housing and Urban Development Ben Carson, dismiss claims about culture, such as about political correctness or about offensive mascots, as petty, unreasonable, or even dangerous.[4]

In this chapter, I review writings primarily from three philosophers whose work overlaps in a way that reveals the cultural roots of justice.

These thinkers help me to illustrate the reasons why we must attend to culture as a force for justice, not focusing only on individuals. I look to Rawls, Rorty, and John Dewey for beginning an inquiry into the cultural conditions necessary for justice. I aim to show that in the convergence of their philosophies, we see how culture can enable or undermine the pursuit of justice, and that we can identify tools in the Pragmatists' writings for addressing some of the challenges in theorizing about justice.

Through sometimes unintended conditions but more often by intentional means, culture can either support or undermine 1) the tolerance versus intolerance of a society; 2) the dehumanization of people; 3) people's ability to see from others' perspectives, or empathy; 4) appreciation for the equality and freedom of other people; 5) the environment in which each person can develop a sense of his or her own self-respect, positive power, and worth; 6) efforts to shame unjust societies and regimes; 7) the recognition of areas of overlapping consensus, valuable for cooperative action; and 8) the democratic way of life necessary for genuinely democratic societies to flourish.

In an excellent book, *Liberalism, Equality, and Cultural Oppression*, Andrew Kernohan advances an argument in favor of what he calls *an advocacy approach* on the part of the liberal state, noting especially that culture can be used to oppress people.[5] His argument focuses especially on equality, my fourth point above, as well as on a portion of what I argue about self-respect, the fifth item I emphasize in this chapter. There is a great deal I agree with in Kernohan's book, but more is needed for justice, I contend, than the advancement of true beliefs about the moral equality of persons. I follow Dewey here in this regard, conceiving of democracy as a way of life, not a small set of beliefs and practices. In this chapter, then, I aim to broaden considerations necessary for justice beyond Kernohan's narrow view. At the same time, there will be points and challenges that arise in later chapters where the implications that Kernohan draws appear overbroad and might thereby call for excessive controls on free speech.[6]

The present chapter is an important early step in my overarching project of arguing for the establishment and maintenance of the cultural conditions necessary for justice. The central challengers to this theory claim that the manipulation of culture is inevitably and unacceptably coercive, a claim that both Kernohan and I reject. I focus in this chapter on the affirmative argument for a culture of justice, setting aside for now the defense against the challenge of the liberal tradition. I show how influential philosophers of culture helped to clarify its role in the pursuit of justice. In advancing the present project, we can also see the usefulness of drawing on insights both from Rawls and the Pragmatists. The latter attended extensively to the mechanisms for reconstructing culture in the democratic era, such as education, cultural criticism, and other forms of public philosophical engagement.

In what follows, I begin by highlighting the resonance between Rawls's and Rorty's outlooks on culture before then turning to their mutual inspiration in Dewey's work, as a philosopher of culture. Next, I turn to distinctions between rationality and culture that Rorty introduced to help clarify his views on the concepts. From there, we can appreciate how he and Dewey can be understood to offer what I would call Pragmatic moral foundations in ethics, especially in the call to diminish suffering. With that in mind, I then turn to the ways in which Rorty especially, but also Rawls and Dewey, put the philosophy of culture to work, in particular with respect to human rights. Finally, I conclude the chapter with considerations on how to rethink important aspects of the liberal tradition at least as we find it in Rawls's influential work.

Rawls's Reflective Equilibrium and Rorty's Resonance on Culture

Bucking expectations, Rorty explained his great appreciation for Rawls's agreement with philosophical Pragmatism. For example, in *A Theory of Justice*, Rawls's most Pragmatic position might be his idea of "reflective equilibrium." Moral theory, he thought, must not be held to an expectation of certain and indubitable premises. Rather, moral theorizing must begin with claims and assumptions that are contingently accepted, and that it may determine to need revising in a back and forth engagement with our various other beliefs.[7]

Rawls was unafraid of making use of contingent claims, much like Peter Singer's argument that widespread yet unnecessary famines and suffering are morally unacceptable.[8] This means that we cannot do otherwise than to draw on the values and assumptions of our culture, at least as a revisable starting point. The present book follows Rawls's lead in this regard. While there may be philosophically interesting questions to talk about for some who enjoy abstraction, we may not arrive at a universally accepted argument against slavery, simply because of the facts of lingering prejudice or to demands for an infinite list of justifications of our premises. This does not mean that we must take proposals to return to past, inhumane practices seriously.[9] Rorty was on the same page with Rawls on this point. He rejected the idea of immutable foundations on which one might seek universal agreement. He also followed Dewey in thinking that it is a mistake to believe that we must justify our moral intuitions to some invented sense of a psychopathic self, which cares only for itself. Rorty cites Dewey, whom he says instructed that "it is easy to detect the fallacy that Dewey described as 'transforming the (truistic) fact of acting *as* a self into the fiction of acting always *for* self.' "[10]

Rawls's reflective equilibrium is reminiscent of Dewey's Pragmatic and empirical theory of inquiry.[11] This is not to call Rawls's cultural awareness sufficient or rich.[12] He certainly was more concerned about it than some approaches to philosophy are, such as those that aim to avoid "application" of philosophy to the real world.[13] He had a great deal to say about culture and therefore appreciated the importance of contingency and social change more than many Kantian moral philosophers before or after him.[14] Rorty shows how Rawls's efforts of this kind followed the spirit of Jefferson's separation of church and state,[15] which Rorty sees as pragmatic and right. It is worth considering next how it is that Dewey came to emphasize culture.

Dewey as a Philosopher of Culture

One way of thinking about how and why Dewey came so thoroughly to focus on culture concerns his early writings in the field of psychology. In Dewey's early days, philosophy and psychology were not treated separately, as they are today. They were even considered one area. What we know as the *Journal of Philosophy* today was once the *Journal of Philosophy, Psychology, and Scientific Methods*.[16] Dewey was especially attentive to the flaws in the simple "stimulus/response" model in psychology. He studied William James's *The Principles of Psychology*[17] with great admiration, but felt dissatisfied about the prevalent outlook referred to as the "reflex arc" concept. That theory explains learning as a matter of reactions or changes in the brain's pathways that are driven by the results of reflexes themselves prompted by external stimuli. The example James used involves the young person in front of a candle, who learns quickly not to return their finger into the flame. The matter that troubled Dewey about that picture, which shows stimuli to be the primary source of action yielding response, was the fact that it isolated the child theoretically, not considering for a moment the fact that they always live in an environment in which countless things, forces, or noises could be stimuli. Dewey's theory of the selectivity of attention is in his view a better way of thinking about initial impulses, and it helps to explain the origin of personality. People are inclined toward certain stimuli over other kinds. In addition, when we watch a new baby kick and reach, there is cause to say that in the beginning was the response, or, for Dewey, the selectivity of attention.

Dewey's influential essay on this matter[18] is rarely noted today, yet it sparked the revolutionary idea that we should create stimulating environments for learning that would have been deemed distracting in older, traditional models of education. It is also among the early inspirations for connecting educational subject matter to students' interests and unique talents. From Dewey's insight in psychology, we see the importance of the social environment—one way of referring to culture—to individual development and education, including in the development of self-respect and of one's powers. Dewey draws and builds on these ideas extensively in his influential philosophy of education, his study of one of the central mechanisms with which we aim to intelligently shape culture for the next generation.

In addition to his interest in education, Dewey also drew considerably on anthropology. In *Freedom and Culture*, for example, Dewey writes, "The state of culture is a state of interaction of many factors, the chief of which are law and politics, industry and commerce, science and technology, the arts of expression and communication, and of morals, or the values [people] prize and the ways in which they evaluate them; and finally, though indirectly, the system of general ideas used by [people] to justify and to criticize the fundamental conditions under which they live, their social philosophy."[19] In this passage, we can understand in part the scope of Dewey's meaning when he refers to democracy as a way of life, as it is not a small set or discrete number of beliefs and practices, but rather an expansive way of thinking whose applications and connections run through one's culture in this broad sense, a point to which I return in chapter 6, considering the establishment of a culture of justice as a way of life.

Dewey has rightly been considered one of the great philosophers of culture.[20] Rorty credits Dewey with the inspiration to take up the theme of culture in a central way.[21] For one of Dewey's influential works, *Experience and Nature*,[22] he began but never completed a revision to the introduction, in which he wrote that in retrospect he would replace the word "experience"—a term he used often—with the word "culture." Among the reasons why "culture" is a better term for Dewey's philosophy is that experience sounds solitary, isolating. I can sit in my living room and experience a movie in a way that creates a dichotomy between the film viewed and the person viewing.

The term "culture" may sound like something that can be consumed, as in visiting a museum on one's own, but it also brings with it a sense of community or of presence within an environment, as well as the kind of feeling that implies the inseparability of the self from that wider whole. Culture, furthermore, refers to a set of conditions, pre-cognitive as well as post-, which envelop persons in sets of needs, beliefs, practices, tools, and habits. "Culture" is also a term that is biological both for Dewey and in the broader sense. For Dewey, the concept of experience, one important for his philosophy, is itself an interaction of organisms with their environments, which include other human beings and their own special interactions as well. In the broader biological sense of the term, we can "culture" cells, furthermore. We set cells in a certain kind of environment in which they grow, flourish, interact in other ways, or die, based on the conditions that suit or conflict with the organisms' evolving needs for living. Dewey was fond of biological understandings and metaphors for thinking about human progress as a kind of growth. The separation of experiencer and subject matter of experience seems to break down in the context of culture, furthermore, such as when we think of persons in a room and what makes up the temperature of that room. Spaces can be cold or warm, but it is familiar that large numbers of people can contribute substantially to warming a room. In other words, persons in a culture or in an environment are thereby part of that culture or environment, affecting it even as they are in turn affected as well.

In a 1947 essay, Dewey sums up his view of the relation between philosophy and culture. He writes,

> My standpoint is that philosophy deals with cultural problems. The principal task of philosophy is to get below the turmoil that is particularly conspicuous in times of rapid cultural change, to get behind what appears on the surface, to get to the soil in which a given culture has its roots. The business of philosophy is the relation that man has to the world in which he lives, as far as both man and the world are affected by culture, which is very much more than is usually thought.[23]

Dewey saw the work of philosophy as cultural critique and participation. This way of thinking was part of his motivation for writing and for speaking often to wide, general audiences. It is why Dewey is thought of as one of America's great public philosophers.[24]

Rorty on Rationality, Culture, and the Moral Weight of Suffering

Given the importance Rawls placed on culture for justice and Dewey's insights about philosophy's role in shaping culture, we can look now to Rorty, a follower of both, who often wrote on culture. In particular, Rorty can help us to avoid unnecessary frustrations that arise when dualisms persist in our philosophy, ones that Rawls and Dewey both sought to get around. Among the ways in which Dewey and I differ from Rorty, however, is in the sharp distinction he made between public or secular "vocabularies" and private or personal ones, an area in which he was sympathetic with Rawls. Dewey's concept of democracy as a way of life saw continuity where Rorty left a dualism in place.[25] On one important dualism, however, Rorty is instructive, offering distinctions between different senses of "rationality" and "culture." His focus on these topics arose out of his background in the philosophy of language. Near the end of his career, Rorty writes explicitly about philosophy "as cultural politics,"[26] but his attention to culture arose much earlier in his writings. The connection between Rorty's early analytic philosophy and his later work is found in the difficult questions raised for the philosophy of language, especially concerning problems of cultural difference. The analytic tradition struggled with questions of translation across cultures, as in the story about the native who yells "Gavagai!" "Gavagai" might refer to the running rabbit he sees, to one of its parts, to the act of running, or some other element of the experience he means to emphasize.[27] In this example drawn from Quine's *Word and Object*, we see how language and culture call for testing out meanings in interaction.

Rorty's and Dewey's attention to culture grows out of the latter's insights in psychology and his consequent philosophy of education. Among the crucial developments undertaken in education is the task of enculturation, educating students about the best practices, scientific developments, and social conditions of their communities, broadly defined, for the sake of preparing them for life's various and changing problems. What troubles many critics of Dewey's philosophy today is precisely the extent to which public schools shape young people's culture. The strictest of such critics want their kids to stay away from public schools. They therefore either send them to private schools of their liking or sometimes put them through a customized curriculum by other means.[28] Some do this as a form of cultural protest against public intrusion into their culture and as an affirmation of their own values. Of course, there are many other reasons to consider homeschool, some of which scholars have argued Dewey might have valued.[29] Dewey's advocacy for public education itself can be understood as the recognition of the value of culture and its intelligent presentation and engagement with citizens for the sake of the public good. In political liberalism like Rawls's, one of the roles of culture in justice is found in the development of persons—in the inculcation of cultural beliefs and attitudes that foster self-respect and a sense of individuals' power to pursue meaningful life plans as equal citizens. If education is among the mechanisms for shaping culture, it remains to consider different conceptions of culture as Rorty explored them.

There are many places to look for Rorty's insights on culture. His essay "Rationality and Cultural Difference"[30] helps to identify understandings of rationality and culture that are problematic and outdated and those that ought to be preserved and put to use. He presents three notions for each of the terms, rationality and culture. He calls *rationality*$_1$ "the ability to cope with the environment by adjusting one's reactions to environmental stimuli in complex and delicate ways. This is sometimes called 'technical reason.'" He differentiates this form of reasoning from *rationality*$_2$, which is his name for "an extra added ingredient that human beings have and brutes do not, [enabling humans to set] goals other than mere survival." *Rationality*$_3$ he characterizes as "roughly synonymous with tolerance—with the ability not to be overly disconcerted by differences from oneself, not to respond aggressively to such differences. This ability goes along with a willingness to alter one's own habits . . . to reshape oneself."[31]

With these three senses of the term rationality, Rorty explains the difference that separates certain groups of thinkers, such as enlightenment Kantians from Pragmatic Deweyans. As Rorty rightly interprets him, Dewey would see rationality$_2$ as overstated, something that assumes too much and ignores the origins of differences in rationality. Dewey sees continuity directly from rationality$_1$ to rationality$_3$. In essence, he rejects the idea that predates Darwin's revolutionary insights, namely that human beings are so characteristically different from other animals as to be categorically distinct from them. Of course, there are differences between humans and non-human animals, but Dewey notes our continuities and sees any developments that separate humans from other animals as contingent beliefs or practices that mask the animal nature of human beings and generally fail to appreciate animals' complex intelligences.

Rorty's distinctions between ideas about rationality inform distinctions he makes about culture in turn. He explains that $culture_1$ "is simply a set of shared habits of action, those that enable members of a single human community to get along with one another and with the surrounding environment as well as they do." $Culture_2$, by contrast, is "the name of a virtue," as in the phrase "to be cultured." Finally, he distinguishes these from $culture_3$, "the overcoming of the base and irrational and animal by something universally human, respect." To say that one $culture_1$ is more "advanced" than another is to say that it has come closer to realizing "the essentially human" than another $culture_1$, that it is a better expression of what Hegel called "the self-consciousness of Absolute Spirit," a better example of $culture_3$. The universal reign of $culture_3$ is the goal of history.[32] Rorty, Dewey, and Rawls each would reject the notion that there is some ultimate or final culture toward which society is progressing, the kind Rorty called $culture_3$.

These three definitions offer ways of thinking about different philosophical traditions and how they have considered issues of culture and rationality. First, it is important to consider that people often make claims about the inherent value of any culture. As Rorty explains, this is in part an argument motivated by the reasonable guilt Westerners feel about brutal colonialism. But the "exaltation of the non-Western and the oppressed seems to [Rorty] just as dubious as the Western imperialists' assurance that all other forms of life are 'childish' in comparison with that of modern Europe."[33] When we think about different cultures and about evaluating one as better than another, more just than another, it is reasonable to ask Rorty whether there can be genuine comparisons.

On the one hand, Rorty believes that there are cultures that "we would be better off without." Among these, he includes "for example, those of concentration camps, criminal gangs, and international conspiracies of bankers."[34] On the other hand, Rorty is quick to add his controversial interpretation of Dewey, writing of Dewey that "He did not think it the function of philosophy to provide argumentative backup, firm foundations, for evaluative hierarchies. He simply took the rhetorics and goals of the social democratic movement of the turn of the century for granted and asked what philosophy might do to further them."[35] At this point,

I see both partial value and partial trouble in Rorty's thinking not just about Dewey, but mainly about evaluation. Rorty believes that it is time people recognize that the firm foundations we have long believed in are really inventions of reason. Dewey would agree with elements of Rorty's critique of tradition, but not all, especially Rorty's rejection of the idea of philosophical foundations,[36] which Dewey reconstructed. Larry Hickman has explained Dewey's sense of "foundations" as different from the immovable, fixed rock metaphor, choosing instead the idea of a movable platform, such as we find on an ocean.[37] The idea of a platform is helpful, since we do stand on foundations of a sort as we experience the world, as we create tools to pursue more complex and refined projects. Whereas Enlightenment thinkers felt that they needed immovable foundations in some abstract idea or divine origin, Hickman explains that Dewey "thought that the moderns had missed the point that naturally occurring ends are the 'platforms' from which it is possible to regard other things."[38] Naturally occurring ends offer platforms for considering and building on cultural ideals. Standing on movable and contingent yet stable foundations, ideas and ideals can be refined and updated in ways increasingly valuable for human life.

In some passages of his work, Rorty seems to agree with the point of the "platform" metaphor, yet he is unwilling to call it a foundation, perhaps given the baggage of the term's history. The second trouble I have with Rorty's point is that he denies evaluative foundations, yet uses one as an evaluative tool time and again. When we look for a basic motive for evaluating another culture, Rorty suggests that we look at its response to suffering. He does not explain to the insensitive person why they should care about suffering in the world. He simply accepts the norm and presents it much in the way that Peter Singer does in "Famine, Affluence, and Morality."[39] What we find in Rorty's attention to suffering, however, is a way of thinking about moral progress. It is also an instrument for moral evaluation and differentiation of more and less acceptable cultures.

Rorty was right about the need for toleration of difference and control of the knee-jerk judgment of others, what he describes in terms of rationality$_3$. In my own youth, derogatory remarks about persons who identified as LGBTQ+ were commonplace, yet in the period of one generation, people's attitudes have changed dramatically in favor of tolerance and respect.[40] Addressing Dewey's lessons regarding the need for flexibility in moral thinking, Rorty writes that

The very mixed bag of results produced by this new flexibility—this increased ability to alter the environment rather than simply fending off its blows—meant, in Dewey's eyes, that we typically solve old problems at the cost of creating new problems for ourselves. (For example, we eliminate old forms of cruelty and intolerance only to find that we have invented new, more insidious forms thereof.) He had no wholesale solution to offer to the new problems we had created, only the hope that the same experimental daring which had created the new problems as by-products might, *if combined with a will to decrease suffering*, eventually produce piecemeal solutions to those new problems.[41]

So, despite all of Rorty's efforts to avoid presenting foundational values, we find in a number of his writings the importance of decreasing suffering. An acquaintance at a conference once asked me whether in moral theory Pragmatists are basically utilitarians, those moral theorists focused on the consequences of choices for aggregate social happiness. The answer is no, but the elimination of suffering where possible is surely a good thing in general. After all, the utilitarian moral theorist believes that moral judgments are right when they follow the demands of a calculus about pains and pleasures. Certainly such a calculus can factor into decision-making for a Pragmatist, but Pragmatists can also be constitutionalists,[42] who think that greater happiness in shutting up Bob should probably not trump his right to speak freely in the public square.

Suffering is the recurring concern in a number of Rorty's works, but especially in his writings on human rights.[43] We can appreciate in his and Dewey's considerations about culture that the diminishment of suffering is central for justice. In addition, we can see the cultural role of rationality$_3$ in shaping the conditions necessary for the moral benefits of tolerance. In that area, he offers some rich arguments with regard to the forces, aims, and tools for reconstructing justice. Whether at the domestic or international level, Rorty's respect for people and their suffering is rooted in his and Dewey's democratic values. He explains Dewey's insights about toleration and its benefits, writing that

As we became more and more emancipated from custom—more and more willing to do things differently than our ancestors for the sake of coping with our environment more efficiently and successfully—we became more and more receptive to the idea that good ideas might come from anywhere, that they are not the prerogative of an elite and not associated with any particular locus of authority. In particular, the rise of technology helped break down the traditional distinction between the "high" wisdom of priests and theorists and the "low" cleverness of artisans—thus contributing to the plausibility of a democratic system of government.[44]

The platform I see in this last passage concerns the Pragmatists' ideas about the best ways of seeking knowledge, as well as the origins of coming to value more and more people's well-being. In Dewey's ideas about logic and inquiry and in Charles Sanders Peirce's essay on fixing belief,[45] we see clear and strong norms for intelligent inquiry, norms that are platforms firm enough to stand on as we pursue increasing levels of intellectual endeavor. As Peirce noted, we certainly can "fix belief" by authority alone, but when we do so, we often end up with beliefs that are hard to maintain, such as when an allegedly immortal king dies. Peirce and Dewey both saw that science proceeds through communal inquiry. Not only is science better and stronger, but so are economies, when more people of varied backgrounds and ways of thinking engage in conversation and commerce.

Pragmatic Foundations—
Democracy, Diversity, and Moral Progress

One can understand Pragmatic cultural foundations in considering elements of social progress, such as in the growth of respect for diversity. Why would business, politics, and science do better as a result of increased diversity? In science, as in business, medicine, and politics, greater diversity in the pool of inquirers is better than more homogeneity. The added benefit comes not only from increases in perspectives on ideas, but also from the competition that tests ideas. In these lessons about humanity and about the platforms on which we stand, there are tools available for achieving greater human progress and for evaluating the strengths, weaknesses, virtues, and vices of different cultures. We see that appreciating all people as possible sources of insight, happiness, industry, and commerce makes for a stronger, smarter, and more humane culture, especially when such democratic values are guided with the aim of enhancing people's well-being and diminishing suffering.

The conclusion we can draw from appreciating the value of diversity in inquiry, ethics, and politics is that cultures that are democratic and tolerant will fare better. In *The Law of Peoples*,[46] Rawls shies away from the claim that cultures must be democratic in order to be legitimate and just, but ultimately that was among the shortfalls of that work, if indeed culture can impede or enable justice. This does not imply that one is justified to intervene militarily in just any or every undemocratic country, but, as Rorty argued in his essay on human rights, it may well be that we ought to intervene culturally, such as in the spread of education and literature—a point that Rawls's strong liberalism would not permit.

In an elegant and metaphorical passage, Rorty offers an insight about the complexity of cultures, conjuring the imagery of a tapestry. He writes,

> The real work of building a multicultural global utopia, I suspect, will be done by people who, in the course of the next few centuries, unravel each culture$_1$ into a multiplicity of fine component threads and then weave these threads together with equally fine threads drawn from other cultures$_1$—thus promoting the sort of variety-in-unity characteristic of rationality$_3$. The resulting tapestry will, with luck, be something we can now barely imagine—a culture$_1$ that will find the cultures$_1$ of contemporary America and contemporary India[47] as suitable for benign neglect as we find those of Harappa or of Carthage.[48]

Here we see Rorty imagining something like a culture-shaping version of Rawls's concept of reflective equilibrium. Rorty's metaphor suggests a way of visualizing the process of aiming to design or establish a specific cultural picture, one that can remove unacceptable or clashing strands, substituting others—and all while striving for a maximally respectful and empowering cultural picture. Rorty is effectively calling for an intelligent reconstruction of culture, a Deweyan aim, which Rawls does not explain how to envision in such explicit language or metaphor.

Putting Culture to Work on Human Rights

Rorty offers his most concrete proposals for reconstructing grossly unjust cultures in his essay on human rights.[49] Of course, he would argue for the need for his proposal at the domestic level in the United States as well. *Human rights* as a term typically invokes international matters, as the

United Nations works on relevant concerns in its Human Rights Office. It is also commonly associated with something like a norm based on rationality$_2$ and rationality$_3$. After all, human rights call for tolerance and respect for all people, and they focus on human beings. They might be said to imply that because of what is distinct in human nature, certain rights correspond with obligations that determine better and worse forms of government and human interaction. In the domain of human rights, a Pragmatist who rejects an exceptionalist outlook on rationality$_2$, seeing it instead as an evolutionary continuity and outgrowth of rationality$_1$, will need to explain on what basis we require rationality$_3$, tolerance, for greatly differing cultures.

In "Human Rights, Rationality, and Sentimentality," Rorty argues that the gross violations of human rights that must be stopped are generally preceded by dehumanization of the oppressed—a decidedly cultural mechanism. When Nazis spoke of Jews as viruses or vermin, they referred to human beings as things that we generally try to kill or exterminate. When Serbs treated Muslims as dogs, they spoke of human beings as animals who could be put down, treated as property, and discarded. In this context, one could expect that concern about "dehumanization" must stem from appeals to the static, enlightenment idea of humanity and rationality$_2$. Rorty avoids that approach. Instead, he again focuses on suffering. Dehumanization is a process whereby people prepare themselves through social conditioning to not feel sympathy for certain other people.[50] Drawing another lesson here, we see the power of language, metaphor, and belief in creating the conditions that dehumanize people and foster injustice.

Rorty sees sentimentality as a contingent development of biology and history. Here we find a difference, I believe, between Rorty and both Dewey and myself, insofar as there is a kind of necessity that comes from contingently developed platforms for Dewey. After all, evolutionarily, those species that attend to the suffering of their fellows gain an evolutionary advantage.[51] People sympathize with others and feel sad when they suffer. If there are any exceptions, the select few who do not feel for others are still entitled to live and be left alone, to some degree, so long as they avoid harming others. The vast majority of people who feel for others as human beings—as animals with rationality$_1$ and rationality$_3$—can protect themselves as necessary from the few unlike them when they become dangerous, or let them be when they are not harming anyone.[52] But, where possible, Rorty believes that it is the responsibility of society to educate people to have the right sentiments. In this sense, a profound moral need is addressed when students read books like *To Kill a Mockingbird*, *The Bluest Eye*, or *The Diary of Anne Frank*.[53] What texts like these do is put the reader in the perspective of the person who is persecuted, who is affected by hatred or lack of respect or sympathy.[54]

Rorty argues that simply identifying as human, biologically speaking, or making some abstract argument about a person's humanity, is unlikely to motivate other people significantly to address suffering, in contrast with telling people's stories. If you want to fight for human rights, he thought, you need to humanize others, caring about some stranger " 'Because this is what it is like to be in her situation—to be far from home, among strangers,' or 'Because she might become your daughter-in-law,' or 'Because her mother would grieve for her.' "[55] The idea is that abstraction makes it easier not to care, while feeling with others, thinking about their stories, caries an emotional force that leads people to care and to act.

Rorty notes the underlying connection between our beliefs about politics and ethics and our sentiments based on stories, histories, and social conditioning. He offers a way of thinking about the possibilities for philosophy to influence culture. First, if he's right, we should disagree with universalists who think that passions and rationality ought to be firmly separated out in thought about ethics. Second, when we think about making a society more just, part of what is needed is a form of education whereby citizens learn to sympathize with others, to see contingent, superficial differences between themselves and others for what they are: irrelevant to people's abilities to flourish or suffer. While there will be disagreement about how sentiments ought to be directed, Rorty does point to mechanisms that influence people, such as literature.

The trouble for Rawls, when he moves to his political conception of justice, is that he seeks to minimize his demands on culture and introduces the problematic distinction between what is private and what is public. The initial distinction relevant here is to consider Rawls's sense of a "public political culture." It arises in *Political Liberalism*, where he explains that offering justification to others about our political beliefs must proceed from matters that are agreed on already. Otherwise, no progress could be made, as it takes a premise one already believes to confer believability on another claim or conclusion to one's arguments.[56]

A worry that arises at this point concerns the freedom of people who hold different religions or comprehensive doctrines. Their motivations can well be called private, such as in seeking to live according to what one believes is right because of private religious revelation. It is an overstatement to say that Rawls would not allow religious speech about private reasons in the public domain, but he would argue that any political discussion should include appeals to reasons that are public and not only private ones. For Rawls, in political settings, proper reasons will rest on matters of overlapping consensus and opinion, which are matters of culture, but not just any element of culture. The practical point to be made here is that agreement about conclusions must start with agreement about premises, at least for systematic public cooperation to function with stability.

Rawls's aim to separate the public and the private with regard to culture is difficult to accept, such as in cases in which one's private culture sees other people as subhuman. The language we use, our beliefs, and our practices have consequences that permeate other behavior and engagements. When judges must be disinterested, they are expected to pay special attention to their own potential for biasing influence, and even to step down from judgment when necessary.[57] The call to limit one's arguments to public culture, to grounds acceptable to all, requires treating others as worthy of such respect. The implications of Dewey's philosophy, by contrast, suggest that some background cultures themselves run counter to the democratic way of life and need to be resisted where possible, and in some way consistent with our other democratic norms—such as through education. For instance, Dewey once argued that intolerance due to politics, race, or color is "treason to the democratic way of life."[58] Rorty is less clear on this kind of matter because of the distinction he retains between the public and the private.[59] Rorty aligns with Rawls in this regard and to that degree, I argue, fails to appreciate Dewey's important point about the continuity at work between the two. Nevertheless, we can see in Rorty's work and in Deweyan educational philosophy the ways in which culture and literature can be employed for the sake of cultivating healthy sentiments necessary for fostering a sense of positive power in all people.

Rethinking Liberalism Pragmatically

Rawls appears at times to take a contextualist approach to his understanding of concepts and how they are shaped by culture. Rorty recognizes and values such moments in Rawls's work, such as where the latter writes,

> The constructionist view accepts from the start that a moral conception can establish but a loose framework for deliberation which must rely very considerably on our powers of reflection and judgment. These powers are not fixed once and for all, but are developed by a shared public culture and hence shaped by that culture. . . . the moral conception is to have a wide social role as a part of public culture and is to enable citizens to appreciate and accept the conception of the person as free and equal.[60]

In each of the passages I have presented so far, the crucial thing I want to highlight is Rawls's frequent references to culture, even if its nature and reconstruction call for further development. In addition, we see in this passage the vital role of the intelligent and purposeful reconstruction of culture aiming to condition people's use of language, concepts, and practices for the sake of developing a sense of each citizen as free and equal. Some of these details he does not spell out in so many words, but he is saying that we must develop people's conceptions about fellow citizens with the help of public cultural forces. With that point, I strongly agree and see demand for further explication.

Contrary to what one might call "non-contextualist" views, Rawls was careful to recognize the importance of community agreement based on present sets of beliefs, however conditioned by a past. It was his aim, of course, to consider how diverse societies, like those we find in the United States of America, can exist with stability despite the many differences in cultural beliefs we find. This was among his central tasks as he explained them in *Political Liberalism*.[61] His goal was never to find truth about ethics or justice independent of what people think about these ideas, differing with scholars such as Russ Shafer-Landau.[62] Instead, he offered ways to think about areas of cultural overlap across difference—as grounds on which to motivate cooperative action. While I would not sharply differentiate public and private culture as he does, the idea of overlapping consensus implied in "public culture" is important for fostering unity and sympathy for others who are different.

The lingering problem with Rawls's distinction between public political culture and background culture is that it does not recognize the power that background beliefs have. When voting on referenda, people are not asked for justifications. Rawls also misses the force that cultural ideas can exert in attacking the self-worth or self-respect of people. After all, while we often think of the Ku Klux Klan as a "hate group," they have long referred to themselves as a religious organization.[63] Of course, Rawls does not defend any which "background culture," as some can be "unreasonable," according to his technical sense of the term, and thus not deserving of the same legitimacy as reasonable religious beliefs. Nevertheless, a norm calling for people to draw on reasonable public cultural values does nothing to address the insidious effects on culture of people's hateful beliefs and practices.

Rorty's solution to such problems is especially long-term in relation to sentimental education. His understanding of sentimental education bears similarities to Rawls's ideas of what he would classify as "reasonable" and of reflective equilibrium. If people had a certain education, they would appreciate the right things in due course. Rorty believes that the best we can do is to tell the stories of suffering, teaching people to feel sympathy for others. An example of Rorty's point involves the fight for civil rights in the United States. In segregated communities, outside reporters were despised along with the African American students who wanted to integrate schools like the University of Mississippi.[64] Those outsider journalists were taking pictures and telling stories of shameful violence and cruelty.[65] It certainly took a great deal of shaming to bring about the slow changes that eventually did come. In such instances, however, the mechanism at work was not to convince people about the biological humanity of others, Rorty would point out, but to shame those in power for not caring or feeling for the oppressed groups in the first place. A version of this argument about the moral force of shame is at work in Kwame Anthony Appiah's argument about how moral change comes about—and shame is a decidedly cultural mechanism.[66]

One concern about Rorty's and Rawls's outlooks on culture to this point regarding the proper sentiments or judgments of what is reasonable parallels Dewey's insights about democracy. Rather than offering foundational justifications, at least in some immutable sense of foundations, each of the three begins by accepting the democratic ideal that every individual matters and is deserving of sympathy, respect, and the chance to develop their faculties. Rather than think some universally persuasive argument could be offered to convince even the psychopath to care about others, the burden of justification must be seen as on the shoulders of the deviant, psychopathic invention of reason—the fancy imagined character whom some armchair philosophers think we need to persuade to be moral. Our laws against murder and child abuse are not controversial. Challenges to them would be radically controversial. By a move along these lines, Dewey noted the historical convergence of the many different modern moral theories on the idea that individuals ought to be respected and valued as having worth. As noted in chapter 1 of their 1908 book *Ethics*, Dewey and James Tufts wrote that

> the worth and dignity of every human being of moral capacity is fundamental in nearly every moral system of modern times. It is implicit in the Christian doctrine of the worth of the soul, in the Kantian doctrine of personality, in the Benthamic dictum, "every man to count as one." It is embedded in our democratic theory and institutions. With the leveling and equalizing of physical and mental power brought about by modern inventions and the spread of intelligence, no State is permanently safe except on a foundation of justice. And justice cannot be fundamentally in contradiction with the essence of democracy.[67]

Those who wish to hold contrary views to these converging moral traditions bear the burden of justification. In the democratic context, burdens of justification presume the worthiness of the persons to whom we justify our actions and decisions. The persons who are unreasonable on Rawls's account, psychopathic or sentimentally deprived on Rorty's view, or undemocratic on Dewey's are those who fail to treat others as full individuals deserving of respect, while nevertheless demanding justification of others' challenges.

Along similar lines, Rawls differentiated in *The Law of Peoples* between reasonable societies and "outlaw societies." Rawls writes that

> outlaw societies were not societies burdened by unfavorable resources, material and technological, or lacking in human capital and know-how; on the contrary, they were among the most politically and socially advanced and economically developed societies of their day. *The fault in those societies lay in their political traditions and the background institutions of law, property, and class structure, with their sustaining beliefs and culture.* These things must be changed before a reasonable law of peoples can be accepted and supported.[68]

In many of Rawls's arguments dealing with the "basic structures" of society, it seems that he is talking about principles and the mechanisms by which society operates through the use of government, regulation, and property. In fact, it is clear in this passage and others that cultural beliefs, such as those involved in anti-Semitism, racism, or misogyny, can have a devastating effect on justice, and therefore conversely opposites like tolerance and respect for people who are different can be highly advantageous for bringing about justice.

Rawls's focus in *The Law of Peoples* is on international contexts for thinking about the right of one society or a set of societies to intervene in another's affairs, but he was also attentive to culture at the domestic level. When contemporary scholars think about human rights, a central subject in Rawls's *The Law of Peoples*, they commonly think about killings, starvations, violations of freedom of speech, incarcerations, and the like. Yet all over the United States, there are people who suffer the consequences of prejudice, on grounds of race, gender, sexuality, and more, but often in subtler forms, such as in inadequate school funding[69] or poorly conceived school disciplinary procedures.[70] To be sure, there are those who have pointed out evidence of overt or direct and deep injustices, such as in the cultural and policy conditions that lead to the disproportionate incarceration of African Americans in the United States compared with white citizens.[71] These points highlight the importance of seeing culture as vital domestically, not only regarding international conflicts. It is worth noting, furthermore, that critics of the United States, like China, Russia, and Iran, point to injustices committed in America when questions arise concerning human rights abuses abroad.[72] Derrick Bell noted just such a force as a contributor to the verdict in *Brown v. Board of Education*.[73]

Whether at the international or domestic levels, it is important to recognize the limits to Rorty's and Rawls's moral arguments. For instance, Rawls writes, "Of course, fundamentalist religious doctrines and autocratic and dictatorial rulers will reject the ideas of public reason and deliberative democracy. They will say that democracy leads to a culture contrary to their religion, or denies the values that only autocratic or dictatorial rule can secure. They assert that the religiously true, or the philosophically true, overrides the politically reasonable. We simply say that such a doctrine is politically unreasonable. Within political liberalism nothing more need be said."[74] There is internal coherence to Rawls's position, but this does not mean that the non-liberal society will be able to accept his position about what is reasonable. Of course, Rawls would respond by saying that those who are unreasonable are not interested in engaging with others in reasonable deliberation, which must treat all individuals with proper respect and as deserving of justification for what is done to them. Claims of national sovereignty and a desire for noninterference from others ring hollow, however, when a nation fails to treat its own people with reasonable respect. At the same time, few nations can escape the challenge of hypocrisy in criticizing others if they themselves fall short of establishing a culture of justice of their own.

Conclusion

Dewey would have opposed military intervention that is not somehow in self-defense or in defense of others. He would have called the idea of "exporting democracy" through military force wishful thinking, although Japan and Germany certainly changed in that direction after World War II.[75] In his 1937 essay "Democracy Is Radical," he argued that "democratic means and the attainment of democratic ends are one and inseparable."[76] Trying to achieve democracy by force misses this lesson, even if a nation must defend itself, such as after Japan's bombing of Pearl Harbor. At the time, Dewey was thinking about claims like those among the Communists of his day, who thought that true democracy was to be achieved through revolutionary violence and a dictatorship. He argued over and over that such approaches were wrongheaded. Elsewhere, he advocated strongly against making war, calling even for outlawing it.[77] His position against war was still consistent with active forms of intervention, but at the cultural and communicative levels. There is cultural force, for example, in making an international heroine out of the young girl who fought for the chance to get an education—Malala Yousafzai.[78] Cultural pressures are powerful and can be applied through public and international attention to problems or to heroes fighting against them. At the same time, conflicts like Russia's war with Ukraine raise questions about the limits of cultural pressures when sufficiently powerful nations are bent on war. In that conflict, however, the Russian people feel deep consequences, culturally speaking, of the change from a cosmopolitan nation to an autocratic one,[79] as well as economically, as the nation's economy was said to be "imploding."[80] Importantly, while economists have been reluctant to try to understand economies in relation to cultural forces, that is changing in a growing body of research that has recognized and begun demonstrating the power of the connection.[81]

As I have said, it is intuitive to look to Rawls's international outlook on justice to find his contributions about culture, but in fact he noted at least in a number of instances in his early work that culture matters profoundly at the domestic level as well. A society and a community fail their youths, he thought, when they regularly raise children to discount their own worth. This happens systematically among the poor, among minority groups, racially or ethnically speaking, as well as among groups that are teased or who come from regions called "backwards," such as Mississippi.[82] Persons with disabilities continue to be dismissed or ridiculed in American culture. There is still some acceptance at least in private settings of reference to bad ideas, as "retarded," for example.[83] One can find initiatives that are trying to combat such uses of language in public schools.[84] It seems that focusing only on society's "basic structures," as Rawls did, would not be enough for justice, unless we mean also its "culture," namely the language we use, the beliefs we hold, and the practices and institutions that grow out of these. It is odd to refer to these as "structures," though in a sense they are. If anything, they are organic and changing structures. Rawls saw the importance especially of self-worth, which is relatable to threats leveled in oppressive conditions. As noted in the introduction, Rawls writes in *A Theory of Justice* that "the value of education should not be assessed solely in terms of economic efficiency and social welfare. Equally if not more important is the role of education in enabling a person to enjoy the culture of his [or her] society and to take part in its affairs, and in this way to provide for each individual a secure sense of his or her own worth."[85] Given what he says here, it is easy to appreciate the threat to justice involved in preventing people from pursuing an education or in ensuring that support for education will be deeply inadequate for disadvantaged citizens.

In the United States, we have compulsory education for all citizens, provided through public schools for those children whose guardians do not choose or have no choice to go to private schools or to participate in homeschooling. In places like Mississippi, however, some school districts have been accused of creating a "school-to-prison pipeline,"[86] and forty-four school districts in 2007 were labeled "dropout factories," the vast majority of which were made up of poor and African American students.[87] While Rorty and philosophers who would not consider themselves to be "ideal theorists" certainly have cause to criticize Rawls's "ideal theory" approach, Rawls had useful resources to offer for incorporating and addressing some real-life facts and forces of culture, and certainly more than he tapped.

As we saw in the introduction, Rawls writes in *A Theory of Justice* that we must "avoid at almost any cost the social conditions that undermine self-respect."[88]

While there is in Rawls's outlook on self-respect a vital issue at the heart of the fight against oppression and anti-democratic social conditions, he falls short of focusing on what his own outlook on this (perhaps) most important primary good implies. As I argue elsewhere,[89] this point turns out to be pivotal in a tension inherent within Rawls's liberalism. If liberalism requires a certain kind of equality of citizenship, such as in mutual respect for each person implicit in what we mean by democracy, then the further liberal norm of needing to minimize intervention into people's lives may protect liberties employed to create an unjust culture. People's lives and culture can include organizations like the Ku Klux Klan and other concerted efforts to subjugate people. The most explicit and overt of these can be targeted for legal reform, to be sure, such as in the rulings against the segregation of public schools and the discussions in recent years about the football team until 2020 named the "Redskins,"[90] yet culture has subtle ways of creating and cultivating hierarchies of citizenship in our language, beliefs, practices, and institutions. Since the time when I first wrote the essay that has become this chapter, the Washington team has changed its name to the "Commanders."[91] Nevertheless, the forces and efforts that threaten democracy look for workarounds to the elimination of past policies like segregation to maintain empowered groups' advantages, such as in the development of segregated private white academies in the South,[92] most of which were created in the 1960s after the *Brown v. Board* decision. Such developments led Derrick Bell to argue that the *Brown* decision was a failure.[93] Elizabeth Anderson proposes a return to efforts at integration but recognizes that the general push has been abandoned.[94]

For reasons such as these, Dewey argued that democracy must be thought of not only as a matter of procedure or of abstract principles. Summing up the central point that Dewey offered, which ought to be heeded today especially in a social and political philosophy attentive to the power of culture, he wrote that "Our original democratic ideas must apply culturally as well as politically . . . If we cannot produce a democratic culture, one growing natively out of our institutions, our democracy will be a failure. There is no question, not even that of bread and clothing, more important than this question of the possibility of executing our democratic ideals directly in the cultural life of the country."[95] It is worth noting that Dewey made this argument in 1932, while the United

States was nearing the height of the Great Depression's 25 percent unemployment rate and consequent challenges for economic, social, and food security. To be sure, in recent years, the United States suffered from a devastating pandemic that put people out of work and led to a loss of more than one million lives and many more abroad. Even in such times of challenge, Dewey thought it vital to ensure that both politics and culture be democratic. At bottom, he argued that nothing, not even such concrete considerations, is more important than the need for establishing a truly democratic and mutually respectful culture. Culture enables or inhibits justice, and so the effects on individuals, practices, policies, and institutions are many and varied. The next steps forward must return to the task of cultural reconstruction, sentimental moral education, and the promotion of self-respect and the conditions necessary for each person to feel and believe in his or her own worth and power to pursue a meaningful and flourishing life.

3

Challenges for a Culture of Justice

Democratic theories of justice reject hierarchies of citizenship. Grave injustices like American slavery, the extermination of Jews in the Holocaust, and apartheid in South Africa were all rooted in beliefs about the inferior status of certain groups of human beings, beliefs that are incompatible with democratic values. Even after slavery was abolished in the United States, troubling practices continued to reinforce the subjugation of some citizens, such as Jim Crow laws. The separation of washrooms and water fountains for black and white citizens was one of the oppressive cultural mechanisms that symbolized and reinforced white supremacy, asserting the second-class status of non-white persons. These practices are examples of conditions that aimed, among other related goals, to diminish or undermine self-respect among oppressed groups or at least to perpetuate systems of privilege. In their attack on individuals' sense of their own positive power in society, such conditions threaten what John Rawls has called a primary good[1]—if not the most important primary good—which is necessary for citizens to fight for the protection of their rights: self-respect.

While there is much disagreement about how to characterize self-respect, there is widespread consensus about its importance. For Rawls and others who emphasize the role of public deliberation and social cooperation in democratic societies, justice is said to depend on people working together, defending their rights, resisting injustice, and otherwise pursuing their own or shared ends, all of which require self-respect. In this book, I argue for understanding the relevant sense of self-respect in terms of individuals' sense of their own worth and positive power in society. When people are oppressed to such an extent and in such a manner that they lose self-respect or a sense of their own positive power in the world, they will not fight for their rights. Given such worries, there is a moral need to avoid and correct for those conditions that undermine self-respect among citizens.

Since a democratic theory of justice calls for fostering self-respect in all citizens, I argue in this book that democracy therefore requires a culture of justice—a culture necessary for the fulfilment of such an obligation. The claim that democratic societies require a culture of justice might appear to be obviously true, but in the present chapter I argue that, while true, it is not obvious, and that the claim requires defense from serious challenges. In addition, recognizing and addressing the impediments to a culture of justice can offer some helpful starting points from which to decipher its nature and content. At the heart of eight challenges that I clarify here is a tension inherent in liberalism between the norm of minimalist intervention into people's lives and culture and the need for certain cultural conditions for fostering in all people a sense of their own worth and positive power in the world.

In demonstrating the challenges to defending what I call the cultural requirement for justice—the moral demand for establishing the conditions necessary for fostering self-respect in all people and a sense of their positive power in the world—I present eight difficulties, which fall into two categories, theoretical challenges and challenges of implementation. To argue for a democratic culture of justice, advocating for its establishment and maintenance, these impediments must be revealed and clarified.

At the outset, I review a few of John Rawls's influential thoughts on the subjects of self-respect and culture. Then I present eight challenges to a culture of justice. Finally, I offer some concluding thoughts about the clarificatory benefits of surveying these challenges and some implications of attending to the need for a culture of justice.

Self-Respect and Culture

Rawls's influence on social and political philosophy in the second half of the twentieth century inspired much of the debate that has arisen about self-respect. He also had a number of valuable considerations to offer on the subject of culture. To appreciate the challenges in the way of establishing a culture of justice, it is necessary to review a few key ideas from Rawls's works, underlying his chief message about self-respect in *A Theory of Justice*. I conclude this section with a look at one of Margaret

Mead's most succinct definitions of "culture," which complements in part what Rawls had to say on the subject, and with which I contextualize the sources of impediments to a culture of justice.

As noted previously, in *A Theory of Justice*, Rawls argued that for the sake of justice, we should "avoid at almost any cost the social conditions that undermine self-respect."[2] While there has been much debate about the nature of self-respect,[3] a guiding question about Rawls's argument here is at least equally difficult to answer: To what extent can or should politics and the pursuit of justice shape or intervene in a culture? At bottom, this question concerns the relationship between social and political philosophy. The liberal tradition in general calls for minimizing government imposition on people, given its basis in consent and individual liberty. Political institutions presently can regulate behavior within certain boundaries, yet beyond those boundaries, there very well could be conditions that threaten some citizens' self-respect. The overarching difficulty, then, is to determine the extent of the cost worth incurring to avoid or redress those conditions that can undermine people's self-respect. We must decide the limits of justified imposition into people's lives and culture that we do not often or always allow presently. A concrete example of this is the controversial decision on the part of the Office of Patents and Trademarks not to renew the trademark protection of the Washington football team's racially offensive mascot.[4] I return to these concerns in the next section, where I differentiate various aspects of the question and challenge.

Rawls recognized the important role of cultural conditions for justice, even if much is still to be examined in the relationship between social conditions, or culture, and politics. He saw culture as the ground from which political justifications must be drawn, for example. In *Political Liberalism*, Rawls wrote, "Since justification is addressed to others, it proceeds from what is, or can be, held in common; and so we begin from shared fundamental ideas implicit in the public political culture in the hope of developing from them a political conception that can gain free and reasoned agreement in judgment."[5] Rawls's ideal of legitimate government rests on culture, though he is specific in referring to "public political culture" as distinct from any one particular group's culture. He reveals a challenge for "public political culture," writing,

> The public political culture may be of two minds at a very deep level. Indeed, this must be so with such an enduring controversy as that concerning the most appropriate understanding

of liberty and equality. This suggests that if we are to succeed in finding a basis for public agreement, we must find a way of organizing familiar ideas and principles into a conception of political justice that expresses those ideas and principles in a somewhat different way than before.[6]

To work from a basis for agreement despite entrenched differences, even in circumstances in which no groups are treated as second-class citizens, calls for the difficult task of establishing beliefs and practices that are based on new ways of thinking acceptable to all. Rawls here foreshadows several of the challenges for achieving a culture of justice, to which I will return. He also touches on a challenge for implementation: namely that intellectual leadership is called for in the construction of new concepts that can bridge the differences commonly found between traditional political conceptions. This need for new concepts is part of what cultural critic John Dewey had in mind in his work *Reconstruction in Philosophy*.[7]

One of the cultural challenges to justice for which Rawls offered an explicit response involved religion. He distinguished between "public political culture" and what he called "background culture." For example, he wrote that

> reasonable comprehensive doctrines, religious or nonreligious, may be introduced in public political discussion at any time, provided that in due course proper political reasons—and not reasons given solely by comprehensive doctrines—are presented that are sufficient to support whatever the comprehensive doctrines introduced are said to support. This injunction to present proper political reasons I refer to as *the proviso*, and it specifies public political culture as distinct from the background culture.[8]

Rawls presented a way of addressing in the political realm difficulties for justice that arise from the social realm of "background culture." He was concerned about reason giving for public deliberation and the effort to respect differences in people's background cultures.

Two further passages are worth revisiting to reveal how profoundly and widely influential culture was for Rawls's approach to justice, stretching from the basic level of constructivism in moral theory to the broad level of international intervention in the affairs of other nations. First, Rawls argued that

The constructionist view accepts from the start that a moral conception can establish but a loose framework for deliberation which must rely very considerably on our powers of reflection and judgment. These powers are not fixed once and for all, but are developed by a shared public culture and hence shaped by that culture. . . . The moral conception is to have a wide social role as a part of public culture and is to enable citizens to appreciate and accept the conception of the person as free and equal.[9]

While Rawls appeared once again appreciative of the role of culture in achieving justice, the task of addressing societies that do not embody the moral conception at work was a challenge for his view, especially at the international level.

In an essay that led to Rawls's last book published in his lifetime, *The Law of Peoples*, culture arose as a vital force in enabling or frustrating the pursuit of justice. In a passage noted already in chapter 2, Rawls wrote,

outlaw societies in the historical cases mentioned . . . were not societies burdened by unfavorable resources, material and technological, or lacking in human capital and know-how; on the contrary, they were among the most politically and socially advanced and economically developed societies of their day. The fault in those societies lay in their political traditions and the background institutions of law, property, and class structure, with their sustaining beliefs and culture. These things must be changed before a reasonable law of peoples can be accepted and supported.[10]

Rawls's claim that some cultures must change before reason and law can properly guide public institutions toward justice seems understandable and correct. At the same time, the liberal tradition in general aims to steer clear of impositions on people's beliefs and culture, as I have said, and hence is in tension with its own ideals here. In addition, his theory appears to call for an understanding of the ways in which culture can be shaped, as well as the development of tools and models for doing so.

Rawls's distinction between "background" culture and "public political culture" suggested different spheres, though he understood that they are continuous with one another, not wholly separate. Richard Rorty appreciated Rawls's work in general and this distinction in particular.

He believed that it is reasonable to differentiate and separate out from political processes of justification matters that Rawls had called "background beliefs." Examples like the meaning of human life were to Rorty "as irrelevant to politics as Jefferson thought questions about the Trinity and about transubstantiation."[11] Even if Rorty and Rawls agreed regarding background culture, it is important to recognize and address the challenges that arise when background beliefs are held by a majority of citizens uninterested in justifying their decisions to those who do not share the same beliefs.

Finally, to conclude this section, an understanding of "culture" is needed to connect with Rawls's ideas here and the overarching points I hope to make in this chapter. Margaret Mead offered a succinct understanding of "culture" in her introduction to Ruth Benedict's influential book *Patterns of Culture*.[12] There, Mead calls culture "the systematic body of learned behavior which is transmitted from parents to children."[13] This learned behavior includes language, beliefs, practices, and the enactment and maintenance of institutions. This definition is not meant to imply that only a child's own parents transmit culture, but that their generation collectively passes on beliefs, practices, and institutions, a "systematic body of learned behavior."

The importance of culture and self-respect for Rawls's approach to justice is profound, even if is interpreted variously by followers and critics. This section aims only to illustrate some of the texts in which matters of self-respect and culture have arisen as essential concerns for politics and justice, and in which challenges emerge.

Challenges to a Culture of Justice

Although my ultimate intent in this book is to clarify and argue in favor of the moral requirement to establish a culture of justice, my task in this chapter is only to demonstrate the need for such a defense, given the theoretical and practical challenges at play. An appreciation of these challenges should reveal some guiding insights about how a culture of justice should be understood. In what follows, I present eight challenges to the case for and establishment of a culture of justice. The eight challenges fall in a general sense into one of two categories. The first five challenges I classify as theoretical and the next three are challenges for implementation.[14]

Theoretical Challenges

Challenge 1: Duty to Oneself

In recognizing the primary importance of self-respect for justice, a challenge emerges with regard to each individual's responsibility for living as a self-respecting person. This first challenge concerns the nature of the self-respect requirement for justice. Does it involve an obligation to oneself? If it implies an individual's responsibility to oneself, the problem is that many thinkers believe justice to be a virtue that has to do with other people, not with oneself alone. Aristotle writes in *Ethics* that "justice and injustice must always involve more than one person."[15] If this is the case, then an individual's participation in the cultivation or embodiment of his or her self-respect is not a matter of justice, at least if understood essentially with regard to him- or herself.

The well-known response here is that self-respect *does* or *can* concern other people, insofar as persons who share an individual's identity characteristics can be negatively affected by the individual who falters with regard to self-respect. This response works for cases that motivate or solidify racism and sexism, as Thomas Hill and others have discussed the matter,[16] but it does not have the same applicability for the self-deprecator who is not identified clearly with a group. For the more difficult cases, Hill argued that from the Kantian point of view, self-respect is a precondition for other duties. Therefore if we have other duties, a duty of self-respect is implicit in those other-oriented duties.

The challenge here is essentially that self-respect seems intuitively to be a self-oriented duty, yet it appears to be relevant to justice only indirectly through our obligations to others. In addition, if self-respect is a precondition for other duties, then that means when others undermine a person's self-respect, such as through oppressive measures, the oppressors are responsible for his or her lack of self-respect. In that context, it seems as though self-respect is relevant, but as an obligation for others not to undermine it, or perhaps even to foster it instead. Consider that communities are sometimes blamed when they have failed to attend sufficiently to the needs of persons who then commit terrible acts of violence.[17] In the case of oppression or of community neglect, if self-respect is a necessity for justice, it is in such circumstances not a matter of one's obligation to oneself or of one's indirect obligation to exhibit self-respect given other-oriented duties. As odd as it sounds, the cultivation and non-impedance of self-respect in these contexts is the fundamental obligation. Therefore, self-respect begins as a social obligation before it becomes a matter of an individual's character.

The central outlook that raises challenges for a culture of justice in connection with the idea of self-respect as a duty to oneself hinges on seeing self-respect primarily as an individual's responsibility. Provocatively, some scholars argue that even when a person is a member of an oppressed group, and thus is not thought to be primarily responsible for threats to his or her own self-respect, that person nevertheless bears the responsibility to be self-respecting and to resist oppression.[18] Such a view fails to appreciate the fact that oppression does not wait until adulthood. Culture conditions people from infancy and is thus more clearly a matter of wider responsibility first and foremost before an individual can reasonably be said to mature into a responsible moral agent.

The next challenge that I present for conceiving of a culture of justice rooted in the self-respect requirement argues that when we focus on self-respect as an individual responsibility in this way, we are blaming the victims of injustice for their unfortunate condition.

Challenge 2: Blaming the Victim

The *blaming the victim* challenge consists of two parts, both of which claim that the cause of injustice is mistaken when one focuses on a culture of justice. The first part concerns the self-respect requirement for justice. The second part concerns the apparent diffusion of responsibility for oppression to the overarching culture, when in fact particular powerful interest groups can sometimes be responsible for injustice.

As noted in describing the first challenge, a common feature in discussions about self-respect is the intuitive attribution of obligations for self-respect to the self. Thus, the basic challenge at work in the first part of the blaming the victim challenge says that attention to the self-respect of oppressed persons is blaming the victims of oppression for their lot in life. The idea of placing central emphasis on individuals' duty of self-respect fails to account for the immense and pervasive power of oppression. It may well be that some people who suffer oppression will nevertheless be sufficiently able to feel and act on self-respect, but this does not mean that all or even many will be able to do so. Consider that some oppressed people are taught to read and some are not. We cannot reasonably say that illiterate people ought to read prior to having the conditions in which they can learn to read.

This first part of the blaming the victim challenge is consistent with claiming that there is an obligation to establish a culture of justice, but it calls for rethinking the nature and role of self-respect. Self-respect is on this view understood as a matter for which the community is responsible, at least in circumstances of oppression or unaddressed and problematic inequality.[19] It seems intuitively correct to think that people *should* be self-respecting—that judging someone as "not self-respecting" is itself to claim blameworthiness. This intuition should be resisted, says the challenge here, however, as it could very well be best to say that self-respect is something that would naturally develop in persons raised and living in the right conditions for the promotion of self-respect. Something like this challenge might have been an implicit motivation for Rev. Jesse Jackson's angry reaction to then-Senator Obama's Father's Day speech in June of 2008. Obama argued that black American fathers needed to be more involved and present in the lives of their children. Charles Blow of the *New York Times* wondered about Jackson's reaction: "he thinks Mr. Obama's speeches on fatherhood have been too hard on black men and not hard enough on The Man?"[20] In his piece, Blow disagrees with Jackson, though Jackson's motivation is not difficult to appreciate. At the very least, it seems harsh to focus attention on the responsibility of people who are highly disadvantaged. In fact, even in his agreement with Obama, Blow concedes, "If Mr. Obama's message of stepping up is 'talking down' [to black people,] then so be it." In such matters, there may well be shared responsibility, yet Jackson or other defenders of the victim of oppression would call first for the alleviation of the cultural forces at work before it is reasonable to blame victims. We do not blame crops for failing to grow in a drought. Nonetheless, Blow appreciates Obama's message, finding it acceptable to upset some people if there are others who need to hear the message.[21]

The second part of the blaming the victim challenge says that focusing on cultural conditions misses the real culprit causing injustice. Cultural conditions in which the victim of oppression participates are important to notice. At the same time, they are sometimes intentionally devised by individuals, groups, or particular power structures that aim to keep power in the hands of already advantaged citizens. An example in the early twentieth century was the filming of D. W. Griffith's *The Birth of a Nation* and the subsequent growth and explicit strategies of the Ku Klux Klan.[22]

To be sure, *The Birth of a Nation* is a film and in that respect a cultural instrument. Nevertheless, the point of the second part of the blaming the victim challenge explains that responsibility for problems of language, beliefs, and practices are not ultimate causes. Instead, it is the intentional *use* of these forces as tools for the benefit of particular groups of people that causes injustice. This version of the challenge says that not only should we relocate the responsibility for injustice away from the victim of it, but in addition we should see that the causes of cultural forces of injustice are really certain groups. The Southern Poverty Law Center at times identifies groups as "hate groups." This second part of the blaming the victim challenge would not deny that cultural forces are at work, but rather emphasizes the blameworthiness for them as stemming from particular groups.

An example will help explain the connection between these two parts to form the blaming the victim challenge. At a conference, a professor of non-white descent explained that when on the job market, his displays of confidence and self-respect as a job candidate were received as arrogance. When he was intentionally self-deprecating, his interviews were more successful, he said, resulting in job offers.[23] There is a history of experiences like this one, such as in connection with the application of the term "uppity" applied to describe African Americans and other non-white citizens in the United States when people pursue careers not often held by non-white persons. This history returned to national attention when a US congressman from Georgia referred to then-Senator Obama as "uppity."[24]

When people stand to lose a great deal, such as potential job offers, for acting in such a way that is generally thought to be self-respecting, the more utilitarian theorists would say that they understand people's inclination to want to cope with their circumstances and to live as well as they can live. The response typically says that in making the most of the situation, oppressed persons are strengthening the hold of oppression. Even if one holds this harder line, however, it should be noted that those who create powerful incentives for an unjust status quo are not attended to when one blames the victim of oppression instead.

Ultimately, the challenge involved in arguing against blaming the victim is partly in agreement with the demand for a culture of justice and partly a challenge to it. It is a challenge to it insofar as it is true that the problem for justice is not simply the general public's language or beliefs or even their individual practices. The bigger problem sometimes comes from people who are perfectly aware that they are fighting to preserve or enhance their own advantage. Therefore, cultural contributions to injustice are really symptoms of underlying interests and power structures, not the proper concern for justice.

With regard to conceiving of a culture of justice and the self-respect requirement, the blaming the victim challenge is of some help. The self-respect requirement can sound as though it is primarily an obligation for individuals, yet the conditions that can undermine it can in so many cases be overwhelming, external, and cultural. What I believe this challenge shows is that the self-respect requirement must be seen first and foremost as an obligation for the wider culture to establish the conditions necessary for fostering individuals' self-respect, and secondarily as an obligation for individuals. Exceptional heroes like Frederick Douglass are not evidence of a lack of impediments to self-respect or that everyone can achieve what he did. Heroes like him are remarkable especially because the odds were so powerfully set against his achievements.

Challenge 3: Negative Liberty

As noted in the first section of this chapter, John Rawls argued that we must "avoid at almost any cost" the conditions that threaten self-respect. The problem with Rawls's formulation is that it sounds as though people will develop self-respect if only a policy of noninterference is adopted. The problem is that self-respect is learned. Just as reading is not learned without positive conditions needed to learn to read, self-respect itself also must be cultivated. If simple noninterference were enough for self-respect, the feral child could be self-respecting. Some positive conditions are necessary for the development and preservation of self-respect, just as food is necessary to avoid the hunger that can distract students from learning in school. School meal programs are provided because some people cannot afford to feed their children sufficiently for them to focus in school. Therefore, if a culture of justice similarly requires positive liberty for its development, a challenge to a culture of justice will come from the strong advocates for restricting public action to the guidelines of *negative liberty*.

The challenge based on negative liberty has two forms of backing, one ideological and one motivated by individuals' interests. The former says that people should take responsibility for themselves. It adds that the costs needed to ensure positive liberties (not sufficiently supported through charity) can only be paid through an imposition of taxation on others. Thus, the negative liberty challenge says that the injustice of a lack of positive liberty on the part of some causes a burden and thereby a harm for others, who often have to support their own children already. To be sure, in the United States public education has its critics, but is also presently universal through high school. The typical reasoning that justifies the imposition of taxes for the sake of public education agrees with the advocate for the negative liberty challenge that individuals ought to take responsibility for their actions, but thinks that people need to be enabled to take such responsibility. The debates that continue concern the extent to which support should be offered.

The success of the negative liberty challenge in the United States typically is limited by conditions for children. For it is not children's fault that their parents are unemployed, impoverished, or otherwise disadvantaged as far as filling young people's needs. The strictest advocate for negative liberty as the only justifiable principle for pursuing a culture of justice would have to say that children's suffering caused by their own parents is not others' responsibility, and therefore is sad, but incorrigible, save by charity. Consequently on this view, therefore, the advocate for restrictions to negative liberty must accept the fact that not all persons are going to develop self-respect, and that this fact is of less importance with regard to democracy and justice than is the protection of individuals' private property.

Challenge 4: Against Patterns

The idea of a culture of justice hinges on the belief that harms can be done by the aggregation of human behaviors in a society. The beliefs, practices, and individual institutions of a society may not on their own appear to be a problem, yet when taken together, they can add up to wreak great harm on all or some citizens. For a simple example, consider government spending that is made impossible either by tax evasion or the public's unwillingness to raise sufficient taxes for its spending commitments. After enough time, the government's resources can[25] collapse. This has happened in Greece, among other places.[26] The individual behavior of people and institutions can have a devastating effect on the wider community. In an analogous way, the wider culture is shaped through the behavior of the whole of individuals all acting on their own. It is on this point that the fourth challenge emerges, the challenge against seeing social patterns as the level at which justice is relevant and meaningful.

The argument here is attributed to Robert Nozick, who in *Anarchy, State, and Utopia* challenged Rawls's ideas about distributive justice. Nozick's argument is worth reviewing because it could be applied to the context of cultural matters. An argument inspired by Nozick's challenge *against patterns* could say that culture is not the appropriate locus for understanding justice.

An example can help illustrate Nozick's argument. If traffic on the highway prevents Tom from getting to the airport in time for his flight, it would be odd to say that others have committed an injustice against Tom. If the traffic were due to teenagers playing a prank, driving slowly together in a coordinated line intended to obstruct cars, then Tom would be a victim of someone's deliberate behavior. An even stronger claim would come from the injured person in an ambulance, who needs to get to a hospital quickly. If the traffic were due to ordinary behavior, however, as in the aggregate effect of all the many cars on the highway traveling freely and following the laws, or even because of an accident and the consequent bottleneck of traffic that it creates, then neither Tom nor the patient in the ambulance would rightly be called victims of an injustice. We would say instead that they were unfortunate. We call such circumstances bad, but not wrong—no one is said to be morally blameworthy. In Tom's case, we might even fault him for lacking the caution to leave sufficiently early for the airport.

Taking another look at the example of difficulties related to traffic patterns can raise questions for too quick an assessment in Nozick's favor. Many causes can lead to traffic accidents that result in problematic traffic patterns, such as vehicle defects all too common today, poor car maintenance,[27] and bad highway design and conditions,[28] among numerous further reasons that can be linked to individuals' or responsible groups' decision-making. The case of the young people playing a prank can be associated with failed moral education at school or at home, furthermore. Those wishing to blame matters on forces beyond anyone's control may be right in some instances, such as in cases of terrible weather, yet Ashley Halsey, writing for *The Washington Post* in 2009, reported that "half of fatal auto crashes" in the United States were due in part to poor highway design or conditions.[29] It is challenging to determine causes and assign blame, but it is also too easy and thus morally dangerous to assume too quickly that matters are in fact entirely unrelated to someone's or the public's responsibilities.

Challenge 5: Equality

The idea that all people need self-respect and that the public ought to foster it maximally in all people depends on the democratic ideal of equality. The ideal of equality is understood by some to be a matter of universality or a norm derived analytically from the demands of democracy, and by others as a guiding value useful for avoiding the terrible injustices that have harmed people in the past when they were not treated equally. To both of these approaches, critics of the moral demand for a culture of justice connected with the self-respect requirement would charge that equality itself is a misguided concept.[30]

Critics of the concept of equality can appreciate the democratic valuation of liberty, but they charge that it is empirically false that people are equal. In fact, Louis Pojman has argued that to claim the equal worth of human beings cannot be accomplished through secular or naturalist arguments. For secularists and naturalists, Pojman argues, "there is reason to give up egalitarianism altogether."[31]

Although Pojman does not attend in particular to the concept of self-respect, if he believes that people are of unequal worth (except perhaps on religious grounds, according to Pojman) and if that is a natural fact of the universe, it becomes understandable why thinkers like Aristotle would find slavery to be a natural phenomenon. Caste and class differentiation has long been the consequence of a differential valuation of human beings. After all, we do not treat things of different moral worth the same. The consequence of a classification of persons, then, denies Rawls's democratic criterion for justice, which says that positions of public authority must reasonably be open to all. In addition, people of lesser moral worth ought not to have self-respect in the ways and proportions proper to people of higher moral worth.

To the democratic ear, these claims are unsettling. To be sure, one consequence of arguments like Pojman's is that the secular approach is simply insufficient, and hence equality might be saved, but only according to outlooks typically inconsistent with secular, religiously non-imposing liberalism. Pojman and other critics do not consider all reasonable arguments for and explanations of the concept of equality, I have argued elsewhere.[32] Nevertheless, the challenge to the concept of democratic equality based on the equal worth of all people represents a line of argument against emphasis on the importance of cultivating self-respect in all people, and hence against a relevant conceptualization of a culture of justice.

In support of Pojman's kind of challenge for views connected with Rawls's liberalism, it is worth noting that Rawls rests his understanding of justice in *A Theory of Justice* on the process of public deliberation and social cooperation. As Martha Nussbaum has noted, cognitively disabled persons cannot participate in the public cooperation and deliberations about justice that he and other liberal social contract theorists consider central to political legitimacy, rights, and justice.[33] At the very least, defenders of a culture of justice who appreciate the moral force of equality and in connection with it the self-respect requirement must contend with the challenge regarding human beings cognitively incapable of deliberation, debate, and fighting for their rights.

CHALLENGES OF IMPLEMENTATION

Challenge 6: Pettiness

In recent years, public attention has been raised over the culturally offensive name of the Washington football team, the "Redskins." Critics believe that the name is racist and that it perpetuates and promotes the idea that Native American peoples were savages, distinguished easily by their skin color. Those who defended the use of the name call their opposition "petty." Others call the critics of the team name "Disgusting!," claiming that "Political correctness is destroying the USA!"[34] Since the initial drafting of this book, the Washington team has chosen a new name, taking eighteen months and "more than 40,000 fan submissions with nearly 1,200 names" proposed. The team is now named the Commanders, and Andrew Golden, writing for the *Washington Post*, notes that the name landed "with a thud" for some fans.[35]

Consider another situation. A man in the workplace wishes to be convivial toward the new women recently hired. He refers to the group as "the girls" and to individuals as "sweetheart." He chats with some of them who like football, and when talking about how players gently spank each other on the behind as a form of encouragement, he illustrates the practice with one of the women.

In connection with both of these circumstances, there are workplace policies and rights at issue, which are typically among the points discussed. I return to the issue of rights and the challenge of protected liberties, like free speech, in presenting the seventh challenge. Before it, however, there is a response to such circumstances that arises sometimes prior to and sometimes beyond or independent of policy and law, which should be recognized.

I call the sixth challenge to the demand for a culture of justice the *pettiness* challenge. It says that attention to identity politics and issues of race or gender discrimination goes too far or proclaims offense too easily, attacking well-meaning people for—according to the challenger—minutia. The law may forbid the coworker from touching another's buttocks, but what about the photographs on his desk, visible to all in the office, of clothed men in his family standing next to women in bikinis? When he is told that the photograph makes others feel uncomfortable, he and others might argue that critics of his behavior are being petty, claiming that they are harmed by matters that, in his mind, have nothing to do with how he treats his colleagues. When such or other examples arise and are related to the need to create a reasonably respectful culture, the common reaction on the part of those criticized is to find such "overreactions" terrible. Therefore, the advocate for establishing a culture of justice must consider the realms in which and the extent to which complaints or moral recommendations ought to be leveled.

Considering the need to recognize the effects of people's use of language, their beliefs, and their practices on justice calls to mind the norm called "political correctness." "Political correctness" is invoked, for example, when a coworker overhears another describing one of his or her customers as "a retard." One need not have cognitive disabilities or be related to a person who does to appreciate the hurtful quality or the deleterious effects on beliefs and practices that certain language and ways of thinking have.

Some authors who raise the pettiness challenge go so far as to claim that the norm of political correctness causes people harm.[36] While it is certainly worth considering whether proposed solutions to injustice themselves would or do cause harm to people, political campaign strategy and messaging, advertising, and editorial "spin" have all made perfectly clear the power of word choice in shaping beliefs, which of course bear consequences for policy. In addition, scholars and public figures like Diane Ravitch can appreciate good initial intentions, yet argue that they sometimes run amok, as when the "language police" problematically "restrict what students learn."[37]

The pettiness challenge is more than a mere dismissal of people's moral—not always legal—demand for using appropriate and respectful language to describe others. The pettiness challenge is more serious and meaningful if interpreted as a challenge to the idea of subtle, diffuse, indirect, or distant harms. Consider the coworker who knows no one with disabilities personally and who hears another employee use the word "retard." If no one around would be immediately hurt by his or her use of the word, some explanation may be needed for appreciating the claim that a harm has been committed. If no harm was done, the challenge says, criticism is pettiness and the critic lacks standing. The pettiness challenge therefore questions not only particular criticisms of the form regarding political correctness, for example, but also the very notion of working to establish a culture of justice, since what he or she sees as minor offenses may well be some of the forces that undermine self-respect in young people. Presently, sexual harassment is typically recognized through a series of small advances and transactions that are unwanted and troubling, even if in subtle, incremental ways. Thus, it may present a way of thinking about the pettiness challenge, given that no one singular offense is thought to be individually of great harm, but the force of many related offenses builds up to a problematic case.

Challenge 7: Protected Liberties

Challenges 6 and 7 both concern offensive speech, actions, beliefs, and practices that constitute threats to the conditions necessary to foster self-respect in all people. Whereas the pettiness challenge suggests that those who raise complaints are claiming injury unreasonably, there are circumstances in which nothing petty is at issue. As noted in the introduction to this book, in February of 2014, a group of students hung a noose and draped an old Georgia state flag, the majority of which display the Confederate battle flag, over the shoulders of the University of Mississippi's statue commemorating James Meredith, the first African American student to enroll in and integrate the university.

As mentioned in the introduction, Geoffrey R. Stone of the University of Chicago Law School argued that the students' acts seemed to him entirely protected by the First Amendment's free speech provision on the grounds that no particular person was threatened by the noose, and neither the noose nor the flag did any lasting physical damage to the statue.[38] As noted previously, the students did plead guilty to misdemeanor offenses involving threats, but the fact is that speech is so profoundly protected in the United States that people leap to the defense of such hateful acts, including experts in constitutional law and freedom of speech. Protected liberties are not limited to speech, furthermore, but concern matters of religion too.

Of course, when it comes to speech, the sale of pornography is directed by policies that generally aim to keep adult content out of the view or reach of minors. At the same time, the protection of free of speech is not unlimited.[39] At bottom, however, it is conceivable that an aggressive effort could be organized to express and cultivate beliefs about the lesser status of some people, such as specific non-white groups, or women, with the intent of creating a culture in which the target population does feel that it is second-class and unworthy of the opportunities and respect that fully valued citizens enjoy. Here we find the central difficulty of challenge 7, concerning *protected liberties*.

There are liberties we protect constitutionally that can be used to harm others and to contribute to a culture that threatens others' self-respect. The protection of the freedom of religion has even been used to permit parents to deny lifesaving medical treatment to their children on religious grounds.[40] Threats to self-respect seem even less controversial by comparison.

To be sure, there are many crucial reasons why we protect the freedom of speech and freedom of religion. At the same time, however, if Rawls is right that we must "avoid at almost any cost the social conditions that undermine self-respect," then some considerations must be raised about how to address threats to self-respect that stem from constitutionally protected liberties. The danger in approaches that would favor limiting speech are the same as those encountered countless times in the past—without the freedom of the noisy whistle that lets out steam, the tea kettle would explode. Nevertheless, the advocate for a culture of justice must think about what force the protections of the freedom of speech and religion will play, or what actions in response they will prompt, in the process of nurturing self-respect in all people.

Both the pettiness challenge and the protected liberties challenge call to mind a reasonable norm advocated by John Lachs, who has highlighted the value of "Leaving Others Alone."[41] There is value in learning to let others be, often, especially if they are not harming anyone. In light of arguments like Lachs's point, the answer might be to seek to correct some behavior while leaving other behavior alone, addressing the problem instead in some other fashion. It is not my aim to flesh out responses to these challenges here, but it helps, I believe, to consider that challenges do not mean matters with which the advocate for a culture of justice must disagree wholly.

Challenge 8: Indoctrination

The eighth and final challenge concerns the implementation of efforts to shape culture for the sake of justice. I call it the *indoctrination* challenge. While the question of how exactly one would try to shape culture is itself an important question that must be addressed, the very idea of trying sounds unnerving to those who believe that government's or private citizens' impositions on each other should be minimal.

Criticism of culture-shaping efforts comes from the political left and right, as well as from the religious and the non-religious. To illustrate the challenge, consider practices in public schools. Public schools are institutions that intentionally develop students' language, beliefs, and practices and are clear examples of culture-shaping institutions. Along such lines, Paolo Freire has written on *Teachers as Cultural Workers*.[42] Conflicts over the Pledge of Allegiance demonstrate the point. In the Pledge, students are led through a recitation of a pledge of one's allegiance to the United States, a first source of conflict, and along the way it adds the phrase "under God," which some citizens see as a form of indoctrination and a violation of the US Constitution's establishment clause.

Today, conflicts about the Pledge center especially on an atheist parent's challenge from the early 2000s.[43] The parent believed that government was imposing a religious point of view on children, including his own, which he saw as a violation of religious freedom. Far less discussed today are the objections that religious believers have raised to the Pledge as early as trials between 1938 and 1940. In an influential case, a Jehovah's Witness had been expelled from school because of his refusal to recite the Pledge. The student believed that the Pledge was indoctrination and a violation of his free exercise of religion.[44] The religious argument had to do with the call to salute an earthly emblem, which to him would mean unfaithfulness to God.[45]

The indoctrination challenge could represent a rejection or at least skepticism of the methods or even of the intention to establish a culture of justice. The communitarian might appreciate the idea of wanting to shape culture, but at a local level, and hence feel wary about any widespread initiatives and their potential encroachment on local control. The classical liberal could worry that the ideas of consent and of the social contract are corrupted by an effort to indoctrinate citizens into any particular outlook.

Conclusion: Initial Benefits and Implications of Advancing a Culture of Justice

In the field of political philosophy, the relationship between political institutions and "background culture" has at times been neglected. In fact, on my first reading of Plato's *Republic* many years ago, I found his ideas about music perplexing. If the poets misled people with their words to speak and believe falsehoods, I understood his concern. But modes of music? I struggled to understand why he was spending time on the subject. Today, I appreciate his principle, but find his call for censorship of the modes of music heavy-handed in the extreme. Baby Einstein music and videos may sound as though they are especially healthy and conducive to child development, yet one study found that parents overestimate the effects of such media, and "infants learn relatively little from infant media."[46] Plato's authoritarianism in the *Republic* remains troubling for me, especially his advocacy for infanticide.[47] Even while we let go of things that Plato appears clearly to have been wrong about, we nevertheless ought to recall and preserve what he was right about. And in particular, I have in mind the fact that he saw an intimate connection between basic and fundamental cultural conditions and forces and their rooted connection to larger matters of social justice. At bottom, then, considering the importance of a culture of justice enables us to clarify the connection between the fields of social and political philosophy, which certainly overlap and are sometimes referred to interchangeably, yet can be distinguished usefully as well.[48]

Where there is merit to defense against those who too quickly complain about offenses to their sensibilities, considering the reasons why a culture of justice is called for and what it requires should help to differentiate how we respond to various cases. In addition, if it turns out that some impediments to a culture of justice are not wholly surmountable, such as in cases in which the freedom of speech is to be defended despite threats to people's self-respect, then the imperative to establish and maintain a culture of justice could motivate counterbalancing efforts that help to redress or mollify threatening forces.

A further benefit worth mentioning here is the fact that attending to the moral demand for a culture of justice helps to frame a variety of concerns for ethics and justice, from broad issues to specific ones. In the big picture, it can help to address the freedom of speech issues and the purposes of public institutions, as in the case of the flag and noose in Mississippi. Universities are sometimes and can more often be guided by statements of value and mission, for example. For particular matters of policy, it can help deliberations about differences in attitudes and practices with regard to such matters as the use of violence as a disciplinary measure for children. States like Iowa and Ohio have banned corporal punishment in schools, while others like Mississippi and Alabama have not. The norm to establish and maintain a culture of justice has wide meaning and implications as well as the potential for valuable guidance in matters local, particular, and of practical importance for life and leadership.

4

Self-Respect, Positive Power, and Stoic Pragmatism

It is easier to build strong children than to fix broken men.

—Frederick Douglass[1]

We need hope. We can't do anything without optimism . . . Our job is to cultivate hope, and that is what I always try to do.

—Angela Davis[2]

Education[3] is among the forces with which disadvantaged people can become empowered. Nevertheless, the public policy nonprofit organization Demos found in 2013 that the median wealth of white high school dropouts was higher than for black college graduates in the United States.[4] In 2020, the Urban Institute reported that black college graduates have a lower homeownership rate than white high school dropouts.[5] The harsh realities of prejudice and limits on opportunity for historically disadvantaged communities motivate debates about how best to prepare, educate, and protect young people. People are sometimes accused of lacking self-respect when they behave outside of mainstream norms, furthermore, such as in wearing pants that sag.[6] To charge disadvantaged communities, however, with a lack of self-respect can seriously miss the mark while also blaming them for the consequences of injustice, for their various ways of coping with or of being self-affirming in a hostile environment. Convention would refer to this as "blaming the victim,"[7] though people may wish to reject the language of "victimhood" in favor of self-affirmation despite social injustice.

In considering unjust societies and the harms they do, I argue in this chapter that justice and democratic liberty for all depend upon a shared, public, cultural obligation that individuals and institutions must strive to fulfill with an attitude of stoic pragmatism. The obligation is to establish the cultural conditions necessary for all to develop self-respect and a meaningful sense of their own positive power. At the same time, it is a moral mistake to judge disadvantaged people for what some believe to be a lack of self-respect when they behave differently from advantaged groups in part as a reaction to injustice. The distinction between self-respect and a sense of positive power helps to clarify my claim here about disadvantaged people and is important for two reasons. The first is that people can be self-respecting while not believing that their society is sufficiently just to be meaningfully altered by their own actions. In this sense, then, what I am concerned about with regard to self-respect and a sense of positive power is the cultural conditions that can influence a set of beliefs about oneself and one's expectations concerning one's interactions with the world. The second reason I attend to a sense of positive power is that self-respect as a concept sounds like an individual's responsibility rather than a shared, cultural responsibility—something that a public must cultivate in each person. Focusing on self-respect, therefore, tends to promote blaming victims over recognizing society's role in maintaining an unjust culture. The sense that people have of their own positive power is partly due to the individual, to be sure, but is conditioned environmentally as well. A "sense of positive power" is a term that John Dewey used in relation to education and its potential effects, and in a utopian society it would be cultivated in all people.[8]

The thesis advanced here addresses deficiencies in modern liberal and libertarian theories of justice, which fail to appreciate cultural obligations necessary for justice. The challenge of achieving a just society in the way I argue is essential here can be daunting, which is why an attitude of stoic pragmatism is important. The ideal of a culture of justice is best approached with a stoic recognition that it may never be met yet is worth fighting for, even if progress can only ever be partial or incremental and often slow in coming. Since some of the conditions necessary for justice require taxation, libertarians are often opponents of such measures. At the same time, the defense or the advancement of liberty depends on self-respect and individuals' sense of their own positive power in society.

Therefore, to expect all to have self-respect and a sense of their own positive power to pursue meaningful life plans requires first that the conditions have been established for all to develop such beliefs on which the expectations of liberty rest.

In what follows, I begin with a brief clarification of the contrast between ancient and modern outlooks on justice before noting the crucial role of self-respect in modern theories of justice. In the tradition, however, there are disagreements about whether self-respect is an individual or a shared obligation. I then present the concept of self-respect in terms of what John Dewey called having a sense of one's own positive power. The latter concept helps to explain the sense in which the obligations for a just culture are shared. I next present contexts and examples of what we might call threats and attacks on self-respect and people's sense of their own positive power from the outside, from advantaged or dominant groups. After that, I address a troubling cultural phenomenon to demonstrate why the distinction between self-respect and positive power matters greatly, particularly in the charge of "acting white,"[9] sometimes, though not always, leveled by people who identify normally as from the same cultural group. The charge of acting white is injurious when leveled against persons wishing to excel in school, for example. At the same time, to tell young people that if they excel in school, their chances are equal to anyone else's for wealth or career success is misleading according to recent findings, such as those from the Demos report. Adding complexity to the concern, the charge can be motivated by a paternalistic or protective cause or one that is meant to be self-affirming despite injustice. Such motivations do not undo the harms that the slur can level, yet they clarify the implications of social injustices and the distinction between self-respect and a sense of one's own positive power. After an analysis of these complexities in the process of trying to develop a sense of positive power in all people, I address the challenge that democratic justice is a far-reaching ideal with the help of John Lachs's concept of stoic pragmatism. Lachs's outlook is important for inspiring a reasonable, cautious optimism about the pursuit of ideals.

Justice, Old and New

On one reading, you might say that the most important virtue in Plato's *Republic* is wisdom, as it should guide all of the other virtues, on the great philosopher's account. The central question of the text, however, concerns the nature of justice. Arguably it is the more important virtue, since justice is having each part of society and each of the other three virtues (wisdom, courage, and moderation) do its part as it should. It means having the proper balance of each role in society and in virtue function as it is meant to do. For Plato's Socrates, furthermore, justice is so important that it can even justify dishonesty, in a few select and vitally important matters, so long as it is wisely guided and aimed at profound social benefit. To the modern ear, trust in leadership to the extent that Plato advocated seems foolish. We have witnessed far too many terrible leaders. We have also behind us the experience of what happens when societies take seriously what the great philosopher suggested in terms of eugenics, which we tragically still find at work today in ethnic cleansings, with reason to raise questions about the development of new gene-editing technologies like CRISPR—a tool in genetic engineering for modifying DNA.[10] In the modern era we prize freedom, furthermore, something that Plato worried about, given the threat that it poses to order and the pursuit of social virtues. We sacrifice a significant degree of control over vice for the priority of freedom and the consent of the governed.

Today we have some remarkable advocates for liberty, such as John Lachs, who present important challenges for those concerned about injustice. Justice is not the only important social virtue, they argue, and sometimes advocacy for it runs too far afield and in fact results in injustice. Philosophers like Robert Nozick and Lachs are right to think that any dreams of equality of incomes or of lives could only be realized through extensive and intrusive imposition from government, contrary to living in a free society. While some grand effort for achieving equality of that kind for citizens is too far-reaching, less radical aims are both more justifiable and more feasible, such as the aim of ensuring for all a set of basic conditions—food, shelter, healthcare, civic education—necessary for developing persons who can and in fact do pursue meaningful life plans.

The advocate for freedom is reasonably concerned about incursions on liberty. It is true that if you ensure that all will have enough to eat and a place to live no matter what people do, some will take little or no responsibility for the work that they might be able to do for themselves. At the same time, persons do not typically like to be thought of as dependent, at least when they need not be, and the desirability for individuals to pursue lives of personal achievement can be cultivated through education. I would add, however, that it is inhumane to stigmatize persons who are dependent on others for their dependency, as some advocates for liberty often do.[11] Some of the reasons for a more generous and understanding attitude are that (a) there are many who depend on others through no fault of their own; (b) at some level we are all at least partly, and at many points in life, highly dependent on others; and (c) valuable liberty and personal responsibility both require environmental conditions that foster and cultivate self-respect and a sense of positive power in the individual.

The ancient attitude toward justice that we find in Plato's *Republic* is surely too heavy-handed for democratic societies, yet it was rightly concerned about the nature and social force of culture on the development of human persons and justice. Plato's Socrates was too restrictive in limiting personal and social liberties, yet people today advocate for various social reforms and restrictions, such as on violent video games[12] as well as on certain forms of pornography.[13] Libertarian inclinations call for minimalist intervention into people's lives and culture, yet there are ways in which culture affects young people profoundly, long before the age of consent. Therefore, we must consider the elements of culture that are necessary for justice. These concern the cultivation of virtues and character traits required for responsibility and meaningful participation in social life.

Self-Respect and Positive Power

Robin S. Dillon edited a collection of essays on the nature of self-respect, but pragmatist philosophy was largely absent from consideration.[14] The literature has clearly differentiated self-respect from "self-esteem,"[15] yet much of the scholarship sees self-respect as a duty to oneself, not as the kind of matter about which Rawls noted a shared, social obligation. What I am concerned with is beliefs about the self and about the social world, and the interactions between them.

In the philosophical pragmatist tradition, a belief is a habit of action. Habits are not themselves merely a state of being, not a mere fact understood as in a descriptive sense verified at a singular point in time. Rather, if belief is a habit of action, then the condition of such a belief would bear meaningful actual or potential consequences in real life. Thus, while in some traditions a belief could also sound passive, it is not so for the philosophical pragmatist idea of habits of action. After all, if one is self-respecting but is unchanged by the fact in terms of one's interactions in the world, except in having a certain static quality of "appreciation" for oneself, it is unclear what difference it would make, hence what it would mean. Esteem bares a similar sense as appreciation, and therefore self-respect could be more meaningfully described as a matter of self-belief or self-doubt, at least according to the pragmatists' sense of belief. One can doubt oneself too much or too little, and one can believe too confidently in one's quality or believe in it too little. For a pragmatist, the test of one's beliefs is to be found in the ways in which one responds or reacts to forces in the world that bear on the relevant belief.

If beliefs about one's expectations regarding interactions with others are helpful for considering the nature of self-respect, the question remains as to what would constitute the proper balance. An anonymous reviewer who commented on an essay on which this chapter draws pointed out to me that racists might have a great deal of belief in themselves or might only believe in themselves modestly. In either scenario, they believe too little in others' value. In this sense, their valuing of themselves might be plentiful or sufficient but excessive in comparison with or in relation to others. Perhaps self-loathing racists make themselves feel better by debasing others or just hating themselves and others too. In all of these cases, the referee noted, good people want such racists to believe in themselves less. We want racists to be more self-doubting. More self-doubt would be appropriate for zealous racists, but those who hate all people in part because of a self-loathing arguably harm others because of their lack of self-respect. For just such a reason, Aristotle argues in the *Nicomachean Ethics* that friendship is based on self-love.[16]

Proper self-belief or self-doubt is not only a matter of degree, however. For Aristotle, one must behave in such a way that achieves not only a quantitative mean but also a qualitative one. In other words, to be courageous is not the absence of fear but fear in the right amount. More precisely, however, we can explain courage as fearing the right things and not the wrong things and then fearing them in the right amounts. A simpler analogy might be found in Aristotle's example of magnanimity. Typically, one ought not to give so much as to make oneself suddenly impoverished and then dependent on others. At the same time, we must not be miserly in giving. But he explained that to be virtuous in giving, one must give the right amount to the right persons for the right reasons, in the right way, and at the right time.[17] Just such a story, I argue, should be told about self-belief or self-doubt. Proper respect for oneself must include the realization that one is fallible. Some self-doubt is necessary for being a good, self-respecting person. At the same time, too much self-doubt is debilitating. One ought to doubt oneself to the right degree, about the right things, at the right times, and for the right reasons. The analogue holds for self-belief. Believing oneself to be superior to other human beings may be an "appreciation" of "the importance of being a person" while failing to recognize the same quality in others in the proper way. Believing in oneself over others, however, is only sensible in very specific conditions, such as when medical doctors believe themselves to be the right person to act in an emergency medical situation over my own limited knowledge and expertise.

Given the importance of democratic equality, Charles Mills addresses concerns about inequality and aspects of Rawls's work all while he also offered his own critique.[18] Mills appreciates elements in Rawls's philosophy but defends a view he calls "black radical liberalism." The premises of Rawls's theory depend on certain norms of cooperative endeavor. The issue that Mills and others have recognized concerns the circumstances in which some people see others as less than fully human or as less deserving of respect. Illustrations of persistent racism that capture to my mind what Mills notes are examples from where I have lived,[19] in which a radical difference is observable in the quality of schooling for white and black students, consequent in part on the effects of poverty, the insufficiency of social and economic support for families, and the underfunding of public schools. As of the time when I lived in Mississippi, more than 40 of the state's roughly 190 school districts were majority black and graduating fewer than 60 percent of their students, with a number of districts graduating only around 40 percent of the students who entered as freshmen.[20]

In connection with such critiques of the tradition of political liberalism, two consequences emerge. The first is that self-respect must be understood not only as a norm about oneself, not merely about the individual. Self-respect must be considered in the context of relations with others. The second is that there are cultural forces that systematically work to categorize persons differently, as superior or inferior. They can be found in crass, overt ideas such as the requirement to use different water fountains and washrooms, as in the old South, but also in the ways in which people are raised from infancy. One children's book published in the United Kingdom told kids about "ten little nigger boys Sitting down to dine—One of them choked himself, and then there were nine." Later, "seven little nigger boys Chopping up Sticks—One chopped himself in half, Then there were six." In another case one was swallowed by a fish, and then the next was hugged by a bear, before the ninth "sitting in the sun" got "shriveled up, Then there was one."[21] Remarkably, on YouTube one can find an old, professionally produced recording of adults and children singing the book to music.[22] The idea was that it was funny when these little children of African-descended peoples died. The modern equivalent that I have read to my children is about monkeys who bump their heads after bouncing on a bed. In the past, children were taught to count while belittling other human beings. One of my former students has told me that to this day she always feels uncomfortable when she hears the word monkey, given that she and others had been called that. It is worth considering further potential concerns about counting books, furthermore, as people might argue that laughing at the pain of animals is also problematic and desensitizing.[23] Perhaps a better solution would be a book or story featuring a variety of people who fall down, with no particular group targeted more than others. Falling down is a human and animal happening. It is not kind to laugh at others' suffering, yet we can sometimes laugh at ourselves when we slip or fall without terrible consequences.

Countless cultural tools were designed to reflect and perpetuate white supremacy. In Mississippi, Governor James K. Vardaman, elected in 1903, once said that "if it is necessary every Negro in the state will be lynched; it will be done to maintain white supremacy."[24] There is no doubt, no exaggeration involved, in the assessment that the United States has intentionally supported unequal citizenship, in fact explicitly fighting for it. In such an environment, Rawls's guiding principles of fair social cooperation appear to miss the point of real-world problems. Some Southern states in the United States have only taken their Confederate battle flags down in 2015. When I began writing this chapter, Mississippi had yet to take any action to change its state flag, which featured an emblem of the Confederate battle flag in its canton, despite the fact that Mississippi was among the most explicit of the states to explain that the defense of slavery was its fundamental cause for seceding from the federal union.[25] In the time since, the state has decided to take down its flag and design a new one after pressure from the George Floyd protests,[26] NASCAR's decision to ban Confederate flags at its events,[27] and the NCAA's decision to ban championship events in Mississippi so long as its flag goes unchanged.[28]

We have a culture in which privileged classes are taught to respect themselves while belittling others. Proper self-respect must not involve seeing oneself as superior to others, save in the way of limited cases of expertise, as I mentioned. Even then, however, it is important to learn from John Dewey's democratic theory that the experts may be wise but do not know "where the shoe pinches," as he would say.[29] Thus, even the expert ought not to have overconfident belief in his or her ability to know all that is relevant for the medical care of another—or, as Dewey's metaphor goes, for the shoemaking we undertake for others.

There are certainly reasons to think that people need self-respect and that it does not develop without the right conditions. David Walker, in his 1830 *Appeal to the Coloured Citizens of the World*, noted that enslaved people in the United States were wretched because of slavery but also because of ignorance.[30] Simply freeing slaves would not render them ready for living happy or virtuous lives. People need proper conditions for personal development. It may be that some extraordinary people, such as Elie Wiesel, were able to maintain their self-respect during the Holocaust, yet bodies can be broken, and standout examples are extraordinary for a reason. In heroic cases, by definition extraordinary, people like Wiesel went into an oppressive condition already having a rich education and respected social position. Walker recognized that ignorance is a wretched condition and dominant groups can keep people ignorant by force and policy. Thus, if self-respect necessitates a degree of knowledge or wisdom, and my sense of proper self-belief implies it, then circumstances in which people are made ignorant are ones that threaten self-respect. It is for this and other reasons that many are deeply concerned about troubling educational inequalities and inadequacies that pervade US public education.[31] If we expect all people to have self-respect and then fail to provide the education and requisite conditions necessary for developing it fully, we are cultivating devastating circumstances that reinforce injustice. Then, with a shift in focus on self-respect to thinking of it as a matter fundamentally of personal responsibility, the dominant classes thereby judge disadvantaged citizens for the effects of unjust social conditions. For the present book and overarching argument, these are examples of the forces creating a culture of injustice against which I argue that we must ultimately fight.

The distinction for which I am arguing in this chapter is the differentiation of self-respect and having a sense of one's own positive power. Persons could have a proper degree of self-respect, such as in terms of self-belief or self-doubt, yet, after experiencing substantial injustice and the frustration of every effort to bring about change, believe with evidence that their society has been designed to undermine their positive power to achieve justice.

The term "a sense of positive power" I derive from one of Dewey's more inventive essays, which the editors at the *New York Times* titled

"Dewey Outlines Utopian Schools." Among the subtitles to the 1933 article is a succinct summary that reads "Sense of Power Is Aim." In a number of writings, Dewey explains the crucial educational importance of cultivating the right attitudes in people. In particular, he wrote in a different essay, "The Supreme Intellectual Obligation," that the obligation he described demands the cultivation in all people of the intellectual attitudes and scientific habits of mind necessary to appreciate wisdom and to put it to use.[32] Attitudes are vital to personal growth, insofar as they are habits of thinking and can be inclinations for the right kinds of intellectual practices.

In his essay about utopian schools, Dewey writes that "through observation, I should say that [in utopia] they ranked the attitude which would give a sense of positive power as at least as basic and primary as the others, if not more so."[33] We find here almost a precedent for Rawls's sense that self-respect is a basic primary good. In Dewey's language, however, a "sense of positive power" does not sound so individualistic as "self-respect" appears to many. For, if I have a sense that I can lift a box, it is because I have experienced my strength and its use in the world, and I have seen boxes like it. I know something about the world and about how it affects me and is affected by me when I have a sense that I can pick up the box. I can be wrong about it or right, but the point is that having a "sense of positive power" more obviously reveals the relationship of oneself to what is beyond oneself, to others and to the world. A sense of one's positive power cannot be only the responsibility of the individual to establish. Dominant groups and their wider culture are responsible also in part for the sense that a disadvantaged citizen has about what their possibilities are in that world. For such reasons, in 2012 the US Department of Justice sued Meridian, Mississippi, for having created a "school-to-prison pipeline."[34] The school system was showing young kids, for grossly inadequate reasons, that their path was leading to incarceration. In such contexts, a self-respecting person might at the same time think that they are deserving of respect but not have a positive sense of their own power because of the force of experience against the latter. Thus, the "sense of positive power" is something limited by others. While it is my understanding that the same can be said of self-respect, its language and tradition in philosophy and in much public discourse point to individual duty. This is why I believe that we must attend especially to the cultivation of a sense of positive power in all people, as an effort for self-respect, seeing the wider culture, the wider public, as an agent in this foundational process for justice.

To illustrate the point, consider the young person who wants to be a medical doctor today but is frustrated at every turn in the aim to graduate high school. Guidance counselors tell her that she is not "wired for college"—one guidance counselor in Mississippi referred to students in that way when I informally surveyed several. In such a context, the option of being a doctor can seem so distant, difficult, or unlikely as to appear impossible. When conditions still leave a young person able to succeed despite discouragements, the few exceptional cases will achieve their goals.

Many high school graduates in Mississippi graduate from high school measurably underprepared for college. The average ACT score for African Americans in the state is 16, and a score above 20 is said to be an important qualifier for likely success in higher education.[35] If we are to fight the structures of injustice that limit people's options in life, we can find a clue in Dewey's book *How We Think*. He writes that "power in action requires largeness of vision, which can be had only through the use of imagination."[36] Through oppression, shaming, and mockery, however, like the children's book I mentioned, a culture can make it more difficult for disadvantaged children to imagine themselves successful in school or in a career. Thus, those who have expansive imaginations despite such challenges are thought Herculean, like the James Merediths of the world.[37]

Many people have warrant for the belief that their society will not permit educational or career success for them or their children. They will not easily have expansive vision, but vision can be enabled through better education and examples of people who are successful. In 2008, for example, Roland Martin on CNN explained that "whenever a kid said, 'I want to be president,' I literally saw black parents say, 'Son, or daughter, you might think of being something else.' I have nine nieces and four nephews, and . . . I can actually say (you can be president) and mean it."[38] In other words, given new circumstances, African Americans in the United States, as well as many people in the country, saw and felt a new possibility open up when President Obama was elected. No longer is it true that only white men have been president. That fact has led many people to doubt less that a woman can be elected president, for example, especially given that Hillary Clinton clinched the popular vote even though she lost the Electoral College count in 2016. The sense of people's positive power while being non-white or non-male has changed, even if it is wise to be cautious about how one interprets that change. Historical barriers can be challenged with respect to persons of various faiths or of none, persons of nontraditional gender identities, sexual orientations, and other historically marginalized groups.[39] In addition, it is vital to see that vision for disadvantaged citizens is not only controlled by the individual. When someone turns the lights out on you, your vision is clearly not only in your own control. Developing a sense of one's positive power is therefore a shared obligation. It also seems clear that one's environment sets many necessary conditions for one to have vision. It determines the lighting as well as the objects one can see in a vision for the future.

The final point to emphasize in this section is the fact that a sense of positive power is crucial for developing the kinds of persons who will be able to cooperate together and to pursue happy, meaningful lives in a more just society. With an understanding of the role of positive power in such undertakings, we can appreciate the importance of culture and of society's role in the formation of people's relevant senses of positive power. Self-respect is often considered too narrowly, with focus on the individual and their character alone. The fuller picture reveals the role of culture in establishing the conditions for justice or injustice. People need many things in order to develop self-respect and a sense of positive power, but at bottom, we must see that the development of these important characteristics and habits of action is a shared social obligation, not an obligation of the individual alone.

Attacks on Self-Respect and People's Sense of Their Own Positive Power

In 2015, I had the opportunity to deliver an early version of this chapter at the Berlin Practical Philosophy International Forum conference. On that trip, I took advantage of the chance to visit the Dachau concentration camp in Bavaria. The gate to the concentration camp reads *Arbeit Macht Frei*, which roughly translates as "Work makes one free." The camps are famous for treating human beings as less than human. The way persons were abused went as far as the gas chamber and subsequent furnaces.[40] For the people living in the camps, systematic belittlements were the order of the day. Persons were faced regularly with the choice between survival and the acceptance of conditions that attacked one's self-respect.

One harsh perspective might think that a self-respecting person would never have survived the Nazi concentration camps. After all, anyone who objected to relevant conditions could easily be disposed of. Cultural forces that threaten self-respect are not always so extreme. There are subtler conditions that were at work in the Southern United States. People had to teach their children to drink from the water fountain marked "colored," not because they thought their children unworthy of first-class citizenship, but for fear of absurd punishments.

It is quite reasonable to tell me, as a grown, educated, and advantaged white man, that when I am insulted or belittled, only I can let others put me down. We have lovely maxims like one from Eleanor Roosevelt, who famously explained that "No one can make you feel inferior without your consent." When I am criticized by others, I can repeat such maxims and remind myself to learn from any substantive criticisms and to ignore or brush off any that do not offer helpful or useful content. An important point is at work in this very line, however: *Consent*. Consent is not something we believe that children are yet capable of giving. Consent is something only adults can offer. This is why, if you are going to make people feel inferior, if you are going to perpetuate a system in which you are advantaged over others, if you are going to fill prisons from which you profit on inequity—you must start when people are young.

Young people in school who grow up so poor that their families cannot feed them before school presently get meals at school. They depend on the public for sustenance. Social messages tell them over and over that they are moochers and should be taking care of themselves. In a great many public schools, when young people misbehave or violate dress codes, they are struck violently in systems that still make extensive use of corporal punishment (nineteen states in the United States).[41] As noted in connection with Merdian, Mississippi, in other schools, police are often called in over infractions great and minor, even for dress code violations.

Where young people are taught that they are not worthwhile, that they are properly punished with violence and policing, literally in both cases, they are taught long before the age of consent that they are not acceptable candidates for social positions that necessitate an education. According to Rajeev Darolia, Peter Mueser, and Jacob Cronin, "about two thirds of state prisoners do not have a high school diploma and assessed numeracy and literacy is substantially lower among the prison population as compared to US households more broadly."[42] If self-respect is something that properly raised adults are expected to have and to embody, what are we to say about people who are systematically "pushed out"[43] of education? These are not people who can consent or choose not to consent to their feeling of inferiority. It is not only some loose or indirect sense in which advantaged classes benefit from the hierarchical treatment of citizens. In fact, the rapid expansion of private prisons has created enormous economic incentives to keep the flow of young people steady into the channels of the juvenile justice system, leading to eventual long-term incarceration later in life.[44] For those who succeed in avoiding recidivism and then look for a job, say, to support their children, they are met with tremendous hurdles as persons without high-school educations and with criminal records. For some, getting a job can be a stroke of immeasurable luck.

While for many thinkers self-respect sounds like an individual responsibility, John Rawls called attention to the extent to which conditions are necessary for developing self-respect. In *A Theory of Justice*, Rawls did not say that at almost any cost we must require that each individual develop self-respect on their own and embody what it requires. Instead, Rawls argued that at almost any cost *we* must avoid those conditions that undermine self-respect.[45] The latter is a matter of social, shared responsibility.

It is true that individuals must be participants in the development of their own self-respect. At the same time, we do not expect feral children to be self-respecting. Certain social conditions are necessary for self-respect. Therefore, the only proper way to understand it is as a matter of shared responsibility. The problem with sharing responsibility is that parties like to blame others, rather than themselves, when matters of shared responsibility are neglected. While this is true, it is unreasonable to blame the victim of injustice for their circumstance. When conditions are just, it is perfectly reasonable to blame persons for falling short of justifiable expectations for their potential. Interestingly, however, the libertarian point of view at the same time wants to avoid compelling anyone to hold certain values, yet wants to fault people for depending on others when they choose dependency over independence, such as athletes, artists, and entrepreneurs.

We must not blame the concentration camp survivors for failing to respect themselves enough not to have fought back. How many of one's neighbors must one watch murdered before it seems reasonable to choose life over a threat to self-respect? So often we blame the victims of threats to self-respect for their conditions simply because there are some who abuse a system.

Having a sense of one's powers in the American South prior to the Civil Rights movement might have meant that a self-respecting person would nevertheless not take the risk of trying to vote. This is because they may have witnessed a beating or a lynching that occurred when their friend or neighbor last tried to vote. The Ku Klux Klan was and remains a terrorist group that aims to strike fear in people who dare to believe themselves equal with whites. Their very outfits allude to ghosts, and their explicit threats take the form of nooses hung as recently as 2014 on the university campus where I was working at the time.[46] In 2022, the January 6 hearings revealed connections between the Ku Klux Klan and the riot in Washington, DC, in 2021 concerning the certification of the presidential election results.[47] Sadly, these forces of hatred and intimidation continue to this day in American life.

Dewey referred to having a "sense of one's positive power" as the idea of understanding and appreciating what one can do in one's social and environmental conditions. Such a sense is not simply a matter for one to decide for oneself. A sense of one's positive power would include those things for which one's capacities and social conditions open up realms of possible action and power. The person who depends on a wheelchair to get around is not lacking in self-respect when they pass on long-jump tryouts. Nevertheless, they develop a sense of their own positive power, given life conditions that are within and beyond one's control.

Consider a far subtler form of pressure, such as in matters of love. In the South, a 2011 report from Public Policy Polling revealed that 46 percent of likely GOP primary voters in Mississippi thought that inter-racial marriage should be illegal.[48] Only 40 percent said that it should be allowed, and 14 percent said that they were unsure. A more just society would not permit limitations on individuals' positive power based on arbitrary and unhealthy reasons. Education should be the realm in which we develop each individual's positive powers to the fullest extent that we can, empowering all young people without stigmatizing the dependency that is unavoidable in youth. If we want all people to be self-respecting, that takes conditions for its establishment. Until those conditions obtain for all citizens, it is harsh to expect the victims of an unjust society to live up to the expectations we have for well-educated, mature adults, encouraged and treated as persons of equal citizenship and worthy of the potential for meaningful life plans.

"Acting White" as Protection, Self-Affirmation, and Harm

I once heard a white Democrat ask an African American woman how she could be interested in opportunities to volunteer for Republicans when someone had offered her information just before the start of a class meeting. He asked her how she could "betray" her people in that way. It was an instance of a white person assuming because of another's race what her political views were, as well as what is best for her. There are circumstances in which, on the basis of historical evidence, we can say that certain African American counties can reasonably be predicted to vote for Democrats in presidential elections, such as when votes are being tallied and projections are running about who is likely to win. Such predictions are based on historical and regional patterns. Something different and troubling happens when we talk about a specific person without historical evidence or prior consultation, assuming that we know their political point of view and interests solely based on their race. In this story, the Democrat was engaged in an instance analogous to the charge that one is "acting white." In his eyes, the woman was defying her people simply by showing interest in hearing from a party not his own, one that he presumed is not a match for the interests of African Americans. In May of 2020, Joe Biden committed a similar offense when he said that black Trump voters "ain't black."[49] The charge of "acting white" or that someone "ain't black" is also raised from one black person to another at times.

A blind reviewer of this work raised the consideration here that conservative figures have weaponized the idea that some kids disdain learning, when sociologists have found "acting white" to have more to do with group loyalty and choices involving engagement and social capital. As Roland Fryer and Paul Torelli argue, ambition and nerdiness are less people's concerns than are choices of social association, affecting social capital.[50] Fryer and Torelli's findings suggest that accusations of "acting white" may indeed have more to do with social associations for those leveling the charge, yet that does not diminish the complexities of feelings for those who are so labeled. As a demonstration of Fryer and Torelli's point, however, black students who excel in black-majority schools are typically not charged with "acting white," since associations in their advanced courses of study do not change the racial makeup of student associations in the way that they do in schools with predominantly white populations. The label "acting white" has multiple meanings, to be sure, and figures on both sides of the political aisle have made problematic use of such norms. Nevertheless, the discomfort and social effects of the phenomenon remain and trouble some students. These are worth considering for the sake of understanding the development of a sense of one's own positive power, as well as for demonstration of the shared nature of the cultivation of such a sense.

PROTECTION

In an environment like the one I have described, in which 46 percent of Mississippi Republican Party voters polled said that they believed interracial marriage should be illegal,[51] one can better understand the impulse of some parents or friends of non-white men and women who might be inclined to protect their children or friends. Parents alive today still have memories of Emmett Till's murder. Till was fourteen years old and was said to have flirted with or whistled at a white woman. The young man was brutally murdered for it in 1955. Many parents and grandparents alive today grew up in a world in which a young man, still a child in the eyes of the law, could be slaughtered over alleged simple flirtation with a white woman. Therefore, when such parents' children or friends consider love interests across races, it is unsurprising to find hesitation and worry for the sake of protecting loved ones. Such worries are not simple prejudices. They are habits of thought and action conditioned by generations of oppressive behavior and injustice from the state and from nongovernmental social practices and institutions, such as churches.[52] In 2012, for example, news of a Mississippi church refusing to host a black wedding, a union of two of its church members, caught international attention.[53]

One way to develop a protective attitude for one's friends and children is to accept the fact that certain dangers are beyond our control as individuals, whereas less dangerous life choices are available. Saying that certain activities, communities, practices, or relationships are for white folks can be intended as an expression of a loving attitude, despite the reinforcement it exhibits for limiting life choices. A person who acts in ways that are at home in environments frequented predominantly by white people might be charged with "acting white," perhaps from a reaction to white people who claimed certain spaces for themselves. Until 2010, some schools in the United States had designated class election offices for white and black students, in which the position of president was always reserved for a white student.[54]

Another version of the protection motive is akin to sources of discouragement or encouragement common to many, if not all, cultures. Consider a mechanic who knows the road through community college vocational training for their son. Their son wants to study art and philosophy. Some parents might be concerned for their children, given that paths different from their own are foreign to them. An attorney I know pressures her daughter strongly to be an attorney also. She can hire her daughter into her own firm, knowing that she will be secure. There are fears in the unknown. When we know little about a field, we worry that our friends, family, or children might fail at an activity that no one we know has pursued successfully. Thus, relevant protective attitudes might apply pressure, gently or firmly, to steer friends and children toward better-known, more familiar, and seemingly safer territory. In so doing, however, we of course run the risk of limiting our friends' or children's happiness. We also reinforce cultural structures, especially when it comes to dominance, privilege, and unequal citizenship. The responsibility, however, is again only partly held by those who feel the compulsion to protect. The far greater responsibility should be placed on those who commit wanton murder, like Till's, or who, from positions of privilege, maintain or reinforce structures of dominance, inequality, and injustice. Parents' sense of their own and their children's positive power may have expanded in the way that Roland Martin's did when President Obama was elected.[55] Nevertheless, when it comes to interracial relationships in Mississippi, the wider culture can maintain a chilling force on the idea that a non-white person is welcome in communities long dominated by white supremacists.

Self-Affirmation

A second motivation for the potentially hurtful charge that a person is "acting white" could also be driven by the experience of unfairness. It can take the form of a defiance of unfair structures, a rejection of them, and a corresponding valuation of one's own identity and practices. A student once mentioned to me that an administrator referred to him as "one of the good ones," by which he could only understand the message as meaning "one of the good black kids." Being called "one of the good ones" suggests the idea of its alternative, that others like him often are not good ones. When the young man behaves in ways that seem right to him, that pursue the development of his abilities and potential, a white authority figure tells him that he is unlike other people of his kind. Again, the source of the charge of acting white can come from the dominant or marginalized group.

At the same time, when people not included in the group known as "the good ones" experience unfairness, presumptions of guilt, quick judgment, or unfair treatment, it is natural and reasonable to reject such conditions as wrong, as unjust. When some people benefit or do well in circumstances one thinks are unjust, such as white people but also educationally successful minorities, those less fortunate can understandably be uncomfortable, with reason, about those who are comfortable and happy in such a system, whether knowingly or unknowingly.

The will to reject injustice is sensible. When avenues for the dominant group's success are largely barred for others, such as in conditions inadequate for a good education, people can be self-affirming through self-creation and pride in their own identity. Remarkable artworks that are referred to as "counterculture" often result, such as in graffiti or music.[56] At the same time, when people become more distant in terms of their cultural experiences, they can find it harder to relate to one another, and choices different from the norm for disadvantaged communities can appear to be judgments of those who have not been as fortunate. The self-affirmation that results can come therefore in the charge of "acting white." Once again, while individuals have a part to play in the development of their own powers, in their sense of self-respect, cultural, and environmental conditions affect what one will perceive to be an option for oneself, what is within one's own power. Thus, the responsibility for the harm done in such charges must rest in large part on often overwhelmingly unjust circumstances.

For a dramatic and troubling example from 2007, consider that in Canton, Mississippi, it was reported that the percentage of high school students retained through their senior year from an entering freshman class was 32 percent.[57] The Canton School District has an almost entirely African American student body, surrounded by a number of more affluent white counties. The vast majority of Canton's students were being channeled into lives that would not have access to those choices for which a high school diploma is necessary. Systematic failure of that degree cannot be attributed to individual students' responsibilities. The culture of poverty, racism, division, oppression, and limited opportunity is clearly blameworthy for its deep, negative impact on the lives of young people there. Their sense of their own positive power is conditioned in part by the wider culture and the forces and negligence of a legislature that underfunds schools, as well as a "justice system" that profits from the incarceration of young men. In the face of such recalcitrant injustice, self-respecting people might reasonably believe that some powers will not be accorded to them, no matter how they act.

The term "uppity" has a related history. Believing oneself to be of worth beyond one's station is the charge involved when one is called uppity.[58] The idea that people have a certain station in life, due, for example, to where they were born or from whom they were born, runs contrary to the belief in social mobility. When one believes oneself to be better than one is, such as in overreaching from one's area of expertise, there can be a case of stepping out of bounds. In a democratic society, we are no longer supposed to accept arbitrary bounds, however, or dismiss a form of great intelligence just because it is considered "blue collar." Scholars have made the case,[59] yet related elitist beliefs persist and can motivate the self-affirming judgment of others who are said to think themselves worthy of unjust privilege or priority. That behavior is deemed a betrayal of the many who suffer injustice and is associated with the dominant group. The will to buck others' disrespectful judgments of these kinds can motivate self-affirmation, even if some of its forms bear meanings that understandably trouble people.

Harm

Two kinds of harm can be at work in the charge of "acting white." The first is unintentional, such as what results from the protection motive. Self-affirming charges can intend no harm, arguably. A devastating version of the charge of acting white concerns the circumstance in which one unintentionally calls things that are virtues, such as knowledge, "white." David Walker rejected such thinking, to be sure, yet when we consider responsibility for the harms at issue conveyed culturally, their source and causes are shared. Once again, the ultimate responsibility for such problems rests in the hands of the people who fail to demand or fund quality schools. Expecting people to be independent and self-respecting without providing the tools through which those virtues are cultivated is cruel. It blames the victim or belittles the person who copes with injustice. It also fails to understand that and how such virtues must be fostered and developed. This harmful version of acting white might stem from a loathing of one's circumstances.

The intentional version of harm can come from an internalization of the oppressive society's values. Not seeing a way to change conditions, one can accept them and come to blame the victims of injustice for their conditions. Such charges are insensitive but play on the emphasis that says that individuals have a part to play in the development of their self-respect. While there is truth to that fact, oppressive conditions can torture a person, literally or metaphorically. In torture, the language of "breaking" a person is familiar. Solitary confinement in prisons has been found to be overused and to be destructive of human personality, for example.[60] If torture and posttraumatic stress are known to be frustrating of human personality, we can also understand the relationship of deep poverty and impediments to developing a sense of positive power.[61] In much of the United States, injustices and unequal citizenship are maintained through economic advantage and disadvantage, accentuated and aggravated by racial and economic differences. Thus, when people show anger at present conditions that are difficult to live through, Aristotle would say that people will have a harder time loving others if they struggle to love themselves. Once again, society therefore has a corresponding, and I argue a greater, responsibility to ensure that all citizens have access to the optimal conditions needed for developing a sense of positive power.

John Lachs's Stoic Pragmatism

John Lachs has long been a champion of liberty. In *The Relevance of Philosophy to Life,* he argues in favor of freedom in end-of-life care and in the sale of human organs.[62] In that work and later, in *Meddling,* he advocates for tolerance, patience, and minding one's own business when it comes to others' affairs.[63] His outlook on the treatment of others typically supports an expansive inclination to allow people to pursue happiness as they will. In understanding something's nature in part as Aristotle did, as a matter of the conditions in which the thing flourishes, Lachs breaks with the Greek philosopher in arguing that human beings do not have a singular nature, but many. He argues for a belief in human *natures*.[64] While he believes that there are many ways to be happy and to pursue a fulfilling life as an individual, there are nonetheless patterns and challenges in life about which stoic philosophy offers valuable lessons for us all. Despite our diversity, he recognizes that there are common needs and difficulties we all face. Illness and death are challenges beyond our control, and all people are subjected to one or both of them eventually.

If we are all to die and face challenges beyond our control, the stoic attitude can help us to accept difficulties, but Lachs also notes that at times the stoic can appear defeatist. While the stoic calls for people to accept the things they cannot change, the modern reaction is familiar, in the call to "change the things I cannot accept."[65] The activist's call revises the stoics' phrase, as the latter can sound fatalistic and pessimistic. In *Stoic Pragmatism*, Lachs recognizes the pessimistic ring in stoic ideals, but also what seems right in them.[66] He contrasts it with the excessive optimism that can be found in American pragmatism, such as in the Deweyan belief in continuous or infinite growth and progress. When we put the two together, we find an answer to the skeptic about ideals. On the one hand, we cannot change everything, yet little changes without optimism. The pragmatist belief in progress is healthy, so long as it is tempered with an acceptance that progress can only ever be partial. The stoic ideal informs good pragmatism but is also in turn spurred into action with pragmatic optimism. After all, how can we know whether we have the power to change circumstances without trying? Any given effort, furthermore, is not evidence that change is impossible. Instead, it either yields some success or is proof that this effort has failed. Thus, in stoic pragmatism, Lachs has identified a way of navigating between cynicism and absolutism about social ideals, as I argued in chapter 1.[67]

At the Berlin Practical Philosophy International Forum, one participant in the conference forum asked me about what he called "the devastating facts" I raised concerning injustices both in American history and in the country today. He wondered whether there is realistically any hope for justice given how deep past and present difficulties have been and remain. Lachs's stoic pragmatism shows the way forward. If one expects perfect justice today, it seems that one will either grow weary of constant failure to meet that ideal or believe that only extreme measures will do. Absolutism or extremism result from the latter and apathy and cynicism from the former. Stoic pragmatism calls us to recognize ideals for what they are, concepts of a perfection that may never be achieved in one's lifetime, yet that can direct our behavior in steps. If we continually take small steps, in time, we can travel a long way. With that outlook a person can champion justice, make progress toward it, yet recognize that always there will be work to be done, more progress to be made. With the right attitude, we can at least feel happy about the difference we have made in a lifetime. A little over a generation ago, my African American students' parents could not have attended the University of Mississippi where I worked for many years. Their mothers could not have attended Princeton University.[68] Until the last twenty years, many women could not have held certain positions in the US military,[69] and many parents hesitated to believe that the United States could elect a president who is not white.[70] Recognizing that so much is left to be done, we can nevertheless take time on occasion to note those moments when progress has been clear.

Stoic pragmatism is vital for the pursuit of a democratically just society, in which all people can grow up in the best conditions possible for developing self-respect and a positive sense of their own power. We will never achieve perfect conditions, and it is likely that the cause of freedom will necessitate variations from the ideal. At the same time, many past causes for hierarchical citizenship have been or can be alleviated. Today, there are many who argue that the United States is not a democracy, but an oligarchy.[71] Some scholars have argued that such problems have arisen because of laws or Supreme Court decisions, such as the *Citizens United* or the *Trump v. United States* cases.[72] Where such arguments are on the mark, advocates for progress can find targets for change.

Lachs's stoic pragmatism is vital for developing a sustained attitude and motivation for progress. At the same time, his wider social philosophy presents challenges to my arguments for the need of a culture of justice and for the belief in shared responsibility for it. Like Robert Nozick, Lachs emphasizes individual responsibility when it comes to moral matters. He accepts the need for governments and for the legal ability to sue organizations, yet he believes that real moral responsibility is always a matter for individuals.

In brief, I argue that we ought to consider the obligations to establish a culture of justice to be shared, since (1) groups of individuals decide policy; (2) individuals make patterns for which together we become responsible in their maintenance or management; (3) each individual can contribute to patterns of shared behavior; yet (4) no particular individual is morally responsible for collective obligations until so specified. Therefore, the moral responsibility that I argue for in this chapter is on such grounds a shared obligation, and the target of that responsibility is the cultivation of a real sense of positive power in all people for the pursuit of meaningful life plans.

Conclusion

While Rawls was right to be concerned about self-respect, the language he chose was problematic in its tendency to be used for blaming those who suffer injustice for their conditions. His own qualifying language notes the social forces connected with self-respect, yet that fact demands more attention than it has received. If his aim in prioritizing self-respect was rooted in an ideal of social cooperation, he was not considering places such as the American South, not to mention much of the United States, where police have used photographs of black men for target practice.[73] The American ideals of self-reliance and industry are meaningful and important but are also insults and reminders of injustice to those for whom real achievement of the aims common to advantaged people is experienced as unrealizable. Important features of what Rawls intended when he wrote about self-respect should not be mistaken for something utterly in the individual's control to develop. To be sure, one should not assume that other people lack self-respect when they fail to believe that society's possibilities for others are realizable for them. The wider culture, the actions of individuals, and the practices of public institutions all weigh in as reasons why people might feel with warrant that their society is unjust, that it does not live up to the proclamation that all people are created equal.

Lachs's insights about stoic pragmatism clarify the attitude with which the public and we individuals who make it up ought to approach the pursuit of our democratic ideals. Those ideals include the need to establish conditions that foster self-respect, understood as a sense of one's own positive power, for all people. In so doing, we fulfill both the democratic ideal of empowering (-cracy, *kratia*) all people (demo-) *and* the libertarian value of individual responsibility, which rests on self-respect and individuals' belief in their positive power. As such, I have argued that liberty for all in democratic societies depends on a shared, public, cultural obligation that individuals and institutions must strive to fulfill with an attitude of stoic pragmatism. That attitude encourages the consideration of all levels of engagement with people, respecting and empowering them, yet with special emphasis on young people. Appreciating stoic pragmatism coupled with the insight from Frederick Douglass with which this chapter began can steer us toward efforts that will yield the greatest progress. For, as Douglass pointed out, "it is easier to build strong children than to fix broken men."[74]

5

Culture, Poverty, and Positive Empowerment

As I noted in the introduction to this volume, Andrew Kernohan significantly advanced the literature on liberalism when he highlighted the power of culture in the pursuit of justice in his book *Liberalism, Equality, and Cultural Oppression*.[1] Kernohan took moral equality as a fact and understood some groups to simply be wrong in their beliefs about the inequalities of people. Critics of such attitudes abound, however, and among the most prominent in philosophy is Louis Pojman, who, with Robert Westmoreland, edited the volume *Equality: Selected Readings*.[2] In that volume, scholars give various accounts of what it means in political thought for people to be equal. The editors' introduction begins with the striking point that "It is an empirical fact that human beings are unequal in almost every way."[3] A compelling point of view neglected in Pojman's and Westmoreland's collection is democratic philosopher John Dewey's, whose outlook I explain in this chapter.

The reason this is important is that where there exists great inequality, as I noted in chapter 3, on the "Impediments to a Culture of Justice," there

An early version of the essay on which this chapter is based was first delivered in February of 2016 as an invited talk for Purdue University's Lectures in Ethics, Policy, and Science. I am grateful especially to Lacey Davidson for the invitation, as well as to support from Purdue University's Office of the Provost, Graduate School, College of Liberal Arts, Brewer Chair in Applied Ethics, Departments of Philosophy and Political Science, College of Agriculture, College of Health and Human Services, and College of Science. The original essay was titled "Culture, Poverty, and Justice: Responsibilities of Individuals and Institutions."

will be difficulties for the task of establishing and maintaining a culture of justice. As I argued in the introduction, such a culture requires maximally fostering self-respect in all people and a sense of their own positive power to pursue meaningful life plans. But if great inequality creates conditions not sufficiently just such that poor and otherwise disadvantaged people lack reason to have confidence that they have the power to pursue meaningful life plans, then without far greater equality there can be no justice. As such, what equality means matters profoundly, and greater equality must be a possibility. At the same time, while Dewey and I argue not merely for the protection of negative liberty, freedom from imposition, but also for positive empowerment, freedom enabled to do and to act, critics exist already who question, challenge, and worry about what they call a culture of dependency.[4] Still others believe that when wealthy white liberals call for cultural progress for the poor, they are exhibiting white European values unfairly and misapplied to people not like themselves. As I explained in brief in the introduction, Alain Locke's philosophical grounding of the Harlem Renaissance calls that kind of challenge into question, supporting the claim that one can be affirming of self-respect and recognition of positive power in the cultures of disadvantaged and minority populations without inherently intending necessarily white, European, or colonial values.[5] The question this chapter seeks to answer is: What conditions might positively empower all people to believe with warrant that the world is sufficiently just, so as to foster confidence that their meaningful life plans are attainable? I argue in this chapter that those conditions involve a supportable understanding of equality, a culture that combats stigmatization of support and dependency on others, and the implementation of policies that ameliorate the lives of persons living in poverty and other forms of disadvantage.

In this chapter, I begin with a brief look at how Dewey understood the concept of democratic equality, when indeed people are all different. Next, I examine Locke's sense of the beauty and powerful potential of a culture even for people who have been historically marginalized and oppressed. Then I address the profound ideological divide in the United States concerning poverty today and address the claims about creating "a culture of dependency." A look at empirical research clarifies the overwhelming evidence that poverty makes countless matters more difficult, even while policies can be modified both to the benefit of the poor and in recognition of some of the concerns that conservatives raise, such as on the pressures of the "benefit cliff."[6] Finally, I conclude the chapter with a sketch of an initial and an obviously incomplete set of policy areas that can have substantial effects on the positive empowerment of all people, including those who live in poverty.

John Dewey's Understanding of Equality Rooted in Individuality, Incommensurability

Dewey would have agreed with Pojman and Westmoreland that, empirically speaking, of course all human beings are unequal. Pojman argues that the tradition of liberalism cannot offer a meaningful cause for calling all people equal without some religious reason of which liberalism is supposed to be independent. Dewey held a pragmatic understanding of the reasons for thinking of people as equals. And it is rooted in appreciation of all of our differences. In 1937, he delivered an address titled "Democracy and Educational Administration," in which he argued that

> The very fact of natural and psychological inequality is all the more reason for establishment by law of equality of opportunity, since otherwise the former becomes a means of oppression of the less gifted . . . [The] democratic faith in equality is the faith that each individual shall have the chance and opportunity to contribute whatever he is capable of contributing, and that the value of his contribution be decided by its place and function in the organized total of similar contributions:—not on the basis of prior status of any kind whatever.[7]

A few years later, in 1939, in Dewey's better-known essay "Creative Democracy—The Task Before Us," the philosopher expands on his earlier sentiment, writing that

> The democratic faith in human equality is belief that every human being, independent of the quantity or range of his personal endowment, has the right to equal opportunity with every other person for development of whatever gifts he has. The democratic belief in the principle of leadership is a generous one. It is universal. It is belief in the capacity of every person to lead his own life free from coercion and imposition by others provided right conditions are supplied.[8]

The language of the "right conditions supplied" is important here, as too often people assume that equality can be achieved merely by eliminating historical barriers to equality. The error in such latter outlooks can be captured in a similar criticism that David Walker raised when people assumed the Emancipation Proclamation meant that former slaves were now equal.[9] Walker argued that freed slaves clearly had need for "material and moral uplift."[10]

In *Democracy and Leadership*, I presented Dewey's case for equality, which can be summed up in terms of each person's incommensurability. At bottom, for Dewey, each person should be understood to be equal because of each person's individuality. Unlike cans of tomato sauce or boulders, each person is a class onto oneself, unlike in the classist thinking of Plato or of feudal societies. Dewey sums up this view in his 1919 essay "Philosophy and Democracy," writing,

> Now whatever the idea of equality means for democracy, it means, I take it, that the world is not to be construed as a fixed order of species, grades or degrees. It means that every existence deserving the name existence has something unique and irreplaceable about it, that it does not exist to illustrate a principle, to realize a universal or to embody a kind or class. As philosophy it denies the basic principle of atomistic individualism as truly as that of rigid feudalism. For the individualism traditionally associated with democracy makes equality quantitative, and hence individuality something external and mechanical rather than qualitative and unique. In social and moral matters, equality does not mean mathematical equivalence. It means rather the inapplicability of considerations of greater and less, superior and inferior. It means that no matter how great the quantitative differences of ability, strength, position, wealth, such differences are negligible in comparison with something else—the fact of individuality, the manifestation of something irreplaceable. It means, in short, a world in which an existence must be reckoned with on its own account, not as something capable of equation with and transformation into something else. It implies, so to speak, a metaphysical mathematics of the incommensurable in which each speaks for itself and demands consideration on its own behalf.[11]

When a car is totaled in an accident, even special cars are understood to be replaceable. A house catching on fire can be rebuilt or alternate housing secured. When the world loses a person, something of significant moral value is lost. Dewey's sense of equality is rooted in the deep meaning that individuality holds for him.

Dewey understood individuality and diversity to be among the crucial evolutionary sources of human beings' powers, connected to his appreciation of Darwin.[12]

Alain Locke on Culture, Self-Respect, and Identity in the Face of Adversity

Dewey's contemporary and fellow pragmatist Alain Locke also valued diversity regarding both individuals and cultures. As I have noted, attending to culture for the sake of justice is not meant as a call for assimilation to white or European culture. In his introduction to *The Philosophy of Alain Locke*, Leonard Harris notes about Locke's important book *The New Negro* that "Locke's version of the New Negro, contrary to [Booker T.] Washington's, emphasized Afro-American cultural continuities with Africa, that is, affirming positively what was valued as inferior by white culture; affirming positively an African identity even though American-ized in many ways; and applauding the folkways, rhythms, symbols, and rituals of black life. In addition, Locke applauded the inevitable urban-ization of blacks while other philosophers romanticized small-town and rural living."[13] Harris points out that just because matters of culture are dismissed or devalued by dominant or oppressive groups, this does not discount their value for others.

In the light of Locke's promotion of tolerance and diversity, my theory must address how the Southern racist might call for appreciation of their culture and Confederate battle flags. The key here is to look again to the thesis of this book, namely that there is a shared, public obligation to establish and maintain a culture that maximally fosters self-respect and a sense of positive power in all people. The affirmation of black or Afro-American cultural arts and contributions is perfectly consistent with people who are different, save insofar as those others wish to denigrate or impede the sense of positive power in others. In other words, the will to inhibit others' senses of their own positive power to pursue meaningful lives is not one of the cultural norms consistent with a culture of justice. This argument is akin to the harm principle. One person's liberty to harm others without their consent is not a form of defensible liberty. So that person's liberty to harm, enslave, or otherwise inhibit another's sense of positive power is not one of the defensible forms of culture that can be expected to be protected. Therefore, for those to whom such values and histories are important, the task must be to identify those cultural norms, histories, and values that are not necessarily embedded in the cultural oppression of another.

Now, it is worth noting that Locke himself was not born of deep poverty, but instead has been referred to as coming from "Philadelphia's black bourgeoisie."[14] It is true that Locke himself was born into some degree of privilege certainly in comparison with poor black Americans of his day. Nevertheless, he moved from considering culture as a matter of what might be called "high culture" to a sense of culture that is for everyone, and he also considered the role of art and cultural discourse in relation to people of all levels of advantage and disadvantage. In his essay "Frontiers of Culture," for example, he acknowledges that "I, too, confess that at one time of my life I may have been guilty of thinking of culture as cake contrasted with bread. Now I know better. Real, essential culture is baked into our daily bread or else it isn't truly culture."[15] In this sense, Locke came around to a sense of culture more akin to Dewey's more environmental sense of the term. Harris notes, furthermore, that "Locke's philosophic conceptions were not supportive of a nativistic or atavistic conception of cultural virtues. Rather, his notion of the New Negro was constituted to alter the nature of public discourse about African people and to re-envision African self-concepts across various social strata."[16] Locke offers a rich example of the cultural leader who rejected the cultural valuations of dominant groups in favor of appreciation of the meaning and power of one's own history. Harris continues, writing that "[Locke] considered African art as the art of grand civilizations at a time when most black and white university-educated scholars believed that African works were either not art or at best the product of primitives unworthy of applause. At a time when the denegration [sic] of black folkways was a national pastime, he considered the folkways of African people as the source of classical artistic texts."[17] In addition, Harris makes clear a very important aspect of Locke's contributions, which helps to explain the power of group identities. Consider the analogue when it comes to the case of a threat against a group or race of people, which was the opening example of the introduction to this book, namely when students at the University of Mississippi draped a noose and old Georgia flag around the neck of the statue of James Meredith. Critics historically have believed that one should prosecute crimes for the harms they do to individuals, not identifying some as "hate crimes."[18] In the case raised in the introduction, the relevant offenders admitted that they intended to threaten and intimidate African Americans at the University of Mississippi as a group.[19]

Just as groups can be threatened and thus be targets of inhibitions to the development of their sense of positive power to pursue meaningful life plans, so too can groups be affirming and empowering in turn. Harris writes of Locke that "he warranted the heuristics of collective identity by culture in conjunction with recognizing the forever-moving process of individual transvaluations and the transpositions of value categories such as truth, beauty, and virtue; rejected reifications of ethnic identities but simultaneously saw self-respect and dignity as being mediated through collective identities."[20] Through such thinking and cultural and intellectual engagements, furthermore, Harris writes that "Locke took pride in his differences" and "was involved in shaping the life-world of his racial group."[21]

It is for reasons and purposes such as Locke's here that it is important to attend to the value of culture for the sake of justice and that such attention should not be understood as something just for privileged classes. After all, when we look to poor and disadvantaged schools, which suffer greatly from insufficient funding,[22] we should not be surprised to hear that matters like art and music are not nearly their priorities, when so many needs deemed to be "basic" go unmet. To be sure, these problems are unacceptable and must be addressed moving forward, yet attention to culture is of profound importance. Harris summarizes the connection here to Locke's thought, writing that "the symbolic creation and re-creation of identity is pictured and portrayed for Locke in art, literature, and drama. He held that the world is subject to remain culturally diverse; that cultural plurality has social advantages that cultural uniformity lacks; that personal concepts of worth such as self-respect, self-pride, and self-esteem, in an already racially and ethnically diverse world, are tied to our valuations of group identities."[23] So when we look to address culture and aim maximally to foster self-respect and a sense of positive power in all people, the point is not to accept some narrowing sense of individualism inherent in liberalism or liberalism's atomization. Rather, Harris writes, "Loyalty to the uplift of the race for Locke was thus, *mutatus mutandis*, loyalty to the uplift of the culture. Locke was not an assimilationist, separatist, instinctivist, nor nativist . . . For Locke, a social identity is conditioned by our individual valuations, but they are not subjectively molded or caused in isolation from our historicity and material condition."[24] For these reasons and more, we must appreciate the potential for anyone to participate in the cultural shaping of his or her group identity and value, yet also recognize the powers and forces of historical and material conditions that can inhibit people's potential and powers.

Testing Ideologies About Poverty and Shaping Culture

In 2012, Matthew Spalding of the conservative Heritage Foundation published "Why the U.S. Has a Culture of Dependency," citing the *Wall Street Journal*'s reporting that in 2011, "49% of the population [in the United States] lives in a household where at least one person gets some type of government benefit."[25] He continues, writing that "the problem is that Washington is building a culture of dependency, with ever-more people relying on an ever-growing federal government to give them cash benefits. This is a growing and dangerous trend." To be sure, it is essential for there to be discussion and consideration, as well as expectations for justifying government expenditures and corresponding efforts to secure revenues to fund them. How and when we decide whether an expenditure is a good or a bad thing is considerably more challenging a question to answer than the mere facts about expenditures. At the same time, Spalding is concerned about culture, about people's thinking and habits, debating about what sorts of policies the public should want for the sake of creating the right kind of culture. However, one must consider the forces that lead people to seek government support, whether such dependency is itself a good thing or a bad thing, and whether present policy designs are the ideal ones for conditioning the kind of culture that is desirable or undesirable.

In December of 2019, Aimee Picchi reported for *CBS News* that "almost half of all Americans work in low-wage jobs," noting that "44% of U.S. workers are employed in low-wage jobs that pay median annual wages of $18,000."[26] And, according to the US Census Bureau, in 2020, 16.1 percent of persons under the age of eighteen live in poverty, and 37.2 million Americans do overall.[27] Additionally, the Centers for Disease Control and Prevention report that "26% (1 in 4) of adults in the United States have some type of disability."[28] With very large numbers of Americans earning low wages, many depending on Medicaid for disability-related needs, and a substantial proportion of children and Americans living below the poverty line, it should not be very surprising that many people seek aid when and where it is offered. At the same time, Spalding includes among the beneficiaries of government support that he has in mind people who receive temporary assistance for needy families, social security, support for higher education, and crop subsidies.[29] Despite this great variety of forms of government support, Spalding takes aim at those that do not require people to be employed to receive the benefits, only a portion of the beneficiaries. But just because a program of support does not require one to be employed to receive it does not mean that we should identify recipients of support as unemployed. In fact, in 2014, NBC News reported that "twenty-five percent of active duty military families get aid from food pantries nationwide, a rare survey about food insecurity among troops finds."[30]

A profound divide has grown in Americans' thinking about the experience of the poor, as noted in the introductory chapter. It bears repeating that a 2014 Pew Research Center poll found that 86 percent of "steadfast conservatives" believed that "the poor have it easy because they can get government benefits without doing anything." And, in stark yet strikingly balanced contrast, 86 percent of "solid liberals" believe that "the poor have hard lives because government benefits don't go far enough to help them live decently."[31] Different political ideologies are certainly rooted in competing values, but it is also important to consider how such thinking can affect others, both in the consequent choices of policies and in the stigma that can result for people who seek support for their needs. In fact, Spalding is explicit that he believes it to be a problem that the United States "is turning into a land where many expect, and see no stigma attached to, drawing regular financial support from the federal government."[32] He wishes that people felt stigmatized. Should members of the military feel bad for their dependence on food aid? Another way to react would be to think that members of the military should be compensated sufficiently such that they would not need the aid, but the same argument could apply to countless other people and professions. Indeed, Fox Business reported in November of 2020 that Walmart and McDonald's are among the largest employers of SNAP and Medicaid recipients.[33] Senator Bernie Sanders condemns these companies for paying "starvation wages,"[34] while defenders of the companies argue that they employ many people who would be on assistance if it weren't for their employment with the companies. The point here is that oversimplification is inherent in rash and blanket judgments, but at the same time, such pronouncements can and do contribute to stigma that can condition people's choices and make people feel as though they are undeserving or not reasonably empowered to pursue meaningful life plans.[35] In *The Shame of Poverty*, Robert Walker writes, "Shame associated with poverty is painful, constrains human agency, and may contribute to the persistence of poverty . . . [and] attempts to manage the shame associated with poverty are often counterproductive in terms of personal efficacy."[36] If Walker is right, then stigmatizing impoverished people for their need for assistance is or can be counterproductive. By contrast, efforts can be made to decrease stigmatization, a matter to which I return in the next section.

Spalding suggests that people do not feel stigma for accepting federal assistance in the United States, but policymakers have gone to great lengths to ensure that some of the most vulnerable recipients of support do. In the last decade, politicians called for drug testing welfare recipients, a move that has been shown both to be off-base in its assumptions and wasteful, fiscally speaking.[37] Darlena Cunha, in *Time* magazine, reports that in Tennessee "only one person in 800 who applied for help tested positive."[38] In addition to costing far more money to test than the process saves, the process is rooted in assumptions about the poor and the explicit intention of people like Spalding to inflict stigmatization, one that says that if you seek assistance, you are a member of a group that makes poor decisions, ones against the law, and that you should feel ashamed. On Spalding's own account, that would be progress.

People like Spalding want our culture to stigmatize dependency on government, yet countless Americans depend on the postal service, public transportation, public schools, public universities, and so much more. When people depend on each other, is this a bad thing? Spalding's presumption is that it is. Philosophers dating back to Plato hold a profoundly different view. Plato argued that cities come to be precisely because people need each other. Plato's Socrates says that "I think a city comes to be because none of us is self-sufficient, but we all need many things."[39] We need each other. No one is an island.

The common reply to the logic I have offered is that people need each other to fill each others' needs, not to depend on each other. This logic fails to appreciate the temporary or seasonal nature of many people's needs. Consider how many jobs were lost in the early days of the COVID-19 pandemic.[40] In addition, people can work their whole lives yet have little in old age. Therefore, some policies aim to respect and support the elderly. And, according to the Census Bureau's report on the 2011 fiscal year budget, 60 percent of funds going out to individuals from Social Security, Medicare, and unemployment insurance in the United States go out to those who paid for them.[41] To those who focus on the remaining 40 percent, it is important to remind people that many face challenges that are not of their own making. I have learned a great deal through personal experience myself in raising a child with severe disabilities.[42]

Many resources can be drawn on to show the troubling effects of poverty. A 2013 release from Princeton University, for example, presented research findings that said that "poverty and all its related concerns require so much mental energy that the poor have less remaining brainpower to devote to other areas of life."[43] In 2015, researchers found that poverty "can lead to a negative spiral of fear and self-loathing," as reporter Dawn Foster summarized the message.[44] In 2016, Lisa Esposito reported for the *U.S. News and World Report* about "the Countless Ways Poverty Affects People's Health," from lowering life-expectancy rates to increased personal injury risks to food insecurity and a lack of mental health supports, to name a few examples.[45] It is little surprise, furthermore, that poverty frustrates the need for safe and secure housing, which is associated with adverse public health conditions.[46] All of these conditions connected with poverty associate with countless other forces impeding people's potential and powers, from schooling to earnings and more. In *Reign of Error*, Diane Ravitch notes that the racial academic achievement gap has narrowed significantly since the 1970s, yet remains substantial and troubling.[47] At the same time, she challenges "our corporate reformers [who] insist that we must 'fix' schools first, not poverty." She responds,

> But the weight of evidence is against them. No serious social scientist believes that rearranging the organization or control or curriculum of schools will suffice to create income equality or to end poverty. The schools did not cause the achievement gaps, and the schools alone are not powerful enough to close them. So long as our society is indifferent to poverty, so long as we are willing to look the other way rather than act vigorously to improve the conditions of families and communities, there will always be achievement gaps.[48]

Ravitch's point—that the expectations policymakers put on public schools often ignore the need to simultaneously address the problems of poverty—is well taken. Still, much can be done to improve schools and address the odds that children living in poverty can have good chances in school. Both matters ought to be addressed simultaneously for the best chances of success. Finally, along with problems for schooling, poverty yields challenges too for employment and career success. In 2016, Eleni Karageorge explained that "Growing Up in High-Poverty Areas Can Affect Your Employment."[49] In 2017, chair of the US Federal Reserve Janet Yellen argued, "Considerable evidence shows that growing up poor makes it harder to succeed as an adult . . . Children who grow up in insecure circumstances, those often experienced in poverty, seem disproportionately likely to experience financial insecurity, as adults."[50]

In exploring the challenge of pursuing a culture of justice, it is important to consider not only the symbolic and stated values that people champion, but also the consequent practices and policy decisions people make as a result of them. Spalding points to the fact that the United States offers support to many people, but also wishes for a culture that would stigmatize such conditions. Even if one can clearly point to some number of troubling cases of people who abuse a system, does that mean that a culture of stigmatization for all who receive help is a good thing? This seems cruel and harmful, especially for those who do not abuse a system designed to help them. Making welfare recipients feel accused or suspected of drug addiction is hurtful, physically invasive, and costly. Moreover, no such measures are put in place for farm subsidies or corporate bailouts of Wall Street.[51]

In their introduction to *The Social Psychology of Stigma*, John Dovidio, Brenda Major, and Jennifer Croker explain that "stigmatization, at its essence, is a challenge to one's humanity—for both the stigmatized person and the stigmatizer. Croker, Major, and Steele (1998) explain that 'a person who is stigmatized is a person whose social identity, or membership in some social category, calls into question his or her full humanity—the person is devalued, spoiled, or flawed in the eyes of others.' "[52] Given this understanding, stigmatization clearly does people harm. It certainly would inhibit people's sense of their own positive power to pursue meaningful life plans. If one sees stigma in a gentler sense, as a matter of cultural force to discourage things that are morally wrong, then it might be considered a gentler cousin of shaming, but presumably for wrongful or troubling behavior. Spalding himself acknowledges that some people deserve public support. If that is the case, how would a culture that intentionally stigmatizes people for seeking public support prevent doing so to people deserving of support? In addition, what one person thinks is deserving can appear undeserving to another, especially on prejudicial grounds, today often referred to in terms of "tribalism."[53] When it comes to establishing and maintaining a culture of justice, it is important to watch out for and resist those forces that aim to stigmatize others for reasonable behaviors even when they involve reliance on others or on public support. No one is an island. We all depend on each other. As many have argued already, the "self-made man" is a myth.[54] I would also add that John Rawls, whose work countless scholars have criticized for a nearly endless variety of reasons, appears to be onto something profoundly morally important in his attention to the least advantaged persons in society, among whom the impoverished certainly fall. The Belmont Report's Ethical Principles and Guidelines for the Protection of Human Subjects of Research call for careful moral attention to the respect for persons and especially for persons who can be considered particularly vulnerable to ethical harm. By the same logic, it is of profound importance to protect the interests of, including the avoidance of stigmatization for, the poor, for people who often have need for public assistance. Cultural and psychological forces can be among the forms of harm for which society and individuals should see themselves as having obligations to diminish or avoid. If that is right, then Spalding and those sympathetic with his arguments should think of other ways of speaking about and reacting to the needs for public assistance that so many Americans have.

As Dovidio, Major, and Croker have argued, it is wrong to stigmatize the recipients of support. A culture of justice must be one that aims to avoid harming people with stigmatization and shaming. Such practices dehumanize others and treat them as undeserving of support that has been made available through difficult political battles fought to address people's needs and challenges. There certainly can be waste in government, but the declaration that there is a culture of dependency ignores the fact that people in society are supposed to depend on one another. It also does harm and is indiscriminate in its injurious shaming of people who need help to have a sense of their positive power to pursue meaningful life plans.

Policies and Practices for
Addressing Material Impediments to a Culture of Justice

As I conclude this chapter, it is worth considering and noting at least briefly a set of practices and policies that have bearing on the lives of vulnerable populations when it comes to fostering a real sense of their positive power in the world. It is not enough to remove barriers to success. People need to eat. They need an education. They need health care, housing, and security. When parents or guardians are able to provide these sufficiently for themselves and their families, this is a good thing, but even for them, it must not be forgotten that people living beyond the poverty line nevertheless benefit from government support of various kinds. While I taught at the University of Mississippi, for example, I had many students who thought that market solutions and offerings are always superior to government resources and productions. It was jarring to them and increasingly fun for me to remind students that I was there as a government employee, supported in part by tax dollars that rendered their college costs lower than had they attended a private institution. Public funds support an ever-decreasing proportion of higher educational costs, but they still create significant cause for students to pursue one of their largest life investments to date at public institutions of higher education.

Forces that can inhibit or foster people's sense of positive power to pursue meaningful life plans include matters from the bottom of Maslow's hierarchy of needs to the top.[55] In February of 2022, for example, NPR reported that advocates are saying that homeless young people are "wildly undercounted."[56] Obtaining the right information about people's physiological and safety needs is already a challenge, and one very important to understanding and then addressing basic needs of people living in profound poverty. In "America's Youngest Outcasts: A Report Card on Child Homelessness," Ellen Bassuk and coauthors point to needs for safe and affordable housing, education and employment opportunity needs, comprehensive assessments of family members, trauma-informed care, identification and treatment of mental disorders including depression, parental supports, developmentally appropriate services for children, and funding for research into child homelessness.[57]

While Spalding may despair at the fact, the 1946 National School Lunch Act, signed by President Harry Truman, has long provided children with free and reduced-price lunches through the US Department of Agriculture. Provisions today include breakfasts too, and advocates championed the provision of meals for all kids, which were provided in 2021 and have been valued for parents' benefit as well.[58] Among the benefits of providing meals to all children is the effect on diminishing stigma for those who participate in the programs. If all kids are offered meals, then poorer children are not differentiated problematically. In addition, as I have noted in earlier chapters, the United States government substantially subsidizes American agriculture as it is. Putting the USDA to work on the provision of healthy meals for all children can support national agricultural needs at the same time as our nutritional needs.

In schools, countless matters can be addressed to make a difference for the sake of establishing and maintaining a culture of justice. For one example that advocates often raise, we can consider the representation of teachers in relation to the student bodies in schools. There are proposals available for recruiting and retaining teachers of color to teach students of color so that all students can see mentors and representatives among their teachers of persons like themselves.[59] A frequent call and hope is for pay to increase for teachers,[60] but in part a cultural shift is needed to see and treat teachers as the professionals they are.[61] As work on this aspect of culture is pursued, it is at the same time important to consider what motivates teachers most. Diane Ravitch has noted research that has shown that teachers would, according to existing studies, largely prefer smaller class sizes over higher teacher pay, as far as their stated priorities have shown. Ravitch writes, "Teachers said that having a smaller class meant more to them than the chance to earn extra money."[62] This does not mean that teachers are not also interested in greater pay and treatment as professionals, but the findings show that their priorities are first to do their best for children, evidence of the values of the profession.

When I have referred to schools, most of the time I have had kindergarten through twelfth-grade schooling in mind, but adult education is also profoundly important and effectual. Jane Addams and Alain Locke were advocates for adult education. Politicians have called for providing all people with free college,[63] while others have promoted free community college in particular.[64] Today a number of states offer community college for free,[65] including especially Tennessee.[66] According to the Tennessee Board of Regents' website, "Tennessee Promise provides Tennessee high school graduates the opportunity to attend a community or technical college free of tuition and mandatory fees . . . [and] is both a scholarship and a mentoring program."[67] It is worth noting that many see community college education as a more vocational track than four-year liberal arts programs, yet community colleges teach arts and humanities as well, and, as Scott Samuelson has argued, plumbers benefit from studying Plato too,[68] not just philosophy majors. At the same time, it is worth noting that a culture of justice calls for establishing the conditions for all people to pursue meaningful life plans, which can include college. As such, the expansion of provision of free community college is certainly a good sign, yet falls short of the widespread need for many to pursue further education, beyond job training, for personal fulfillment and growth. For this reason, it is not enough to endorse culturally the expansion of job training programs, and instead it is right to call for the provision of opportunity for education for all, a provision that many other countries offer today.[69]

It is worth noting that there have been initiatives pleasantly named that have raised cause for scrutiny and criticism, such as Georgia's HOPE Scholarship.[70] The Georgia scholarship has been said to provide support primarily to students from largely middle-class families rather than lower-income families. At the same time, poorly designed or unfairly implemented programs are not evidence that better programs could not be crafted.

Historian of American education Patricia Albjerg Graham has argued that among the challenges to offering quality education to all Americans is a profound underinvestment in educational research. In her book *Schooling America*, Graham writes:

> In a nation that has traditionally believed in research and development in other fields, there has been precious little "R" on which to base the "D" in education. During the Reagan, Bush, and Clinton years the federal government, the primary funder of educational research, reduced its expenditures for this activity by 82 percent, according to a National Academy of Sciences study led by Richard Atkinson, former head of the National Science Foundation and later president of the University of California. Diane Ravitch, former assistant secretary of education, placed the drop at 90 percent from 1975 to 1995.[71]

Indeed, there are endless criticisms of public schools, blaming them for far more than makes sense. Nevertheless, politicians have slashed the resources that could usefully supply insight about how to use the money we spend on schooling more wisely and justly. Where funding is available, it generally focuses on interventions, akin to wanting to develop new medicines without the benefit of basic research in the sciences.[72]

When it comes to education in the United States, critics are quick to point fingers and suggest their preferred ideologically driven solutions. For instance, it is commonly assumed that public schools are failing and that privatization is a viable solution. Ravitch, appointed first to the US Department of Education by George H. W. Bush, is an advocate who decries the privatization movement as a hoax on the American people. She also points out that American students are performing better on tests than they ever have before. In addition, she shows how the disaggregation of educational data demonstrates that purported modest growth is actually better understood as remarkable growth in the narrowing of the racial achievement gap, combined with growth for those on average more privileged in schools, namely white Americans.[73] While there remain legitimate concerns about the achievement gap that ought to be eliminated, substantial progress has been made on its narrowing since 1973.[74] In addition, if Americans wish to rise in the international rankings of student performance,[75] the greatest gains to be made would be from achieving greater equity and support for the country's most disadvantaged students. As noted above, Ravitch has argued that the way to achieve this goal is through attention to poverty and policies to aid people who live in its conditions.[76]

One area of concern aggravating the problems of poverty is the phenomenon of the "benefits cliff." It is the idea that one can be a recipient of public benefits for which a small difference in earnings or circumstances can suddenly mean a dramatic loss of public support. This means that people will have strong cause to beware of changing their circumstances in such a fashion that could risk the loss of substantial public benefits. In simplest terms, one proposed outlook on the matter would be the recommendation that benefits recede more in the form of a slope than a cliff where possible. In "Balancing at the Edge of the Cliff," for example, Theresa Anderson and her coauthors suggest such an idea when they propose that "benefits could not drop so quickly after an increase in earnings or offer a grace period for families to stabilize their new employment situation."[77] They also propose the possibility that "if tax credits were distributed throughout the year instead of in a lump sum annually, it may help families incorporate this income into their monthly budgeting."[78] Anderson and her coauthors' report for the Urban Institute also proposes mechanisms for easing understanding of how and when benefits change, such as online calculators, an idea echoed by Meghan McCann and Josephine Hauer in "Moving on Up: Helping Families Climb the Economic Ladder by Addressing Benefits Cliffs," a report for the National Conference of State Legislatures.[79] Interestingly, McCann and Hauer note the potential power of "fostering culture and system changes in the public and private sectors," though none of their recommendations calls for stigmatizing persons in need. They call for changes to cultural considerations related to "employer engagement, cost-benefit analysis, goal setting, career planning and coaching, and student access to SNAP."[80] Anderson and her coauthors also note the potential power of employer flexibility.[81] None of the recommendations of scholars and experienced administrators points to the usefulness of stigmatization, and the moral weight against it should be clear at this point.

There will of course always be mixed results when it comes to efforts to help people who face the challenges of poverty. At the same time, it is worth noting that some programs have demonstrated significant benefits for disadvantaged youths, such as Head Start, a program launched in 1964 in President Lyndon Johnson's "war on poverty." Early studies that showed remarkable benefits of such programs have been called into question, yet the Brookings Institution's Economic Studies Fellow Lauren Bauer writes that "The Head Start Impact Study reanalyses and the decades of research on Head Start show that on a variety of outcomes from kindergarten readiness to intergenerational impacts, Head Start does work, particularly for students who otherwise would not be in center-based care."[82]

In the big picture, what is needed is not just one or another policy measure, but rather a cultural shift. American leaders value power, money, corporations, and guns, regularly disavowing the importance of children's safety and education, caregiving, and teaching. The United States falls far behind other nations in terms of respect for the need for parents to attend to newborn babies.[83] Many in the United States oppose choice for mothers' reproductive health[84] yet fail to consider the value of paid parental leave[85] or policies that would make children safer from gun violence at school.[86] The norm of expecting gratitude for military personnel is established,[87] though the country should do better, including for veterans, as noted above, yet the same appreciation has waned for teachers[88] and caregivers.[89] A culture that promotes power and wealth first and foremost and discounts the work of caring and educating others is one that promotes injustice. It undermines many people's chances in the pursuit of meaningful life plans. Individual efforts in policy are not enough to bring about change, but a set of policies together, along with real efforts to change a culture, can move the country in the direction of greater justice. Fostering a sense of service to others is one area of policy not broached in this chapter, but could take the form of universal public service,[90] which some other countries require, encouraging more interaction and practices of contributing to one's society. Many more efforts can be pursued, but together the aims of justice call for an overarching effort to support one another, rather than stigmatizing some people's needs for support, when in fact we all depend on others.

This quick run-through of practices and policies that generally target persons living in poverty conditions demonstrates that a wide variety of efforts can be enacted with the aim of fostering maximally in all people a sense of their own positive power. Critics like Spalding suggest that people lose initiative to do for themselves when resources are provided for them, but Head Start and school lunch programs demonstrate that this is not the case. And it is important to recall that countless people receive benefits from public, shared support for the people's needs, including any and all people who attend public colleges and universities. This includes Representative Paul Ryan, who worried about a culture of dependency yet attended the public Miami University in Oxford, Ohio, for his under-graduate education.[91]

The purpose of this section and of this chapter in the end is to consider an array of ways in which cultural values, practices, and policies can have an effect on whether or not a society is genuinely doing all that it can to establish and maintain a culture of justice. It is certainly justifi-able to debate different policies and proposals, including to always expect strong justification for shared endeavor and spending. At the same time, it is of profound importance to defend society's most vulnerable people and of great consequence for justice that cultural efforts be made to avoid stigmatization and promote people's sense, by positive means, that they indeed have the power to pursue meaningful life plans without troubling impediments or lack of reasonable social support.

6

Obligations for Culture as Public and Shared

If justice requires the establishment and maintenance of a culture that maximally fosters self-respect and a sense of positive power in all people, as I have argued, then it is important to consider who bears the responsibility for it. In chapter 5, I argued in favor of policies and public support for alleviating the challenges of poverty, highlighting especially the public obligation to enable all people to develop a justified sense of their own positive power to pursue meaningful life plans. The aim there was not to deny that responsibility for culture is shared, but rather to emphasize the weight and central import of ensuring that where and when people exercise their responsibilities and make efforts to participate maximally and ideally in developing a shared culture of justice, their hard work has a fair chance of bearing fruit. In that sense, the first and greatest responsibility for fostering a culture of justice, I believe, is the public obligation, one that society must work to fulfill by means of public schools, fair policing and trials, supportive and empowering public practices and policies, and through public expression of values. While on my view the greatest obligation for establishing a culture of justice is public, nevertheless

This chapter is based in part on an essay I first delivered at Michigan State University in February of 2016. I am grateful to Kyle Whyte and his former colleagues in the Philosophy Department at Michigan State University, who generously invited me to give this presentation. Whyte has moved to the University of Michigan since I first wrote the essay that became this chapter. Flaws in this chapter and book are all my responsibility, but I have benefited from insights that Whyte and his colleagues offered me.

individuals and private groups bear great power in contributing to the shaping of culture. As such, they also bear important responsibility as well, even while people deserve protections for the liberty to think, disagree, and debate public matters in ways that challenge the goals of a culture of justice. The obligation then for the shared contributions to culture is best understood as a moral one, which all people bear for contributing to a just democratic society. The corresponding expectation hinges on the idea that John Dewey introduced, and that Ruth Anna Putnam examined with care,[1] that democracy is a way of life, and not just a political one or merely a social one. Putnam notes the striking claim Dewey made in 1939 that "democracy is a personal way of individual life."[2] For Dewey, democracy is more than a political mechanism. It is cultural and moral, and more fundamentally so than it is political. In this chapter, I therefore argue that the powers that establish, maintain, and change culture are shared among individuals and institutions, and, correspondingly, obligations for culture are also public and shared.

In what follows, I begin with a response to one of the greatest critics of public or shared obligations, especially when it comes to seeking to address social or economic patterns, namely Robert Nozick. Next, I examine the moral aspect of the shared obligation to establish a culture of justice, as I understand it in terms of Dewey's idea that democracy is a personal way of individual life. In a similar fashion, then, I see the establishment of a culture of justice, in addition to being a task for states and public institutions, as a personal way of individual life, in which people should call themselves and others to task morally for ensuring that society fosters maximally in each person a sense of his or her own positive power to pursue meaningful life plans.

Patterns of Justice and Responsibility for Culture

If the legitimacy of government rests on the consent of the governed, then it is thought that a government's actions and commitments ought to be minimal to avoid clashes with the people. Liberal societies focus on freedom of the individual and root obligations negatively, with the goal of leaving people as maximally free as possible so long as they do not harm others or limit the liberty of others. As I argued in chapter 3, there are tensions inherent in liberalism that clash with the expectation of equal citizenship and respect for all. Enabling liberty for some and not others also fails to heed the same concern noted about the need for the consent of the governed. We cannot ask some people to accept gross injustices for the privileging and benefit of others. At the same time, government is not the only contributor to the perpetuation of cultural forces that can inhibit or enable justice. Individuals acting freely can actively engage in prejudicial behavior that can threaten other people's sense that they have a fair chance at pursuing meaningful life plans. A key example is in the activity of speech, expression, on which the next chapter focuses. For now, my aim is to consider the devil's advocate, the claim that we should not be looking for justice at the level of culture, and hence that is public and shared. Robert Nozick famously challenged the claim that justice should be expected at the level of patterns.

In *Anarchy, State, and Utopia*, Nozick acknowledges that there can be ways in which activities are compelled unjustly. He writes, "If an existing society was led to by an actual history that is unjust, then so is that society."[3] At the same time, however, he contends that through the free actions of individuals, patterns of economic distribution can emerge that some people will call objectionable. Nozick believes that if there was fairness in the transactions between people, then there is no injustice in the pattern that emerges from "justice in transfer."[4]

The examples that help to illustrate Nozick's claim work especially well when we contrast the earnings of public schoolteachers and those of famous basketball players. Nozick gave Wilt Chamberlain as an example.[5] Some people believed it to be outrageous that basketball players would earn millions of dollars while schoolteachers would struggle to make ends meet. Nozick argues that no injustice produced this difference in incomes, but that it arises instead from the patterns of individuals' free behavior.

In the higher-education context, university presidents and chancellors have more recently earned salaries in excess of $1 million, like Nathan Hatch of Wake Forest University or Gordon Gee of the Ohio State University. John R. Boatright has offered ways of determining reasons for thinking that executive compensation can be either defensible or not, yet substantial sums of money generally raise cause for scrutiny.[6] Years ago, it was thought scandalous that Gee earned in excess of $6 million per year as president of the Ohio State University in 2013. Consider that at the time the average student loan burden upon graduating from the university was $26,000.[7] It is fair to ask whether the educational context is different, such as for the reason that Boards of Trustees are involved and nonprofit educational institutions are not driven in the same way as other markets.

While this is a reasonable consideration, it nevertheless motivates even more curiosity over the reason why the relevant executives then would need to be paid such large sums. A danger of such executive compensation, furthermore, is that it reinforces the notion of treating education as a commodity, as a mere market matter, rather than one about personal and social fulfillment.

Jordan Weissman asks and answers his question about Gordon Gee's 2013 salary, "This State College President Earned $6 Million Last Year. Should You Be Mad?," clearly in the affirmative.[8] All while some leaders of public institutions and stars of sports teams make huge sums of money, in critically important areas like education, newspapers around the country use the metaphor of schools "hemorrhaging teachers."[9] To be sure, there is a variety of factors that contribute to teacher dissatisfaction, but low salaries are among the first considerations raised, with fingers pointed at people earning astonishingly large sums of money in contrast.

Nozick's point makes more sense concerning the star athlete, who earns money for private entities, with customers voluntarily giving their money to watch a game and enjoy an evening. Systems are at work in the case of university presidents that are less relevant to the context he wishes to imagine, one of individuals acting freely with no unfairness or injustice in the transfer of their goods. It is imaginable that someone could earn a huge sum of money without having caused a great injustice to others, he proposes, so we can start with him in accepting the claim for the sake of argument. If we grant Nozick this point, then it is at least conceivable that there could be patterns that emerge from the free actions of individuals about which some people will complain, but for which no injustice was intended or arguably done, at least by the mere difference in distribution.

Nozick's assumption, however, is that we can look to the level of individual transactions for questions of justice, correcting those matters for which some compulsion occurred that should not have. As such, if he is right, then it does not make sense to look for justice at the level of patterns of individuals' behavior. After all, no one intended either a desired or undesirable outcome of the pattern of individuals' freely chosen behavior, except that it be free from coercion. So no one can be blamed, is the belief, when patterns emerge that some people do not like.

There are at least three significant problems with Nozick's argument. I call them the due diligence challenge, the lessons learned challenge, and the orphan challenge.

The due diligence challenge concerns the fact that people who plan an activity, such as a musical concert like Woodstock in the late 1960s, should see themselves as having an obligation to anticipate problems and possible ways in which people or environments might be harmed. The harm I have in mind is the damage that was done in terms of tons of waste and to the fields in the area. One could argue that countless individuals littered and damaged the landscape, but organizers are supposed to plan—their due diligence. Woodstock was a cultural phenomenon as well as a business endeavor, after which many lawsuits arose.[10] Even if one could argue that the event was not one for which harm was intended, there is an expectation, or there should be understood to be one, that people will do their due diligence to ensure that harm does not come to others. If people do not, we cannot genuinely say that there is justice in transfer.

If we imagine that something truly unexpected were to occur as a result of the pattern of free individuals' behavior, we can say that we learned a lesson. The fact that problems can emerge as a result of people's free choices means that even if we do not punish or blame anyone at first, we can nevertheless call for changes for the future. Nozick is particularly concerned about coercion, but coercion is not always required of efforts to "nudge" more people toward behavior that advances the common good, that enables justice.[11] While rules that save countless lives on the road rankled some people,[12] no substantial campaign remains with the aim of combating seatbelt laws. On that score, even if there were, the people who accept greater risk in driving without seatbelts would have to contend with the moral challenges regarding the greater dangers and costs involved in insurance and medical care that individuals' free choices can impose on others. No one is an island. The lessons learned challenge replies to Nozick that society may decide that a tragic number of deaths is unacceptable and can therefore justify efforts to alleviate harms, to prevent unnecessary deaths that can be anticipated.

The orphan challenge is my greatest concern when it comes to libertarian arguments about justice. Imagine a family is walking by the side of a road and a driver hits the parents, killing them as well as the driver. There are now orphans. Freely chosen actions result in harming some people. The person who committed the harm had negative assets on balance, and so no money of theirs can be used to care for the children. In a libertarian world, no one in particular has an obligation to tend to the orphaned children. On libertarian grounds, there is no public obligation to care for them. People can therefore go about their business, exhibiting justice in transfer with regard to each of their duties and responsibilities freely chosen. In the process, unsupervised children can walk into the road or simply die of exposure and starvation by the side of the road. If individuals' transactions were the only real source of consideration for justice, then the children would have nothing to offer and would perish.

One point of view suggests that the motivation to universalize obligation and to care about the dignity of humanity requires religion. Louis Pojman argues as much in his essay "On Equal Human Worth: A Critique of Contemporary Egalitarianism" in *Equality: Selected Readings*.[13] He claims that liberalism lacks the substance for offering anything like a robust justification for people's equality and inherent worth. In the same collection, Pojman and his coeditor Robert Westmoreland include Nozick's own contribution, excerpted from *Anarchy, State, and Utopia*, titled "Justice Does Not Imply Equality."[14] In that passage, Nozick argues that people who advocate for equality merely presume without argument that equality in material conditions is to be expected.

In the end here, we see that Nozick wants to know why people who believe themselves to have no interest in contributing to shared public expenses for the needs of orphans should be compelled to do so. His challenge recalls Peter Singer's imagined skeptic in a now famous essay, "Famine, Affluence, and Morality." Singer bites the bullet and acknowledges that he may not have an argument that can sufficiently convince the skeptic that hundreds of thousands of people dying of starvation is a bad thing, morally speaking.[15] He writes,

> I begin with the assumption that suffering and death from lack of food, shelter, and medical care are bad. I think most people will agree about this, although one may reach the same view by different routes. I shall not argue for this view. People can hold all sorts of eccentric positions, and perhaps from some of them it would not follow that death by starvation is in itself bad. It is difficult, perhaps impossible, to refute such positions, and so for brevity I will henceforth take this assumption as accepted. Those who disagree need read no further.[16]

Singer's approach here supports Pojman and Nozick's challenges to the liberal justification for human worth. It is worth considering for the sake of a culture of justice, however, what might be reasons that could be offered for thinking that it matters whether everyone has a fair chance at the pursuit of their own meaningful life plans, free from the cultural threats that others can bring to bear.

There are three interrelated reasons why the skeptic should care to feel their obligation to contribute to a culture of justice, caring about things beyond their narrow, private interests, and hence feeling their share of responsibility. The broadest is the biological argument. Human beings have evolved in such a manner as to tend to each other's needs when we are hurt or in need of help.[17] If the majority of human beings tended not to care for people in need, and given how helpless babies are, humanity would not have fared well over time. One might think that a biological argument is compelling, but biology recognizes the profound importance of variation, and hence while it is advantageous evolutionarily for human beings to care for each other, it is also perfectly natural that some or even many people not care for others. Those in the minority are beneficiaries of others' kindness, however, which should not be missed. And, so long as it is a significant majority who do care for others, then biology will be satisfied for survival. But biology also begets us the exceptions, the variations. The corresponding key is that not too many human beings end up unconcerned about the suffering of others. That minority, however, will proclaim an injustice whenever they are called to care for or support causes for which they do not care. Yet there is a biological basis for considering the worth of each person, at least on the whole, as a general matter, even if universal concern is unlikely or impossible. The biological outlook represents a reasonably realistic approach to garnering the consent of the many.

A second reason for caring about shared obligation, such as to the orphan or to one's part in a culture of justice, can be found in Plato's *Republic*, in which he argues that the city comes to be because people need each other. This argument could be understood as a version of the biological argument. Plato's Socrates claims, "I think a city comes to be because none of us is self-sufficient, but we all need many things."[18] People concerned with the worth and dignity of each person worry about basing a person's value on their social productivity for others. When President Obama in the health care debates called for end-of-life planning to address the costs of care, critics raised concerns about "death panels."[19] Such were scare tactics, to be sure, but the norm underlying them is that we should respect our elders and not just kill them off for the sake of a few dollars. Republican Lieutenant Governor Dan Patrick of Texas has also been criticized for saying "there are more important things than living and that's saving this country," concerning risks to the elderly of lifting mask mandates during the coronavirus pandemic.[20] The lieutenant governor wanted people to get out and buy things, to stimulate the economy, which was struggling during the time of the pandemic. He too faced criticism for sacrificing grandma to the economy. The idea that people should be protected so long as they are contributing to a nation's economy is a crass reason to be concerned about others, but it also illustrates a way of justifying a lack of concern for one's fellows. And while I noted Plato's interest in the fact that people need each other, he also famously advocated for killing imperfect babies in the *Republic* by leaving them to die of exposure.[21] On the whole, Plato thought that people who were a drain on society should be sacrificed. Thus, his outlook would face similar challenges to the cries of "death panels." So while it is true that people need each other, it is crude to care for people only for their use value.

A third argument concerns the virtues of gratitude and friendship, which also could be interpreted as a variant or offshoot of the biological argument. While religiously, rather than biologically, inspired, St. Thomas of Aquinas argued that self-love is the basis for the love of others.[22] The incredible vulnerability of human beings in youth depends on parents or guardians who will tend to babies' and young people's needs, going to great lengths out of love or care that far exceeds what is returned. The love of a parent or guardian may indeed exceed the kind of care that a friend would offer, yet even for friends, Aristotle argued in the *Nichomachean Ethics*, the point is to love, not to be loved. In Book VIII of the *Ethics*, Aristotle writes:

> Friendship . . . seems to lie in the loving, rather than in the being loved. This is shown by the delight that mothers take in loving; for some give their children to others to rear, and love them since they know them, but do not look for love in return, if it be impossible to have both, being content to see their children doing well, and loving them, though they receive from them, in their ignorance, nothing of what is due to a mother.[23]

It is not surprising that in youth, children fail to appreciate what their guardians do for them. It is more troubling, however, when adults fail to see all that others did for them in their time of youth. As such, under healthy conditions, it should be hoped that a person grown to maturity would develop a sense of obligation to give back to those who are vulnerable as a form of "paying forward" the gratitude that one ideally should feel to those who raised them. A colder form of this argument takes a Hobbesian outlook, such that care for others is inspired by prudence, given that any of us can become disabled or dependent on others in an instant, falling down stairs or in a car accident. Any who wish to live into old age are scheduled for their period of need for others' help in time.

Viewed in relation to the virtues of gratitude and friendship, someone who lacks concern for others' needs appears shameful. This is perhaps why Peter Singer's response to the skeptic about people's suffering is as famous and understandable as it is. A person who demands justification for having to contribute in a small way to taxation for the sake of tending to the needs of orphaned children should likely feel some amount of shame. It is true that it can be troubling to shame people for many matters, such as being overweight[24] or for their disabilities,[25] yet Kwame Anthony Appiah has argued that one of the crucial mechanisms prompting moral revolutions is honor.[26] People are proud of the reasons they believe that they are deserving of honor and feel ashamed about those matters for which no one should feel proud, that are not deserving of honor. For a significant news cycle, not just Americans, but the entire world protested the murder of George Floyd,[27] for example, and shortly thereafter the state of Mississippi finally voted to change its now-former state flag, which bore a Confederate battle flag emblem in its canton. Savannah Smith, writing for NBC News, reports that

> the debate around Mississippi's state flag is not new, but with the governor's signature it finally reached a conclusion after many failed attempts to change it. The difference this year, according to [State Representative Robert] Johnson, was the bipartisan leadership by first-term legislators. "We've never had anything start in the Legislature that way, and it just became a perfect storm," Johnson said, referring to the protests across the country for police reform and against racism, spurred by George Floyd's killing while in the custody of Minneapolis police.[28]

The change did not come quickly or easily until a tipping point rooted in shame over the idea of unquestionable evidence of institutionalized racism, instilled in government, symbols, and American culture.

When it comes to the thesis of this book concerning a culture of justice, the reasons stated so far all contribute to my argument's overarching purpose. While it is true that culture is a term applicable in small and narrow ways, such as in referring to a subculture or pop culture, it is also the case that culture can be understood in a broad sense, as in the wider culture. Culture as a term is akin to the mathematician's term "set." Culture is a set, as we have defined in earlier in this book, including symbols, language, beliefs, practices, and institutions passed down from one generation to the next. That set can be understood narrowly or in the broadest sense. And in such senses, we can think about cultural environments as fish tanks, such that we all swim in the water. We share in the character and effects of what is contributed to the culture, to the environment. In that sense, the contributions one makes to caring for others, about their well-being, to tending to those in need, may indeed be motivated by a Hobbesian prudence for one's own future potential needs. Even if some, many, or all people's care for others is rooted in prudence, virtue ethical education calls for the hope that people would turn such practices into behaviors of friendship and gratitude, which people would ideally come to want for their own sake. In addition, culturally, we can aspire to a greater future beyond our lifetimes, as in the Indian proverb "Blessed is he who plants trees under whose shade he will never sit."[29] Examples of such thinking include public libraries,[30] universal education,[31] and endowed scholarships and programs aiming in the long term for a more just and humane culture into the future.

One might object to the arguments that I have given so far that there will never be universal agreement that people should care about others' suffering. Several points are worth making in response. First, just as in aiming for a healthy country, universal vaccination is not required; just a significant majority is necessary.[32] Second, it is far better for opponents of care for others to be visible and vocal so that their concerns can be taken seriously and heard. On the one hand, critics generally help to reveal what could be improved on when it comes to programs and efforts that need improvement. On the other hand, as I have noted about Dewey's argument elsewhere, it can be a great value to democracy to be put on the defensive. It is a problem when people merely parrot ideas without understanding them. When democracy is challenged, people have to reckon with ideas to keep them alive, fresh, and in mind. This means that democracy and ethics take constant effort.

A Culture of Justice as a Way of Life

John Dewey was known for championing the idea that democracy is a way of life. At bottom, the shared, public obligation to establish and maintain a culture that maximally fosters self-respect and a sense of positive power in all people to pursue meaningful life plans is essentially one that aims to empower all people, to be democratic. It too calls for both public institutions and for individuals to take part in the shaping of the culture needed for justice. In this way, Dewey as a moral and political philosopher is the important figure to turn to in contrast with the many thinkers who argue for justice merely in terms of procedure and political mechanisms. If, as I have argued, there is a public and *shared* obligation to establish and maintain a culture of justice, then we need to also consider what it means to enact a culture of justice as a way of life for groups and individuals.

As noted earlier in this chapter, Ruth Anna Putnam points to one of Dewey's more famous essays to highlight what some might believe to be a peculiarity of his argument, namely the idea that democracy must be a "personal way of individual life." The line arises in "Creative Democracy—The Task Before Us," where Dewey writes:

> We have had the habit of thinking of democracy as a kind of political mechanism that will work as long as citizens were reasonably faithful in performing political duties . . . Of late years we have heard more and more frequently that this is not enough; that democracy is a way of life. This saying gets down to hard pan. But I am not sure that something of the externality of the old idea does not cling to the new and better statement. In any case we can escape from this external way of thinking only as we realize in thought and act that democracy is a personal way of individual life; that it signifies the possession and continual use of certain attitudes, forming personal character and determining desire and purpose in all the relations of life.[33]

Putnam points to one of Dewey's earliest statements about democracy, namely his 1888 essay "The Ethics of Democracy," to note that already he had articulated a view that proclaimed the moral foundations of democracy, necessary on Dewey's view, for any political procedure or mechanisms.

Dewey writes there that "democracy, in a word, is a social, that is to say, an ethical conception, and upon its ethical significance is based its significance as governmental. Democracy is a form of government only because it is a form of moral and spiritual association."[34]

In much of Dewey's thought and in this last passage, we hear the language of spiritualism, and in "Democracy Is Radical," he refers to faith. In the latter, he writes, "The revival of democratic faith as a buoyant, crusading and militant faith is a consummation to be devoutly wished for. But the crusade can win at the best but partial victory unless it springs from a living faith in our common human nature and in the power of voluntary action based upon public collective intelligence."[35] Here we see a connection, a parallel between Dewey's outlook on democracy and the kind of concern that I have drawn from John Rawls's *A Theory of Justice* early on in this book. Rawls argues that it is essential that "at almost any cost" we avoid those forces that undermine self-respect. For, as Rawls writes,

> When we feel that our plans are of little value, we cannot pursue them with pleasure or take delight in their execution. Nor plagued by failure and self-doubt can we continue in our endeavors. It is clear, then, why self-respect is a primary good. Without it nothing may seem worth doing, or if some things have value for us, we lack the will to strive for them. All desire and activity become empty and vain, and we sink into apathy and cynicism.[36]

For Dewey, the point is more general, that for democracy to be meaningful, it must spring from a living faith in human nature. The worry that Rawls reveals here is that privileged classes of people can feel faith and potential for their lives, all while contributing to a culture that belittles, demeans, or threatens others' real sense of possibility for their lives.

The connection to make here is that in addition to fostering a faith in human potential for public collective intelligence, a culture of justice demands attention to the ways in which culture, both at the social and political as well as the individual level, can contribute to threatening people's sense of their own positive powers. Here it is worth noting that today some people will likely snicker at the idea that anyone might have a real faith in public collective intelligence. Political polarization is at an all-time high.[37] The idea of truth untouched by political manipulation is met with the language of "alternative facts" and the idea that we now live in a "post-truth" world.[38] In addition, even as an independent press verified and publicized the election of Joe Biden to the presidency against incumbent President Donald Trump, a number of Americans rioted, resulting in the loss of seven lives in 2021.[39] Putnam notes in her essay that it is often said that "The ballot is . . . a substitute for bullets,"[40] yet there are reasons to worry that more bullets will continue to fly so long as Americans fail to have faith in our common human nature. In fact, as I write this paragraph, National Public Radio reports that "It's 19 Weeks Into the Year and America Has Already Seen 198 Mass Shootings," including the most recent in which ten people were killed in a racially motivated killing spree.[41]

In light of troubling news and developments, the simplest answer is that it is clear that we can do better, and yet at the same time, there have been far more troubling practices in US history. Dewey writes, "Put into effect," democracy as a way of life "signifies that powerful present enemies of democracy can be successfully met only by the creation of personal attitudes in individual human beings; that we must get over our tendency to think that its defense can be found in any external means whatever, whether military or civil, if they are separated from individual attitudes so deep-seated as to constitute personal character."[42] The creation Dewey has in mind must take place in many ways and at many levels. To be sure, there is a powerful need to retrieve American public schools from the scourges of high-stakes standardized testing and its overbearing accountability culture, as well as the privatization movement, as Diane Ravitch has powerfully argued in several books.[43] At the same time, there are countless things individuals can do in their own interactions with others every day, with social media contacts, with coworkers and friends, to embody a culture that believes and makes real the sense that all people should be treated with respect and with the attitudes that convey that each person deserves a fair chance at pursuing meaningful life plans. It is in this sense, then, that each person must see their part in the contributions we each make to a culture that can enable or inhibit the pursuit of justice. As such, while a culture of justice is an obligation for everyone, that does not mean it is an obligation for no one in particular. It is an obligation for each and every one of us. If some or many choose and wish to perpetuate cultural injustice, that means that the rest need to work all the harder for the establishment of a culture of justice and to invite our fellows into the fold of working toward the culture on which justice depends.

7

Free Speech and the Cultivation of Hatred

In this book, I have argued that there is a shared, public obligation to establish and maintain a culture of justice, one that maximally fosters self-respect and a sense of positive power in all people to pursue meaningful life plans. Such a culture also calls for protections of the freedom of speech, yet speech can be used in a manner that threatens a culture of justice. In this context, this chapter attends to the legal, political, and social aspects of the obligations of a culture of justice with regard to the expression and cultivation of hate or discrimination associated with hate, as in hate crimes law. I argue that present understandings of the protections of the freedom of speech in the United States fail to appreciate sufficiently the harms that threatening speech can do and that there is a shared, public obligation to respond with cultural force to instances of the expression and cultivation of discriminatory ideas. At the heart of my analysis is John Dewey's concept of "cultivation," which can help to contrast instances of the mere consideration of hateful ideas from those cases and organizations that seek to grow and render active the prejudicial

I first delivered an early draft of the essay that has grown into this chapter in March of 2018 at the Midsouth Philosophy Conference at Rhodes College in Memphis, TN. I am grateful to the thoughtful feedback that I received there. Next, I delivered a more developed version of the essay at the Instituto de Filosofia da Nova—IFILNOVA, Faculdade de Ciências Sociais e Humanas, Universidade Nova de Lisboa in Lisbon, Portugal, in March of 2022. I am grateful especially to Dina Serra Luz Mendonça, who invited and hosted me on the trip and offered rich feedback, along with rich interactions with her students and colleagues at the New University of Lisbon.

impulses that Dewey calls treasonous to democracy. At the same time, among the problems and challenges in this context is the inadequacy of the term "hate" when the problem at issue pertains more appropriately at times to unjust discrimination, whether impassioned or coldly calculating and dehumanizing.

I begin with a review of some basic and broad justifications for the profound need to be protective of the freedom of expression. Then I return to the matter of threats to groups, something discounted in the case with which this book opened, namely the noose incident at the University of Mississippi, where freshmen hung an old Georgia flag and a noose around the statue of James Meredith, the man who first integrated the university. Next, I clarify and explain a distinction important to Dewey, the great philosopher of democracy, differentiating the expression of hateful ideas from the "cultivation" of hatred or discriminatory practices. Finally, I briefly survey a variety of ways in which people can fight for a culture of justice at the political and social levels.

Central Motivations for Maximally Free Speech

There are at least four major reasons why we ought to maximally protect the freedom of speech. Maximal protection, however, is nevertheless consistent with some constraints. These reasons bear reviewing to highlight central democratic norms. While more can be offered, the four reasons revisited here include the Marketplace of Ideas argument, the Teakettle argument, the Basic Democratic Freedom argument, and the Both Ways argument.

The Marketplace of Ideas. In "The Marketplace of Ideas: A Legitimizing Myth," Stanley Ingber explains that the idea in question arose in debates among English philosophers John Milton and John Stuart Mill.[1] He writes that "Justice [Oliver Wendell] Holmes first introduced the concept into American jurisprudence in his 1919 dissent to *Abrams v. United States*: 'the best test of truth is the power of thought to get itself accepted in the competition of the market.'"[2] If truth and wisdom are to be important for leading a good society, then one view is to believe that an open competition of ideas will yield the truth as a result of the competition. Competition is thought to be the best way to garner the truth. One might think that intelligence must be fostered by a kind of encouraging culture of mutual respect, as is typically a hope in educational settings, yet John Stuart Mill, in *On Liberty*, wrote, "Truth, in the great practical concerns of life, is so much a question of the reconciling and combining of opposites that very few have minds sufficiently capacious and impartial to make the adjustment with an approach to correctness, and it has to be made by the rough process of a struggle between combatants fighting under hostile banners."[3] When we consider the combative ways in which expression tends to be employed with regard to contentious issues, Mill already had such concerns in mind. Ideas can seem beyond the pale and can be totally unpopular, yet sometimes win out. The history of science is rich with such instances, from Galileo's conflict with the Catholic Church to the ongoing cultural debates in the United States over the teaching of evolutionary theory.[4]

Given the value of entertaining competing ideas, constraint on speech yields a diminishment of available information, and freedom means that inquiry can proceed even into subject matters that the majority prefer not to hear or consider. Protections like tenure in the academy are meant in part to empower diversity of opinion and exploration despite the unpopularity of some beliefs or questions. These protections are real and important, especially as we can see that even in 2022, political leaders like Texas's Lieutenant Governor Dan Patrick have announced plans to "phase out tenure in Texas' public colleges and universities, and to revoke tenure for those who teach critical race theory."[5] More recently, President Trump "is waging war against DEI in schools"[6] and threatened that "All Federal Funding will STOP for any College, School, or University that allows illegal protests."[7]

The notion of the marketplace of ideas, however, does not mean that any which manner of expression must be protected. It is one thing to have the opportunity in newspapers and public street corners to express one's views. The idea of advocacy near voting booths can be considered a form of intimidation,[8] for example, and is not necessitated for protections of the marketplace of ideas. Where you protest might be rhetorically relevant, but the marketplace of ideas does not necessarily require that all or any which avenue for persuasion be open to all. The marketplace argument also doesn't protect all subject matters, such as the case of yelling "Fire!"[9] in a theater. Perhaps even more troubling is that the strength of the marketplace argument is threatened by misinformation and the spread of falsehoods. You might think that people will choose their news sources, voting with their feet, as they say, but misinformation about COVID-19 has been found to have led to hundreds of deaths.[10] A serious challenge for the marketplace argument, then, is the old saying that "a lie can travel halfway around the world while the truth is still putting on its shoes."[11]

Beyond the threat of misinformation, it is worth noting that marketplaces can also be aggressive and drown out the less powerful. Ingber argues that the marketplace of ideas argument rests on a myth about personal autonomy, when in fact society is governed by the powerful who work to preserve the status quo. While such arguments are worth considering, the silencing of speech could be used against the political minority, and hence can be counterproductive, a point to which I return in discussing the Both Ways argument. In addition, while powerful forces will weigh heavily on the scales of their preferred outcomes in the competition of ideas, allowing space for expression is necessary for any effort to counter such forces. In sum, the guiding belief at work in the notion of the marketplace of ideas is likely to be overoptimistic with regard to belief in the outcome of open and public debate, yet it is difficult to trust in any authority to exhibit the detachment necessary to limit speech justly. As such, worries like Ingber's call for education and social organization to resist the forces for partiality and twisting of the truth, matters to which I return in the final section of this chapter. For now, it bears repeating that even if the central hope of the marketplace of ideas is too optimistic, a modest amount of realism leads to reasonable worries about who might be the fair arbiter of what causes and truths ought to be given how much attention and promotion. If anything, a healthy skepticism here prompts people to prioritize freedom when it comes to expression. Nevertheless, while freedom of expression is to be protected, that does not mean that all theories deserve a hearing, as David Hildebrand has argued,[12] nor do all outlooks deserve the promotion of a platform for their amplification, as many colleges and universities have argued with respect to speakers on campus.[13]

Avoiding the Teakettle. The Teakettle argument suggests that if a person or group has no opportunity to speak, they may believe themselves to have no other outlet for their energies than exploding. If you stop up the outlets of a teakettle, heating the water inside creates a bomb. Allowing an outlet for steam may create an unpleasant whistle but diffuses the otherwise very dangerous energies inside.[14] The claim suggests that we must beware not to limit people to no other course of action than violence, though it makes assumptions that I argue are questionable. Unlike the Marketplace of Ideas argument, which concerns the necessities of self-governance, the Teakettle argument is more of a social contract argument. We agree to let others have the chance to express themselves, even distastefully, to prevent them from acting violently, offering them another outlet for their energies.

The Teakettle argument, then, is not about nobility, but prudence. In the metaphor, the pressure valve offers an avenue of release, something one can do in order to not have to resort only to destructive force.

To be sure, there is a threat at work in the Teakettle argument of which there is cause to beware. Essentially, the argument threatens violence if persons are not permitted to express their sometimes distasteful views. In the American Civil Rights movement, Dr. Martin Luther King Jr. responded to constraints on speech with clarification that his group's efforts involved only nonviolent protest. In his "Letter from a Birmingham Jail," King acknowledged that his aim was disruption, and in the end he accepted the claim that his efforts were extremist, but only in the sense that Jesus was "an extremist in love."[15] King illustrates that resistance to speech need not be seen as justifying violence. People who work to cultivate hatred do not deserve a hearing or protections simply because they otherwise threaten violence. In fact, threats of violence are among the clear instances that can justify limitations on speech. Speaking of logical justification, furthermore, philosophers consider an argument that involves a threat of force to justify a conclusion to be a logical fallacy, namely the *argumentum ad baculum*, an "argument to the stick."[16]

While King's example demonstrates a limitation to the Teakettle argument, other examples point to instances of violence that many think of as justified today, such as in the Boston Tea Party. The much more recent Tea Party movement made use of symbols of that early American history, such as in the use of flags bearing the symbol of the coiled snake, with the warning "Don't tread on me." That expression presents a warning, which sounds threatening, but defenders would argue that people are prepared to defend themselves. There can therefore be a line of distinction at work in the threat that one will defend oneself versus being the instigator of harm. The Teakettle argument in a sense buys into the worry that failing to permit a person to speak justifies violent threats. At the same time, one can envision circumstances such that making someone wait for their chance to speak can delay justice or permit a harm to take place that might arguably warrant the claim that the prohibition of speech is akin to an attack worthy of a response like self-defense. Thus, the Teakettle argument is at least a controversial justification for the freedom of expression, but one that could seem justifiable depending on the exigency of circumstances about which the speech is relevant. Nevertheless, one could reasonably challenge the claim that violence would be the justifiable response to constrained expression.

The Basic Democratic Freedom argument. The Marketplace of Ideas argument is not without some conflict even among defenders of the freedom of speech. Dewey famously argued for incredibly far-reaching protections for freedom of expression, then elsewhere seems to have been in conflict with such freedom, as I note when discussing the concept of cultivation later in this chapter. In "The Basic Values and Loyalties of Democracy," Dewey wrote:

> In short, a primary, perhaps the primary, loyalty of democracy at the present time is to communication . . . The freedom which is the essence of democracy is above all the freedom to develop intelligence; intelligence consisting of judgment as to what facts are relevant to action and how they are relevant to things to be done, and a corresponding alertness in the quest for such facts. To what extent we are actually democratic will in the end be decided by the degree to which the existing totalitarian menace awakens us to deeper loyalty to intelligence, pure and undefiled, and to the intrinsic connection between it and free communication: the method of conference, consultation, discussion, in which there takes place purification and pooling of the net results of the experiences of multitudes of people. It is said that "talk" is cheap. But the hundreds and hundreds of thousands of persons who have been tortured, who have died, who are rotting in concentration camps, prove that talk may also be tragically costly, and that democracy to endure must hold it immensely precious.[17]

This passage reveals the soaring value of free expression for Dewey's democratic theory. We must be loyal to free speech, Dewey argues, and it may well be *the* primary loyalty for democracy. At bottom, the reason concerns the development of intelligence, regarding things to be done, as he says. It is worth noting that here too, the truth matters again, as it does in those dangerous instances of misinformation noted above and as philosopher Michael Lynch cautions readers.[18]

Concerning leadership, in "Creative Democracy—the Task Before Us," Dewey writes, "The democratic belief in the principle of leadership is a generous one. It is universal. It is belief in the capacity of every person to lead his own life free from coercion and imposition by others provided right conditions are supplied." In Dewey's democratic theory, then, people have need of intelligence, which he took to be a shared, dynamic process of inquiry, for the sake of leading their own lives, for getting things done, let alone for participation in wider public affairs relevant to their lives or the public interest. As such, the freedom to develop intelligence is not merely important in principle or for protection against teakettle threats, but for the public good. This line of thinking bears similarities to the Marketplace of Ideas argument. To be sure, misinformation is a threat to public intelligence, but, as Dewey would say, the "cure for the ills of democracy is more democracy."[19] Of course, this does not mean that we respond to misinformation with more misinformation. In the full passage in which Dewey invokes the old idea about democracy, he makes this clear, writing:

> The old saying that the cure for the ills of democracy is more democracy is not apt if it means that the evils may be remedied by introducing more machinery of the same kind as that which already exists, or by refining and perfecting that machinery. But the phrase may also indicate the need of returning to the idea itself, of clarifying and deepening our apprehension of it, and of employing our sense of its meaning to criticize and re-make its political manifestations.[20]

In short, misinformation and the forces of social media influence from other nations with political agendas need to be met with criticism and a remaking of tools and methods of communication. How this remaking will happen, however, will take not just experts with their black-box algorithms, but public discussion and debate about how such platforms function and how the public can better protect itself from threats, including of the form of speech and popular online memes.[21]

The Both Ways argument.[22] Like the Teakettle argument, the Both Ways argument is also prudential. Rather than taking the form of a threat issued if one's speech is limited, the Both Ways argument warns that groups and movements you care about and wish to defend may find their relevant speech curtailed by the very mechanisms that one believes are justified in curtailing others' speech. It worries that granting power to curtail speech opens the door to the control of speech that should be defended.

Two circumstances are worth considering when it comes to cases of speech constraints that might "go both ways." In 2019, for example, US Supreme Court Justice Clarence Thomas argued that the landmark libel ruling in *New York Times v. Sullivan* bears revisiting. The case concerned a 1964 ruling overturning a lower court's decision in favor of L. B. Sullivan, a city commissioner who claimed an ad the *New York Times* published on behalf of the Committee to Defend Martin Luther King and the Struggle for Freedom in the South was libelous. As commissioner, Sullivan held the role of supervisor of the police. Sullivan claimed that the advertisement's criticism of the police implied criticism of him. To be sure, people can hurt each other when spreading falsehoods, and as Matthew L. Schafer and Jeff Kosseff note, "The ad was not without its issues," which they illustrate with a number of inaccuracies in the details included in the advertisement.[23] Of course, these included which song was reportedly sung on the state capitol steps, where the police in fact were stationed at a relevant time, and the number of times Martin Luther King Jr. had been arrested.

The *Sullivan* case decided unanimously that for criticism of a public figure to be considered libelous, a heightened standard of evidence is required for curbing speech and seeking damages. Writing for the *New York Times*, Adam Liptak explains, "Thanks to the Sullivan decision, it is indeed hard for public figures to win libel suits. They have to prove that something false was said about them, that it harmed their reputation, and that the writer acted with 'actual malice' . . . To prove actual malice under the Sullivan decision, a libel plaintiff must show that the writer knew the disputed statement was false or had acted with 'reckless disregard.' "[24] In the initial case, advocates for civil rights were sued successfully at first, with an award of $500,000 in Sullivan's favor. The Supreme Court's decision to overrule the lower court came down through a unanimous opinion authored by Justice William Brennan in favor of higher evidentiary expectations for the curtailment of speech critical of public figures.

Schafer and Kosseff call for Congress to protect speech and the central aspects of the *Sullivan* decision, since it "and the cases that came after it . . . hang in the balance now more than ever before."[25] Back in 2016, then-presidential candidate Donald Trump detailed his plan to curb freedom of the press by means of harsher libel laws. According to Daniel Politi in *Slate*, Trump made this vow: "I'm going to open up our libel laws so when they write purposely negative and horrible and false articles, we can sue them and win lots of money . . . So when the *New York Times* writes a hit piece, which is a total disgrace, or when the *Washington Post* . . . writes a hit piece, we can sue them and win money instead of having no chance of winning because they're totally protected."[26] While

Justice Thomas has argued in favor of revisiting *Sullivan*, he had little support until Justice Neil Gorsuch more recently departed from his earlier affirmations of the opinion, claiming that it "has come to leave far more people without redress than anyone could have predicted."[27]

Whether the Court chooses to revisit Sullivan or not, there is certainly danger in empowering public figures to mire their critics in protracted lawsuits. Whether the powerful win or not, bleeding their often poorer adversaries dry in legal costs can itself be the win they seek, exerting the quieting effect they want simply with the threat of such a lawsuit. Schafer and Kosseff explain that "even despite *Sullivan,* several plaintiffs still manage to succeed. Short of a jury verdict in their favor, libel plaintiffs can measure their success in years-long defense costs that can easily exceed $1–2 million depending on the case. For plaintiffs seeking retribution more than redress, putting a defendant through the time and trouble is well worth the squeeze."[28] There is need to protect people from wanton harms to their reputations, as well as a crucially important need to be able to criticize government actions. As such, it is dangerous for libel laws to enable too much curtailment of critics. When one considers causes for protecting speech or curtailing it, the wealthy have a remarkably powerful mechanism to curtail others' speech in libel laws. In this sense, while we may wish to curtail some deeply troubling speech, it will be vital to specify a limiting principle, such that speech that should be curtailed is, while unpleasant and upsetting speech critical of public figures may indeed need to be permitted unless a heightened level of evidence is offered, meeting the expectations set in *Sullivan.*

As the writing of this book concluded, tensions flared up around the country around protests about the conflict in Israel and Palestinians in Gaza. Columbia University came into the spotlight as "allegations of antisemitism arose during pro-Palestinian protests against Israel's actions in the war in Gaza," writes the Associated Press.[29] Since in the present book I am concerned with threats to self-respect that often take the form of expressions of hatred or of the subjugation of one people to another, the case of the conflict concerning Gaza raises an even stronger complexity for my argument, given that the argument for curtailing others' speech is rooted in the language of discrimination. Those who might criticize the actions of a particular nation are understandable, yet can be labeled "antisemitic" if the criticisms target the actions of Israel. This is clearly problematic, since it seems that it identifies any criticism of a Jewish population or group as hinging on or based on wanton prejudice against an ethnic group. But, of course, any group or government can make mistakes and be deserving of, even in need of, criticism.

The problem with feeling justified in curbing speech is that the self-same justification, in calling for prohibitions on discriminatory speech, can be used against those who may well have justified cause for criticism, which need not have anything to do with hatred of the target group's religious identity. In that sense, the need to defend free speech goes both ways. If you want to protect speech that is needed and justified, then that can necessitate the protection of like communication on others' parts, even if it appears to level criticisms against populations that historically have been attacked. As I have said, then, we can understand just how important it is to craft a limiting principle for speech that would protect vitally important communication, such as the freedom needed to criticize powerful public officials while curtailing the most troubling speech that can undermine a culture of justice. Later in this chapter, I indicate my support for such a proposal. Even if it were never adopted in the United States, however, that doesn't conclude the matter, since hot water can be cooled with cold, and justice can therefore call for protected yet troubling speech to be answered with countervailing messages in turn.

Speech Threatening to Groups

With important reasons to protect free expression in mind, there are nevertheless causes for limiting speech, and in this section, I address one form of expression that legal scholars believe is defensible, but controversially so.

Presently, there are prohibitions on some forms of threatening and intimidating speech. For example, *Virginia v. Black et al.* (2003) found that "a State, consistent with the First Amendment, may ban cross burning carried out with the intent to intimidate."[30] Despite such rulings, however, some subtler threats go unimpeded, and others face very gentle proscription.

Mari J. Matsuda's essay "Public Response to Racist Speech: Considering the Victim's Story" in *Words That Wound* opens with a passage from Patsy Sims's book *The Klan*, which recounts the following story: "A Black family enters a coffee shop in a small Texas town. A white man places a card on their table. The card reads, 'You have just been paid a visit by the Ku Klux Klan.' The family stands and leaves."[31]

In this instance, we see an example of a case of speech that many will think should be protected. How can it be more than mere expression?

What harm does it do? If one were to have been paid a visit by this or that group of Mormons, Buddhists, or Catholics, it would hardly constitute a threatening message. In small-town Texas, however, and given the Klan's history of intimidating, threatening, and murdering people,[32] the mere message of visitation by the Klan clearly represents a threat to an African American family. It is one thing if people talking to each other at a restaurant were Klansmen. It is another for a particular family to be approached, however. Such a distinction is important for considering the case in which a statue, a symbol of an African American civil rights leader, could be used in an effort to threaten a group of people.

In the first chapter of this book, I presented the example of the circumstance in Mississippi, in which freshmen at the University of Mississippi hung an old Georgia flag, two-thirds of which bear the symbol of the Confederate battle flag, and a noose around the statue of James Meredith. Meredith was the first African American student to integrate the university. As noted in the introduction to this book, Geoffrey Stone argued that the act of speech was defensible on grounds of the First Amendment, even though it "was by any measure, deeply disrespectful and hateful."[33]

In the introduction, I explained that a young African American woman, a student, at the University of Mississippi had come to visit me at her friend's recommendation. She was in tears and did not know whether she could stay at the university. She felt afraid, threatened, and unwelcome. It is important to note that many institutions can offer basic courses to students, to be sure. If a student were to feel uncomfortable at one institution, he or she could attend another, often including within the same state. That argument does not hold water in defending threatening speech, however, for universities often have programs unduplicated in their own state, such that to choose not to attend a given university can mean foreclosing on a life option for oneself, if out-of-state tuition were too costly for a move. The example I offered in the introduction was about majoring in pharmacy, though other choices could be considered. States like Mississippi only have one School of Pharmacy, and hence only one institution in which one can study to be a pharmacist while paying in-state tuition. The young woman's visit occurred only a day or so before I encountered Stone's essay in the *Huffington Post*, offering me a startling context in which to read his insensitive interpretation of the protections of speech in the United States, or perhaps his accurate defense of an outrageously insensitive legal history.

As a top constitutional law scholar at the University of Chicago, Stone had crafted an "official statement for [his] own university—The

University of Chicago—on the institution's Principles of Free Expression." He acknowledges of course that the freedom of speech is not absolute. A clear case in which speech can be limited is when it is threatening. Concerning the noose incident, Stone writes that

> as offensive as this act was, it does not *quite* fit the conventional definition of a "threat." To constitute a "threat," an individual's speech must not just put people in fear, but must (a) be directed at specific individuals and (b) be unambiguous. "If you don't give me your money, I will kill you," if stated in circumstances in which the statement would reasonably be taken seriously, is a "threat." Hanging a noose on the door of an African-American student's dorm room, in circumstances in which the message would reasonably be taken as a threat, is also . . . a "threat." But is it a "threat" to hang a noose around the neck of a statute of James Meredith?

Stone offers in his answer two examples to challenge people's intuitions on the matter. First, he writes,

> The Supreme Court has dealt with a somewhat similar situation. The Court has held that burning a cross on the lawn of an African-American family that just moved into a previously all-white community is punishable as a "threat," but that burning a cross at a Ku Klux Klan rally cannot be deemed a "threat" and is, indeed, constitutionally protected speech—even though the very existence of the rally and the cross-burning will quite predictably be seen by some people as threatening.

Then he continues,

> Another example is the Nazi march in Skokie, a predominantly Jewish suburb of Chicago, in the late 1970s. Someone who hangs a swastika on the front lawn of a Jewish family, in circumstances in which the family would reasonably understand it as a "threat," can constitutionally be punished, but the Nazis have a First Amendment right to march through downtown Skokie, carrying swastika banners, because, although their message might be deeply offensive and frightening to the Jews

in Skokie, it does not constitute an unambiguous "threat" to particular individuals. There is a difference between a rallying cry, however offensive, and a threat.

For these reasons, Stone argues, the situation at the University of Mississippi "is not as clear-cut as most people seem to think."

One point on which I agree with Stone in part is in his conclusion, and I return to the matter at the end of this chapter. He writes, "Perhaps the university, its students, its faculty and its alumni should see this as an opportunity for 'open discussion' rather than 'inhibition,' as an occasion on which to reaffirm the deeper values of the university and, in the words of Chancellor Jones, an opportunity for the university to renew its 'commitment to promoting the values that are engraved on the statue—Courage, Knowledge, Opportunity, and Perseverance.' " Stone's idea here is good, whether or not we accept his understanding of the speech protections of the First Amendment. In fact, as a former professor at the University of Mississippi, I can attest to the fact that the campus engaged in frequent conversations and meetings of just this sort, after the many conflicts that arose in my time working there. One of the cultural efforts that can be employed in combating hurtful speech, I believe, is just the sort of dialogue that Stone proposes here, but his idea that it must occur "rather than inhibition" is the part with which I disagree in the case of the noose incident.

When Stone claims that the noose incident does not quite fit the conventional definition of a threat, he must mean that either the threat was not directed at specific individuals or that it was ambiguous. I suggest that the hanging of a noose around the symbol of the first African American student to integrate the University of Mississippi is no more ambiguous than the burning of a cross on a family's lawn. It is certainly a message of intimidation, in fact one that appears less ambiguous than the burning cross. Between 1865 and 1950, it is estimated that 6,500 African Americans were lynched in "racial terror killings" in the United States.[34] And, unlike a cross, a noose is understandably "a potent symbol of hate," as Alaa Elassa writes for CNN.[35] Nooses have been used widely in American history to commit terrorizing racial killings and are used as symbols of a threat. Such a message is so clear that a man who wore a T-shirt to the voting booth bearing the symbol of a Confederate battle flag, overlayed by the image of a noose, and reading "Mississippi Justice," was fired from his position as a hospital employee in Memphis, Tennessee, in 2018. After concluding an investigation into the matter, Regional One Health released a statement explaining that "Regional One Health holds employees to a high standard. We are committed to upholding our mission to provide compassionate care and exceptional services to all. This includes fostering a safe and protected work and care environment for all. Behaviors contrary to these principles are unacceptable and will not be tolerated."[36] Of course, in this instance, it is important to note that the First Amendment concerns the actions of government that may not infringe on one's freedom to speak. Laying off a worker for speech that expresses values in conflict with one's professional ethics and expectations is not an instance of the violation of the First Amendment, though it is important to consider the dangers of employers' potential unjustified causes for terminating employees. As Elizabeth Anderson has argued, employers rule our lives, and it is often the case that employees should be protected from termination just because in their private lives they express ideas that the company dislikes.[37] In the case of the "Mississippi Justice" noose T-shirt, however, it is difficult to imagine justly carried out triage of patients when an employee's beliefs expressed even only in their private life include valuing lynching associated with the Confederacy.

It is difficult to accept Stone's justification for thinking a noose around a symbol of an African American alumnus at the University of Mississippi is ambiguous, though he included that point in his challenge to the claim that the instance does not quite fit the conventional definition of a threat. What is more understandable, though still odd, in my view, is the idea that Stone believes that it is important for a threat to "be directed at specific individuals." The language of "specific individuals" suggests that a threat to members of a group of people may not be specific enough for it to be a threat. At the same time, the threat can understandably be interpreted as targeting African American students at the University of Mississippi. It is thereby not an ambiguous target group. A noose is a symbol and instrument of hate, terror, and murder, and the statue of James Meredith is the symbol of the integration of African American students enrolling in the University of Mississippi. The message is loud and clear: that African American students do not belong and should feel threatened. In 2020, the University of Mississippi reported an enrollment of 2,806 African American students, 12.9 percent of its 21,676 overall enrolled student body.[38]

As I claimed in the introductory chapter, either Stone must be wrong or the law is. Perhaps historically the law has indeed been carried out in the ways he explains, but, if so, how can this stand? The justification I can imagine for his point of view would have to suggest that "African American students and employees" on campus at the University of Mississippi are not a sufficiently specific group of individuals to warrant understanding the message as a threat. Do mass murderers like Dylan Roof have a clear sense in advance of whom exactly they target when they commit their murders? Such acts target groups of people, kinds of people. So, if Stone is right historically about First Amendment jurisprudence, then a new precedent is needed.[39]

My experience of meeting a young African American woman who felt not only afraid but also threatened at the University of Mississippi presented me with palpable reason to find Stone's claims shocking. As I noted in the introductory chapter, furthermore, two of the three young men in question from the University of Mississippi noose incident pled guilty to misdemeanor charges for "using a threat of force to intimidate African-American students and employees."[40] To be sure, the misdemeanor charges were a compromise from the original felony charges first leveled against them. As I noted in the introduction, Austin Reed Edenfield, the second of the young men charged, admitted "that he knew the rope and flag would be threatening and intimidating to black students," according to the *New York Times*.[41]

One reaction to the noose incident shocked me, when a representative of a funding organization that promotes the freedom of expression said that "the kids just had a bad lawyer." If they had simply been counseled right and early enough, they would have gotten away with what they did. This would mean that Stone was right and that had the offenders simply been counseled more carefully, they would have been protected either because their speech was sufficiently ambiguous or because their expression was not directed at particular individuals. They would then have gotten away with terrifying the young African American woman whom I have mentioned, who felt profoundly threatened and understandably moved to tears. Indeed, many of my African American students when I taught at the University of Mississippi had a similar story to tell me about a family member strongly counseling them not to attend "Ole Miss," saying, "You'll get killed!" The students would tell me that they brushed off such worries, but the noose incident made such reactions harder to do.

If someone were to threaten to place a bomb in a building on a university campus, not yet chosen, at 1:00 p.m. the next day, it seems absurd to imagine that the lack of specificity of the victims to be killed would mean that the speech should be defensible. At the same time, the intended victims of the threat of the noose incident were more targeted than that. It was not directed merely at any which members of a university campus who might visit a given building, but instead at select members of a group who participate in the campus. One might think that the bomb at 1:00 p.m. is more precise as a means, at least in its timing, but with a history of lynching, the message of a noose is equally specific about means, if not about the day and time.

It is important to consider at this point Stone's logic in terms of the relationship of legality and morality. Stone noted that he believed the offending students' actions to be wrong, but not illegal. There is a long history in moral theory of challenging disconnections of this sort, particularly when people are harmed significantly. Martin Luther King Jr. famously echoed a notion that dates back to St. Thomas of Aquinas, which says that an unjust law is no law at all.[42] The point is not to legally prohibit all activities thought immoral, but rather to challenge the idea that just because the laws presently protect a behavior, they should continue to do so. The law may protect a matter now, but that is not justification for preserving the law, since laws can be unjust. By the same token, just because past speech was protected by First Amendment law does not mean that precedents should be decisive for the future. We can establish new laws, new precedents. Ultimately, morality should check our laws, not the other way around, even if many moral matters are to remain debated and reasonable disagreement should be allowed. The question is whether in fact disagreement about the threats discussed here is truly reasonable. I argue that in the case of the noose incident, it is not.

The idea of "hate speech" laws and prohibitions, controversial though they may be, is that great harm can be done to groups of people and society when others promulgate hatred and systemic discrimination. It implies that groups of people can be threatened and intimidated. I have mentioned already my sense of the limitation of terms like "hate" for this purpose, given that one can be cool-headed in discriminating grossly against others. Hate suggests emotional energy. Expressions of dehumanization appear at least as troubling if not more so when they seem obvious to a calm communicator and thinker. Opponents of hate speech laws generally believe that speech that can be prohibited should be prohibited no matter whom it targets, that the group nature of the threat is irrelevant, perhaps in the same way that the bomb threat should be proscribed.[43] In contrast, the international community has raised concerns over hate speech, and efforts in the United Nations have targeted the writing of policies for identifying and proscribing hate speech.

The United Nations Rabat Plan of Action proposes a set of six tests for hateful expression, which can guide decision-making about whether speech should be limited. Note that adoption of such a proposal need not open doors for the harshening of libel laws and in that sense passes one important test of the Both Ways argument. The Rabat Plan of Action suggests

> a high threshold for defining restrictions on freedom of expression, incitement to hatred, and for the application of article 20 of the ICCPR [(the International Covenant on Civil and Political Rights)]. It outlines a six-part threshold test taking into account (1) the social and political **context**, (2) status of the **speaker**, (3) **intent** to incite the audience against a target group, (4) **content** and form of the speech, (5) **extent** of its dissemination and (6) **likelihood** of harm, including imminence.[44]

There is much to debate about the methods and tools for limiting speech that discriminates and thereby undermines people's sense that their life plans are meaningfully worth pursuing.

In the United States, people who believe that hate speech laws are unreasonable and illegitimate fail to consider law that already exists, namely the Violent Interference with Federally Protected Rights, 18 U.S.C. §245 of the Civil Rights Act of 1968, which reads: "Criminal Interference with Federally Protected Rights—Section 3631 makes it a crime to use, or *threaten to use force* to willfully interfere with any person because of race, color, religion, or national origin and because the person is participating in a federally protected activity, such as public education, employment, jury service, travel, or the enjoyment of public accommodations, or helping another person to do so."[45] While it is acknowledged already that threats are a form of speech that is justifiably proscribed by law, this passage of the Civil Rights Act of 1968 connects the matter of speech and threats to discrimination against any person because of race, color, religion, or national origin. A threat to a group of people on such a basis would thereby, I argue, constitute a threat to persons who are members of such groups. While vocal critics reject proposals for hate speech laws, arguably the Civil Rights Act of 1968, in this passage, offers a form of evidence that some such laws are already on the books, proscribing threatening speech on the basis of "race, color, religion, or national origin." As such, some form of what is advocated for exists already and thus bears some precedent in the United States. Whether to broaden the relevant proscriptions is the question, and in the case of "hate crimes" law, passage has already been successful and has born weight in criminal cases and sentencing.[46]

When it comes to harms to others, expression is one key element of the danger to a culture of justice, as in the case of threats, but individuals and groups can also make efforts to actively cultivate a culture in which people are prompted to express and enact hateful ideas. This distinction is evident in an essay by Dewey, in which he raises the concept of cultivation in passing, yet a key difference can be identified between such cultivation and expression alone. I turn now to that useful distinction, since nonthreatening expression that does not affirmatively cultivate hatred or discriminatory ideas, such as a discussion of the Ku Klux Klan's ideas in a college history course, ought to be maximally free, yet the cultivation of beliefs treasonous to democracy and that incite hateful or discriminatory acts certainly warrants consideration[47] for proscription.

Expression versus Cultivation

Earlier in this chapter, I referenced Dewey's essay "The Basic Values and Loyalties of Democracy" to show his profound defense of the freedom of expression. He argued that perhaps the primary loyalty of democracy is to free communication. In that essay, he also writes, "There are still many, too many, persons who feel free to cultivate and express racial prejudices as if they were within their personal rights, not recognizing how the attitude of intolerance infects, perhaps fatally as the example of Germany so surely proves, the basic humanities without which democracy is but a name."[48] Here, Dewey tells us that people are wrong to think that it is within their personal rights to "cultivate and express racial prejudices." In the context of an essay in which Dewey proclaims free communication to be the primary and most fundamental loyalty of democracy, it can appear jarring on first encounter to read this passage, in which he says that people should not feel free to express and cultivate some given ideas.[49]

To be sure, Dewey advocated on the one hand for soaring protection for the freedom of expression as an element of the development of democratic intelligence. On the other hand, people should not feel free to cultivate and express certain ideas treasonous to democracy. An uncharitable interpretation might suggest that Dewey was simply inconsistent and trying to protect only the speech he liked, that was consistent with democracy, while proscribing the speech to which he objected, without warrant. There are two ways of interpreting Dewey more charitably, however. The first concerns his justification for the crucial value of free expression in democratic societies, and the second involves his concept of "cultivation."

As we have seen already in this chapter, in his defense of maximally free expression, Dewey based his justification in "the freedom to develop intelligence; intelligence consisting of judgment as to what facts are relevant to action and how they are relevant to things to be done, and a corresponding alertness in the quest for such facts."[50] If the aim of democracy's loyalty to communication is indeed the development of intelligence, then some forms of expression, such as threats, most certainly can set up barriers to the development of intelligence. In another essay, "Creative Democracy—The Task Before Us," Dewey explains how dangerous prejudice and hatred are for democracy. He writes,

> When I think of the conditions under which men and women are living in many foreign countries today, fear of espionage, with danger hanging over the meeting of friends for friendly conversation in private gatherings, I am inclined to believe that the heart and final guarantee of democracy is in free gatherings of neighbors on the street corner to discuss back and forth what is read in uncensored news of the day, and in gatherings of friends in the living rooms of houses and apartments to converse freely with one another. Intolerance, abuse, calling of names because of differences of opinion about religion or politics or business, as well as because of differences of race, color, wealth or degree of culture are treason to the democratic way of life. For everything which bars freedom and fullness of communication sets up barriers that divide human beings into sets and cliques, into antagonistic sects and factions, and thereby undermines the democratic way of life. Merely legal guarantees of the civil liberties of free belief, free expression, free assembly are of little avail if in daily life freedom of communication, the give and take of ideas, facts, experiences, is choked by mutual suspicion, by abuse, by fear and hatred. These things destroy the essential condition of the democratic way of

> living even more effectually than open coercion which—as the example of totalitarian states proves—is effective only when it succeeds in breeding hate, suspicion, intolerance in the minds of individual human beings.[51]

Here Dewey offers us a response to those concerned about the coercion that could be leveled against hateful or discriminatory speech. Coercion is a threat to democracy, but one less dangerous, in his view, than abuse and intolerance on the basis of "race, color, wealth or degree of culture." Both are threats to democracy, yet barriers to the development of intelligence and to the conditions necessary for the democratic way of life render "merely legal guarantees of civil liberties" hollow, of "little avail." Free communication "choked by mutual suspicion, by abuse, by fear and hatred" destroys "the essential condition of the democratic way of life."

What we gain from Dewey's remarks so far is that abusive and hateful expression can be quite dangerous for democracy, and as such should be the subject of careful scrutiny. When allowed, it should be primarily insofar as it contributes to the development of intelligence, but were it, for example, to lead to barriers, as when a young African American student came to my office in tears, feeling threatened and as though she must leave her university of choice, sensitivity to these effects is warranted. Studying the history of such ideas and their effects, or permitting a person to express the ideas, would be one thing, but what of organizational efforts to promote hatred or abusive discrimination? On my view, the Ku Klux Klan should neither be granted the honorific nor benefit governmentally from the status of a nonprofit organization or the protections of trademark for symbol or marks that contribute to the cultivation of hatred or abusive or discriminatory beliefs and practices. The reason is simple, that such an organization is predicated on treason to democracy.

In the case of the young men at the University of Mississippi, their lawyers raised the defense that their fraternities were awful organizations that developed their hateful feelings. In September of 2015, *The Oxford Eagle*'s Alyssa Schnugg wrote:

> In a document filed by [Harris's attorney] before the sentencing, he suggested Harris' resentment toward people of color began when a black football coach failed to make him starting quarterback as was promised and instead selected a black quarterback.

His attorney says the incident left Harris with a "bitter taste in his mouth" for not being allowed to compete for the starting position.

That hatred and disrespect was [sic] *cultivated* by the fraternity that he described as a "segregation club, a disgusting organization promoting a disgusting culture."[52]

Here we see an example of the defense of a perpetrator of threatening and injurious speech incorporating an additional or allegedly ultimate cause, in the organizational development, the cultivation, of disrespectful, racist ideas and actions. If Harris's defense lays blame on the organization in a case in which the defendant pled guilty, we see that it is not only the victims of hateful or discriminatory acts who would raise charges against the cultivation of such expression, but also the perpetrators. Young men who acknowledge their guilt and intent to intimidate and threaten African American students and employees at the University of Mississippi also have acknowledged that efforts to cultivate their harmful actions are in part responsible for what they did.

Matt Zapotosky of the *Washington Post* in 2016 reported that "Sigma Phil [sic] Epsilon has since shuttered its University of Mississippi chapter."[53] Had the national organization not shuttered the chapter, I argue that the University of Mississippi should have investigated it, as should any further relevant authorities, to enforce whatever rules ought to prevent the cultivation of hatred and abusive or discriminatory ideas and practices. Such practices surely conflict with the reasonable expectations of codes of student conduct relevant to the proper participation of students in the work of a public institution of higher education. As I note in the next section, they clearly conflict with the explicit statement of values known as the University of Mississippi Creed, whose values are said to guide foundationally the work of the institution and its community expectations.[54] I have in mind such statements of values when I think about government speaking, communicating matters important for a culture of justice. In this context, we have a case useful for examining Dewey's distinction between expression and cultivation, for which a definition of "cultivation" is needed.

I propose a preliminary definition of "cultivation" for our context. In this definition, for brevity I use the term "hatred" despite the caveat I have mentioned already, that it is a placeholder term for abusive, discriminatory, and harmful beliefs and speech acts that are treasonous to democracy, as Dewey has argued. For the purposes of raising a distinction between expression and cultivation, I argue that the cultivation of hatred is the *persuasive* effort to develop hateful antagonisms on the basis of religion, race, ethnicity, or sexual orientation that set up barriers to free communication and interplay and that undermine the democratic way of life.

I accentuate the importance in the concept of cultivation of the term "persuasive" for an integral reason, for which I am indebted to a former colleague.[55] There are laws against speech calling for the overthrow of government—seditious speech. Yet that speech has been protected legally, though ironically, on the basis of whether or not that speech is persuasive, whether it gets traction. When seditious speech is ineffectual, it is defended. When it prompts action, it is proscribed.[56] This seems paradoxical, but in fact when we consider Dewey's idea about the development of intelligence, we can appreciate the point. Perhaps in someone's seditious speech we can identify cause or ideas for the improvement of governmental behavior or practices. At the same time, when such speech leads people to actions that aim at violent overthrow of the government, there is defensible cause to limit that speech. By the same token, when people express ideas to consider that can be understood as intellectual yet undemocratic, it is different to hear or express the idea than it is to cultivate belief in such ideas through action that begets the widespread development of such beliefs. For instance, in the case of a fraternity, we already have an example of an organization whose behaviors have been considered contributory to a disgusting culture that promoted students' preexisting hatred, encouraging them and setting them in an environment in which they would act and threaten others.

Critics might reasonably worry about permitting speech that is undemocratic but does not constitute either a threat or the cultivation of hate or discriminatory ideas and practices. Why would a thinker defend the right to express undemocratic ideas? Dewey offers us an answer in his essay, "Social Absolutism." He writes that

> it may be that the best thing which can happen to the ideal of democracy is to be put on the defensive. For then it will no longer remain a vague optimism, a weak benevolent aspiration, at the mercy of favorable circumstances. It may become a compact, aggressive and realistic intelligence directing circumstance. Such an idea will recognize that its one great enemy is the hankering of men for unity of existence, aim and law in

whatever form it may offer itself. It will recognize the infinite variety of human nature, and the infinite plurality of purposes for which men associate themselves together. It will recognize that progress is never in one line, but comes when a variety of things move along together. It will take its stand on the conviction that this movement comes about by many-sided interaction in which lee-way is given each force and principle for an experimental development.[57]

Dewey here presaged Stone's point, that those who present intellectual challenges to democracy can thereby offer cause for dialogue and consideration of values. Rather than accepting catchphrases and warm feelings alone, people can exercise their reasoning and communication abilities to weigh and understand for themselves how and why democracy matters. At the same time, while expression that does not rise to the level of cultivation may remain protected, those who seek to pursue justice with regard to injurious speech can look to examples like the American Civil Rights Act of 1968 and to concerns about the cultivation of injurious discrimination as causes to call for change and the redress of harms.

Cultural Responses to the Cultivation of Hatred and Discrimination

Much of the scholarship and of what I have said so far has focused on legal action that can be leveled with regard to threatening and injurious speech on grounds of discrimination often referred to as hateful, but, as Stone suggested in his essay for the *Huffington Post*,[58] there are other means for responding to such harms. The three categories I propose for combating the cultivation of discriminatory beliefs, speech, and actions for the defense of a culture of justice are legal, political, and social. The legal and the political have some areas of overlap, insofar as political actions can be challenged on grounds of legal rights. At the same time, some actions that could be called political may also overlap with the category of the social. These proposed categories and terms are not meant to be presented as hard distinctions, as mutually exclusive, but instead as rough ones intended to group approaches to the advancement of a culture of justice. I have touched on a number of legal matters, furthermore, such as in states' attempts to punish speech acts like the noose incident at the

University of Mississippi. I conclude this chapter with some considerations of the political and social actions that can be engaged in for the sake of promoting a culture of justice in defense against those who promote abusive and either hateful or coldly discriminating ideas and policies.

Political Defenses of a Culture of Justice

While a legal effort to address speech-related attacks on a culture of justice could involve criminal charges, as in the cases of threats to people or groups of people, political approaches on the part of governmental offices and representatives are also available, though they can be subject to legal challenge in turn. The initial policy decision and practice may be understood as political, and the subsequent conflict about it in the courts would turn on legal decision-making, to be sure. For an example, imagine an abusive symbol that "hate groups" might use to cultivate hatred, as on clothing, and for which they may wish to register trademark, to prevent others from profiting on their business endeavor, to gain sales for the cultivation of hatred. Should the US Patent and Trademark Office be required to register the trademark for any message or symbol, regardless of its contribution to the cultivation of abusive, discriminatory, or hateful messages? It is one thing to permit expression that might be said not to cultivate such beliefs and attacks on others, but the government can speak, as scholars have argued.[59] One way that the government speaks is in the selection of that which it values and protects. The business interests of racist organizations that cultivate their values in others is not in the public interest for any society intending to foster and maintain a culture of justice. As such, it is understandable when the Patent and Trademark Office questions applications for the registration of trademark.

There are cases that ought perhaps to be defensible, however, even when language might be called an epithet or racist. Consider the case involving "the Slants," a derogatory term historically leveled against people of Asian descent.[60] Some people may purposefully aim to "reclaim" words, as the band has argued, or to buck stereotypes, intending to disarm the oppressor in a matter of injustice.[61] There will be conflicts over which cases ought to be thought defensible and which should not, but the thesis of this book is intended to offer an avenue for considering the norms underlying such decision-making. When we consider expression as a tool for the development of intelligence, we can contrast that with cultivation that impedes or breaks down the interplay of discourse and intelligence pooling for the sake of mutual public benefit.

A similar matter was at work in the US Supreme Court's decision to support the state of Texas, which denied the request of the Sons of Confederate Veterans to print a Confederate battle flag on state license plates. Again, a legal case arose, but that was after the political consideration of the interests of the state of Texas in its decisions about what kind of culture it hoped to foster and maintain. In that case, Justice Clarence Thomas in an unusual move sided with the liberal justices to agree that Texas should not have to print that plate.[62] It could make the decision that the state is not obligated to support and endorse messages that cultivate discrimination and hatred. In this instance we have a clear case in which the liberal norm of minimalist intervention in people's lives is challenged when the state speaks, when the decision is made that some points of view are sufficiently harmful to the public interest that the state can make a value judgment, a call about what kind of culture state powers and tools can and cannot be used to promote or maintain. For the *Atlantic*, Garrett Epps sums up the decision at work in *Walker v. Texas Division, Sons of Confederate Veterans, Inc.*, writing,

> Remarkably enough, [Justice Thomas] joined the Court's four moderate-liberals—Justices Ruth Bader Ginsburg, Stephen Breyer, Sonia Sotomayor, and Elena Kagan—to provide a decisive vote to allow the state of Texas to refuse to print a specialty license plate bearing the much-loved and hated Confederate battle flag. In an opinion by Breyer, the 5-4 majority held that a government can, with few limits, decide to convey any license-plate message it wants, and bar any that it disapproves. This isn't "content-based" regulation of speech; the plate is speech by the government itself, and the First Amendment does not apply.[63]

This decision acknowledges explicitly that government speaks and that it may decide what it wishes to say. While other organizations may petition to have their messages printed on license plates, the printing of a message constitutes by this decision a message of the state. We might by the same token, then, question the messages of monuments that are placed in public squares, such as the "Nearly 100 Confederate Monuments Removed in 2020," according to Rachel Treisman of NPR News.[64]

Political action with regard to promoting a culture of justice in defense of attacks on it can include the removal of troubling monuments, the changing of building names, the denial of hurtful symbols or imagery in petitions for license plates, and many more possibilities. In addition to these decisions to remove or deny matters, there are also possibilities for positive public affirmation. One such example is the Ronald McNair Scholars Program, which is publicly funded at the federal level in the United States.[65] Ronald McNair was an African American physicist, Presidential Scholar, Ford Foundation fellow, and the second African American to fly in space. He died in the US Challenger space shuttle explosion. The McNair Scholars Program was designed "to prepare undergraduate students for doctoral studies through involvement in research and other scholarly activities. McNair participants are either first-generation college students with financial need, or members of a group that is traditionally underrepresented in graduate education and have demonstrated strong academic potential. The goal of the McNair Scholars Program is to increase graduate degree awards for students from underrepresented segments of society."[66] McNair was an outstanding scientist and a sixth-degree black belt in karate, in addition to having been an astronaut. Higher education remains highly imbalanced racially speaking and in other ways in many fields, especially in graduate study. Thus, the federally funded McNair Scholars program aims affirmatively to promote access for people who have been underrepresented in positions of educational and scientific influence. I see such a program as an effort to combat a culture that historically has kept advancement in many fields inaccessible in a variety of ways.

Beyond individual programs such as the one honoring McNair, many institutions have drafted explicit statements of the values by which they are intended to operate. Among these are colleges and universities, including state institutions. As I have noted, the University of Mississippi has an explicit document referred to as the "UM Creed." The University of Kentucky, where I work now, also has an official creed, which is quite similar. The UM Creed reads as follows:

> The University of Mississippi is a community of learning dedicated to nurturing excellence in intellectual inquiry and personal character in an open and diverse environment. As a voluntary member of this community:

> I believe in respect for the dignity of each person

> I believe in fairness and civility

I believe in personal and professional integrity

I believe in academic honesty

I believe in academic freedom

I believe in good stewardship of our resources

I pledge to uphold these values and encourage others to follow
my example.[67]

Similarly, the University of Kentucky's Creed, which is found on the website
of the Office of Student Conduct, reads:

As a Wildcat,

- I *promise* to strive for academic excellence and freedom by
promoting an environment of creativity and discovery.

- I *promise* to pursue all endeavors with integrity and compete
with honesty.

- I *promise* to embrace diversity and inclusion and to respect
the dignity and humanity of others.

- I *promise* to contribute to my University and community
through leadership and service.

- I *promise* to fulfill my commitments and remain accountable
to others.

We believe in the University of Kentucky and will forever
honor our alma mater.[68]

As I note in considering social efforts to foster and maintain a culture of
justice, and to fight in its defense, I witnessed the invocation of the UM
Creed on numerous occasions in moral response to conflicts involving
racism and other discriminatory tensions. Students, staff, faculty members,
and administrators have called attention to the creed in a manner that
criticized troubling behavior, such as behavior in conflict with a culture
of justice, and to promote a more humane and just culture.

A former colleague and friend from my time at the University of Mississippi wondered whether a public institution like the university should have a creed at all. Should a public institution proclaim or expect students to share in a statement of its values in this way, he wondered? There certainly can be reason to worry about the stymying of differences in point of view. One could raise concerns of indoctrination, for example. Consistent with the belief in the need for minimalist governmental intervention in people's lives, inherent as an aspect of liberalism, one might believe that a creed such as those I have shared just now would impinge on the freedom of and equal access to public education for those who would not assent to such beliefs. As I noted in the introductory chapter as well as in chapter 3 on the impediments to a culture of justice, however, it is important to consider the ways in which some aspects of liberalism can be at work in threatening other important aspects of the tradition. In particular, if each person is to have access to public educational institutions, there are values that must be in place in the guidance of such institutions.

Values undergird the work of education and of public endeavor. If one person wishes to have one's values respected even when those values conflict with the fair and equal treatment of others, that person expects the public and its institutions to maintain and advance their subjugation of others. That is clearly an expectation of a right inconsistent with the demands of a culture of justice, and one that the public should feel no compulsion to honor. To do the work of public education should be understood to entail values and virtues involving respect for the dignity of each person, for example. There must be expectations for the conduct of students, faculty, staff, and administrators, such that a statement of values offers fundamental guidance and clarity of vision and mission. As such, I argue that a potentially powerful political effort to establish and maintain a culture of justice would be for public institutions to reexamine and reassert, in meaningful ways, the power and importance of the values that underlie what they do and why they do it. In sum, I contend not only that statements of value like the UM Creed are defensible, but also that the public and its representatives should see the clarification and advancement of proper values in such statements as an imperative. To those who do not adhere to religious beliefs, the word "creed" might feel troubling, but as Dewey argued in *A Common Faith*, one can identify and cultivate a meaningful belief in a faith in important human values without limiting oneself to beliefs in supernatural beings or powers.[69]

I have raised the idea of statements of values or of "creeds" in discussion of political efforts to combat forces that attack a culture of justice, such as in hate speech, but one might reasonably wonder why we should think of these statements as political. At bottom, I mention these moral tools here because educational institutions run by the state act on behalf of the public and in many ways speak. The entrances to university campuses often include monuments, such as those donated by alumni and community groups. The places where such symbols are located can often be considered honorific and hence can constitute politically powerful forms of state speech. As such, examination of building names, statues in prominent public spaces, and statements of values encapsulating the moral norms that undergird the work of the institution all are matters guided or influenced or even spoken by representatives of the state. Consider, for example, that in 2017, the Jefferson Davis Elementary School in Jackson, Mississippi—named after the first and only president of the Confederate States—with a student population that is 98 percent African American, was renamed for President Barack Obama, the first African American president of the United States.[70]

In 2015, furthermore, the "core values of the University of Texas at Austin," which include "learning, discovery, freedom, leadership, individual opportunity, and responsibility," were said to be "in direct contradiction" with "the presence of the Jefferson Davis statue" on campus, according to a statement passed by the U.T. Austin Student Government Assembly.[71] The students at U.T. Austin argued both that "Jefferson Davis held that African-Americans repeatedly [sic] were morally and intellectually inferior to white" and "argued vociferously that the institutions of American slavery were beneficial." The document, authored by courageous student leaders, concludes that "the University of Texas at Austin as a public institution of the State of Texas that represents a diverse population should not condone or promote Jefferson Davis' values that are offensive to the student body . . . It is obvious that Jefferson Davis was racist against African Americans; and, . . . The University of Texas at Austin Student Government fully endorses the removal of the Jefferson Davis statue from campus."[72] Statements of values on the part of political institutions serve as invaluable tools for calling leaders to account. For a far more famous example, note that Martin Luther King Jr. appealed to the US Declaration of Independence in his "I Have a Dream" oration in his reference to "all men" being equal.[73] By the same token, Malcolm X appealed to the Second Amendment in his promotion of the self-defense rights of African Americans.[74] In a variety of ways, leaders of movements have appealed to statements of public and institutional values that help to illustrate and support causes for justice. At the same time, some efforts and movements draw on political tools and statements such as those I have mentioned, but are enacted through what might be thought of as social or nongovernmental groups and actions, like King's and others'. I therefore conclude with some examples of the ways in which individuals and social groups can contribute to establishing, maintaining, or defending a culture of justice from speech and cultivating acts that contribute to injustice and treason to democracy.

Social Defenses of a Culture of Justice and a Note on the Both Ways Argument

As I argued in chapter 6, the obligation to establish, maintain, and defend a culture of justice is public and shared. That means that individuals should feel called to speak up and act, including when others are speaking and acting in ways that threaten justice. A number of efforts are worth calling attention to as especially social, if not technically legal or political efforts. For example, these include speaking up in turn in defense of democracy and justice, protesting or counterprotesting matters of injustice, organizing or signing petitions, giving to fundraising campaigns for organizational efforts to champion justice, marching to proclaim values and to call attention to problems, and raising expectations for our peers and engaging in two-way peer education.

It is true that big companies maintain remarkable control over the communicative landscape, with their money for advertising, public relations, legal teams, and more. At the same time, individuals with time and a computer can write and submit editorials and letters to the editor for their local and national newspapers, aiming to make a difference to the dialogue about publicly important matters. In 2015, for example, I published a few op-eds calling for Mississippi to change its flag, including "Sometimes Heritage Does Harm" and "Mr. Bryant, Take Down the Flag."[75] When you consider how much it would cost to take a full-page advertisement out in a newspaper today, you can get a sense of what value one gains, communicatively, at least in comparison with dollars spent on the space, for publishing an article. While any one individual may only feel that they have made a small difference, getting a finite number of people who read the piece to think for a few minutes about what they have written, there are many of us who wish for justice and who can contribute to discourse. No one individual needs to make a big difference for the whole to make one together.

I recall a moving experience at the University of Mississippi, furthermore, when members of the Ku Klux Klan planned to protest the removal of the song "From Dixie with Love" from the roster of the university's marching band on football game days. Crowds at the football games had been using the concluding cadence of the medley to shout "The South will rise again!"[76] When the chancellor pulled the song and the Klan announced its plans to protest, hundreds of undergraduate students mobilized in three days' time to prepare a counterprotest with the catchphrase "Turn your back on hate!" I participated alongside my students, got a free "Turn Your Back on Hate!" T-shirt and a copy of the UM Creed, and together we read aloud the UM Creed many times in counterprotest with our backs to the Klansmen, who were on campus to protest on a football game day. It was unnerving to see the SWAT team members who were there in full body armor with weapons of war to keep the peace, ensuring the safety of protestors and community members. Nevertheless, the whole tenor of the day was profoundly different from what one could imagine of a game day in which the Klan alone might have protested.

Two other counterprotests are worth mentioning. For one form, consider the "locked arm" counterprotests against members of the Westboro Baptist Church. In 2010, Judson Berger of Fox News reported that "Arizonans [Rallied] to Prevent Westboro Church Disruption of Shooting Victims' Funerals."[77] Berger writes, "The Kansas-based Westboro church is notorious for showing up at the funerals of dead soldiers and other high-profile gatherings wielding anti-gay signs." Counterprotestors sought to "cordon off the family from the protests." The Westboro Church's leader, Fred Phelps, "believes that tragic events like the deaths of soldiers are punishment for tolerance of homosexuality." In response, a Facebook group organizing a counterprotest explained, "We will create a wall of humanity to allow the families who've lost their loved ones to hold their funerals in peace, held with dignity, and surrounded in love."[78]

Considerably larger than such counterprotests was one in Massachusetts in 2017. That year, young white male "white nationalists" had marched with tiki torches through Charlottesville on the campus of the University of Virginia.[79] A few days later, a "small number of right-wing 'Free Speech Rally' demonstrators" in Boston, Massachusetts, prompted a massive counterprotest of thousands of people who came out "shouting anti-Nazi and anti-KKK slogans" in response.[80]

Finally, back at the University of Mississippi, when I was there, President Obama had won a second term as president in 2012, and some epithets were shouted after the results were reported.[81] The next night, students and the university's Chancellor Dan Jones organized a "We Are One Mississippi" candlelight walk, referred to also as the "unity march," calling attention to the fact that the behavior of the night before was not an example of the university's and its community's values. This was another instance in which the UM Creed was drawn on explicitly, as "the group read aloud . . . 'I believe in the respect and dignity of each person.' "[82]

At this point, the Both Ways argument for protecting free speech arises again, as it represented one of the greatest challenges for my view, arguably.[83] The examples I have focused on here have involved nonviolent communication, certainly in a physical sense, yet words can wound in metaphorical yet deeply real and meaningful ways.[84] A friend and colleague has asked me concerning this chapter whether one should "punch a Nazi."[85] Certainly in the cases in which physical violence is at stake, people should have the right to defend themselves, yet when the violence is verbal, symbolic, communicative, and not physical, the battle should be understood to be communicatively cultural and concerning ideas, values, symbols, and language. The potential and power to communicate opens opportunity for the benefits of community building or the rectification of injustice. Just talking to Nazis in Germany when they were killing people would not have brought about change, to be sure. At the same time, fighting communicative culture with physical force involves an abandonment of the potential and power of communication and democracy. It represents a failure to believe that ideas of justice and their communication can win out. It also invites violence in return, and at that point in justifiable self-defense.

Champions of civil rights defend freedom of expression in part because its limitation was used so many times by those in power against those seeking justice—the heart of the Both Ways argument. By the same token, we can expect violence to be used against the minority, against those seeking justice, should violence be taken up as the latter's tactic for change. As I argued in chapter 1, progress will only ever be incremental, yet a balance must be struck between cynicism and absolutism, one of giving up and one of tearing down. If a cultural conflict can be addressed through communication, then employing physical violence is to trade one injustice for another, something that will garner morally justified opponents. So vigilantism in punching a physically nonviolent Nazi should be prohibited, but that Nazi's speech and actions should be scrutinized with a test of whether it rises to the level of the cultivation of hatred. A society that does not fight treason to democracy in this way invites the punching of Nazis, as the Teakettle argument might analogously be extended. Deference to the cultivation of hatred because it is speech is injustice and fails to redress the great harm that can be committed through the cultivation of hatred.

It is important to return to the challenge introduced earlier about the Both Ways argument. If a person intends to criticize a group that historically has been oppressed or marginalized, it is important that the criticism not cultivate further hatred or discrimination. The idea can be clarified with the help of thinking about the logical fallacy referred to as *ad hominem*, or *to the man*, today referred to as *to the person*. The idea is that when a person claims a speaker to be wrong because of some circumstantial fact about them, the logic bells should be ringing. To tell a white man that he's wrong about his claim because he is white would mean nothing to a black man who might say the same sentences. Imagine a person criticizing a white person for advocating for color-blind policies, who then asks, "What would you say to Ward Connerly, the black former University of California Regent and anti-affirmative action activist?" The point here is that the same words spoken by Mr. White logically are not different from the same words being spoken by Connerly. Rhetorically and situationally there can be important differences between speakers, but the point is that it is logically a mistake to say that a conclusion doesn't follow from a given premise because of who said it. Therefore, we instruct students not to commit ad hominem attacks in order to avoid poor reasoning. By the same token, when a given group that historically has been subjected to injustice then is thought to commit some moral mistake, it is important not to foment hatred or antidemocratic sentiment while advocating for justice.

Groups in conflict, even violent conflict, can become close friends and allies in time if they genuinely aim in the conclusion of conflict to promote the good of all. The United States and Japan have a very close and mutually beneficial relationship despite the killing of hundreds of thousands of people with nuclear weapons. What I am describing is neither easy nor simple. When generations of families were formed through the rape of slaves,[86] separation and sales, later plagued by Jim Crow and criminalization and mass incarceration, suffering people can understandably worry about the "White Devil." As I noted in chapter 4, people can be self-respecting yet, because of an aim of protection of their children, worry about their boys flirting with girls of other races. We must recall that such messages can intend protection for their families. In response, when people worry about white guilt,[87] the question is whether in fact youths come to lose their sense of positive power in life to pursue meaningful life plans. Diminished pride in the horrifying actions of one's white ancestors does not meet the threshold of troubling speech. It is important to be proud of moral actions, not viciousness. Those who wish to silence the teaching of history that reveals past injustices claim psychological injury but thereby promulgate ignorance in the name of nationalism. As a white male myself, I find the actions of slave owners and Jim Crow politicians indeed evil. Calling out immoral action is one thing, but, as with Japan, we all must think about the long run, about how to hold onto our democracy and about what kind of culture we wish to leave for our grandchildren.

This chapter began with considerations involving a legal protection of speech, proceeding to thoughts about legal efforts for justice, and then political and social. A final thought concerns the individual. In addition to marches and gathered efforts, individuals can make a difference, such as when we call our friends, family, and peers to consider ways of speaking and acting that are more consistent with the shared values we should all embody. The point is not to exhibit "virtue signaling" or "greater than thou" attitudes, but rather to point out to each other that use of words like "retarded" or "gay" are not the words to use to speak generally about something undesirable. When friends call attention to matters undeserving of it, we can suggest, as David Hildebrand has, that not every theory deserves a hearing.[88] At the same time, it is important to listen to those with whom we disagree and be open to learning from them in turn. These final thoughts may sound like platitudes, yet they are norms for guiding a culture. Some of these ideas are hotly criticized as well, both by Ben Carson in his criticisms of "political correctness" and in op-eds by the editorial board of the *New York Times*, which say that Americans have a free speech problem.[89] In the next chapter, I turn to the norm of political correctness in particular, a far subtler concern than those about hate speech or speech that is abusive or discriminatory, for the concept is inaccurately named and its relevant norms are often too vague, points I take to be in some sympathy with the editors of the *New York Times*. For now, I hope that this chapter has revealed ways in which discriminatory speech can be combated, especially when it takes the form of the cultivation of discriminatory and hateful beliefs and practices that are treasonous to democracy. Approaches to combating such forces can be legal, political, or social, and in any effort for justice, there will be need for short-term and long-term endeavors. No one individual is particularly responsible or compelled to act most profoundly, yet, as I have argued in chapter 6, the obligation to establish, maintain, and defend a culture of justice should be understood to be public and shared.

8

Correcting Political Correctness

US Senator Bernie Sanders has argued that although Donald Trump "said some outrageous and painful things," he won his 2016 campaign for president because "people are tired of the same old politically correct rhetoric."[1] In 2015, then-candidate Trump admitted, "I'm so tired of this politically correct crap."[2] That year, Dana Milbank argued that the GOP turned political correctness "into the mother of all straw men."[3] While it is true that in 2018 more Republicans expressed sentiment "against political correctness," at 76 percent, according to *Christian Today*'s reporting on a Marist Institute of Public Opinion poll, 45 percent of Democrats did too, even though 55 percent wanted "more sensitivity to be shown in expressing opinions."[4] Comedians like Steve Harvey have said that political correctness "has killed comedy,"[5] though critics retort that "the old guard is being left behind in a world that no longer finds bigotry funny."[6] As I mentioned in the introduction, past presidential candidate Ben Carson has sounded the gravest warning when he has said that "political correctness . . . is going to destroy our nation."[7]

I first published a short essay with this same title as Eric Thomas Weber, "Correcting Political Correctness," *Philosophers Magazine* 1 (2016): 113–14. I have included that early short essay in the appendix to this book. In addition, I am grateful to Mike Austin and the Department of Philosophy and Religion at Eastern Kentucky University, whose faculty invited me to deliver an early version of the longer essay that became this chapter for the 2019 Ron Messerich Distinguished Lecture in Philosophy and Religion at Eastern Kentucky University in February of 2019 in Richmond, Kentucky.

Many people on both sides of the political aisle bemoan the call for political correctness yet at times get reasonably upset when others commit offenses of speech, symbolism, or action that raise concerns of injustice or trampling on treasured practices or ideals. Some people are concerned about those who call women "babe" in the workplace[8] and others, unimpressed at other times, become enraged over the "war against Christmas."[9] In this chapter, I hope to show first that the ways in which we think about the norms we call "political correctness" can be misapplied and be based on problematic, inaccurate language, and second, that these ways relate to valuable norms that we ought to recognize more precisely and appreciate for guiding respectful public conduct in the effort to establish a culture of justice.

I begin with a focus on why we really need to talk about political correctness. Next, I present a sense of the problems it raises. Then I suggest ways in which we can rethink the concept to better guide what we ought to be considering more precisely when it comes to cultural interactions in the public sphere. Ultimately, this chapter examines one of the aspects of individuals' and institutional leaders' shared and public obligations to establish a culture of justice that does not rise to the level of censored expression, yet that certainly prompts criticism and calls for change. In the final section of this chapter, I show how the alternative language I propose, of "cultural respectfulness," draws on the central thesis of this book and also builds on the idea of what Axel Honneth has called the "struggle for recognition."[10] The task at issue is to call attention to the need for developing new habits for how individuals and groups talk about other people and cultural matters in ways that show respect for others' concerns, suffering, and need for humane treatment. It is no surprise that such conflicts rankle older and more conservative outlooks, as old habits die hard and the development of new ways of thinking and speaking takes efforts that often clash with people's sensibilities, values, or feelings of embarrassment about their ignorance of others' concerns.

Why Talk about Political Correctness?

The *Oxford English Dictionary* defines "politically correct" as an adjective, meaning "*(a)* appropriate to the prevailing political or social circumstances (in early use not as a fixed collocation); *(b) spec.* (originally *U.S.*, sometimes *depreciative*) conforming to a body of liberal or radical opinion, esp. on social matters, usually characterized by the advocacy of approved causes or views, and often by the rejection of language, behaviour, etc., considered discriminatory or offensive."[11] Here we see two versions of "political correctness" that are at odds. The concept of political correctness, in my view, is best understood first in terms of why we should talk about it. Philosophical pragmatists have pointed out that one's purposes for thinking about an idea have important consequences for what we mean by it. William James famously poked fun at philosophers who debated what it might mean to "go around" a squirrel on a tree.[12] It might mean to go to the north, the east, the south, and the west of it, but, as anyone who has tried knows, and as boxers might recognize, doing so does not mean that we have gotten to the side of the squirrel, to its back, its side, and its front again. The boxer wants to get around their opponent, and "getting around" something that moves is not about cardinal directions of north, east, south, and west, but about the front, the side, the back, and so on. So why we need to know something often matters profoundly for understanding what it is. The pragmatist theory of meaning is of profound importance to a subject like political correctness, therefore, since it makes little sense to imagine a pure, Platonic sense of "political correctness" in its ultimately real sense. It is a term that has been coined and used with significant variation and loosely captures a family of ideas and behaviors, making it easier to caricature as inconsistent and foolish.[13]

As I have noted, former neurosurgeon and 2016 presidential candidate Ben Carson has argued that political correctness is "dangerous." He warned, "Political correctness will destroy us if we don't wake up."[14] His remarks were offered in defense of then–fellow candidate Donald Trump's proposal of a "Muslim ban." Carson further explained his view, saying, "We should all be careful about what we say, but the fact of the matter is, let's not get so concerned about how offended our enemies are." Carson here either committed a straw man fallacy or a fallacy of ambiguity in suggesting that those who find a proposal offensive are concerned about offending terrorists or hostile foreign national leaders, or he lumped any Americans offended by Trump's proposal into the category of enemies.

Carson's worries about political correctness may be misapplied in this case, yet Americans of many stripes and points of view feel exhausted about calls for being culturally respectful of others. The organization More in Common released a major report in 2018 on a poll they conducted called "Hidden Tribes: A Study of America's Polarized Landscape."[15] They found that while "82 percent of Americans agree that hate speech is a problem in America today, . . . 80 percent also view political correctness as an issue."[16] They found the latter result in respondents' answers to the question of their agreement or disagreement with the statement "Political correctness is a problem in our country."[17] The one group least in agreement with fellow Americans on this matter is made up of "progressive activists," among whom 30 percent still see political correctness as a problem.[18]

Many examples of political correctness arise about domestic matters rather than about concerns over immigration. For example, as mentioned in chapter 7, a man went to vote in November of 2018 in Olive Branch, Mississippi, a suburb of Memphis, Tennessee, just on the other side of the Mississippi border, wearing a T-shirt that read "Mississippi Justice" and prominently featuring a Confederate battle flag with the image of a hanging noose overlaying the flag. A photo of the man at the voting booth made its way via Twitter to the news cycle, which shortly thereafter reported that Regional One Health in Memphis had terminated the man's employment as an emergency medical technician.

On the theme of Confederate symbols, in Oxford, Mississippi, Justice Victory reported for the *Clarion Ledger* of Jackson that "pro-Confederate groups" were "fed up with political correctness BS," concerning changes considered progressive at the University of Mississippi. Confederate 901, which identifies itself as a political organization, explained its February 2019 protest, writing:

> This is an event to draw the line in the sand!!! For over a decade the administration and faculty [at the University of Mississippi] have completely disregarded and disrespected the traditions of a once great southern university. Far to [sic] long the administration has kowtowed to the minority left leaning students and basically have done everything that they have demanded . . . If you are fed up with this Political Correctness BS and sick and tired of this mess happening then please join us on FEB. 23, 2019 at the monument in the groove [sic].[19]

There are many in the South who wish to claim that appreciation for Confederate symbols has to do with states' rights and Southern heritage. The cases featuring nooses, however, clearly present threatening symbols honoring tools of mob violence that were used in slaughtering thousands of black Americans across the South in terrorizing mob rule processes with no resemblance to a justice system. How a hospital could permit a man to publicly present himself in such a threatening shirt, symbolizing his violent racist values, while pretending that he is ready to care for any and all patients whom the hospital intends to treat is unanswerable. Hence, as I noted in chapter 7, the man was fired from his position with Regional One Health of Memphis.[20]

The case of Southern heritage and pride with respect to Confederate statues and imagery in the name of heritage, denying connection to slavery and white supremacy, might be a more defensible argument, were it not refuted so clearly in historical documents,[21] such as Mississippi's declaration of its causes for secession. The state legislature of Mississippi explained its motivation for joining the Confederacy in 1861 as follows:

> In the momentous step which our State has taken of dissolving its connection with the government of which we so long formed a part, it is but just that we should declare the prominent reasons which have induced our course. Our position is thoroughly identified with the institution of slavery—the greatest material interest of the world. Its labor supplies the product which constitutes by far the largest and most important portions of commerce of the earth. These products are peculiar to the climate verging on the tropical regions, and by an imperious law of nature, none but the black race can bear exposure to the tropical sun.[22]

It is one thing for people unaware of this history to learn it and then be judged for embracing it henceforth. But, to proclaim the values of the Confederacy in Mississippi, denying the relevance of slavery, all in the name of heritage, is a contradiction too bald to stand up to scrutiny. When I lived in Mississippi, furthermore, and called attention to noble causes for pride in the South, such as in James Meredith's heroic efforts to enroll at the all-white University of Mississippi, discussions of heritage of that nature inspired some people I met to search for other company.

Not all cases of calls for political correctness are defensible. Critics of "political correctness" often consider its norms to be a kind of micromanagement of people's lives. A "Bias-Free Language Guide" produced at the University of New Hampshire offered a good example of overstepping.[23] The "Bias-Free Language Guide," now removed from the university's website, said that the word "American" is "problematic," for example. I am presently teaching a course on education in American culture at the University of Kentucky. Imagine trying to teach the course without using the word "America." Intentions may have been good in designing the guide, but its removal from the university's website has received no great attention from free speech activists or academics.

At the same time, the fact that an effort to strive for a just culture was imperfect or unsuccessful does not imply that the goal of striving for such a culture is wrongheaded. Consider two further and recent examples over which there will be more debate and controversy. The first example concerns what have long been referred to as "brown bag lunches" as a name for meetings for which each person is to bring his or her own lunch in order to talk about some kind of shared business somewhat informally. The second example involves public school curricula and selection of shared readings for literature courses.

The phrase "brown bag lunch" may sound innocuous to many Americans. To some, however, it recalls a painful history. The "paper bag test" refers to a discriminatory practice of judging people on the basis of whether they are lighter or darker than a brown paper bag.[24] The matter is connected to a history that involved the question of whether a person of African American descent could "pass" as white.[25] Later, fraternities and sororities and social groups would make use of the "paper bag test" or hold a "bag party," into which only persons lighter than a brown bag would be let in.[26] Given such discriminatory history, in 2013 the Office for Civil Rights in Seattle, Washington, according to Amanda Taselaar in *Time* magazine, "suggested that government workers refrain from using the common term," namely "brown bag lunch," "because it could be offensive to some people." Taselaar continues, explaining, "City leaders usually designate bring-your-own-lunch meetings as brown bag lunch meetings, but have decided that 'lunch-and-learn' or 'sack lunch' are more appropriate alternatives." Also according to Taselaar, "While the city has its reasons for balking at the words, some Seattle residents told [the] KOMO [news network] that they think the proposed language goes too far."[27]

This example may frustrate some people for a number of reasons. The first is that it might seem like micromanaging people's every word choice. Second, the wonder is what exactly is the harm? Why are people really complaining about subtle uses of language? This criticism raises the charge that some people are "snowflakes."[28] Third, along with micromanaging is a worry about policing. If the Mississippi Justice T-shirt wearer can be fired for his free expression, do such threats accompany concerns over plain language like invoking the color of one's lunch sack? I will return to this example, but a reasonable reply can begin with two steps. First, we can point out that not everyone's use of language is called into question here. Instead, the matter concerned public offices. These are to be open and welcoming to all, unlike a private family picnic in the backyard at home. Second, the cost of using different language is very low. A few years ago, I ran the colloquium series in my department at the University of Kentucky. The one worry I had in raising this concern was simply whether past organizers might feel judged for using what used to be usual language to refer to informal lunch gatherings. One can suggest a change without necessarily condemning past practices, however. If people were unaware of a worry, being made aware of it is an important step for future responsibility. Given that, tolerance and patience with people whom we ask to try new things is important. New generations may know more than past ones about some developments, such as the dangers of cigarette smoke. We need not infer that past generations sought to harm their children by means of secondhand smoke. Worries about not judging our parents should not keep us from making our children's environments smoke free when possible.

I let my colleagues know about the 2013 development in Washington state, asking whether there would be any objection to using the term "Lunch and Learn" for our meetings that used to be called "brown bag" events, and no one flinched. It was settled. Perhaps in another group of people, someone might have moaned or rolled their eyes, but the cost to them verges on zero. As such, the person reluctant to adapt has little reason to complain. If anything could motivate hesitation, it could be expenses incurred due to the replacement of printed materials that include outdated language. The good news is that with more happening online, rather than in print, such a matter is rarely relevant any longer, as changes can often be made to content online in a matter of moments. In addition, the price of printed materials is nowhere near the cost of bad publicity or lawsuits.

The second example concerns common texts taught in schools. *The Adventures of Huckleberry Finn* and *To Kill a Mockingbird* have long served as texts for English courses or summer reading assignments, but some school districts have chosen to drop them.[29] The books have arguably been valuable for the movement away from past prejudices to the greater democratic equality of all people. Some critics in recent decades have questioned whether it remains appropriate to teach kids a text that repeatedly uses the term "N-word Jim," uncensored, to describe one of its key characters. The books might be redeemable or defended, but it is reasonable at least to ask whether or not perhaps it is time to find other texts or to allow for more variety in selecting literature that can speak to more kids, addressing themselves better to the generations of students in school today. Similarly, Shakespeare's *Romeo and Juliet* may continue to be loved and read, but is *The Taming of the Shrew* essential reading today?[30] Is it unreasonable to question the starvation of a young woman and fanning of her vanity as methods for rendering her more obedient and respectful? I recall being startled about the popularity of the text when I read it in my own youth. It is perfectly reasonable to raise questions about what we are teaching kids. Reasonable intellectual and moral conservatives wish to preserve what is right and good from tradition, not just any which aspect of our history just because it has been an element of our past.

All of these examples point to the kind of conflict at work in thinking about political correctness. In some of the most troubling cases, such as in the case involving the ACLU, which I discussed briefly in the introduction, concrete and heavy consequences are noted as a result of cultural symbols. Recall that the ACLU argued that an African American defendant in a death penalty case cannot reasonably expect a fair trial in a courthouse over which the Confederate battle flag is flying.[31] Many cases of political correctness concern far smaller or subtler worries about offenses to people's sensibilities. The matter of culture and its relation to justice runs the gambit. Thus, it is essential for my purposes to examine how and why we ought to think about both the blunt and striking forms of cultural injustice and the subtler, more controversial ones involved in calls for political correctness.

What Is the Problem with Political Correctness?

Several problems emerge systematically as a result of calls for political correctness. The first is that the very tools some people invoke to protect vulnerable populations can be used to target them as well. For example, concern over racial slurs can be motivated to protect people against their damaging use. At the same time, some people who are subjects of those slurs make use of them in ways that are said to be intended to "reclaim" the relevant term, to use oppressive language in a mode of defiance for the sake of resisting oppression. A controversial example involves the band that calls itself "the Slants," which I mentioned in chapter 7. The group is an Asian-American rock band based in Portland, Oregon, which made use of a slur commonly applied to persons of Asian descent. When they sought to register the trademark for their band name, the US Patent and Trademark Office opposed the registration. The case went all the way to the US Supreme Court, which decided unanimously in favor of allowing the group to keep its name.[32]

In another case, the Trademark Office opposed the reregistration of the Washington Redskins, another controversial decision, but one not notably based on its use by oppressed people for their own reclaiming of language. The matter in this latter case concerned the fact that some groups have called for the Trademark Office not to renew the registration of the team's trademark. "What does it matter that some people refer to a team name like the 'Redskins'?" one might ask. The matter is starker when we imagine the request to trademark a name like the Mississippi Black-skins or an uncensored version of the Alabama N-words. Registration of trademark is arguably a form of governmental protection of an entity's right to profit exclusively from the use of a mark for trade purposes. The US Congress is granted the right to regulate commerce among the states, and other policies can be used to decide what practices and processes may be deserving or undeserving of state support or protection. As I said in chapter 7, I argue that the Ku Klux Klan should not be afforded the governmentally provided benefits of incorporation as a nonprofit organization. A museum of the Ku Klux Klan, which has historical and hence educational value, is quite different in purpose, insofar as it promotes democracy and not hate. A project is growing to turn the historically troubling "Redneck Shop" into the Echo Project, a "community center and racial reconciliation museum . . . [featuring] KKK memorabilia."[33] As noted in chapter 7, some practices of government are said to speak, to support or not support relevant activities.[34,35]

In each of these cases, the problems of political correctness become clear. First, political correctness often appears not to be about political procedures or mechanisms. This may not be true, depending on how expansive is one's intended meaning of "political." At the same time, using the language around the holiday season of "Merry Christmas" may seem to many people to have little to do with their everyday conceptions of politics. Philosophers may like to explain how the word politics concerns the "polis," which really has to do with the city, what is public.[36] Yet when people refer to politics today, they typically do not have in mind sports mascots, the names of rock and roll bands, or the choices that people make about holiday greetings. Again, it may be that we ought to correct people's senses of the disconnect between these terms, but it is at least counterintuitive for most people to think of such things as political. Below I present two of my own stories about just such a feeling.

I am the son of a French mother and an American father. I learned a great deal about French culture growing up, including the language. I also remember how strange it sounded to me when I learned that France has a minister of culture. An American libertarian recently asked me whether I favor the idea of a "culture czar." The very idea sounds strange. Does that mean that we ought not to address problems in our culture? The French do not think so. They also have the "Académie Française," the "official custodians of the French Language."[37] The idea of official custodians of a language for Americans sounds absurd in part because if there were such a thing, it would probably be thought to have to do with English, and there is already a country that might claim authority in the matter other than the United States. According to Harmeet Kaur of CNN, furthermore, "FYI: English Isn't the Official Language of the United States," she wrote in June of 2018.[38] The United States is a nation of immigrants, so our cultures and languages are intermingled. A country of approximately 330 million people has a National Endowment for the Arts, federally funded with $162.4 million in 2020,[39] yet the city of Vienna alone, with a population under 2 million people, invested $280 million in the same year, and Austria's national cultural budget was $466 million, for a nation of fewer than 9 million people.[40] To be sure, the United States does not centralize control of language or culture, even if some think that we ought to regarding language[41] or loyalty to the flag.[42]

A second case struck me when I first studied philosophy. An art major learned I studied philosophy early on and told me that she didn't like Plato. He opposed artists and poets in his vision of the just society, she explained. I had yet to read Plato's *Republic* at the time, so I rushed to understand what she was talking about. Not only would Plato ban the poets from society, but, as I noted in chapter 3, he also argued for control of not just the messages of music, as in today's complaints about rap and rock and roll, but even the modes of music that aren't based in the major or minor scales. I was bewildered that Plato would see problems and cause to control artists so thoroughly, squelching freedom of expression. The idea was strange and unsettling. At the same time, today, I see that many of our arguments about culture and virtue are simply a matter of degree on the same continuum. People bemoan the absence of prayer in school. They oppose the messages of rap and heavy metal music for the threats they pose to young people's character. Plato went too far, but many Americans today think that some degree of control over culture is morally necessary.

While the modes of music that we should allow people to play may not be real matters of political concern, we ought nevertheless to think carefully about those mechanisms that influence children. We no longer permit cigarette companies to advertise their products by means of the Flintstones cartoons, as they did in the 1960s, even though that rule is a restriction on business and free expression.[43] Some matters of culture are clearly too important to leave to chance and free choice. At the same time, some critics around the world[44] and some in the United States[45] find Americans strange for permitting pharmaceutical companies to run advertisements.

If the first problem with political correctness concerns the notion of whether or not what is at stake is political, the remaining term is still problematic and misleading, namely "correctness." In conventional thinking about math problems, when asked for the sum of 2 + 3, the answers 1, 2, 3, and 4 are all incorrect. The answer 5 is correct.[46] There is a definite and determinate answer. Some people find philosophy and ethics frustrating because they like what they believe to be the objectivity and clarity of answers in subjects like basic math. There's no gray area in the answer choices I have just proposed. Newcomers to the study of philosophy or civics sometimes throw their hands up when matters admit of shades of gray, what we call matters of degree. If answers are not very precise and specific, people get frustrated, thinking that what we're talking about itself is foggy, fuzzy, or meaningless. Aristotle famously taught, however, that it is a mistake to expect more precision in a subject matter than the subject matter allows.[47] If we ask at what point a person becomes rich, the matter is clearly an issue about which precision cannot be clear-cut and highly specific. The more precise one's determination of being in the category "rich," the more easily others can challenge the claim. For example, at one time, owning a home that is worth one million dollars may have clearly suggested that one is rich. Today, however, living in California in a very modest home can require a plot valued at such an amount.[48] It was announced in 2019 that the total cost of attending Duke University for a single year is approaching $75,000.[49] So the small family in California leveraging sizeable educational loans for a kid in college in North Carolina may balk at being called "rich," even if their three-bedroom home on a small plot is valued at one million dollars.

Correctness in the philosophical tradition is typically associated with a norm concerning knowledge referred to as correspondence theory. The idea is that what we say or believe does or does not accurately correspond with the relevant meaning of the belief or statement. Things are as we believe them to be, in a direct way, it is thought, one that typically is understood in connection with singularity of interpretation. When we make social or evaluative claims however, such as in suggesting that a certain spoon is a "dessert spoon," which we might claim implies that it is to be used last in a meal, few would think that in all contexts it makes sense to reserve the use of that spoon for elaborate meals, in which it must always be used last. My priority in the drawer is for a spoon to be clean, for instance.

When it comes to contexts typically associated with political correctness, therefore, it can be misleading to use the term "correctness," as if there were a singular correct way of speaking or acting with regard to the symbol or person in question. For instance, when we see someone of African descent in the United States, at one time such a person would have been referred to as "colored" or as a "Negro," the former of which remains in the acronym of the NAACP. In more recent years, "black" and "African American" have supplanted the earlier terms, and sometimes these are used interchangeably or together to capture a group of people alternatively referred to or self-identifying, as in the US Department of Health and Human Services' terminology.[50] While some people are unsure of how to refer to others, this is because of distinctions that include the fact that some black people in the United States are not American. Nigerians I know who come to study in the United States understand themselves to be black, of African descent, but not as African American. To the average person who may or may not need to refer to another person's identity, it may or may not appear to matter that they understand such a history. However, a given person may not choose to select a box that reads "African American" if they are not American. Understanding this fact simply points to the challenge of thinking that there is one, singular, and universally correct way of referring to a person on the basis of race when they are of African descent in the United States.

Frustration over the call for "correctness" therefore is onto something right when it imagines the standard to be unreasonable, in a sense, expecting more precision at times in a subject matter than the subject matter allows. "Correctness" of the degree at work in 2 + 3 is too high of an expectation, and what can sometimes help is greater vagueness. At the same time, James Murray's work in progress articulates concern for excessive aggregation of the term "black," which can enable diversity policies and practices that do little to grow inclusion of people who are American descendants of slavery. He points out that this can happen when black immigrants are hired or admitted into colleges and universities, increasing racial diversity while masking the continued inaccessibility of higher education for descendants of American slaves.[51]

A further challenge arises in the call for precise correctness, which is that it is difficult for people to know the intricacies of the kinds of terminology that a great variety of groups prefer or demand as a form of what Axel Honneth has referred to as "recognition."[52] One example is the recent term "Latinx," which avoids the binary of "Latino" and "Latina," yet, according to ABC News, "One poll shows only 4% of U.S. Latinos use the non-binary term, Latinx."[53] Challenges of these kinds irk some people, who feel as though they are being criticized by others demanding attention, respect, and subordination of the majority's speech and values, while others are seeking recognition for their identities that can be trampled by so many who seem not to care. At bottom, Dewey would see reactionary attitudes as an unwillingness to continue the task of lifelong education that democracy implies and requires. A devil's advocate would reply that such calls concern small matters of excess sensitivity about little to nothing, on their view, and as such are really pernicious political strategies meant to undermine the rightful dominance of traditional moral or religious claims. It is one thing to expect people to keep learning and inquiring together about democratic challenges and problems, but "correctness" as a term bears a ring that indeed connotes a specificity of expectation that is too high. A variety of terms and respectful ways of speaking may well be appropriate, and, as such, a narrow view of what kind of language can and should be tolerated may in truth be appropriate primarily for academic, legal, and policy writing, rather than for everyday language expectations of ordinary communication.

Even if "political correctness" is not the right term, we nevertheless need some language that can address for us the clearer cases of conflict. An emergency medical technician should be expected to treat their patients with equal respect or else we ought to be able to be successful in suing the relevant public hospital. If that is right, then there are things that individuals can do that may seem personal or unrelated to their jobs, that nevertheless may indicate cause for apology, redress, or termination of employment. If the government can choose what license plates to make or not make, at least with respect to deeply important and problematic cases that do not deserve the endorsement of government, as I noted in chapter 7 about the Confederate license plate case,[54] then we need terminology and a theory for understanding how and when to apply the relevant norms that have been poorly captured with the language of "political correctness."

Rethinking Political Correctness as Cultural Respectfulness

If "political correctness" is not the optimal term for identifying the norms that I suggest are needed, I am called to propose alternatives. First, although problems with political correctness may be "political" in some broad, loose, or technical and academic sense, we do understand the relevant concerns to be cultural. Symbols like Confederate battle flags, football mascots, nooses, uses of language, and selections of readings for public school curricula all have bearing on culture. The sphere in which we are concerned is cultural. We must be culturally correct, but "correct" is not the right word.

If "correctness" isn't correct, we need to think about what we mean. There are sometimes several ways of acting that are unacceptable, and one or several that are not. The problem isn't that one or another is *the* right one. Rather, it's that some are appropriate and some are not. "Appropriate" is too vague, however, and lacks the clear connection to moral values that is implied by valuable uses of "political correctness." Instead, I propose "respectful." Respect is a moral norm and a democratic one. The US Constitution is meant to respect persons, despite its own troubling historical flaws including the notion of fractional persons,[55] and government is to treat each person fairly according to the law.[56] Respect for law is understood to be important, and respect is a key notion central to the Belmont Report, a core document in the bioethics tradition for guiding respectful research on human subjects.[57]

In short, rather than using the terminology of "political correctness," I suggest that the crucial norm at work about appropriate uses of symbols and language is "culturally respectful." Political correctness, then is better referred to as "cultural respectfulness."

Among the important aspects of being culturally respectful is the recognition that individuals do not on their own determine the full meaning of their communications, whatever their intents. Meanings are shared, and responsibility for them is public and shared. It is in this sense too that there is a shared and public obligation to establish and maintain a culture of justice, one that works to ensure a cultural respect for enabling each person to develop self-respect and a sense of their own positive power to pursue meaningful life plans.

To be sure, a new term like "cultural respectfulness" will not in itself resolve the conflicts that will continue to arise over people's uses of symbols and language and others' sensibilities and genuine feelings of offense. At the same time, dissatisfaction over the "straw man" of political correctness calls for a clearer and stronger justification of what is right in the expectation that people make efforts to be respectful of others' cultural identities and values in ways that embody the sorts of public and shared obligations to establishing a culture of justice as a way of life, as I discussed in chapter 6.

As I have said, aiming to establish and maintain a culture of justice involves various levels of concern and consideration about the shared environments in which we live, work, and raise our children. Correctness is too specific of an expectation for a vaguer category of appropriateness, and culture is the sphere of matters in which respectfulness should be expected. It is my hope that the argument of this book has presented a framework for understanding what sorts of obligations the expectations involved are and how they can be justified, at bottom. Much more work is needed on the many applications and spheres of conflict that will arise concerning the pursuit of a culture of justice. It appears to me at least that many scholars and writers are working in these various areas to offer enriching ways of thinking about how to be more carefully respectful and supportive of the conditions necessary for establishing and maintaining a culture of justice.

Cultural Respectfulness as Experimentation and Informal Education

John Dewey believed that education is going on all around us all the time. Schools are formal, institutionalized contexts in which purposeful education is organized and structured, but outside of schools, people continue to be educated for better or worse, and with significant influence from powerful parties interested in driving thinking for their own aims. In this book, I have agreed with and supported John Rawls's claim that it is vital to safeguard against threats to people's self-respect, adding the Deweyan consideration that active effort and support are needed to empower people to develop a sense of their own positive power to pursue meaningful life plans. At the same time, through everyday activity, communication, and policymaking, people can intentionally or unintentionally threaten others' sense of their own value. In *The Struggle for Recognition*, Axel Honneth identifies three forms of social interaction in which a person's sense of his or her own value can be threatened, namely relationships of intimacy, familial or not; legal recognition; and the recognition of solidarity. He sums these up with the terms "love, rights, and solidarity."[58] The flip side of respect garnered with regard to each of these areas, he explains, includes "violation of the body, the denial of rights, and the denigration of ways of life."[59] These distinctions are useful for considering forms of cultural respect and disrespect in engagements that typically raise questions about what is popularly called political correctness.

I agree with Honneth on an ideal that may never be achieved but is a useful aspiration, in the sense raised in chapter 1 of this book, of an evolving regulative ideal, namely his sense of "social solidarity." He writes that social solidarity would be achieved when "every member of a society is in a position to esteem himself or herself."[60] On my outlook, drawing on chapter 1, justice is understood as an evolving regulative ideal. As such, social solidarity will never fully be achieved, yet it can be strived for, and society can come closer to it step by step.

As I finished the initial draft of this chapter, President Biden recently declared that "white supremacy is a poison" after yet another racially motivated killing spree in Buffalo, New York.[61] Consider that just over a decade ago, 46 percent of Mississippi Republicans said that interracial marriage should be illegal.[62] Only seven years later, the "Hidden Tribes" report noted that 82 percent of Americans believed that hate speech is a problem, as noted earlier in this chapter.[63]

One way to think about people's frustration with the need for cultural respectfulness can be to think of it in terms of the challenges of experimentation and learning. Learning new things is difficult and sometimes uncomfortable if a person lacks the right attitudes. This is part of the reason that Dewey so often spoke of keeping the right attitudes for democracy and for engaging in public inquiry. In particular, people who think of themselves as grown, beyond schooling, think of themselves as established and developed, done with education. The example I offered earlier in this chapter, of the "Lunch and Learn," represented a very easy transition in my experience, but it also took place about seven years after the conflict in Seattle, Washington, where the story started. In addition, my context involved an academic community, one that is supposed to include people with the scientific attitudes and habits of mind to be ready to listen to others and learn. A proposal for how to speak in a new way had already been considered, tried, tested, and used successfully elsewhere, furthermore, making it easy for my colleagues and me to adopt new language.

New challenges have arisen today regarding how to speak about persons with disabilities, some of whom prefer that others use "people-first language," referring to someone as a person first and with a disability second, in contrast with calling someone an "epileptic."[64] Of course, the approach of using "people-first" language has its critics and is a matter still in development.[65] Also challenging are those contexts still in development today for which a variety of uses of language are called for regarding senses of gender that do not conform to the binary of "he or she." Some persons wish to be referred to in a singular form of "they," for example, and culturally respectful persons work toward greater understanding and practice of the use of pronouns different from how they were introduced to them in their youth.[66] Critics not only do not feel comfortable making efforts to be respectful of others, but assert that alternate ways of understanding gender from the traditional binary are "riddled with contradictions."[67] In these first examples of conflict, we see concerns over uses of language and lack of solidarity, but there are also legal challenges related to them as well, such as in cases of transgender athletes and bans on their participation in sports.[68]

Those fighting for recognition and enlisting friends and partners bear the weight of various forms of disrespect, as well as the tasks of working to figure out new ways of speaking and acting that help to garner respect and recognition for their identities and values in the public sphere. There is no obvious formula for achieving success, but the search for clearer and easier ways of enabling people to think, speak, and behave respectfully pays dividends. At the same time, ease and simplicity can obscure important subtleties and distinctions important to people. The tragedy of fighting for a more culturally respectful world is that people are afraid of change and scapegoat others in their manifestos and conspiracy theories, like "replacement theory."[69] On the one hand, critics of any movement or effort can be understood to provide useful insight about what the challenges and targets are for educating people and building new habits in solidarity with others. On the other hand, when political pundits with broad viewership take up and promote white supremacist conspiracy theories about an intent to "replace" white people in the United States with persons of color, it is important to call out such figures, as NBC News has done recently with Tucker Carlson of Fox News.[70]

The challenges at stake in pursuing cultural respectfulness depend on a lack of the attitudes that Dewey said are needed for democracy. Democracy as a personal way of individual life calls for a kind of openness to hear people out about their concerns. When conflicts arise over girls' sports, dialogue, engagement, and even legal struggles are to be expected. A culture of justice calls for people to be respectful and consider their uses of language and the harms of mockery and dehumanization, but such a call is needed precisely because experience shows that we can expect such harms to occur. The vocal opponents of change in various areas generally dismiss political correctness precisely because it is about talk and things that are not tangible, that in their eyes do no real harm, yet Honneth notes that disrespect and a lack of recognition commonly inspire and motivate "violation of the body," violence. Matthew Shepard's murder was a tragic yet influential moment in the movement to recognize persons who are gay.[71] George Floyd's murder prompted protests against police violence and an appreciation of why many have fought for concern over the loss of black lives in the United States.[72] Sadly, violence reached a record high against transgender and gender nonconforming people in the United States in 2021.[73]

The irony about "political correctness," or cultural respectfulness, is that in a sense it is the element of pursuing a culture of justice that people most commonly dismiss as unimportant, ridiculous, or dangerous. Political philosophers tend to focus on principles, policies, legal mechanisms, and institutions, yet at bottom, Dewey was right, I believe, in arguing that political democracy is only meaningful to the extent that it rests on a democratic ethics, on a society and culture that adopt and value the attitudes that call for mutual respect and dialogue. I end this book here on the subject of political correctness because in a sense it captures the extent of how challenging it can be to bring about change with regard to culture for the sake of being more humane, of working to ensure that all people are supported in the development of their self-respect and their sense of positive power to pursue meaningful life plans. The dismissiveness of some people about the lack of concreteness and unimportance of the concerns of "snowflakes," about the use of language and of pronouns, misses the clear connection between such thinking and the dehumanization and murder of others. Even when people are not killed, but are harassed, that too is a violation and form of violence, if not physical, that is abusive and disrespectful, discounting the meaningfulness of another's sense of the worth of pursuing their life plans. At the same time, creative thinking and experimentation, as well as persistence in the effort at self-education and the education of others for the sake of new and more just habits of thought, speech, and action, are the constant imperative of a culture of justice. While the task that I have described here is daunting, there are a great many people to whom we can make appeals for consideration and recognition. Individuals can take some solace in the fact that the pursuit of solidarity means that with effort and time, many more people can be enlisted to build and maintain a more respectful culture of justice

Notes

Introduction

1. Jerry Mitchell, "Ole Miss Student Charged for Defacing Meredith Statue," *Clarion Ledger* (Jackson, MS), March 27, 2015, https://www.usatoday.com/story/news/nation/2015/03/27/ole-miss-meredith-statue-vandalism/70562446/.

2. Geoffrey R. Stone, *Perilous Times: Free Speech in Wartime—From the Sedition Act of 1798 to the War on Terrorism* (New York: W. W. Norton, 2004).

3. Geoffrey R. Stone, "The Noose, Ole Miss, and Free Speech," *Huffington Post*, February 19, 2014, https://www.huffpost.com/entry/the-noose-ole-miss-and-fr_b_4820588.

4. "The law" here is meant in the general sense, including court precedents.

5. Therese Apel, "Deryl Dedmon, Two Others Sentenced from 7-50 Years in Hate Crime," *Clarion Ledger* (Jackson, MS), February 10, 2015, https://www.clarionledger.com/story/news/2015/02/10/deryl-dedmon-two-others-to-be-sentenced-in-hate-crime-tuesday/23166397/.

6. For his guilty plea, prosecutors agreed to drop the felony charge.

7. See Bracey Harris, "Ex-Ole Miss Student Sentenced for Noose on Statue," *USA Today*, September 17, 2015, https://www.usatoday.com/story/news/nation/2015/09/17/ex-ole-miss-student-sentenced-noose-statue/72376068/; Susan Svrluga, "Former Ole Miss Student Pleads Guilty to Hanging Noose Around Statue Honoring the First Black Student," *Washington Post*, March 24, 2016, https://www.washingtonpost.com/news/grade-point/wp/2016/03/24/former-ole-miss-student-pleads-guilty-to-hanging-noose-around-statue-honoring-the-first-black-student/.

8. Svrluga, "Former Ole Miss Student Pleads Guilty to Hanging Noose."

9. See James Taranto, "Durham, We Have a Problem," *Wall Street Journal*, July 30, 2015, https://www.wsj.com/articles/durham-we-have-a-problem-1438279548; and Janelle Ross, "The Story Behind the University of New Hampshire's 'Bias-Free Language Guide,'" *Washington Post*, July 30, 2015, https://www.washingtonpost.com/news/the-fix/wp/2015/07/30/the-story-behind-the-university-of-new-hampshires-bias-free-language-guide/?utm_term=.d154c4136193.

10. Diane Ravitch, *The Language Police: How Pressure Groups Restrict What Students Learn* (New York: Vintage Books, 2003), 3.

11. Katie Lobosco, "Ben Carson: Political Correctness Is Going to 'Destroy Our Nation,'" CNN Politics, October 22, 2019, https://www.cnn.com/2019/10/22/politics/ben-carson-transgender-political-correctness/index.html.

12. Ibid.

13. Andrew Kernohan, *Liberalism, Equality, and Cultural Oppression* (New York: Cambridge University Press, 1998).

14. Suzanne Ito, "Confederate Flag at Louisiana Courthouse Taints Death Penalty System with Racial Bias," ACLU Speak Freely, May 10, 2011, https://www.aclu.org/blog/smart-justice/mass-incarceration/confederate-flag-louisiana-courthouse-taints-death-penalty.

15. It is worth noting that the *Chicago Manual of Style* has not used the hyphen between the words African and American for years, but when quoting from sources, the original source may. See Merrill Perlman, "AP Tackles Language About Race in This Year's Style Guide," *Columbia Journalism Review*, April 1, 2019, https://www.cjr.org/language_corner/ap-style-guide-race-black-vs-african-american.php.

16. ACLU, "Confederate Flag to Be Removed from Outside Louisiana Courthouse," ACLU News Release, November 4, 2011, https://www.aclu.org/press-releases/confederate-flag-be-removed-outside-louisiana-courthouse.

17. Jeff Ferrell, "Confederate Flag Comes Down Friday," KSLA News 12, November 3, 2011, https://www.ksla.com/story/15955226/caddo-parish-commission-votes-to-remove-confederate-flag/.

18. Ibid.

19. Ibid.

20. Chris Lyon, "Caddo Parish Commission Votes to Remove Confederate Monument at Courthouse," *Heliopolis: Shreveport News and Culture*, October 19, 2017, https://heliopolis.la/caddo-parish-commission-votes-remove-confederate-monument-courthouse/.

21. The same argument was given in Mississippi concerning the continuing popularity of corporal punishment among parents, despite extensive evidence that the practice does long-term harm. See Eric Thomas Weber, *Uniting Mississippi: Democracy and Leadership in the South* (Jackson: The University Press of Mississippi, 2015); and Robert D. Sege, Benjamin S. Siegel, Council on Child Abuse and Neglect; Committee on Psychosocial Aspects of Child and Family Health, "Effective Discipline to Raise Healthy Children," *Pediatrics* 142, no. 6 (2018) 1–10, https://pediatrics.aappublications.org/content/pediatrics/142/6/e20183112.full.pdf. Leaders in Mississippi also argued that calls for the state flag to be changed should be answered with a public referendum on the flag, which resulted earlier in votes to keep it as is. See Luke Ramseth, "Mississippi Flag: Where Do Governor, Lieutenant Governor Stand on Confederate Emblem?," *Clarion Ledger*,

April 11, 2019, https://www.clarionledger.com/story/news/politics/2019/04/11/mississippi-flag-candidates-stances-removing-confederate-symbol/3415376002/.

22. Lex Talamo, "Caddo Confederate Monument Vote Close, Leaning for Removal," *Shreveport Times*, October 17, 2017, https://www.shreveporttimes.com/story/news/2017/10/17/caddo-confederate-monument-vote-close-leaning-removal/772654001/.

23. Dennis Romero and Anthony Cusumano, "Death Sentence Upheld for Dylann Roof, Who Killed 9 in South Carolina Church Shooting," NBC News, August 25, 2021, https://www.nbcnews.com/news/us-news/death-sentence-upheld-man-who-killed-9-south-carolina-church-n1277667.

24. Daniel Politi, "Dylann Roof Burns U.S. Flag, Details White Supremacist Worldview in Shocking Online Manifest," *Slate*, June 20, 2015, https://slate.com/news-and-politics/2015/06/dylann-roof-details-white-supremacist-worldview-in-shocking-online-manifesto.html.

25. See Christopher Ingraham, "How the Confederacy Lives On in the Flags of Seven Southern States," *Washington Post*, June 21, 2015, https://www.washingtonpost.com/news/wonk/wp/2015/06/21/how-the-confederacy-lives-on-in-the-flags-of-seven-southern-states/; and Rosalind Bentley, "After Dylann Roof, What's the Fate of the Confederate Flag?," *Atlanta Journal-Constitution*, January 9, 2017, https://www.ajc.com/news/crime—law/after-dylann-roof-what-the-fate-the-confederate-flag/HaCtiPvplkXOdQbn6jAhAN/.

26. Jon Schuppe, "South Carolina Gov. Nikki Haley Signs Bill Removing Confederate Flag," NBC News, July 9, 2015, https://www.nbcnews.com/storyline/confederate-flag-furor/gov-haley-sign-bill-removing-confederate-flag-n389231.

27. Charles J. Dean, "Alabama Gov. Bentley Removes Confederate Flags from Capitol Grounds," *Birmingham News*, June 24, 2015, https://www.al.com/news/2015/06/confederate_flag_removed_from.html.

28. Eric Thomas Weber, "Weber: Sometimes Heritage Does Harm," *Clarion Ledger*, June 27, 2015, https://www.academia.edu/attachments/38038257/download_file?s=work_strip.

29. Eric Thomas Weber, "What a Flag Has to Do with Justice," *Prindle Post*, July 8, 2015, https://www.prindlepost.org/2015/07/what-a-flag-has-to-do-with-justice/.

30. I sat watching student leaders debate whether to ask the university to take down the flag, with student after student acknowledging that they have never spoken to someone who had expressed the harm that the flag does to them. Two-thirds of the mostly white Associated Student Body leadership voted to ask the university to take down the flag. Next, when it came to the Confederate monument in a later meeting, the vote to move it to the cemetery on campus, out from the center of campus, was unanimous. Hadley Hitson, "Unanimous: ASB Senate Votes to Move the Monument," *Daily Mississippian*, March 6, 2019, https://thedmonline.com/unanimous-asb-senate-votes-to-move-the-monument/.

31. Alexandra Starr, "University of Mississippi Orders State Flag Removed," NPR, October 26, 2015, https://www.npr.org/sections/thetwo-way/2015/10/26/451955764/university-of-mississippi-orders-state-flag-removed.

32. Bracey Harris, "KKK Protests 'Take Down the Flag' Rally at Ole Miss," *Clarion Ledger*, October 15, 2015, https://www.clarionledger.com/story/news/2015/10/16/ole-miss-students-rally-remove-state-flag-campus/74046586/.

33. Eric Thomas Weber, "Students' Flag Request Was 'Emotional' but Courageous," *Clarion Ledger*, October 30, 2015, https://www.clarionledger.com/story/opinion/columnists/2015/10/30/students-flag-request-emotional-but-courageous/74885008/.

34. See Eric Thomas Weber, *Democracy and Leadership: On Pragmatism and Virtue* (Lanham, MD: Lexington Books, 2013); and *Uniting Mississippi: Democracy and Leadership in the South* (Jackson: University Press of Mississippi, 2015).

35. Joanna gave me permission to mention her by name.

36. Dean, "Alabama Gov. Bentley Removes Confederate Flags."

37. Michael J. Rosenfeld, "Moving a Mountain: The Extraordinary Trajectory of Same-Sex Marriage Approval in the United States," *Socius* 3 (2017): 1–22.

38. Eddie Murphy and Bruce Gowers, *Eddie Murphy "Delirious"* (Beverly Hills, CA: Entertainment Studios, 1983).

39. See for example Tim Teeman, "Why Did Matt Damon Think Calling Gay Men 'F*ggots' Was Ok?," *Daily Beast*, August 2, 2021, https://www.thedailybeast.com/why-did-it-take-matt-damons-daughter-to-stop-him-calling-gay-men-the-f-slur.

40. Kami Chavis Simmons, "Subverting Symbolism: The Matthew Shepard and James Byrd, Jr. Hate Crimes Prevention Act and Cooperative Federalism," *American Criminal Law Review* 49 (2012): 1863–1912.

41. Isaac Chotiner, "Why the Marriage-Equality Movement Succeeded," *New Yorker*, June 10, 2021, https://www.newyorker.com/news/q-and-a/sasha-issenberg-on-the-fight-for-marriage-equality.

42. I have in mind here the striking down of *Roe v. Wade*. See Nina Totenberg and Sarah McCammon, "Supreme Court Overturns Roe v. Wade, Ending Right to Abortion Upheld for Decades," NPR.org, June 24, 2022, https://www.npr.org/2022/06/24/1102305878/supreme-court-abortion-roe-v-wade-decision-overturn.

43. James Barragán, "In Roe Decision, Justice Clarence Thomas Invites New Legal Challenges to Contraception and Same Sex Marriage Rights," *Texas Tribune*, June 24, 2022, https://www.texastribune.org/2022/06/24/roe-wade-clarence-thomas-contraception-same-sex-marriage/.

44. Associated Press, "Supreme Court Won't Hear Case Involving Transgender Rights," *U.S. News and World Report*, November 1, 2021, https://www.usnews.com/news/health-news/articles/2021-11-01/supreme-court-wont-hear-case-involving-transgender-rights.

45. David Firestone, "Mississippi Votes by Wide Margin to Keep State Flag That Includes Confederate Emblem," *New York Times*, April 18, 2001, https://www.nytimes.com/2001/04/18/us/mississippi-votes-wide-margin-keep-state-flag-that-includes-confederate-emblem.html.

46. Rick Rojas, "Mississippi Voters Approve Flag with Magnolia Instead of Confederate Symbol," *New York Times*, November 4, 2020, https://www.nytimes.com/2020/11/03/us/politics/mississippi-voters-approve-flag-with-magnolia-instead-of-confederate-symbol.html.

47. Veronica Stracqualursi, "Mississippi Ratifies and Raises Its New State Flag Over the State Capitol for the First Time," CNN, January 13, 2021, https://www.cnn.com/2021/01/12/politics/mississippi-new-state-flag-flown/index.html.

48. Jake Tapper, Sara Sidner, Omar Jimenez, W. Kamau Bell, Anthony Barksdale, and Elie Honig, "Derek Chauvin Sentenced to 22-1/2 Years for George Floyd's Murder. Aired 4-5p ET," *CNN The Lead with Jake Tapper*, June 25, 2021.

49. Matt Barnum and Kalyn Belsha, "Protests, Donations, Lesson Plans: How the Education World Is Responding to George Floyd's Killing," Chalkbeat, June 2, 2020, https://www.chalkbeat.org/2020/6/2/21278591/education-schools-george-floyd-racism.

50. Elizabeth A. Harris, "In Backlash to Racial Reckoning, Conservative Publishers See Gold," *New York Times*, August 15, 2021, https://www.nytimes.com/2021/08/15/books/race-antiracism-publishing.html.

51. See Heidi Przybyla and Adam Edelman, "States Weigh a Raft of Proposed Laws to Limit Race, Sexuality Lessons in Schools," NBC News, January 28, 2022, https://www.nbcnews.com/politics/politics-news/states-weigh-raft-proposed-laws-limit-race-sexuality-lessons-schools-n1288108; Daylyn Gilbert, "Racial Reckoning withing the Classroom," *Harvard Political Review*, January 6, 2021, https://harvardpolitics.com/racial-reckoning-classroom/; Nick Anderson and Susan Svrluga, "From Slavery to Jim Crow to George Floyd: Virginia Universities Face a Long Racial Reckoning," *Washington Post*, November 26, 2021, https://www.washingtonpost.com/education/2021/11/26/virginia-universities-slavery-race-reckoning/.

52. I owe aspects of my understanding of culture to Margaret Mead and Ruth Benedict, in Ruth Benedict, *Patterns of Culture* (1934; repr., New York: Mariner Books, 2005), xiii. In Mead's preface to Benedict's book, she refers to culture as the "systematic body of learned behavior which is transmitted from parents to children." It is worth noting that different fields of study may concern themselves with different aspects or senses of the term "culture" and for their own various reasons. For example, Ralf Michaels writes in "Legal Culture" that "Legal culture stands between law and culture, with unclear borders in both directions. According to a widespread understanding, legal culture represents that cultural background of law which creates the law and which is necessary to give meaning to law." See Ralf Michaels, "Legal Culture," in *Oxford Handbook*

of European Private Law, ed. Basedow, Hopt, and Zimmermann (London: Oxford University Press, 2012), https://scholarship.law.duke.edu/cgi/viewcontent.cgi?article=3012&context=faculty_scholarship.

53. John Dewey, *Democracy and Education*, in *The Middle Works of John Dewey, 1899–1924: 1916*, ed. Jo Ann Boydston, vol. 9 (Carbondale: Southern Illinois University Press, 2008).

54. Corey Brettschneider, *When the State Speaks, What Should It Say? How Democracies Can Protect Expression and Promote Equality* (Princeton, NJ: Princeton University Press, 2012).

55. Maria Armoudian, "Where the Bucks Don't Stop," *Australasian Journal of American Studies* 37, no. 1 (2018): 25–62.

56. John Dewey, "The Future of Philosophy," in *The Later Works of John Dewey*, ed. Jo Ann Boydston, vol. 17 (Carbondale: Southern Illinois University Press, 2008), 466–70, LW.17.467.

57. Alain Locke, "The Ethics of Culture," in *The Philosophy of Alain Locke: Harlem Renaissance and Beyond*, ed. Leonard Harris (Philadelphia: Temple University Press, 1989), 435–41, 435.

58. In "Frontiers of Culture," he acknowledges that he has come to reevaluate his sense of culture as something that is more expansive, something that all people experience as part of their daily lives. There, he writes that "I, too, confess that at one time of my life I may have been guilty of thinking of culture as cake contrasted with bread. Now I know better. Real, essential culture is baked into our daily bread or else it isn't truly culture." See Alain Locke, "Frontiers of Culture," in *The Philosophy of Alain Locke: Harlem Renaissance and Beyond*, ed. Leonard Harris (Philadelphia: Temple University Press, 1989), 229–36, 230–31.

59. Arnold Rampersad, "The Book That Launched the Harlem Renaissance," *Journal of Blacks in Higher Education* 38 (Winter 2002–2003): 87–91.

60. Alaine Locke, "The Ethics of Culture," 435–36.

61. For many years teaching students how to write, it bothered me to see the use of "their," a plural pronoun, associated with "a person," a singular. Other languages make use of a gender-neutral singular pronoun, however, which is quite useful, and matters of gender today have called for some rethinking of the matter. At the same time, the *Oxford English Dictionary* notes a use of the "singular 'they'" that dates back to 1375. As such, there is significant precedent for the use of "A person . . . they." See Dennis Baron, "A Brief History of the Singular 'They,'" [blogpost] Oxford English Dictionary, September 4, 2018, https://public.oed.com/blog/a-brief-history-of-singular-they/. Others have endorsed such usage, such as *Merriam-Webster's Dictionary* and the style guide of the American Psychological Association. See "Singular 'They,'" Merriam-Webster.com, September 2019, https://www.merriam-webster.com/words-at-play/singular-nonbinary-they; and "Singular 'They,'" *APA Publication Manual*, 7th. ed., 2019, Section 4.18.

62. John Rawls, *A Theory of Justice* (Cambridge, MA: Harvard University Press, 1971), 101.

63. Rawls, *Theory*, 440. Emphasis added.

64. John Rawls, *Political Liberalism* (New York: Columbia University Press, 1996).

65. Joshua Forstenzer, "Deweyan Democracy, Robert Talisse, and the Fact of Reasonable Pluralism," *Transactions of the Charles S. Peirce Society* 53, no. 4 (2017): 553–78, 556.

66. An example of reconciliation in religious conflict could be useful here, such as in regard to the saying "spare the rod, spoil the child," a simplification of biblical scripture. The thought for many is that it means that one must hit one's children to avoid spoiling them. The question of which rod is at issue reveals the insight that it is the shepherd's rod. The good shepherd does not punish or seek to hurt one's sheep, but rather to tap them to give direction. The latter interpretation is nonviolent and the former is violent. Assuming that one must dismiss the scripture if one is a Christian advocate for nonviolence misses the incredible potential variety of interpretations of doctrines. Assuming irreconcilability could well indicate a lack of imagination, a cynicism concerning the potential for democracy to yield solutions to conflicts where people could not see them before.

67. I am indebted to Tibor Solymosi for calling my attention to the tapestry metaphor, which we can find in a number of writings, including Larry Hickman's foreword to a work on John Dewey and Chinese education. See Larry A. Hickman, foreword to *John Dewey and Chinese Education*, ed. ZHANG Huajun and Jim GARRISON (Boston: Brill, 2022), ix–xi, xi. Capitalization here is listed as in the original.

68. See Josh Corngold, "John Dewey, Public School Reform, and the Narrowing of Educational Aims," *Philosophy of Education* (2010): 237–40; Pamela Bolotin Joseph, Nancy Stewart Green, Edward R. Mikel, and Mark A Windschitl, "Narrowing the Curriculum," ch. 2 in *Cultures of Curriculum*, 2nd ed., ed. Pamela Bolotin Joseph (New York: Routledge, 2011), 36–54; and Kelly V. King and Sasha Zucker, "Curriculum Narrowing: Policy Report," Harcourt (San Antonio, TX: Harcourt Assessment, 2005), http://images.pearsonclinical.com/images/PDF/assessmentReports/CurriculumNarrowing.pdf.

69. See M. Victoria Costa, "Rawlsian Civic Education: Political Not Minimal," *Journal of Applied Philosophy* 21 (2004): 1–14; J. S. Johnston, "Rawls's Kantian Educational Theory," *Educational Theory* 55 (2005): 200–18; and Eric Thomas Weber, "Rawls, Dewey, and Education," *Human Studies* 31 (2008): 361–82. Costa writes that Rawls "advocates a rather minimal conception of civic education" (1) on which her theorizing expands, and Johnston writes that Rawls "had neither a robust nor a coherent theory of education" (204).

70. Violet M. Williams, *Ten Little Nigger Boys* (London: Raphael Tuck and Sons, 1956), 1, 3, 9. A variety of editions exists, including one from 1866.

71. Derek McCulloch, "TEN LITTLE NIGGER BOYS," YouTube video, posted by "EMGColonel," September 18, 2017, https://www.youtube.com/watch?v=vioBurOEefo&t=83s. Original post was removed. This link here is to the latest

posting of the music. If this one is removed again, a search on the name in YouTube is likely to find the music posted elsewhere.

72. Helen Jill Fletcher and Janet P. D'Amato, *10 Little Indians: A Counting Song and Counting Book Record* (A Peter Pan Book and Record, 1960).

73. Steven M. Young, "Beyond Neutrality," *University of Toronto Law Journal* 49 (1999): 151–65, 156.

74. Ibid., 159.

75. Thomas E. Hill, Jr. "Servility and Self-Respect," *Monist* 57, no. 1 (1973): 87–104.

76. Polycarp Ikuenobe, "Culture of Racism, Self-Respect, and Blameworthiness," *Public Affairs Quarterly* 18, no. 1 (2004): 27–55.

77. Barbara Ehrenreich, *Bright-Sided* (New York: Metropolitan Books, 2009).

78. Today, "average annual starting salaries of our recent graduates range from $105,000 and $122,000," according to the Careers in Pharmacy page of the program. "Careers in Pharmacy," University of Mississippi, https://pharmacy.olemiss.edu/careers-in-pharmacy/.

79. As I clarify in the pages to come, I borrow the term "stoic pragmatism" from John Lachs's book by the same name. When I refer in this book to the philosophical tradition known as Pragmatism, I capitalize the name, unless it is in quoted material or in Lachs's terminology. See John Lachs, *Stoic Pragmatism* (Bloomington: Indiana University Press, 2012).

80. Paul Ryan, "The War on Poverty: 50 Years Later: A House Budget Committee Report," Washington, DC: House Budget Committee, 2014.

81. Anna Maria Santiago, "Fifty Years Later: From a War on Poverty to a War on the Poor," *Social Problems* 62 (2015): 2–14.

82. John Donne, "No Man Is an Island," in "Preface," *Devotions Upon Emergent Occasions and Death's Duel* (New York: Vintage Press, 1999), xvii.

83. John Lachs has long been a strong advocate for liberty, while at the same time always seeing the interconnectedness of human beings. See John Lachs, *Intermediate Man* (Indianapolis, IN: Hackett, 1981) and John Lachs, *Freedom and Limits* (New York: Fordham University Press, 2014). See also Brian Miller and Mike Lapham, *The Self-Made Myth: And the Truth about How Government Helps Individuals and Business Succeed* (San Francisco: Berrett-Kochler Publishers, 2012). Finally, see also Ester Bloom, "The Self-Made Man Is a Myth, Arnold Schwazenegger Tells Students," CNBC.com, May 15, 2017, https://www.cnbc.com/2017/05/15/arnold-schwarzenegger-channels-elizabeth-warren-in-u-of-houston-speech.html.

84. Craig Cruse and David Powers, "Estimating School District Poverty with Free and Reduced-Priced Lunch Data," US Census Bureau, Small Area Estimates Branch, 2006, https://www.census.gov/library/working-papers/2006/demo/cruse-01.html.

85. See Amy Ellen Schwartz and Michah W. Robart, "Let Them Eat Lunch: The Impact of Universal Free Meals on Student Performance," Syracuse University Center for Policy Research, 235 (2017), https://surface.syr.edu/cpr/235.

86. Robert Nozick, *Anarchy, State, and Utopia* (1974; repr., New York: Basic Books, 2013).

87. "Heights and Views," National Capital Planning Commission, https://www.ncpc.gov/topics/heights/.

88. John Dewey, "The Basic Values and Loyalties of Democracy," in *America's Public Philosopher: Essays on Social Justice, Economics, Education, and the Future of Democracy* (New York: Columbia University Press, 2021), 57–58.

89. Stone, *Perilous Times: Free Speech in Wartime, From the Sedition Act of 1798 to the War on Terrorism*.

90. Lachs, *Stoic Pragmatism*.

91. Fareed Zakaria, "The Downward Path of Upward Mobility," *Washington Post*, November 9, 2011, https://www.washingtonpost.com/opinions/the-downward-path-of-upward-mobility/2011/11/09/gIQAegpS6M_story.html.

92. John Dewey, "Creative Democracy—The Task Before Us," in *America's Public Philosopher*, ed. Eric Thomas Weber (New York: Columbia University Press, 2021), 62.

93. Joel Westheimer, *What Kind of Citizen? Educating Our Children for the Common Good* (New York: Teachers College Press, 2015).

Chapter 1

1. David Walker, *Appeal to the Coloured Citizens of the World*, ed. Peter Hinks (1829; repr., University Park, PA: Pennsylvania State University Press, 2000).

2. Derrick Bell, *Silent Covenants: Brown v. Board of Education and the Unfulfilled Hopes for Racial Reform* (New York: Oxford University Press, 2005).

3. Derrick Bell, *Faces at the Bottom of the Well: The Permanence of Racism* (New York: Basic Books, 1993).

4. Bell's *Silent Covenants* makes the most extensive case for this. In addition, Elizabeth Anderson has more recently argued in favor of integration as a moral imperative, though recognizing that *Brown*, while well intended in her view, was indeed insufficient to achieve integrated communities. Elizabeth Anderson, *The Imperative of Integration* (Princeton, NJ: Princeton University Press, 2010).

5. Another version of this outlook gives up on the meaningfulness of justice in worldly affairs. Such a religious response sees justice as something only possible in the afterlife, as divine justice.

6. Martin Luther King Jr., "Love, Law, and Civil Disobedience," in *The Essential Writings and Speeches of Martin Luther King, Jr.*, ed. James M. Washington (New York: HarperCollins, 1986), 43–53, 52. The phrase is believed to have originated from abolitionist preacher Theodore Parker, according to John Haynes Holmes, "Salute to Montgomery," *Liberation* 1, no. 10 (1956): 5. I am indebted for this latter reference to Clayborn Carson, senior ed., *The Papers of*

Martin Luther King, Jr., Volume 3: Birth of a New Age (Los Angeles: University of California Press, 1997), 486.

7. Martin Luther King, Jr. "Letter from a Birmingham Jail," in *Why We Can't Wait* (New York: Signet Classics, 1963), 77–100.

8. See editors, "The 2014 Race Card: Democratic Appeals to Racial Division Are Worse than Ever," *Wall Street Journal*, October 26, 2014, http://www.wsj.com/articles/the-2014-race-card-1414192776; and Tanya Young Williams, "I'm Tired of Talking about Racism and a Judge's Bid to Abolish the Grand Jury," *Huffington Post*, December 12, 2014, http://www.huffingtonpost.com/tanya-young-williams/im-tired-of-talking-about_b_6304140.html.

9. The Sentencing Project, *Report of the Sentencing Project to the United Nations Human Rights Committee: Regarding Racial Disparities in the United States Criminal Justice System* (Washington, DC: The Sentencing Project, August 2013), http://sentencingproject.org/doc/publications/rd_ICCPR%20Race%20and%20Justice%20Shadow%20Report.pdf.

10. The Sentencing Project, "New Report Finds Imprisonment Rate of Black Men Has Fallen by Nearly 50% Since 2000, but Pushback Threatens Continued Progress," news release, SentencingProject.org, October 11, 2023, https://www.sentencingproject.org/press-releases/new-report-finds-imprisonment-rate-of-black-men-has-fallen-by-nearly-50-since-2000-but-pushback-threatens-continued-progress/.

11. Ibid.

12. As cited in Carlton Waterhouse, "Avoiding Another Step in a Series of Unfortunate Legal Events," *Boston College Third World Law Journal* 26, no. 2 (2006): 207–65, 208.

13. Nirupama Rao, "Mahatma Gandhi's 'Light' Guided Martin Luther King, Jr.," *Politico*, March 7, 2013, http://www.politico.com/story/2013/03/mahatma-gandhis-lightguided-martin-luther-king-jr-88581.html.

14. Sharon Lerner, "A School District That Was Never Desegregated," *Atlantic*, February 5, 2015, http://www.theatlantic.com/education/archive/2015/02/a-school-district-that-was-never-desegregated/385184/.

15. Emily Richmond, "Schools Are More Segregated Today than During the Late 1960s," *Atlantic*, June 11, 2012, http://www.theatlantic.com/national/archive/2012/06/schools-are-more-segregated-today-than-during-the-late-1960s/258348/.

16. David Remnick, "Charleston and the Age of Obama," *New Yorker*, June 19, 2015, http://www.newyorker.com/news/daily-comment/charleston-and-the-age-of-obama.

17. Michelle Alexander, *The New Jim Crow* (New York: The New Press, 2012).

18. John Dewey, "Democracy Is Radical," in *The Later Works of John Dewey*, vol. 11 (1937; repr., Carbondale: Southern Illinois University, 1987), 296–99.

19. Martin Luther King Jr., *Stride Toward Freedom: The Montgomery Story* (1958; repr., New York: Beacon Press, 1986), 39.

20. See Anna R. Schechter and Jon Schuppe, "Confederate Flag Rally Tests a Diminished Ku Klux Klan," MSNBC.com, July 18, 2015, http://www.msnbc.com/msnbc/confederate-flag-rally-tests-diminished-ku-klux-klan; Eric Thomas Weber, "What a Flag Has to Do with Justice," *Prindle Post*, July 8, 2015, http://www.prindlepost.org/2015/07/what-a-flag-hasto-do-with-justice/; Therese Apel, "Deryl Dedmon, Two Others Sentenced from 7-50 Years in Hate Crime," *Clarion Ledger*, February 12, 2015, http://www.clarionledger.com/story/news/2015/02/10/deryl-dedmon-two-others-to-be-sentenced-in-hate-crime-tuesday/23166397/; and Simon McCormack, "Dylann Roof Charged with 9 Counts of Murder," *Huffington Post*, June 19, 2015, http://www.huffingtonpost.com/2015/06/19/dylan-roof-confesses_n_7620314.html.

21. King, "Love, Law, and Civil Disobedience," 52.

22. John Dewey, *A Common Faith* (1933; repr., New Haven, CT: Yale University Press, 2013).

23. Gideon Yaffe, "More on 'Ought' Implies 'Can' and the Principle of Alternate Possibilities," *Midwest Studies in Philosophy* 29 (2005): 307–12.

24. John Lachs, *Stoic Pragmatism* (Bloomington: Indiana University Press, 2013).

25. Karl Popper, *The Open Society and Its Enemies* (Princeton, NJ: Princeton University Press, 2013).

26. See Martin Gilens and Benjamin I. Page, "Testing Theories of American Politics: Elites, Interest Groups, and Average Citizens," *Perspectives on Politics* 12, no. 3 (2014): 564–81; and Zachary Davies Boren, "The US Is an Oligarchy, Study Concludes," *Telegraph (UK)*, April 16, 2014, http://www.telegraph.co.uk/news/worldnews/northamerica/usa/10769041/The-US-is-an-oligarchy-study-concludes.html.

27. He even calls it permissible for them to tell a profound, indeed a noble, lie, calling themselves to believe it too. That kind of leadership is most clearly unchecked, with the protection of deception and secrecy.

28. Mount Vernon Ladies' Association, "Ten Facts about Washington and Slavery," http://www.mountvernon.org/george-washington/slavery/ten-facts-about-washington-slavery/.

29. As in Gilens and Page, but see also Nicholas Confessore, "Koch Brothers' Budget of $889 Million for 2016 Is on Par with Both Parties' Spending," *New York Times*, January 27, 2015, A1; and Bailey Williams, "Sen. Bernie Sanders Calls U.S. Politics 'Oligarchy'; Considers Run in 2016," Medill News Service—United Press International, March 9, 2015, http://www.upi.com/Top_News/US/2015/03/09/Sen-Bernie-Sanders-calls-US-politics-oligarchy-considers-run-in-2016/8711425927237/.

30. John Dewey and James Tufts, *Ethics (1908)*, in *The Collected Works of John Dewey, The Middle Works*, ed. Jo Ann Boydston, vol. 5 (Carbondale: Southern Illinois University Carbondale, 1978), 466.

31. Eric Thomas Weber, *Uniting Mississippi: Democracy and Leadership in the South* (Jackson: University Press of Mississippi, 2015).

32. Terry Frieden, "Mississippi Town Sued over 'School-to-Prison Pipeline,'" CNN, October, 26, 2012, http://www.cnn.com/2012/10/24/justice/mississippi-civil-rights-lawsuit/.

33. Plato, *Republic*, Book V, 460c.

34. I am thinking of Peter Singer and his outlook on exceptional cases of profound medical problems that produce deep suffering. See Helga Kuhse and Peter Singer, "Debate: Severely Handicapped Newborns," *Law, Medicine, and Healthcare* 14, no. 3–4 (1986): 149–53. While there are some interesting debates today, note that Plato believed it justifiable to terminate the lives of healthy infants if they were born to parents who were "inferior" to those he called "golden" or "silver" citizens of the good city in the *Republic*, Book V, 460c.

35. Michael Levin, "Why Homosexuality Is Abnormal," *Monist* 67 (1984): 251–83.

36. John Lachs, "Human Natures," *Proceedings and Addresses of the American Philosophical Association* 63, no. 7 (1990): 29–39.

37. Ray Sanchez and Ed Payne, "Charleston Church Shooting: Who Is Dylann Roof?" CNN.com, June 19, 2015, http://www.cnn.com/2015/06/19/us/charleston-church-shooting-suspect/.

38. Lewis E. Lehrman, *Lincoln at Peoria, The Turning Point: Getting Right with the Declaration of Independence* (Mechanicsburg, PA: Stackpole Books, 2008).

39. Of course, not all evolution is progress, but can simply sometimes be cumulative change.

40. Robert C. Neville, *The Highroad Around Modernism* (Albany: State University of New York Press, 1992), 25.

41. Ibid.

42. Peter Manicas's review of Joseph Brent's *Charles Sanders Peirce: A Life* sums up the point succinctly. See Peter Manicas, "*Charles Sanders Peirce: A Life* (Review)," *Biography* 17, no. 1 (1994): 63–66, 64. For more detail, see Joseph Brent, *Charles Sanders Peirce: A Life* (Bloomington: Indiana University Press, 1998), especially the introduction, 26–81.

43. Charles Sanders Peirce, "Some Consequences of Four Incapacities," in *The Collected Papers of Charles Sanders Peirce*, ed. Charles Hartshorne and Paul Weiss (Cambridge, MA: Harvard University Press, 1932–1935), vol. 5, standard notation: CP.5.265.3.

44. For a few, see CP.1.70, CP.2.148, and CP.2.761. It is worth noting that Peirce often said he was correcting Laplace's errors, where the latter's theory is "false and harmful" (CP.2.761).

45. Pierre Simon Laplace, *Théorie Analytique des Probabilités* (Paris: Imprimerie Royale, 1847).

46. See also Robert Burch, "Charles Sanders Peirce," *Stanford Encyclopedia of Philosophy*, 2010, http://plato.stanford.edu/entries/peirce/, especially section 7. See

also "Charles Sanders Peirce—Biography," The European Graduate School, Library, Biography, http://www.egs.edu/library/charles-sanders-peirce/biography/. Burch explains Peirce's contributions in some depth, and the European Graduate School's library biography of Peirce refers to him as "one of the founders of statistics."

47. Charles S. Peirce, "The Fixation of Belief," *Popular Science Monthly* 12 (November 1877): 1–15, CP.5.384n.

48. Peirce add this footnote: "Fate means merely that which is sure to come true, and can nohow be avoided. It is a superstition to suppose that a certain sort of events are ever fated, and it is another to suppose that the word fate can never be freed from its superstitious taint. We are all fated to die."

49. Charles S. Peirce, "How to Make Our Ideas Clear," *Popular Science Monthly* 12 (January 1878): 286–302, CP.5.407. Emphasis in the original.

50. Charles S. Peirce, "Truth," ch. 4 in *The Collected Papers,* vol. 5, *Pragmatism and Pragmaticism, Book 3, Unpublished Papers*, ed. Charles Hartshorne and Paul Weiss (Cambridge, MA: Harvard University Press, 1934), CP.5.565.

51. Ibid., CP.5.566. Emphasis in the original.

52. James H. Jones, *Bad Blood: The Tuskegee Syphilis Experiment, New and Expanded Edition* (New York: The Free Press, 1993).

53. See Neil C. Manson and Onora O'Neill, *Rethinking Informed Consent in Bioethics* (New York: Cambridge University Press, 2007); and Susanne Uusitalo and Barbara Broers, "Rethinking Informed Consent in Research on Heroin-Assisted Treatment," *Bioethics* 29, no. 7 (2015): 462–69.

54. Charles S. Peirce, "Some Consequences of Four Incapacities," *Journal of Speculative Philosophy* 2, no. 3 (1868): 140–57, CP.5.265.2. Emphasis in original.

55. Eyder Peralta, "PA Judge Sentenced to 28 Years in Massive Juvenile Justice Bribery Scandal," NPR.org, August 11, 2011, http://www.npr.org/sections/thetwo-way/2011/08/11/139536686/pa-judge-sentenced-to-28-years-in-massive-juvenile-justice-bribery-scandal.

56. I have in mind, of course, the 45th president of the United States. See Norman Eisen and Fred Wertheimer, "Finally, a Road Map to Hold Trump Accountable," CNN.com, March 30, 2022, https://www.cnn.com/2022/03/30/opinions/trump-road-map-accountability-january-6-eisen-wertheimer/index.html; Bill McCann, "Will 'Teflon Don' Ever Be Held Accountable," *Austin-American Statesman*, April 7, 2022, https://www.statesman.com/story/news/2022/04/07/opinion-donald-trump-ever-held-accountable/9472134002/; Jason Lemon, "Trump Indictment in Georgia Expected Before DOJ Charges," *Newsweek*, July 21, 2022, https://www.newsweek.com/donald-trump-georgia-indictment-prediction-laurence-tribe-1726833; and Harper Neidig and Rebecca Beitsch, "DOJ Has Multiple Possible Paths to Trump Indictment," *The Hill*, July 27, 2022, https://thehill.com/homenews/house/3576858-doj-has-multiple-possible-paths-to-trump-indictment-heres-what-it-could-look-like/.

57. John Feinblatt, "A Bad Week for the NRA," *Huffington Post*, October 3, 2014, http://www.huffingtonpost.com/john-feinblatt/a-bad-week-for-the-nra_b_5929188.html.

58. Ta-Nehisi Coates, "The Case for Reparations," *Atlantic*, June 2014, http://www.theatlantic.com/features/archive/2014/05/the-case-for-reparations/361631/.

59. Indeed, in 2021, the state of Mississippi adopted the "In God We Trust" flag, "The New Magnolia," taking down the former flag bearing the Confederate Battle flag emblem in its canton. This occurred in the wake of the murder of George Floyd.

Chapter 2

1. Percy Bysshe Shelley, "A Defence of Poetry," in *English Essays: Sidney to Macaulay*, vol. 27 of *The Harvard Classics*, ed. Charles W. Eliot (New York: P.F. Collier & Son, 1909–1914), 345–77, 377.

2. For example, we can see an early version of this tendency in Rawls's "Two Concepts of Rules" essay, which has inspired the view we call "rule utilitarianism"—an outlook that aims to reconcile the importance of utilitarianism and deontological ethics as different elements in the justification of rules and of practices followed within such rules. John Rawls, "Two Concepts of Rules," *Philosophical Review* 64, no. 1 (1955): 3–32.

3. Robert Nozick, *Anarchy, State, and Utopia* (New York: Basic Books, 1974), 160–64.

4. Dana Milbank, "Doctor of Divisiveness," *Washington Post*, May 29, 2014, A2. Milbank refers in particular to Ben Carson.

5. Andrew Kernohan, *Liberalism, Equality, and Cultural Oppression* (New York: Cambridge University Press, 1998).

6. For example, I can agree with Kernohan when he claims that "The advocacy state, unlike the neutral state, can engage in the project of cultural reform," while wondering about how far-reaching and specific he means to be when he writes that "an advocacy state should oppose advertising that represents women in positions subordinate to men" (101). In fairness, he probably means this in the sense of women having lesser moral worth, but it can be very difficult to decide which communications imply a differential moral worth of the people alluded to or included in the communication. Advertising featuring a male boss over a female employee represents a woman in a position subordinate to a man, but not necessarily making a claim about their differential moral worth. On the other hand, if one were never to see women as bosses, doctors, or other professionals, there could be said to be an aggregate harm of the kind that Kernohan points out. The worries that one might reasonably have about Kernohan's statement include concern over how one might carry out the "opposition" he calls for. I return to the matter of free speech in chapter 7.

7. John Rawls, *A Theory of Justice* (Cambridge, MA: Harvard University Press, 1999), 44.

8. Peter Singer, "Famine, Affluence, and Morality," *Philosophy and Public Affairs* 1, no. 3 (1972): 229–43.

9. I am indebted to David Hildebrand, "Does Every Theory Deserve a Hearing?," *Southern Journal of Philosophy* 44, no. 2 (2006): 217–36.

10. Richard Rorty, *Philosophy and Social Hope* (New York: Penguin Books, 1999), 77.

11. Rawls noted explicitly his debt to Nelson Goodman for the theory underlying reflective equilibrium, in *Theory*, 18. He cited Nelson Goodman, *Fact, Fiction, and Forecast* (Cambridge, MA: Harvard University Press, 1955), 65–68. Attending to the philosophy of culture, Morton White has recently clarified Goodman's role in the tradition of a pragmatic philosophy of culture, in which Dewey was a great inspiration. See Morton White, *A Philosophy of Culture: The Scope of Holistic Pragmatism* (Princeton, NJ: Princeton University Press, 2002), especially ch. 7.

12. A number of critics have made this point clear, such as Charles W. Mills, "Retrieving Rawls for Racial Justice? A Critique of Tommie Shelby," *Critical Philosophy of Race* 1, no. 1 (2013): 1–27. Mills notes Elizabeth Anderson's abandonment of "ideal theory," a label capturing Rawls's theory of justice. See Elizabeth Anderson, *The Imperative of Integration* (Princeton, NJ: Princeton University Press, 2010). Both Mills and Anderson see in Rawls and in most scholarship that draws on Rawls a troubling dearth of consideration about issues of race in justice.

13. Gerald Gaus, "Should Philosophers 'Apply Ethics'? By 'Applying Ethics,' Do Philosophers Actually Succeed in Corrupting Philosophy?," *Think* (Spring 2005): 63–67.

14. A remarkable exception is Christine Korsgaard's account of Kant, one of the most attractive available on this score. Sounding pragmatic, Korsgaard writes, "Realism, I argue, is a reactive position that arises in response to almost every attempt to give a substantive explanation of morality. It results from the realist's belief that such explanations inevitably reduce moral phenomena to natural phenomena. I trace this belief and the essence of realism to a view about the nature of concepts—that it is the function of all concepts to describe reality. Constructivism [, which she defends,] may be understood as the alternative view that a normative concept refers schematically to the solution to a practical problem." See Christine M. Korsgaard, "Realism and Constructivism in Twentieth-Century Moral Philosophy," in *Philosophy in America at the Turn of the Century*, ed. Robert Audi (APA Centennial Supplement "Journal of Philosophical Research," 2003), 99–122, 99.

15. Richard Rorty, "The Priority of Democracy to Philosophy," in *Objectivity, Relativism, and Truth: Philosophical Papers*, vol. 1 (1991; repr., New York: Cambridge University Press, 2008), 175–96, 175.

16. This is according to the journal's Web site, http://www.journalof philosophy.org/generalinfo.html.

17. William James, *The Principles of Psychology*, vols. 1 and 2 (1890; repr., New York: Dover Publications, 1950).

18. John Dewey, "The Reflex Arc Concept in Psychology," *Psychological Review* 3, no. 4 (1896): 357–70.

19. John Dewey, *Freedom and Culture*, in *The Collected Works of John Dewey, The Later Works*, ed. Jo Ann Boydston, vol. 13 (Carbondale: Southern Illinois University Press, 2008), 79.

20. Beyond Rorty, many others have pointed this out. For one example, see Morton White, *A Philosophy of Culture*.

21. Richard Rorty, *Philosophy as Cultural Politics: Philosophical Papers*, vol. 4 (New York: Cambridge University Press, 2007).

22. John Dewey, *Experience and Nature*, in *The Collected Works of John Dewey, The Later Works*, ed. Jo Ann Boydston, vol. 1 (1925; repr., Carbondale: Southern Illinois University Press, 2008).

23. John Dewey, "The Future of Philosophy," an address delivered to the Graduate Department of Philosophy, Columbia University, New York, NY, November 13, 1947, in *The Collected Works of John Dewey, The Later Works*, ed. Jo Ann Boydston, vol. 17 (Carbondale: Southern Illinois University Press, 1990), 467.

24. See Eric Thomas Weber, "Lessons from America's Public Philosopher," *Journal of Speculative Philosophy* 29, no. 1 (2015): 118–35; and John Dewey, *America's Public Philosopher: Essays on Social Justice, Economics, Education, and the Future of Democracy*, ed. Eric Thomas Weber (New York: Columbia University Press, 2021).

25. See Lauren Swayne Barthold, "Rorty, Religion, and the Public-Private Distinction," *Philosophy and Social Criticism* 38, no. 8 (2012): 861–78.

26. Rorty devoted the fourth collection of essays to this theme. See Rorty, *Philosophy as Cultural Politics*.

27. This example, famous in the tradition, comes from W. V. O. Quine. See Willard Van Orman Quine, *Word and Object* (Cambridge, MA: MIT Press, 1960), 29. Quine writes, "The utterances first and most surely translated in such a case are ones keyed to present events that are conspicuous to the linguist and his informant. A rabbit scurries by, the native says 'Gavagai,' and the linguist notes down the sentence 'Rabbit' (or 'Lo, a rabbit') as tentative translation, subject to testing in further cases."

28. See Henry T. Edmonson III, *John Dewey and the Decline of American Education* (Wilmington, DE: ISI Books, 2006). For the latter case I have in mind some people's reasons for homeschooling—to avoid public schools' cultural influence. See Shane Ralston, "A Deweyan Justification for Homeschooling," ch. 5 in *John Dewey's Great Debates—Reconstructed* (Charlotte, NC: Information Age Publishing, 2011), 73–86.

29. Ralston, "A Deweyan Justification for Homeschooling."

30. Richard Rorty, "Rationality and Cultural Difference," in *Truth and Progress: Philosophical Papers*, vol. 3 (New York: Cambridge University Press, 1998),

186–201. The piece was originally published in 1992 in vol. 42 of *Philosophy East and West*.

31. Ibid., 186–87.

32. Ibid., 188–89.

33. Rorty, "Rationality and Cultural Difference," 190.

34. Ibid., 189.

35. Ibid., 193.

36. Timm Triplett, "Rorty's Critique of Foundationalism," *Philosophical Studies* 52, no. 1 (1987): 115–29.

37. Larry A. Hickman, *John Dewey's Pragmatic Technology* (Bloomington: Indiana University Press, 1990), 72.

38. Ibid.

39. Singer, "Famine, Affluence, and Morality." In this essay, Singer admits that it may be unfeasible to offer a universally convincing account of why it is terrible for vast numbers of people to starve to death unnecessarily, but he thinks that assuming it to be a bad thing is not at all unreasonable.

40. Alison Avery et al., "America's Changing Attitudes toward Homosexuality, Civil Unions, and Same-Gender Marriage: 1977–2004," *Social Work* 52, no. 1 (2007): 71–79.

41. Rorty, "Rationality and Cultural Difference," 192–93, emphasis added.

42. Shane Ralston, "Can Pragmatists Be Institutionalists? John Dewey Joins the Non-ideal/Ideal Theory Debate," *Human Studies* 33, no. 1 (2010): 65–84.

43. Richard Rorty, "Human Rights, Rationality, and Sentimentality," in *Truth and Progress: Philosophical Papers*, vol. 3 (New York: Cambridge University Press, 1998), 167–85.

44. Rorty, "Rationality and Cultural Difference," 192.

45. See Charles S. Peirce, "The Fixation of Belief," in *The Essential Peirce: Selected Philosophical Writings*, ed. Nathan Houser and Christian Kloesel (1877; repr., Indianapolis: Indiana University Press, 1992), 109–23. See also John Dewey, *Logic: The Theory of Inquiry*, in *The Collected Works of John Dewey, The Later Works*, ed. Jo Ann Boydston, vol. 12 (1938; repr., Carbondale: Southern Illinois University Press, 1986).

46. John Rawls, *The Law of Peoples* (Cambridge, MA: Harvard University Press, 2001).

47. Rorty composed this essay for presentation at the Indian Institute for Philosophy at Mount Abu before it was published in *Philosophy East and West*. This explains his references to America and India here.

48. Rorty, "Rationality and Cultural Difference," 201.

49. Rorty, "Human Rights, Rationality, and Sentimentality."

50. It is worth noting that concern for animals and criticism of factory farming are gaining support, but even with such growing sympathy for animals, they are treated differently from human beings nonetheless. Whether or not we ought to treat chickens humanely, we do not enter into contracts with them. At

the same time, with good reason, human activists and lawyers come to represent animals and other non-human agents or entities, seeking to act on and advocate for their best interests.

51. See Charles Darwin, *The Descent of Man* (New York: Penguin Classics, 2004) and Geoffrey M. Hodgson, "The Evolution of Morality and the End of Economic Man," *Journal of Evolutionary Economics* 24 (2014): 83–106.

52. John Lachs, "Leaving Others Alone," *Journal of Speculative Philosophy* 18, no. 4 (2004): 261–72.

53. Harper Lee, *To Kill a Mockingbird* (New York: Harper Perennial, 2002); Toni Morrison, *The Bluest Eye* (New York: Random House, 2007); and Anne Frank, *The Diary of a Young Girl* (Garden City, NY: Doubleday, 1952).

54. Here we have a chance to answer those who ask whether Pragmatist ethics is essentially utilitarian. If utilitarianism in general denies the importance of special relationships, such as in prioritizing a slight increase in my child's happiness over a larger increase to another person's happiness, then we can say that Pragmatists are not utilitarian in that way. In at least many versions of utilitarianism, it is important to fight the force of one's emotional inclinations to prioritize one's loved ones, denying the moral force of sentiments and relationships. Unlike that feature of utilitarianism or related emphasis on reason in the dismissal of emotion in deontology, Pragmatism sees emotions as part of who we are, and elements of ourselves that we can condition. Just as we can condition our reason to function better than it does without education, the same can be said of our emotions. Both are important, as both are part of who and what we are as human beings.

55. Rorty, "Rationality and Cultural Difference," 184–85.

56. John Rawls, *Political Liberalism* (New York: Columbia University Press, 1996), 100–1.

57. Amanda Frost, "Keeping Up Appearances: A Process-Oriented Approach to Judicial Recusal," *University of Kansas Law Review* 53 (2004): 531–94.

58. John Dewey, "Creative Democracy—The Task Before Us." In *America's Public Philosopher*, ed. Eric Thomas Weber, 59–65 (New York: Columbia University Press, 2021). Also published in the standard edition of *The Collected Works of John Dewey* in LW.14.224–31, 227.

59. I am grateful to my colleague and sometimes editor Tibor Solymosi for pointing out here that in Rorty's hard distinction between public and private, he appears especially Western, as China emphasizes privacy considerably less than do people in the United States. When they do, furthermore, social harmony is typically considered more important than individual rights. See Luisa Tam, "Why Privacy Is an Alien Concept in Chinese Culture," *South China Morning Post*, April 2, 2018, https://www.scmp.com/news/hong-kong/article/2139946/why-privacy-alien-concept-chinese-culture.

60. John Rawls, "Kantian Constructivism in Moral Theory," *Journal of Philosophy* 77, no. 9 (1980): 515–72. Republished in *John Rawls: Collected Papers*, 347.

61. In the introduction, he asks, "How is it possible that deeply opposed though reasonable comprehensive doctrines may live together and all affirm the political conception of a constitutional regime?" Rawls, *Political Liberalism*, xx. I must point out a dissatisfaction with how Rawls thought of political philosophy and stability. In *Justice as Fairness: A Restatement*, he points to the Federalist Papers as an example of political conflict leading to political philosophy, the purpose for which, he says, is political stability. Yet, as Rawls points out himself, the tension in the Federalist Papers about the issue of slavery, yielding philosophical debate, failed to generate the constitutional stability that would have avoided a Civil War. The end of the war created stability, of course, though as a former citizen of the state of Mississippi, I can attest to the lingering animosities that remain over compulsion to remain in the Union. What may be political stability today is accompanied by deeply troubling cultural instabilities and divisions, which, I argue in *Uniting Mississippi*, are sources of some of the state's deepest moral difficulties. Most look with reverence on the Federalist Papers, and with much good reason, but the nation's founding might be worth considering as a failure of philosophy to resolve conflicts that were and remain at the heart of the country's cultural sources of injustice. See John Rawls, *Justice as Fairness: A Restatement* (Cambridge, MA: Harvard University Press, 2001) and Eric Thomas Weber, *Uniting Mississippi: Democracy and Leadership in the South* (Jackson: University Press of Mississippi, 2015).

62. Russ Shafer-Landau, *Moral Realism: A Defense* (New York: Oxford University Press, 2003).

63. Shadee Ashtari, "KKK Leader Disputes Hate Group Label: 'We're a Christian Organization,'" *Huffington Post*, March 21, 2014, http://www.huffingtonpost.com/2014/03/21/virginia-kkk-fliers_n_5008647.html.

64. French journalist Paul Guihard, for example, was shot and killed, along with Oxford, Mississippi, native Ray Gunter, on the day that James Meredith enrolled at the University of Mississippi. See Deborah Purnell, "U.S. Marshals Share Recollections of Ole Miss Integration at Program," *University of Mississippi News*, October 2, 2012, https://news.olemiss.edu/u-s-marshals-share-recollections-of-ole-miss-integration-at-program/.

65. See William Doyle, *An American Insurrection: James Meredith and the Battle of Oxford, Mississippi, 1962* (New York: Anchor Books, 2003).

66. Kwame Anthony Appiah, *The Honor Code: How Moral Revolutions Happen* (New York: W.W. Norton, 2011).

67. John Dewey and James Tufts, *Ethics*, in *The Collected Works of John Dewey, The Middle Works*, ed. Jo Ann Boydston, vol. 5 (1908; repr., Carbondale: Southern Illinois University Press, 1978), 466.

68. Rawls, *The Law of Peoples*, 106, emphasis added.

69. See for example Daniel J. Losen and Kevin G. Welner, "Disabling Discrimination in Our Public Schools: Comprehensive Legal Challenges to Inappropriate

and Inadequate Special Education Services for Minority Children," *Harvard Civil Rights-Civil Liberties Law Review* 36 (2001): 407–60.

70. Catherine Y. Kim, Daniel J. Losen, and Damon T. Hewitt, *The School-to-Prison Pipeline: Structuring Legal Reform* (New York: New York University Press, 2010). See especially ch. 5, "Criminalizing School Misconduct."

71. Michelle Alexander, *The New Jim Crow: Mass Incarceration in the Age of Colorblindness* (New York: The New Press, 2012).

72. Shane Croucher, "China, Russia, and Iran Chide U.S. Over Racism While Persecuting Minorities in Their Own Countries," *Newsweek*, June 8, 2020, https://www.newsweek.com/china-russia-iran-us-protests-racism-persecution-minorities-1509341.

73. Derrick Bell, "Brown v. Board of Education and the Interest-Convergence Dilemma," *Harvard Law Review* 93, no. 3 (1980): 518–33.

74. Rawls, "The Idea of Public Reason Revisited," *Collected Papers*, 613.

75. I am grateful to a blind reviewer for noting this worthwhile point. Dewey would welcome such a critique, I believe, and would likely note the importance of intending an end to conflict and a transition to international friendship and the mutual uplift of the peoples at stake. Dewey rejected the idea of the United States serving as a police officer to the world, yet the ideas of protecting and serving others that are taglines for such functions are worthwhile attitudes that ought to accompany conflict resolution.

76. John Dewey, "Democracy Is Radical," in *The Later Works of John Dewey*, vol. 11 (Carbondale: Southern Illinois University Press), 296–99, 299.

77. John Dewey, "Ethics and International Relations," *Foreign Affairs* 1 (1923): 85–95, republished in MW.15.53–65.

78. See John D. Sutter, "Malala Is the New Symbol of Hope," CNN.com, October 13, 2014, http://www.cnn.com/2014/10/10/opinion/sutter-nobel-prize-malala/.

79. Pjotr Sauer, "Cosmopolitan No More: Russians Feel Sting of Cultural and Economic Shift," *Guardian*, May 20, 2022, https://www.theguardian.com/world/2022/may/20/russians-feel-sting-of-cultural-and-economic-rift-sanctions-ukraine.

80. Jeffrey Sonnenfeld and Steven Tian, "Actually, the Russian Economy Is Imploding," *Foreign Policy*, July 22, 2022, https://foreignpolicy.com/2022/07/22/russia-economy-sanctions-myths-ruble-business/.

81. Luigi Guiso, Paola Sapienza, and Luigi Zingales, "Does Culture Affect Economic Outcomes?," *Journal of Economic Perspectives* 20, no. 2 (2006): 23–48; Jim Granato, Ronald Inglehart, and David Leblang, "The Effect of Cultural Values on Economic Development: Theory, Hypotheses, and Some Empirical Tests," *American Journal of Political Science* 40, no. 3 (1996): 607–31; and Roberta Gatti, "Yes, Culture Matters for Economic Development," *World Bank*, March 28, 2016, https://www.worldbank.org/en/news/feature/2016/03/28/yes-culture-matters-for-economic-development.

82. See Meg Laughlin, "Polishing Mississippi," *St. Petersburg Times (Florida)*, December 17, 2006, 1D. See also Patrik Jonsson, "A Bid to Buff Mississippi's Image," *Christian Science Monitor*, December 12, 2006, 2.

83. It is reasonable to challenge this understanding, suggesting that the use of the word is inappropriate, yet as recently as 2021, authors have argued against the use of the term, suggesting that the need for changing the culture remains. See Andrew Pulrang, "It's Time to Stop Even Casually Misusing Disability Words," *Forbes*, February 20, 2021, https://www.forbes.com/sites/andrewpulrang/2021/02/20/its-time-to-stop-even-casually-misusing-disability-words/?sh=404de22c7d4e.

84. See Brian Willoughby, "Speak Up at School: How to Respond to Everyday Prejudice, Bias and Stereotypes—A Guide for Teachers," Teaching Tolerance, a Project of the Southern Poverty Law Center, Montgomery, Alabama, 2012, http://www.tolerance. org/sites/default/files/general/Speak_Up_at_School.pdf. See also Robin M. Smith and Mara Sapon-Shevin, "Disability Humor, Insults, and Inclusive Practice," *Social Advocacy and Systems Change* 1, no. 2 (2008–2009): 1–18.

85. Rawls, *Theory*, 87.

86. Terry Frieden, "Mississippi Town Sued over 'School-to-Prison Pipeline,'" CNN.com, October 26, 2012, http://www.cnn.com/2012/10/24/justice/mississippi-civil-rights-lawsuit/.

87. Johns Hopkins Researchers, "Dropout Factories: Take a Closer Look at Failing Schools Across the Country," Associated Press, 2007, http://hosted.ap.org/specials/ interactives/wdc/dropout/.

88. Rawls, *Theory*, 386. Emphasis added.

89. Eric Thomas Weber, *Rawls, Dewey, and Constructivism: On the Epistemology of Justice* (London: Continuum Publishing, 2010).

90. Theresa Vargas, "U.S. Patent Office Cancels Redskins Trademark Registration, Says Name Is Disparaging," *Washington Post*, June 18, 2014, https://www.washingtonpost.com/local/us-patent-office-cancels-redskins-trademark-registration-says-name-is-disparaging/2014/06/18/e7737bb8-f6ee-11e3-8aa9-dad2ec039789_story.html.

91. Ryan Homler, "A Timeline of the Washington Football Team's Name Change Saga," NBCSports.com, July 3, 2021, https://www.nbcsports.com/washington/football-team/timeline-washington-football-teams-name-change-saga.

92. Sarah Carr, "In Southern Towns, 'Segregation Academies' Are Still Going Strong," *Atlantic*, December 13, 2012, www.theatlantic.com/national/archive/2012/12/in-southern-towns-segregation-academies-are-still-going-strong/266207/. See also Kenneth T. Andrews, "Movement-Counter Movement Dynamics and the Emergence of New Institutions: The Case of 'White Flight' Schools in Mississippi," *Social Forces* 80, no. 3 (2002): 911–36.

93. Derrick Bell, *Silent Covenants: Brown v. Board of Education and the Unfulfilled Hopes for Racial Reform* (New York: Oxford University Press, 2005).

94. Elizabeth Anderson, *The Imperative of Integration* (Princeton, NJ: Princeton University Press, 2010).

95. John Dewey, "Politics and Culture," *Modern Thinker* 1 (1932): 168–14, 238, republished in LW 6.40–48.

Chapter 3

1. John Rawls, *A Theory of Justice* (1971; repr., Cambridge, MA: Harvard University Press, 1999), 386.

2. Rawls, *A Theory of Justice*, 386.

3. For one of many examples, some authors challenge Rawls's apparent identification of self-respect with self-esteem. See David Sachs, "How to Distinguish Self-Respect from Self-Esteem," *Philosophy and Public Affairs* 10, no. 4 (1981): 346–60. Sachs argues that one can have too much self-esteem, such as in arrogance, but not too much self-respect.

4. "Retire American Indian Team Nicknames? #TellUSAToday," editorial collection of Twitter Responses, *USA Today*, May 6, 2014, http://www.usatoday.com/story/opinion/2014/05/06/native-american-nicknames-redskins-tellusatoday-your-say/8785465/.

5. John Rawls, *Political Liberalism* (New York: Columbia University Press, 1993), 100–1. Hereafter referred to as *PL*.

6. Rawls, *PL*, 9.

7. John Dewey, *Reconstruction in Philosophy*, in *The Collected Works of John Dewey, The Middle Works, 1899–1924: 1920*, ed. Jo Ann Boydston, vol. 12 (Carbondale: Southern Illinois University Press, 1988).

8. John Rawls, "The Idea of Public Reason Revisited," *University of Chicago Law Review* 64, no. 3 (1997): 765–807, 783–84.

9. John Rawls, "Kantian Constructivism in Moral Theory," *Journal of Philosophy* 77, no. 9 (1980): 515–72, 561.

10. John Rawls, "The Law of Peoples," *Critical Inquiry* 20, no. 1 (1993): 36–68, 62.

11. Richard Rorty, "The Priority of Philosophy to Democracy," in *Objectivity, Relativism, and Truth* (New York: Cambridge University Press, 1991), 175–96, 180.

12. Ruth Benedict, *Patterns of Culture* (1934; repr., New York: Mariner Books, 2005).

13. Margaret Mead, "Preface," in Benedict's *Patterns of Culture*, xiii.

14. I offer these categories not because I believe there to be hard distinction between matters of theory and matters of implementation, as clearly there can be overlap. Each challenge just seems to fit slightly more easily in one category than the other.

15. Aristotle, *The Nichomachean Ethics* (New York: Penguin Classics, 1953), Book V, 20–21, 142.

16. Thomas Hill, "Servility and Self-Respect," *Monist* 57, no. 1 (1973): 87–104.

17. John Douglas, *The Anatomy of Motive* (New York: Simon and Schuster, 2012), 6.

18. See Carol Hay, *Kantianism, Liberalism, and Feminisim: Resisting Oppression* (New York: Palgrave MacMillan, 2013); Carol Hay, "A Feminist Kant," *New York Times: The Stone*, December 8, 2013, http://opinionator.blogs.nytimes.com/2013/12/08/a-feminist-kant/); Bernard Boxill, "Self-Respect and Protest," *Philosophy and Public Affairs* 6, no. 1 (1976): 58–69; and Bernard Boxill, "The Responsibility of the Oppressed to Resist Their Own Oppression," *Journal of Social Philosophy* 41 (2010): 1–12.

19. The latter may sound vague. For a concrete example, consider having as one's only option, financially speaking, a public school for one's children with, at one time, a retention rate from freshman year to senior year of high school of 32 percent (Canton County School District, in Canton, MS). Johns Hopkins Researchers, "Dropout Factories: Take a Closer Look at Failing Schools across the Country," Associated Press, 2007, http://hosted.ap.org/specials/interactives/wdc/dropout/. "Dropout factories" arguably track young people into prison or lives of poverty or near-poverty, while experimental schools have shown just how successful students living in poverty can be in school. See Terry Frieden, "Mississippi Town Sued over 'School-to-Prison Pipeline,'" CNN, October, 26, 2012, http://www.cnn.com/2012/10/24/justice/mississippi-civil-rights-lawsuit/, and Billy Watkins, "Rural, Poor, Successful: Every Arkansas KIPP Delta Grad Accepted into College," *Clarion Ledger*, March 7, 2013, http://www.clarionledger.com/article/20130217/OPINION03/302170002/.

20. Charles M. Blow, "Talking Down and Stepping Up," *New York Times*, July 12, 2008, http://www.nytimes.com/2008/07/12/opinion/12blow.html.

21. There are critics who argue that the call to action for black fathers is based on a mistaken stereotype. The claim is that even if heads of households are mothers for many black Americans, "70% of black dads said they bathed, diapered or dressed [their] kids every day, compared with 60% of white fathers and 45% of Latino fathers." See Emily Alpert Reyes, "Survey Finds Dads Defy Stereotypes about Black Fatherhood," *Los Angeles Times*, December 20, 2013, http://articles.latimes.com/2013/dec/20/local/la-me-black-dads-20131221.

22. See Melvyn Stokes, *D. W. Griffith's* The Birth of a Nation (New York: Oxford University Press, 2007) and Sheryll D. Cashin, "Democracy, Race, and Multiculturalism in the Twenty-First Century: Will the Voting Rights Act Ever Be Obsolete?," *Washington University Journal of Law and Policy* 22 (2006): 71–105, 80.

23. Out of respect, I keep this person's identity undisclosed.

24. Brent Staples, "Barack Obama, John McCain, and the Language of Race," *New York Times*, September 22, 2008, A22.

25. The word "can" has been added since the original essay on which this chapter is drawn. The reason is, that while examples of collapse can be found, as in the case of Greece that follows, in fact, so long as nations continue to make their debt

payments, it is possible for debt to continue to increase indefinitely. See Matthew O'Brien, "Why the U.S. Government Never, Ever Has to Pay Back All Its Debt," *Atlantic*, February 1, 2013, https://www.theatlantic.com/business/archive/2013/02/why-the-us-government-never-ever-has-to-pay-back-all-its-debt/272747/; Frances Coppola, "Everything You've Been Told About Government Debt is Wrong," *Forbes*, April 17, 2018, https://www.forbes.com/sites/francescoppola/2018/04/17/everything-youve-been-told-about-government-debt-is-wrong/?sh=5e36b34314f4; and "Putting on Weight; Government Debt—Governments Can Borrow More Than Was Once Believed," *Economist*, September 12, 2020, 58.

26. See Harriet Alexander and Fiona Govan, "Beware Greeks Who Will Not Pay Their Income Tax," *Sunday Telegraph*, June 26, 2011, 28–29; Jennifer Steinhauer, "California, Nearly Broke, Edges Nearer Brink," *New York Times*, February 17, 2009, A14; and Douglas Stanglin, "Arizona Puts State Buildings on Sale to Plug Deficit," *USA Today*, January 12, 2010, http://content.usatoday.com/communities/ondeadline/post/2010/01/arizona-puts-state-buildings-on-sale-today-to-fill-empty-coffers/1#.U5ezOPldUnX.

27. The Place, "Does Poor Car Maintenance Lead to Accidents? Yes and These May Be the Top 2 Culprits!" Fox 13 Salt Lake City, April 29, 2021, https://www.fox13now.com/the-place/does-poor-car-maintenance-lead-to-accidents-yes-and-these-may-be-the-top-2-culprits.

28. Ashley Halsey III, "Bad Highway Design, Conditions Contribute to Half of Fatal Auto Accidents in U.S.," *Washington Post*, July 2, 2009, https://www.washingtonpost.com/wp-dyn/content/article/2009/07/01/AR2009070101700.html.

29. Ibid.

30. A number of essays representing this view are collected in Louis Pojman and Robert Westmoreland, *Equality: Selected Readings* (New York: Oxford University Press, 1997). See especially Robert Nozick's essay, "Justice Does Not Imply Equality," 102–3, the editors' "Introduction: The Nature and Value of Equality," 1–16, and Pojman's "On Equal Human Worth: A Critique of Contemporary Egalitarianism," 282–98.

31. Pojman, 283.

32. See Eric Thomas Weber, *Democracy and Leadership: On Pragmatism and Virtue* (Lanham, MD: Lexington Books, 2013), especially ch. 7.

33. Martha Nussbaum, *Frontiers of Justice: Disability, Nationality, Species Membership* (Cambridge, MA: The Belknap Press of Harvard University Press, 2006).

34. "Retire American Indian Team Nicknames? #TellUSAToday" [Editorial collection of Twitter Responses], *USA Today*, May 6, 2014, http://www.usatoday.com/story/opinion/2014/05/06/native-american-nicknames-redskins-tellusatoday-your-say/8785465/.

35. Andrew Golden, "The Commanders Name Lands 'With a Thud' for Some Washington Fans," *Washington Post*, February 2, 2022, https://www.washingtonpost.com/sports/2022/02/02/washington-commanders-fan-reaction/.

36. See Sally Satel, *P.C., M.D.: How Political Correctness Is Corrupting Medicine* (New York: Basic Books, 2002) and Jeff Sharlet, "'F—k Your Feelings': In Trump's America, the Partisan Battle Flag Is the New Stars and Stripes," *Vanity Fair*, September 8, 2020, https://www.vanityfair.com/news/2020/09/trump-partisan-battle-flag-is-the-new-stars-and-stripes.

37. Diane Ravitch, *The Language Police: How Pressure Groups Restrict What Students Learn* (New York: Vintage Press, 2003). See also Morgan Trau, "As the School Year Begins, Calls for Book Bans Begin to Accelerate in Ohio," *Ohio Capital Journal*, August 9, 2022, https://ohiocapitaljournal.com/2022/08/09/as-the-school-year-begins-calls-for-book-bans-begin-to-accelerate-in-ohio/.

38. Geoffrey R. Stone, "The Noose, Ole Miss, and Free Speech," *Huffington Post*, February 20, 2014, http://www.huffingtonpost.com/geoffrey-r-stone/the-noose-ole-miss-and-fr_b_4820588.html.

39. *United States* v. *Williams*, 553 U. S. 285 (2008). The case was an instance of the protection of limits on the "pandering" of child pornography.

40. Seth M. Asser and Rita Swan, "Child Fatalities from Religion-Motivated Medical Neglect," *Pediatrics* 101, no. 4 (1998): 625–29.

41. John Lachs, "Leaving Others Alone," *Journal of Speculative Philosophy* 18, no. 4 (2004): 261–72. Lachs continues this reasoning in *Meddling: On the Virtue of Leaving Others Alone* (Bloomington: Indiana University Press, 2014).

42. Paolo Friere, *Teachers as Cultural Workers* (Boulder, CO: Westview Press, 1998).

43. *Newdow v. Cong.*, 383 F. Supp. 2d 1229 (E.D. Cal. 2005), *sub nom.* Newdow v. Rio Linda, No. 05–17257 (9 Cir. 2007).

44. *Minersville School District v. Gobitis*, 310 U.S. 586 (1940).

45. The student's motivation hinged especially on Exodus 20:4–6, which commands that God's followers neither create solemn images nor bow down to them nor serve them.

46. Judy S. Deloache, Cynthia Chiong, Kathleen Sherman, Nadia Islam, Mieke Vanderborgth, Georgene L. Troseth, Gabrielle A Strouse, and Katherine O'Doherty, "Do Babies Learn from Baby Media?," *Psychological Science* 21, no. 11 (2010): 1570–74.

47. Plato, *Republic*, trans. G. M. A. Grube (Indianapolis, IN: Hackett Publishing, 1992), 460c.

48. Here I have in mind John Lachs's rich work in social philosophy, such as John Lachs, *Intermediate Man* (Indianapolis, IN: Hackett, 1981) and Lachs, *Meddling*.

Chapter 4

1. See Marian Wright Edelman, "The Cradle to Prison Pipeline: America's New Apartheid," *Harvard Journal of African American Public Policy* XV, summer issue (2009): 67–68, 67.

2. Simone Hattenstone, "Angela Davis on the Power of Protest: 'We Can't Do Anything without Optimism," *Guardian*, March 5, 2022, https://www.theguardian.com/us-news/2022/mar/05/angela-davis-on-the-power-of-protest-we-cant-do-anything-without-optimism.

3. This chapter is the product of two related, previously published papers, synthesized here for the larger purpose of this book. It is worth noting here that in combining the two papers, some matters of scholarly interest and connection have been removed or shortened for the purposes of the flow of this chapter and book. Where there is interest in reading more detail about relevant academic matters, please see the original two papers from which they were derived, the citation information for which is listed in the acknowledgments section at the opening of this volume.

4. Matt Bruenig, "White High School Dropouts Have More Wealth than Black and Hispanic College Graduates," *Huffington Post*, December 6, 2017, https://www.huffpost.com/entry/white-high-school-dropout_b_5881838.

5. Jung Hyun Choi and Laurie Goodman, "Why Do Black College Graduates Have a Lower Homeownership Rate Than White People Who Dropped Out of High School," *Urban Wire, The Urban Institute*, February 27, 2020, https://www.urban.org/urban-wire/why-do-black-college-graduates-have-lower-homeownership-rate-white-people-who-dropped-out-high-school.

6. Gene Demby, "Sagging Pants and the Long History of 'Dangerous' Street Fashion," NPR.org, September 11, 2014, http://www.npr.org/sections/code switch/2014/09/11/347143588/.

7. See William Ryan, *Blaming the Victim* (New York: Vintage Press, 1976); Edward W. Said and Christopher Hitchens, eds., *Blaming the Victims: Spurious Scholarship and the Palestinian Question* (1988; repr., New York: Verso Press, 2001); and Susan E. Wright, "Blaming the Victim, Blaming Society, or Blaming the Discipline: Fixing Responsibility for Poverty and Homelessness," *Sociological Quarterly* 34, no. 1 (1993): 1–16.

8. John Dewey, "Dewey Outlines Utopian Schools," *New York Times*, Sunday, April 23, 1933, Education, 7. It is worth noting here that Dewey was not a Utopian thinker, but he wrote and delivered this address around the height of the Great Depression. Perhaps his aim was to inspire some hope in a troubling time.

9. See James Q. Wilson, "Convincing Black Students that Studying Hard Is Not 'Acting White,'" *Journal of Blacks in Higher Education* 39 (2003): 85–88; Karolyn Tyson, William Darity, and Domini R. Castellino, "It's Not 'a Black Thing': Understanding the Burden of Acting White and Other Dilemmas of High Achievement," *American Sociological Review* 70, no. 4 (2005): 582–605; Devon W. Carbado and Mitu Gulati, *Acting White? Rethinking Race in "Post-Racial" America* (New York: Oxford University Press, 2015); and Tommy J. Curry, "George Floyd Jr as a Philosophical Problem: Why Disaggregated Data Should Guide How

Philosophers Theorize Black Male Death," *Harvard Review of Philosophy* XXVIII (2021): 171–91.

10. Carl Zimmer, "CRISPR, 10 Years On: Learning to Rewrite the Code of Life," *New York Times*, June 27, 2022, https://www.nytimes.com/2022/06/27/science/crispr-gene-editing-10-years.html.

11. An example of this is in the attitude of Ayn Rand, who refers to people as "moochers." See Richard Brodsky, "Moochers, Makers, Boehner, Rand, and Obama: Getting to a Real Debate with the Tea Party," *Huffington Post*, January 23, 2014, http://www.huffingtonpost.com/richard-brodsky/moochers-makers-boehner-r_b_4077188.html.

12. Brad Bushman, "Do Violent Video Games Play a Role in Shootings?," CNN.com, September 18, 2013, http://www.cnn.com/2013/09/18/opinion/bushman-video-games/.

13. David Stout, "Supreme Court Upholds Child Pornography Law," *New York Times*, May 20, 2008, http://www.nytimes.com/2008/05/20/washington/19cnd-scotus.html.

14. Robin S. Dillon, ed., *Dignity, Character, and Self-Respect* (New York: Routledge, 1995).

15. David Sachs, "How to Distinguish Self-Respect from Self-Esteem," *Philosophy and Public Affairs* 10, no. 4 (1981): 346–60. This essay offered a valuable challenge to a passage in Rawls's *Theory* in which he appears to identify the two concepts with one another.

16. Aristotle, *Nicomachean Ethics*, trans. David Ross (New York: Oxford University Press, 2009), bk. IX, sec. 4.

17. Ibid., bk. IV.

18. George Yancy and Charles Mills, "Lost in Rawlsland," *New York Times—The Stone*, November 16, 2014, https://opinionator.blogs.nytimes.com/2014/11/16/lost-in-rawlsland.

19. When I originally wrote this sentence, I was living in Mississippi.

20. Robert Balfantz and Johns Hopkins Researchers, "Dropout Factories."

21. Violet M. Williams, *Ten Little Nigger Boys* (London: Raphael Tuck and Sons, 1956), 1, 3, 9. A variety of editions exist, including one from 1866.

22. Derek McCulloch, "TEN LITTLE NIGGER BOYS," YouTube video, 1:31, "Medley 4 (see description) (feat. Stanley Riley, Leslie Woodgate, Doris Gambell)," posted by "joe seph," December 12, 2013, http://www.youtube.com/watch?v=SfNdwFwV6Ao. If this specific video has been removed, searching for the title is likely to yield the same or similar productions.

23. I am grateful here to editor and friend Tibor Solymosi for pointing out the reasonable concern that one could raise over "species-chauvinism" with regard to mammals closely related to human beings. Animal rights authors and activists do raise concerns over the need for greater sympathy with respect to animal suffering. See Josephine Donovan, "Attention to Suffering: Sympathy as a

Basis for Ethical Treatment of Animals," ch. 6 in *The Feminist Care Tradition in Animal Ethics*, ed. Carol J. Adams and Josephine Donovan (New York: Columbia University Press, 2007), 174–97.

24. "Biography: James K. Vardaman," *American Experience*, PBS, 2008, http://www.pbs.org/wgbh/americanexperience/features/biography/flood-vardaman/.

25. Convention of the Mississippi Legislature, "An Address Setting Forth the Declaration of the Immediate Causes which Induce and Justify the Secession of Mississippi from the Federal Union and the Ordinance of Secession," Jackson: Mississippi Book and Job Printing Office, 1861, https://archive.org/details/addresssettingfo01miss.

26. Giacomo Bologna, "Mississippi Voted to Keep Its State Flag in 2001. A Lot Has Changed Since Then," *Clarion Ledger*, June 8, 2020, https://www.clarionledger.com/story/news/politics/2020/06/08/mississippi-flag-confederate-emblem-time-reconsider-protests-george-floyd/5318216002/.

27. Alan Blinder, "NASCAR's Confederate Flag Ban Faces a Test in Alabama," *New York Times*, June 20, 2020, https://www.nytimes.com/2020/06/20/sports/autoracing/nascar-confederate-flag-ban-talladega.html.

28. Matt Bonesteel, "NCAA Bans Championship Events in Mississippi Because of Its Flag," *Washington Post*, June 19, 2020, https://www.washingtonpost.com/sports/2020/06/19/sec-issues-ultimatum-mississippi-over-state-flag-that-features-confederate-symbol/.

29. John Dewey, "Democracy and Educational Administration," in *The Later Works of John Dewey*, ed. Jo Ann Boydston, vol. 11 (Carbondale: Southern Illinois University Press, 1987), 218–19.

30. David Walker, *Appeal to the Coloured Citizens of the World* (1830; repr., Baltimore: Black Classic Press, 1993).

31. See Jonathan Kozol, *Savage Inequalities: Children in America's Schools* (New York: Broadway Books, 2012) and Anne Walters, "Inequities in Access to Education: Lessons from the COVID-19 Pandemic," *CABL: The Brown University Child and Adolescent Behavior Letter* 36, no. 8 (2020): 8.

32. John Dewey, "The Supreme Intellectual Obligation," *Science Education* 18 (February 1934): 1–4.

33. Dewey, "Dewey Outlines Utopian Schools," 7.

34. Terry Frieden, "Mississippi Town Sued over 'School-to-Prison Pipeline,'" CNN, October 26, 2012, https://www.cnn.com/2012/10/26/us/mississippi-town-sued-over-school-to-prison-pipeline/index.html.

35. Ben Wolfgang, "Scores Show Students Aren't Ready for College," *Washington Times*, August 17, 2011, http://www.washingtontimes.com/news/2011/aug/17/scores-show-students-not-ready-college/. I should add here that I am in agreement with those who would challenge the value of standardized testing as a measure for such things as college preparedness, especially since indicators like high school GPA are at least as good indicators and are less culturally biased. Nevertheless, a

person with a modest GPA and a high ACT score is more likely to be retained in college from freshman to sophomore year. My point, in short, is not that the ACT is a good or appropriate tool for measuring college preparedness, but just that it is purported to be one and bears some predictive usefulness. I side with those who advocate for a move away from standardized testing of that sort.

36. John Dewey, *How We Think*, in *The Later Works of John Dewey, 1925–1953: 1933*, ed. Jo Ann Boydston, vol. 8 (Carbondale: Southern Illinois University Press, 2008), 224.

37. Meredith integrated the University of Mississippi in what has been called the last battle of the Civil War. See William Doyle, *An American Insurrection: James Meredith and the Battle of Oxford, Mississippi, 1962* (New York: Anchor Books, 2003).

38. Roland Martin, "A Remarkable Night for the Country: Analysts React to Obama's Victory," CNN.com, November 5, 2008, http://edition.cnn.com/2008/POLITICS/11/05/analysts.react/index.html.

39. In a recent conversation with an acquaintance, I was told that the United States is not ready for a gay man to be president. I encountered similar disbelief that the state of Mississippi would ever change its state flag and indignation at the idea that the Washington "Redskins" would change their name, yet in the time since I began writing this book, these changes have taken place.

40. The tour at Dachau suggested that these had not yet been used there, though they were installed, and similar ones had been used at concentration camps outside of Germany.

41. Christina Caron, "In 19 States, It's Still Legal to Spank Children in Public Schools," *New York Times*, December 13, 2018, https://www.nytimes.com/2018/12/13/us/corporal-punishment-school-tennessee.html.

42. See Rajeev Darolia, Peter Mueser, and Jacob Cronin, "Labor Market Returns to a Prison GED," *Economics of Education Review* 82 (2021): 1–27, 2. See also Denise McKeon, "Research Talking Points on Dropout Statistics: High School Attendance, Graduation, Completion, & Dropout Statistics," National Education Association, February 2006, accessed November 2023, http://www.nea.org/home/i3579.htm; and Caroline Wolf Harlow, "Education and Correctional Populations. Special Report," NCJ 195670, Washington, DC: United States Department of Justice, Bureau of Justice Statistics, 2003.

43. Originally, I had used the expression "channeled into educational failure," but that language continues to place blame on students, whereas "push out" notes the force compelling people directionally. See Monique Morris, Mankappr Conteh, and Melissa Harris-Perry, *Pushout: The Criminalization of Black Girls in Schools* (New York: The New Press, 2018).

44. Todd R. Clear, "A Private-Sector, Incentives-Based Model for Justice Reinvestment," *Criminology & Public Policy* 10, no. 3 (2011): 585–608.

45. Rawls, *Theory*, 386.

46. Bracey Harris, "Ex-Ole Miss Student Sentenced for Noose on Statue," *USA Today*, September 17, 2015, http://www.usatoday.com/story/news/nation/2015/09/17/ex-ole-miss-student-sentenced-noose-statue/72376068/.

47. Ja'han Jones, "The MAGA Movement is a KKK Re-up. The Latest Jan. 6 Hearing Proves It," MSNBC, July 13, 2022, https://www.msnbc.com/the-reidout/reidout-blog/summary-jan-6-hearing-kkk-rcna37960.

48. See Erik Hayden, "Poll: 46 Percent of Mississippi GOP Want to Ban Interracial Marriage," Atlantic Newswire, April 7, 2011, http://www.thewire.com/national/2011/04/mississippi-republicans/36455/; and Dean Debnam, "MS GOP," Public Policy Polling, April 7, 2011, 1–17, https://www.publicpolicypolling.com/wp-content/uploads/2017/09/PPP_Release_MS_0407915.pdf.

49. David Swerdlick, "Biden Said Black Trump Voters 'Ain't Black.' That's a Double Standard," *Washington Post*, May 22, 2020, https://www.washingtonpost.com/outlook/2020/05/22/biden-charlamagne-trump-black/.

50. Roland Fryer and Paul Torelli, "An Empirical Analysis of 'Acting White,'" *Journal of Public Economics* 94 (2010): 380–96.

51. Ibid., 1; Larry McShane, "Interracial Marriage Should Be Illegal, Say 46% of Mississippi Republicans in New Poll," *New York Daily News*, April 8, 2011, https://www.nydailynews.com/news/national/interracial-marriage-illegal-46-mississippi-republicans-new-poll-article-1.111449.

52. John Blake, "Why Sunday Morning Remains America's Most Segregated Hour," CNN Belief Blog, October 6, 2010, http://religion.blogs.cnn.com/2010/10/06/why-sunday-morning-remains-americas-most-segregated-hour/.

53. Ed Pilkington, "Mississippi Church Bans African American Wedding after Complaints," *Guardian*, July 29, 2012, https://www.theguardian.com/world/2012/jul/29/mississippi-church-african-american-wedding.

54. Nate Jones, "Want to Be Class President in Mississippi? You Need to Be White," *Time*, August 27, 2010, http://newsfeed.time.com/2010/08/27/want-to-be-class-president-in-mississippi-you-need-to-be-white/.

55. Roland Martin, "A Remarkable Night for the Country: Analysts React to Obama's Victory," CNN.com, November 5, 2008, https://edition.cnn.com/2008/POLITICS/11/05/analysts.react/.

56. It is worth noting that many efforts to achieve and maintain a culture of justice might be labeled "countercultural," to the extent that they are combating or resisting the cultural forces contributing to injustice. I am indebted to friend and editor Tibor Solymosi for calling my attention to this point.

57. Robert Balfantz and Johns Hopkins Researchers, "More Information on the Methodology, Data and Terms Used in the AP Dropout Factory Story," Center for Social Organization of Schools, 2007, http://web.jhu.edu/CSOS/images/AP.html.

58. Molly K. Hooper, "GOP Rep.: Obamas Part of 'Uppity' Class," *USA Today*, September 4, 2008, http://usatoday30.usatoday.com/news/politics/election2008/2008-09-04-westmoreland_N.htm.

59. Mike Rose, *The Mind at Work: Valuing the Intelligence of the American Worker* (New York: Penguin Books, 2014).

60. Sarah Shourd, "Tortured by Solitude," *New York Times*, November 6, 2011, SR4.

61. Anandi Mani, Sendhil Mullainathan, Eldar Shafir, and Jiaying Zhao, "Poverty Impedes Cognitive Function," *Science* 30 (August 2013): 976–80.

62. John Lachs, *The Relevance of Philosophy to Life* (Nashville, TN: Vanderbilt University Press, 1995), especially part 4, ch. 15–21, 163–208.

63. John Lachs, *Meddling: On the Virtue of Leaving Others Alone* (Bloomington: Indiana University Press, 2014).

64. Lachs, *Relevance*, 228–42.

65. The line is generally attributed to Angela Davis.

66. John Lachs, *Stoic Pragmatism* (Bloomington: Indiana University Press, 2012).

67. See ch. 1 in this volume, which was first published as Eric Thomas Weber, "Justice as an Evolving, Regulative Ideal," *Pragmatism Today* 6, no. 2 (2015): 105–16, http://www.pragmatismtoday.eu/winter2015/10%20Weber.pdf.

68. According to Princeton University's blog, "Three female African American transfer students graduated in the class of 1972." See April C. Armstrong, "African Americans and Princeton University," Mudd Manuscript Library Blog, Princeton University Archives and Public Policy Papers Collection, May 27, 2015, https://blogs.princeton.edu/mudd/2015/05/african-americans-and-princeton-university/.

69. Adam Gabbatt, "Women in Combat: Pentagon to Overturn Military Ban," *Guardian*, January 24, 2013, https://www.theguardian.com/world/2013/jan/23/pentagon-overturn-ban-women-combat.

70. In 2000, "only 38 percent of those polled said the country was ready for a black president." In 2008, the number reached 68 percent. See CBS, "CBS Poll: Ready for a Black President?," CBS News, June 4, 2008, https://www.cbsnews.com/news/cbs-poll-ready-for-a-black-president/.

71. Many have written popular pieces arguing this point, though a Princeton study was perhaps one of the most influential scholarly essays to make the point. See Martin Gilens and Benjamin I. Page, "Testing Theories of American Politics: Elites, Interest Groups, and Average Citizens," *Perspectives on Politics* 12, no. 3 (September, 2014): 564–81. The worries about oligarchy have only increased since the United States reelected President Trump. See Robert Reich, "In the Global Clash Between Democracy and Oligarchy, the U.S. Is Switching Sides," *Guardian*, February 20, 2025, https://www.theguardian.com/commentisfree/2025/feb/20/trump-musk-oligarchy-russia-far-right.

72. See Atiba R. Ellis, "*Citizens United* and Tiered Personhood," *John Marshall Law Review* 44, no. 3 (2011): 717–49; and *Trump v. United States*, October 2023, https://www.supremecourt.gov/opinions/23pdf/23-939_e2pg.pdf.

73. Peter Edwards, "White Clergy Offer Their Photos for Target Practice; Twitter Campaign a Response to Miami Police Snipers Using Black Men's Mug Shots," *Toronto Star*, January 27, 2015, A10.

74. Edelman, "The Cradle to Prison Pipeline," 67.

Chapter 5

1. Andrew Kernohan, *Liberalism, Equality, and Cultural Oppression* (New York: Cambridge University Press, 1998).

2. Louis Pojman and Robert Westmoreland, eds., *Equality: Selected Readings* (New York: Oxford University Press, 1996).

3. Ibid., 1.

4. See Paul Ryan, "The War on Poverty: 50 Years Later: A House Budget Committee Report," Washington, DC: House Budget Committee, 2014; Justin Murray, "Why It's So Hard to Escape America's Anti-Poverty Programs," Foundation for Economic Education (Fee.org), March 30, 2020, https://fee.org/articles/why-its-so-hard-to-escape-americas-anti-poverty-programs/; and Eli Steele, "Rooftop Revelations: Can a Government that Helped Create a Culture of Dependency Reverse the Damage?," FoxNews.com, February 10, 2022, https://www.foxnews.com/opinion/rooftop-revelations-can-a-government-that-helped-create-a-culture-of-dependency-reverse-the-damage.

5. Arnold Rampersad, "The Book that Launched the Harlem Renaissance," *Journal of Blacks in Higher Education* 38 (Winter 2002–2003): 87–91.

6. Peter Coy, "The 'Benefits Cliff' Discourages People from Making More Money," *New York Times*, November 10, 2021, https://www.nytimes.com/2021/11/10/opinion/benefits-cliff-welfare.html.

7. John Dewey, "Democracy and Educational Administration," in *The Later Works of John Dewey*, ed. Jo Ann Boydston, vol. 11 (Carbondale: Southern Illinois University Press, 2008), 217–25, 220.

8. John Dewey, "Creative Democracy—The Task Before Us," in *The Later Works of John Dewey*, ed. Jo Ann Boydston, vol. 14 (Carbondale: Southern Illinois University Press, 1988), 224–30, 226–27.

9. See David Walker, *Appeal to the Coloured Citizens of the World*, ed. Peter Hinks (University Park: Pennsylvania State University, 2002); and Ian Finseth, "David Walker, Nature's Nation, and Early African-American Separatism," *Mississippi Quarterly* 54, no. 3 (2001): 337–62.

10. Finseth, "David Walker," 343.

11. John Dewey, "Philosophy and Democracy," in *The Middle Works of John Dewey*, ed. Jo Ann Boydston, vol. 11 (Carbondale: Southern Illinois University Press, 1982), MW.11.41–53, 52.

12. John Dewey, "The Influence of Darwin on Philosophy," in *The Middle Works of John Dewey*, ed. Jo Ann Boydston, vol. 4 (Carbondale: Southern Illinois University Press, 2008), MW.4.3–15.

13. Leonard Harris, "Rendering the Text: Introduction," in *The Philosophy of Alain Locke: Harlem Renaissance and Beyond*, ed. Leonard Harris (Philadelphia: Temple University Press, 1989), 3–27, 6.

14. Tobi Haslett, "The Man Who Led the Harlem Renaissance—and His Hidden Hungers," *New Yorker*, May 14, 2018, https://www.newyorker.com/magazine/2018/05/21/the-man-who-led-the-harlem-renaissance-and-his-hidden-hungers.

15. See Alain Locke, "Frontiers of Culture," in *The Philosophy of Alain Locke: Harlem Renaissance and Beyond*, ed. Leonard Harris (Philadelphia: Temple University Press, 1989), 229–36, 230–31.

16. Harris, "Rendering the Text," 6.

17. Ibid., 10.

18. For one of many examples, see James B. Jacobs and Kimberly A. Potter, "Hate Crimes: A Critical Perspective," *Crime and Justice: A Review of Research* 22 (1997): 1–50.

19. Susan Svrluga, "Former Ole Miss Student Pleads Guilty to Hanging Noose Around Statue Honoring the First Black Student," *Washington Post*, March 24, 2016, https://www.washingtonpost.com/news/grade-point/wp/2016/03/24/former-ole-miss-student-pleads-guilty-to-hanging-noose-around-statue-honoring-the-first-black-student/.

20. Harris, "Rendering the Text," 11.

21. Ibid.

22. See Laura Meckler, "Study Finds Black and Latino Students Face Significant 'Funding Gap,'" *Washington Post*, July 22, 2020, https://www.washingtonpost.com/education/study-finds-black-and-latino-students-face-significant-funding-gap/2020/07/21/712f376a-caca-11ea-b0e3-d55bda07d66a_story.html; and Clare Lombardo, "Why White School Districts Have So Much More Money," NPR, February 26, 2019, https://www.npr.org/2019/02/26/696794821/why-white-school-districts-have-so-much-more-money.

23. Harris, "Rendering the Text," 15.

24. Ibid., 20–21.

25. Matthew Spalding, "Why the U.S. Has a Culture of Dependency," Heritage Foundation, Commentary: Poverty and Inequality, September 21, 2012, https://www.heritage.org/poverty-and-inequality/commentary/why-the-us-has-culture-dependency.

26. Aimee Picchi, "Almost Half of All Americans Work in Low-Wage Jobs," NBC News, December 2, 2019, https://www.cbsnews.com/news/minimum-wage-2019-almost-half-of-all-americans-work-in-low-wage-jobs/.

27. US Census Bureau, "National Poverty in America Awareness Month: January 2022," Census.gov, January 2022, Release Number CB22-SFS.013, https://www.census.gov/newsroom/stories/poverty-awareness-month.html.

28. Disability and Health Branch of the CDC, "Disability Impacts All of Us," Centers for Disease Control and Prevention, September 16, 2020, http://cdc.gov/ncbddd/disabilityandhealth/infographic-disability-impacts-all.html.

29. Spalding, "Why the U.S. Has a Culture of Dependency."

30. Editors, "Hungry Heroes: 25 Percent of Military Families Seek Food Aid," NBC News, August 17, 2014, https://www.nbcnews.com/feature/in-plain-sight/hungry-heroes-25-percent-military-families-seek-food-aid-n180236.

31. Pew Research Center, Beyond Red vs. Blue: The Political Typology," June 2014, https://www.pewresearch.org/politics/wp-content/uploads/sites/4/2014/06/6-26-14-Political-Typology-release1.pdf, 44.

32. Spalding, "Why the U.S. Has a Culture of Dependency."

33. Thomas Barrabi, "Walmart, McDonald's Among Largest Employers of SNAP, Medicaid Recipients: Report," Fox Business, November 18, 2020, https://www.foxbusiness.com/markets/walmart-mcdonalds-largest-employers-snap-medicaid-recipients.

34. Ibid.

35. Chaim I. Waxman, *The Stigma of Poverty: A Critique of Poverty Theories and Policies* (New York: Pergamon Press, 1977).

36. Robert Walker, *The Shame of Poverty* (New York: Oxford University Press, 2014), 1, 190.

37. Darlena Cunha, "Why Drug Testing Welfare Recipients Is a Waste of Taxpayer Money," *Time*, August 15, 2014, https://time.com/3117361/welfare-recipients-drug-testing/.

38. Ibid.

39. Plato, *Republic*, Book II, 369b.

40. Misty L. Heggeness et al., "Tracking Job Losses for Mothers of School-Age Children During a Health Crisis," Census.gov, March 3, 2021, https://www.census.gov/library/stories/2021/03/moms-work-and-the-pandemic.html.

41. Joy Moses, "The Facts About Americans Who Receive Public Benefits: Misperceptions About Poverty in Our Country Complicate Effective Policymaking," Center for American Progress, December 2011, https://cdn.americanprogress.org/wp-content/uploads/issues/2011/12/pdf/public_benefits_pdf.pdf?_ga=2.33085566.179903058.1647009053-54787874.1646749890. Moses cites US Census Bureau, March Supplement 2011.

42. Eric Thomas Weber, "Stoic Pragmatism for Parenting a Child with Disabilities: An Essay Addressing Philosophers, Parents, Teachers, and Educational Policymakers," in *Disability and American Philosophies* (London: Routledge Press, 2022), 182–98.

43. See Morgan Kelly, "Poor Concentration: Poverty Reduces Brainpower Needed for Navigating Other Areas of Life," News, Princeton.edu, August 29,

2013, https://www.princeton.edu/news/2013/08/29/poor-concentration-poverty-reduces-brainpower-needed-navigating-other-areas-life; and Anandi Mani, Sendhil Mullainathan, Eldar Shafir, and Jiaying Zhao, "Poverty Impedes Cognitive Function," *Science* 341 (August 2013): 976–80.

44. Dawn Foster, "How Being Poor Can Lead to a Negative Spiral of Fear and Self-Loathing," *Guardian*, June 30, 2015, https://www.theguardian.com/society/2015/jun/30/poverty-negative-spiral-fear-self-loathing.

45. Lisa Esposito, "The Countless Ways Poverty Affects People's Health," *U.S. News and World Report*, April 20, 2016, https://health.usnews.com/health-news/patient-advice/articles/2016-04-20/the-countless-ways-poverty-affects-peoples-health.

46. Kathryn M. Leifheit et al., "Severe Housing Insecurity During Pregnancy: Association with Adverse Birth and Infant Outcomes," *International Journal of Environmental Research and Public Health* 17, no. 8659 (2020): 1–12.

47. Diane Ravitch, *Reign of Error: The Hoax of the Privatization Movement and the Danger to America's Public Schools* (New York: Vintage Press, 2014), 50–62.

48. Ibid., 62.

49. Eleni X. Karageorge, "Growing Up in High-Poverty Areas Can Affect Your Employment," US Bureau of Labor Statistics, March 2016, https://www.bls.gov/opub/mlr/2016/beyond-bls/growing-up-in-high-poverty-areas-can-affect-your-employment.htm.

50. Patrick Gillespie, "Growing Up Poor Makes It Harder to Succeed: Janet Yellen," CNN Business, March 23, 2017, https://money.cnn.com/2017/03/23/news/economy/fed-yellen-income-inequality-poor-success-study/.

51. Steven Strauss, "Shouldn't We Drug Test CEOs of Banks Receiving Federal Aid?," *Huffington Post*, April 7, 2013, https://www.huffpost.com/entry/drug-test-ceos_b_3034127.

52. John F. Dovidio, Brenda Major, and Jennifer Crocker, "Stigma: Introduction and Overview," in *The Social Psychology of Stigma*, ed. Todd F. Heatherton et al. (New York: The Guilford Press, 2003), 1–28, 1.

53. Amy Chua, "How America's Identity Politics Went from Inclusion to Division," *Guardian*, March 1, 2018, https://www.theguardian.com/society/2018/mar/01/how-americas-identity-politics-went-from-inclusion-to-division.

54. See Heike Paul, "Expressive Individualism and the Myth of the Self-Made Man," in *The Myths That Made America: An Introduction to American Studies* (Bielefeld, Germany: Transcript Verlag, 2014); Mike Myatt, "Self-Made Man—No Such Thing," *Forbes*, November 15, 2011, https://www.forbes.com/sites/mikemyatt/2011/11/15/self-made-man-no-such-thing/; John Swansburg, "The Self-Made Man: The Story of America's Most Pliable, Pernicious, and Irrepressible Myth," Slate.com, September 29, 2014, http://www.slate.com/articles/news_and_politics/history/2014/09/the_self_made_man_history_of_a_myth_from_ben_franklin_to_andrew_carnegie.html; Irvin G. Wyllie, *The Self-Made Man in America: The Myth of*

Rags to Riches (New Brunswick, NJ: Rutgers University Press, 1954); Matt Johnson, "The Psychology of the Self-Made Man: Can a person Be Solely Responsible for Creating Their Own Fortune?," *Psychology Today*, March 27, 2021, https://www.psychologytoday.com/us/blog/mind-brain-and-value/202103/the-psychology-and-mythology-the-self-made-man; and Jim Cullen, "Problems and Promises of the Self-Made Myth," *Hedgehog Review* 15, no. 2 (2013): 8+, https://hedgehogreview.com/issues/the-american-dream/articles/problems-and-promises-of-the-self-made-myth.

55. See Abraham H. Maslow, *Motivation and Personality* (New York: Harper and Row, 1954); and David Lester, "Measuring Maslow's Hierarchy of Needs," *Psychological Reports: Mental and Physical Health* 113, no. 1 (2013): 15–17.

56. Camila Beiner, "Homeless Youth and Children are Wildly Undercounted, Advocates Say," NPR.org, February 15 2022, https://www.npr.org/2022/02/15/1073791409/homeless-youth-and-children-are-wildly-undercounted--advocates-say.

57. Ellen L. Bassuk, Carmela J. DeCandia, Corey Anne Beach, and Fred Berman, "America's Youngest Outcasts: A Report on Child Homelessness," American Institutes for Research, National Center on Family Homelessness, Waltham, MA, November 2014, https://www.air.org/sites/default/files/downloads/report/Americas-Youngest-Outcasts-Child-Homelessness-Nov2014.pdf.

58. Priya Fielding-Singh, "Free School Meal Programs Don't Just Feed Hungry Kids—They're a Major Win for Moms," *Washington Post*, August 13, 2021, https://www.washingtonpost.com/opinions/2021/08/13/universal-free-school-meals-moms-california-maine/.

59. Kate Rix, "Schools Need Teachers of Color. This Is How to Retain Them, Educators Say," NBC News, December 20, 2021, https://www.nbcnews.com/news/education/schools-need-teachers-color-retain-educators-say-rcna7732.

60. Juan Perez, "Governors Want to Boost Teacher Pay," *Politico*, January 24, 2022, https://www.politico.com/newsletters/weekly-education/2022/01/24/governors-want-to-boost-teacher-pay-00001091.

61. Robert Bruno, "When Did the U.S. Stop Seeing Teachers as Professionals?," *Harvard Business Review*, June 20, 2018, https://hbr.org/2018/06/when-did-the-u-s-stop-seeing-teachers-as-professionals.

62. Ravitch, *Reign of Error*, 242.

63. Danielle Douglas-Gabriel, "Tuition-Free College Movement Gains Momentum, Despite Biden's Stalled Plan," *Washington Post*, March 5, 2022, https://www.washingtonpost.com/education/2022/03/05/tuition-free-college-states/.

64. Madeleine Ngo, "After Dropping Free Community College Plan, Democrats Explore Options," *New York Times*, October, 22, 2021, https://www.nytimes.com/2021/10/22/us/politics/free-community-college-democrats.html.

65. Robert Farrington, "These States Offer Tuition-Free Community College," *Forbes*, March 25, 2020, https://www.forbes.com/sites/robertfarrington/2020/03/25/these-states-offer-tuition-free-community-college/.

66. Benjamin Wermund, "The Red State that Loves Free College: How Tennessee Is Making Bernie Sanders' Favorite Education Idea a Reality," *Politico*, January 16, 2019, https://www.politico.com/agenda/story/2019/01/16/tennessee-free-college-000867/.

67. Tennessee Board of Regents, "Tennessee Promise," College System of Tennessee, https://www.tbr.edu/initiatives/tn-promise.

68. Scott Samuelson, "Why I Teach Plato to Plumbers," *Atlantic*, April 29, 2014, https://www.theatlantic.com/education/archive/2014/04/plato-to-plumbers/361373/.

69. See Amy Gibbons, "The Countries Offering Students Free (or Somewhat Affordable) University Education," *Independent*, December 5, 2016, https://www.independent.co.uk/student/study-abroad/free-university-education-courses-study-abroad-brexit-erasmus-students-germany-copenhagen-france-a7457576.html; and Katie Lobosco, "Americans Are Moving to Europe for Free College Degrees," CNNMoney.com, February 23, 2016, https://money.cnn.com/2016/02/23/pf/college/free-college-europe/.

70. Michael Lanford, "The Political History of the Georgia HOPE Scholarship Program: A Critical Analysis," *Policy Reviews in Higher Education* 1, no. 2 (2017): 187–208.

71. Patricia Albjerg Graham, *Schooling America: How the Public Schools Meet the Nation's Changing Needs* (New York: Oxford University Press, 2005), 199.

72. See Craig A. Tovey, "In Defense of Basic Research," *Science* 355, no. 6327 (2017): 804; and Abraham Flexner, *The Usefulness of Useless Knowledge* (Princeton, NJ: Princeton University Press, 2017).

73. See Ravitch, "The Facts About Test Scores" and "The Facts About the Achievement Gap," in *Reign of Error*, 44–62.

74. Ibid., 51–52.

75. Drew Desilver, "U.S. Students' Academic Achievement Still Lags That of Their Peers in Many Other Countries," Pew Research Center, STEM Education & Workforce, February 15, 2017, https://www.pewresearch.org/fact-tank/2017/02/15/u-s-students-internationally-math-science/.

76. Ravitch, *Reign of Error*, 62.

77. Theresa Anderson et al., "Balancing at the Edge of the Cliff: Experiences and Calculations of Benefits Cliffs, Plateaus, and Trade-Offs," Urban Institute, 2022, https://www.urban.org/sites/default/files/publication/105321/balancing-at-the-edge-of-the-cliff.pdf, viii.

78. Ibid., ix.

79. Meghan McCann and Josephine Hauer, "Moving on Up: Helping Families Climb the Economic Ladder by Addressing Benefits Cliffs," National Conference of State Legislatures, August 20, 2019, https://www.ncsl.org/Portals/1/Documents/cyf/Benefits-Cliffs_v03_web.pdf, 8.

80. Ibid.

81. Anderson et al., "Balancing at the Edge of the Cliff," viii.

82. Lauren Bauer, "Does Head Start Work? The Debate Over the Head Start Impact Study, Explained," Brookings.edu, June 14, 2019, https://www.brookings.edu/blog/brown-center-chalkboard/2019/06/14/does-head-start-work-the-debate-over-the-head-start-impact-study-explained/.

83. Gretchen Livingston and Deja Thomas, "Among 41 Countries, Only U.S. Lacks Paid Parental Leave," Pew Research Center, December 16, 2019, https://www.pewresearch.org/fact-tank/2019/12/16/u-s-lacks-mandated-paid-parental-leave/.

84. Eleanor Klibanoff, "U.S. Supreme Court Rules There's No Right to Abortion, Setting Up Texas Ban," *Texas Tribune*, June 24, 2022, https://www.texastribune.org/2022/06/22/supreme-court-abortion-texas/.

85. Krystin Arneson, "Why Doesn't the U.S. Have Mandated Paid Maternity Leave?," BBC, June 28, 2021, https://www.bbc.com/worklife/article/20210624-why-doesnt-the-us-have-mandated-paid-maternity-leave.

86. Laurel Wamsley, "The U.S. Is Uniquely Terrible at Protecting Children from Gun Violence," NPR, May 28, 2022, https://www.npr.org/2022/05/28/1101307932/texas-shooting-uvalde-gun-violence-children-teenagers.

87. Rep. Mark Green, "Every Military Family Deserves Our Gratitude," *The Hill*, November 27, 2020, https://thehill.com/blogs/congress-blog/politics/527737-every-military-family-deserves-our-gratitude/.

88. Alexandra Robbins, "Teachers Deserve More Respect," *New York Times*, March 20, 2020, https://www.nytimes.com/2020/03/20/opinion/sunday/teachers-coronavirus.html; and Brenda Iasevoli, "Building Respect for Teachers: What Can Be Done?," HMHco.com, November 4, 2021, https://www.hmhco.com/blog/building-respect-for-teachers-what-can-be-done.

89. Liz Empson and Matthew Yarnell, "Enough Is Enough: PA. Needs to Protect Seniors, Respect Caregivers," *Pennsylvania Capital-Star*, June 6, 2021, https://www.penncapital-star.com/commentary/enough-is-enough-pa-needs-to-protect-seniors-respect-caregivers-opinion/.

90. Bill Chappell, "Should Young Americans Be Required to Do Public Service? Federal Panel Says Maybe," NPR, January 23, 2019, https://www.npr.org/2019/01/23/687715869/should-young-americans-be-required-to-do-public-service-federal-panel-says-maybe.

91. Editors, "Paul Ryan," Biography.com, April 2, 2014, https://www.biography.com/political-figure/paul-ryan.

Chapter 6

1. Ruth Anna Putnam, "Democracy as a Way of Life," in *Pragmatism as a Way of Life: The Lasting Legacy of Willian James and John Dewey*, by Hilary Putnam and Ruth Anna Putnam, ed. David MacArthur (Cambridge, MA: The Belknap Press of Harvard University Press, 2017), 439–52.

2. John Dewey, "Creative Democracy—The Task before Us," in *The Later Works of John Dewey*, ed. Jo Ann Boydston, vol. 14 (Carbondale: Southern Illinois University Press, 224–30, 225–26.

3. Robert Nozick, *Anarchy, State, and Utopia* (1974; repr., New York: Basic Books, 1999), 293.

4. Ibid., 150–53.

5. Ibid., 161.

6. John R. Boatright, "Executive Compensation: Unjust or Just Right?," in *Oxford Handbook of Business Ethics*, ed. George G. Brenkert (New York: Oxford University Press, 2010), 161–200.

7. Jordan Weissman, "This State College President Earned $6 Million Last Year. Should You Be Mad?," Slate.com, May 20, 2014, https://slate.com/business/2014/05/college-president-pay-is-it-too-high.html.

8. Weissman, "This State College President Earned $6 Million Last Year. Should You Be Mad?"

9. See Marlon A. Walker, "Despite Pay Hikes, School Districts Still Hemorrhaging Teachers," *Atlanta Journal-Constitution*, July 19, 2019, https://www.ajc.com/news/local-education/despite-pay-hikes-school-districts-still-hemorrhaging-teachers/wj3I0VLffX9JJCDiBZtMSI/; and Alex Kajitani, "Fixing the Teacher Shortage Begins with Stopping the Bleeding," EdWeek.org, December 2, 2015, https://www.edweek.org/leadership/opinion-fixing-the-teacher-shortage-begins-with-stopping-the-bleeding/2015/12. See also Diane Ravitch, *Reign of Error: The Hoax of the Privatization Movement and the Danger to America's Public Schools* (New York: Alfred A. Knopf, 2014), 132.

10. See Jan Hodenfield, "After Woodstock: Money and Smiles—The Aftermath of the Party of the Year," *Rolling Stone*, October 4, 1969, https://www.rollingstone.com/music/music-news/after-woodstock-money-and-smiles-182998/; and Ray Cavanaugh, "Max Yasgur Rented Out His Farm for Woodstock. His Neighbors Sued Him," *Time*, August 14, 2019, https://time.com/5645555/woodstock-max-yasgur/. According to Cavanaugh, "The festival organizers faced a string of lawsuits and had to spend hundreds of thousands of dollars on cleanup."

11. Richard H. Thaler and Cass R. Sunstein, *Nudge: Improving Decisions About Health, Wealth, and Happiness* (New Haven: Yale University Press, 2008).

12. Daniel Ackerman, "Before Face Masks, Americans Went to War Against Seat Belts," *Business Insider*, May 26, 2020, https://www.businessinsider.com/when-americans-went-to-war-against-seat-belts-2020-5.

13. Louis Pojman and Robert Westmoreland, eds., *Equality: Selected Readings* (New York: Oxford University Press, 1997), 282–98.

14. Ibid., 102–4.

15. Peter Singer, "Famine, Affluence, and Morality," *Philosophy and Public Affairs* 1, no. 3 (1972): 229–43.

16. Singer, "Famine, Affluence, and Morality," 231.

17. See Michael Balter, "Human Altruism Traces Back to the Origins of Humanity," *Science*, August 27, 2014, https://www.science.org/content/article/human-altruism-traces-back-origins-humanity; Sharon E. Kessler, Tyler R. Bonnell, Joanna M. Setchell, and Colin A. Chapman, "Social Structure Facilitated the Evolution of Care-Giving as a Strategy for Disease Control in the Human Lineage," *Nature* 8 (2018): 1–14, https://www.nature.com/articles/s41598-018-31568-2.pdf; Samuel Paul Vesslère, "Caring for Others Is What Made Our Species Unique," *Psychology Today*, October 28, 2015, https://www.psychologytoday.com/us/blog/culture-mind-and-brain/201510/caring-others-is-what-made-our-species-unique; and Alison Gopnik, "How Humans Evolved to Care for Others," *Wall Street Journal*, April 16, 2020, https://www.wsj.com/articles/how-humans-evolved-to-care-for-others-11587045511.

18. Plato, *Republic*, Book II, 369b.

19. Julie Rovner, "Kill Grandma? Debunking a Health Bill Scare Tactic," NPR.org, August 12, 2009, https://www.npr.org/2009/08/12/111729363/kill-grandma-debunking-a-health-bill-scare-tactic.

20. Alex Samuels, "Dan Patrick Says 'There Are More Important Things than Living and That's Saving This Country,'" *Texas Tribune*, April 21, 2020, https://www.texastribune.org/2020/04/21/texas-dan-patrick-economy-coronavirus/.

21. Plato, *Republic*, Book V, 459e and especially 460c. See also Karen Brennan, "Evidence of Infanticide and Exposure in Antiquity: Tolerated Social Practice, Uncontrolled Phenomenon or Regulated Custom?," *University College Dublin Law Review* 2 (2002): 92–119.

22. David M. Gallagher, "Thomas Aquinas on Self-Love as the Basis for Love of Others," *Acta Philosophica* 8 (1999): 23–44.

23. Aristotle, *Nichomachean Ethics*, trans. F. H. Peters (London: Kegan Paul, Trench, Trübner & Co, 1906), Book VIII, VIII.viii.27–34.

24. Charlotte Curran, "The Ethics of Fat Shaming," *Philosophy Now* 144 (July 2021): 10–12.

25. Eliza Chandler, "Interactions of Disability Pride and Shame," in *The Female Face of Shame*, ed. Erica L. Johnson and Patricia Moran (Bloomington: Indiana University Press, 2013), 74–86.

26. Kwame Anthony Appiah, *The Honor Code: How Moral Revolutions Happen* (New York: W. W. Norton, 2011).

27. See Robin Wright, "Fury at America and Its Values Spreads Globally," *New Yorker*, June 1, 2020, https://www.newyorker.com/news/our-columnists/after-the-killing-of-george-floyd-fury-at-america-and-its-values-spreads-globally; Karen Tumulty, "How George Floyd Speaks to the Shame of Our History and the Promise of Our Future," *Washington Post*, June 9, 2020, https://www.washingtonpost.com/opinions/how-george-floyd-speaks-to-the-shame-of-our-history-and-the-promise-of-our-future/2020/06/09/8ff43956-aa6e-11ea-94d2-d7bc43b26bf9_story.html.

28. Savannah Smith, "Why Mississippi Voted to Change Its Flag After Decades of Debate," NBC News, June 30, 2020, https://www.nbcnews.com/news/us-news/why-mississippi-voted-change-its-flag-after-decades-debate-n1232607.

29. The earliest reference I could find for this proverb came from an Algerian article in French by M. Trotter, "Australian Trees and Algerian Deserts," *Pall Mall Gazette*, London, 1868. Acknowledgement to "Notes sur l'Eucalyptus et Subsidiairement sur la Nécessité du Reboisement de l'Algérie," Column 2, 11, London (British Newspaper Archive and Newspapers.com).

30. Karrie Jacobs, "Why Libraries May Never Stop Being People Places," *New York Times*, April 21, 2022, https://www.nytimes.com/2022/04/21/style/libraries-outdoor-public-space.html.

31. Rebecca Winthrop, "Universal Education Is an Investment for America," Brookings.edu, September 24, 2009, https://www.brookings.edu/blog/up-front/2009/09/24/universal-education-is-an-investment-for-america/.

32. Serpil Erzurum, "How Much of the Population Will Need to Be Vaccinated Until the Pandemic Is Over?," ClevelandClinic.org, May 5, 2021, https://health.clevelandclinic.org/how-much-of-the-population-will-need-to-be-vaccinated-until-the-pandemic-is-over/.

33. John Dewey, "Creative Democracy—The Task Before Us," in *America's Public Philosopher*, ed. Eric Thomas Weber (New York: Columbia University Press, 2021), 59–65.

34. John Dewey, "The Ethics of Democracy," in *The Early Works of John Dewey* ed. Jo Ann Boydston, vol. 1 (Carbondale: Southern Illinois University Press, 2008), 227–49, 240.

35. John Dewey, "Democracy Is Radical," in *America's Public Philosopher*, ed. Eric Thomas Weber (New York: Columbia University Press, 2021), 19–23.

36. John Rawls, *A Theory of Justice* (Cambridge, MA: Harvard University Press, 1971), 101.

37. See Thomas B. Edsall, "America Has Split, and It's Now in 'Very Dangerous Territory,'" *New York Times*, January 26, 2022, https://www.nytimes.com/2022/01/26/opinion/covid-biden-trump-polarization.html; and Drew Desilver, "The Polarization in Today's Congress Has Roots that Go Back Decades," *Pew Research Center*, March 10, 2022, https://www.pewresearch.org/fact-tank/2022/03/10/the-polarization-in-todays-congress-has-roots-that-go-back-decades/.

38. Lee McIntyre, *Post-Truth* (Cambridge, MA: MIT Press, 2018).

39. Chris Cameron, "These Are the People Who Died in Connection With the Capitol Riot," *New York Times*, January 5, 2022, https://www.nytimes.com/2022/01/05/us/politics/jan-6-capitol-deaths.html.

40. Putnam, "Democracy as a Way of Life," 448.

41. Saeed Ahmed, "It's 19 Weeks Into the Year and America Has Already Seen 198 Mass Shootings," NPR.org, May 15, 2022, https://www.npr.org/2022/05/15/1099008586/mass-shootings-us-2022-tally-number.

42. Dewey, "Creative Democracy—The Task Before Us," 62.

43. Diane Ravitch, *The Death and Life of the Great American School System: How Testing and Choice Are Undermining Education* (New York: Basic Books, 1994); Diane Ravitch, *Reign of Error: The Hoax of the Privatization Movement and the Danger to America's Public Schools* (New York: Vintage Press, 2014); and Diane Ravitch, *Slaying Goliath: The Passionate Resistance to Privatization and the Fight to Save America's Public Schools* (New York: Vintage Press, 2020).

Chapter 7

1. Stanley Ingber, "The Marketplace of Ideas: A Legitimizing Myth," *Duke Law Journal* 1 (1984): 3.

2. Ibid.

3. John Stuart Mill, *On Liberty* (1859; repr., Indianapolis, IN: Hackett, 1978), 46.

4. For discussion of Darwin's uneasy acceptance with particular attention to the development of American Pragmatism, see Louis Menand, *The Metaphysical Club: A Story of Ideas in America* (New York: Farrar, Straus, and Giroux, 2001), 103.

5. Seth Masket, "Texas' College Tenure Decision Undermines One of America's Proudest Accomplishments," NBCNews.com, March 9, 2022, https://www.nbcnews.com/think/opinion/texas-tenure-attack-america-s-colleges-embarrassing-ncna1291314.

6. Ingrid Jacques, "Trump Is Waging War Against DEI in Schools," *USA Today*, March 5, 2025, https://www.usatoday.com/story/opinion/columnist/2025/03/04/trump-dei-college-stanford-barnard-protests/80849201007/.

7. Alex Morey, "Statement on President Trump's Truth Social Post Threatening Funding Cuts for 'Illegal Protests,'" Fire.org, March 4, 2025, https://www.thefire.org/news/statement-president-trumps-truth-social-post-threatening-funding-cuts-illegal-protests.

8. Institute for Constitutional Advocacy and Protection (ICAP), "Fact Sheet: Protecting Against Voter Intimidation," Georgetown University Law Center, https://www.law.georgetown.edu/icap/wp-content/uploads/sites/32/2020/10/Voter-Intimidation-Fact-Sheet.pdf.

9. Carlton F. W. Larson, "Should 'Fire' in a Theater: The Life and Times of Constitutional Law's Most Enduring Analogy," *William and Mary Bill of Rights Journal* 24 (2015): 181–212.

10. Alistair Coleman, "'Hundreds Dead' Because of COVID-19 Misinformation," BBC News, August 12, 2020, https://www.bbc.com/news/world-53755067.

11. The saying is often attributed incorrectly to Mark Twain, when in fact it "appears to be descendant of a line published centuries ago by the satirist Jonathan Swift," according to Niraj Chokshi. See Niraj Chokshi, "That Wasn't Mark

Twain: How a Misquotation Is Born," *New York Times*, April 26, 2017, https://www.nytimes.com/2017/04/26/books/famous-misquotations.html. The author noted the irony that the saying is so often misattributed to Twain.

12. David Hildebrand, "Does Every Theory Deserve a Hearing? Evolution, Intelligent Design, and the Limits of Democratic Inquiry," *Southern Journal of Philosophy* 44, no. 2 (2006): 217–36.

13. See Rebecca Roman, "When Free Speech Isn't Free: The Rising Costs of Hosting Controversial Speakers at Public Universities," *University of Chicago Legal Forum* 2020 (2020): 451–76; Alyson R. Hamby, "You Are Not Cordially Invited: How Universities Maintain First Amendment Rights and Safety in the Midst of Controversial On-Campus Speakers," *Cornell Law Review* 104, no. 1 (November 2018): 287–316; and Leil Levy, "No-Platforming and Higher-Order Evidence, or Anti-Anti-No-Platforming," *Journal of the American Philosophical Association* 5, no. 4 (2019): 487–502.

14. David R. Dewberry, Ann Burnette, Rebekah Fox, and Pat Arneson, "Teaching Free Speech Across the Communication Studies Curriculum," *First Amendment Studies* 52, no. 1–2 (July 2018): 80–95.

15. Martin Luther King Jr., "Letter from a Birmingham Jail," *Atlantic Monthly* 212, no. 2 (1963): 78–88.

16. Once again, I am indebted to my colleague and friend Tibor Solymosi, who commented on my draft and noted the connection to the study of logic, which catalogs fallacies of reasoning, including this form. See John Woods, "*Argumentum ad Baculum*," *Argumentation* 12 (1998): 493–504. The italics in the article title are presented here as in the source.

17. John Dewey, "The Basic Values and Loyalties of Democracy," *American Teacher* 25 (May 1941): 8–9. Republished in LW.14.275–78.

18. See Michael P. Lynch, *Know-It-All Society* (New York: Liveright, 2020) as well as his forthcoming book, on which I was fortunate to hear one of his presentations, namely Michael P. Lynch, *On Truth in Politics: Why Democracy Demands It* (Princeton, NJ: Princeton University Press, 2025).

19. John Dewey, "Search for the Great Community," ch. 4 of *The Public and Its Problems*, in *The Collected Works of John Dewey, Volume 5*, ed. Jo Ann Boydston (Carbondale: Southern Illinois University Press, 1988), LW.2.325–50, 325.

20. Ibid.

21. For one of many outlooks on considering the challenge of the development of democratic intelligence in the time of social media misinformation, see Nabiha Syed, "Real Talk about Fake News: Towards a Better Theory for Platform Governance," *Yale Law Journal Forum* 127 (2017–2018): 337–57.

22. I am grateful to a blind reviewer for noting their sense that perhaps the Both Ways argument is even more persuasive, in the sense that we allow deeply troubling speech because we wish to protect other speech that might potentially be curtailed in like manner.

23. Matthew L. Schafer and Jeff Kosseff, "Protecting Free Speech in a Post-*Sullivan* World," *Federal Communications Law Journal* 75, no. 1 (2022): 4.

24. Adam Liptak, "Justice Clarence Thomas Calls for Reconsideration of Landmark Libel Ruling," *New York Times*, February 19, 2019, https://www.nytimes.com/2019/02/19/us/politics/clarence-thomas-first-amendment-libel.html.

25. Schafer and Kosseff, 2.

26. Daniel Politi, "Donald Trump Vows to Curb Press Freedom Through Harsher Libel Laws," *Slate*, February 27, 2016, https://slate.com/news-and-politics/2016/02/donald-trump-vows-to-curb-press-freedom-through-libel-laws.html.

27. Devan Cole, "Justice Thomas Renews Attacks on Landmark First Amendment Decision in Fiery Dissent," CNN, June 27, 2023, https://www.cnn.com/2023/06/27/politics/clarence-thomas-first-amendment-libel-new-york-times-supreme-court/index.html.

28. Schafer and Kosseff, 2.

29. Associated Press, "Timeline of the Nationwide Protest Movement that Began at Columbia University," APNews.com, May 6, 2024, https://apnews.com/article/israel-palestinian-campus-protests-timeline-f7cd3abe635f8afa4532b7bed9212b56.

30. *Virginia v. Black et al.* (2003), https://www.law.cornell.edu/supct/html/01-1107.ZS.html.

31. Mari J. Matsuda, "Public Response to Racist Speech: Considering the Victim's Story," *Words That Wound: Critical Race Theory, Assaultive Speech, and the First Amendment*, ed. Mari J. Matsuda, Charles R Lawrence III, Richard Delgado, and Kimberle Williams Crenshaw (Boulder, CO: Perseus Press, 1993), 17; Patsy Sims, *The Klan* (Lexington: University Press of Kentucky, 1996).

32. Hella Pick, "KKK Men Charged with Murder," *Guardian*, August 8, 1964, https://www.theguardian.com/world/1964/aug/08/usa.hellapick.

33. Geoffrey R. Stone, "The Noose, Ole Miss, and Free Speech," *Huffington Post*, April 22, 2014, https://www.huffpost.com/entry/the-noose-ole-miss-and-fr_b_4820588.

34. Alex Fox, "Nearly 2,000 Black Americans Were Lynched During Reconstruction," *Smithsonian*, June 18, 2020, https://www.smithsonianmag.com/smart-news/nearly-2000-black-americans-were-lynched-during-reconstruction-180975120/. Fox points to two reports that together add up to the estimate. See Equal Justice Initiative, "Reconstruction in America: Racial Violence after the Civil War, 1865–1876," Report, Montgomery, AL, 2020, https://eji.org/wp-content/uploads/2020/07/reconstruction-in-america-report.pdf; and Equal Justice Initiative, "Lynching in America: Confronting the Legacy of Racial Terror, Third Edition," Report, Montgomery, AL, 2017, https://eji.org/wp-content/uploads/2005/11/lynching-in-america-3d-ed-110121.pdf.

35. Alaa Elassar, "Why the Noose Is Such a Potent Symbol of Hate," CNN.com, June 23, 2020, https://www.cnn.com/2020/06/23/us/noose-hate-symbol-racism-trnd/index.html.

36. Staff, "Hospital Employee Fired After Photo of Him Wearing 'Mississippi Justice' T-Shirt While Voting Goes Viral," *Action News 5*, November 9, 2018, https://www.actionnews5.com/2018/11/08/hospital-employee-fired-after-photo-him-wearing-mississippi-justice-t-shirt-while-voting-goes-viral/.

37. Elizabeth Anderson, *Private Government: How Employers Rule Our Lives (and Why We Don't Talk About It)* (Princeton, NJ: Princeton University Press, 2019).

38. Lisa Stone, "UM Releases Enrollment for Fall 2020," *University of Mississippi News*, November 3, 2020, https://news.olemiss.edu/um-releases-enrollment-for-fall-2020/.

39. I am indebted to Tibor Solymosi for his valuable comment here, in which he noted that "conventions can be useful tools so long as they aid us in enriching our understanding of the problems we currently face; but too often conventions are not tools for inquiry but roadblocks to it."

40. See Bracey Harris, "Ex-Ole Miss Student Sentenced for Noose on Statue," *USA Today*, September 17, 2015, https://www.usatoday.com/story/news/nation/2015/09/17/ex-ole-miss-student-sentenced-noose-statue/72376068/; Susan Svrluga, "Former Ole Miss Student Pleads Guilty to Hanging Noose Around Statue Honoring the First Black Student," *Washington Post*, March 24, 2016, https://www.washingtonpost.com/news/grade-point/wp/2016/03/24/former-ole-miss-student-pleads-guilty-to-hanging-noose-around-statue-honoring-the-first-black-student/.

41. Svrluga, "Former Ole Miss Student Pleads Guilty to Hanging Noose."

42. David A. Love, "MLK Disobeyed Unjust Laws. The State of America Today Requires that We Not Forget That." NBC News, January 17, 2022, https://www.nbcnews.com/think/opinion/mlk-disobeyed-unjust-laws-state-america-today-requires-we-not-ncna1287569.

43. Jonathan Turley, "No, the U.S. Does Not Need European-Style Hate Speech Laws," *USA Today*, November 8, 2019, https://www.usatoday.com/story/opinion/2019/11/08/no-us-not-need-european-style-hate-speech-laws-column/4157833002/.

44. United Nations Human Rights Office of the High Commissioner, "One-Pager on 'Incitement to Hatred': The Rabat Threshold Test," United Nations, OHCHR.org, April 20, 2020, https://www.ohchr.org/en/documents/one-pager-incitement-hatred-rabat-threshold-test. Emphasis in the original.

45. US Department of Justice, "Hate Crime Laws: About Hate Crimes," Justice.gov, n.d., https://www.justice.gov/crt/hate-crime-laws. Emphasis added.

46. Liz Baker, "A Jury Finds Ahmaud Arbery's 3 Killers Guilty of Federal Hate Crimes," NPR.org, February 22, 2022, https://www.npr.org/2022/02/22/1082225480/ahmaud-arbery-hate-crimes.

47. I use the word consideration here because what ought or ought not to be proscribed should not be decided too quickly or easily, as in cases in which groups seek to "reclaim" a term or buck the effects of epithets, like the n-word or as in the band name "the Slants," involving a musical group including persons of Asian descent. See Bill Chappell, "The Slants Win Supreme Court

Battle Over Band's Name in Trademark Dispute," NPR.org, June 19, 2017, https://www.npr.org/sections/thetwo-way/2017/06/19/533514196/the-slants-win-supreme-court-battle-over-bands-name-in-trademark-dispute.

48. Dewey, "The Basic Values and Loyalties of Democracy."

49. When I first considered this apparent tension in the essay, I consulted two of my former professors who taught courses on Dewey's work, Larry A. Hickman and Tom Alexander, now emeritus professors at Southern Illinois University Carbondale. Both of them suggested to me that the key distinction at work concerned cultivation. I am grateful to each of them for their guidance to focus on cultivation.

50. Dewey, "The Basic Values and Loyalties of Democracy."

51. John Dewey, "Creative Democracy—The Task Before Us," in *America's Public Philosopher*, ed. Eric Thomas Weber (New York: Columbia University Press, 2021), 59–65. Also published in the standard edition of *The Collected Works of John Dewey*, LW.14.224–31.

52. Alyssa Schnugg, "Federal Prison for Harris," *Oxford Eagle*, September 18, 2015, https://www.oxfordeagle.com/2015/09/18/federal-prison-for-harris/. Italicized emphasis added.

53. Matt Zapotosky, "Ex-Ole Miss Student Admits Helping Put Noose on Statue of Civil Rights Figure," *Washington Post*, March 24, 2016, https://www.washingtonpost.com/news/post-nation/wp/2016/03/24/ex-ole-miss-student-admits-helping-put-noose-on-statue-of-civil-rights-figure/. The passage should read "Sigma Phi Epsilon."

54. University of Mississippi, UM Creed, https://olemiss.edu/info/creed.html.

55. Jack Nowlin was my colleague at the University of Mississippi when I was there, and he too has since moved on. He is responsible for none of my errors or flaws in interpretation or argument, of course.

56. See Sarah Sorial, "Can Saying Something Make It So? The Nature of Seditious Harm," *Law and Philosophy* 29, no. 3 (2010): 295. See also *Brandenburg v. Ohio* (1969), which ruled: "Since the statute, by its words and as applied, purports to punish mere advocacy and to forbid, on pain of criminal punishment, assembly with others merely to advocate the described type of action, it falls within the condemnation of the First and Fourteenth Amendments. Freedoms of speech and press do not permit a State to forbid advocacy of the use of force or of law violation except where such advocacy is directed to inciting or producing imminent lawless action and is likely to incite or produce such action. Whitney v. California, 274 U.S. 357, overruled." *Brandenburg v. Ohio*, 395 U.S. 444 (1969), Justia, U.S. Supreme Court, https://supreme.justia.com/cases/federal/us/395/444/.

57. John Dewey, "Social Absolutism," in *The Collected Works of John Dewey: The Middle Works, Volume 13*, ed. Jo Ann Boydston (Carbondale: Southern Illinois University Press, 1983), 315–16.

58. Stone, "The Noose, Ole Miss, and Free Speech."

59. Corey Brettschneider, *When the State Speaks, What Should It Say? How Democracies Can Protect and Promote Equality* (Princeton, NJ: Princeton University Press, 2012).

60. Sarah Jeong, "Should We Be Able to Reclaim a Racist Insult—as a Registered Trademark?," *New York Times*, January 17, 2017, https://www.nytimes.com/2017/01/17/magazine/should-we-be-able-to-reclaim-a-racist-insult-as-a-registered-trademark.html.

61. Chappell, "The Slants Win Supreme Court Battle Over Band's Name in Trademark Dispute."

62. Garrett Epps, "Clarence Thomas Takes on a Symbol of White Supremacy," *Atlantic*, June 18, 2015, https://www.theatlantic.com/politics/archive/2015/06/clarence-thomas-confederate-flag/396281/.

63. Ibid.

64. Rachel Treisman, "Nearly 100 Confederate Monuments Removed in 2020, Report Says; More than 700 Remain," NPR.org, February 23, 2021, https://www.npr.org/2021/02/23/970610428/nearly-100-confederate-monuments-removed-in-2020-report-says-more-than-700-remai.

65. See Cheryl Bailey Gittens, "The McNair Program as a Socializing Influence on Doctoral Degree Attainment," *Peabody Journal of Education* 89 (2014): 368–79.

66. "About," McNairScholars.com, https://mcnairscholars.com/about/.

67. University of Mississippi, UM Creed.

68. University of Kentucky Office of Student Conduct, University of Kentucky Creed, https://www.uky.edu/studentconduct/university-kentucky-creed, last accessed April 27, 2022.

69. John Dewey, *A Common Faith* (1934; repr., New Haven, CT: Yale University Press, 2013).

70. Associated Press, "Jefferson Davis School in Mississippi Renamed in Honor of Barack Obama," *Birmingham News*, October 18, 2017, https://www.al.com/news/2017/10/mississippi_renames_jefferson.html.

71. Student Government Assembly, "AR 35: In Support of Removing the Jefferson Davis Statue at UT," University of Texas at Austin, March 24, 2015, https://repositories.lib.utexas.edu/bitstream/handle/2152/42815/9AR%2035.pdf?sequence=1. The document records that the statement was passed by "handvote."

72. Ibid.

73. Martin Luther King Jr., *A Testament of Hope: The Essential Writings and Speeches*, ed. James M. Washington (New York: Harper One, 2003), 217–20.

74. Chad Kautzer, "Notes for a Critical Theory of Community Self-Defense," in *Setting Sights: Histories and Reflections on Community Armed Self-Defense*, ed. scott crow (Oakland, CA: PM Press, 2018), 3548.

75. Eric Thomas Weber, "Sometimes Heritage Does Harm," *Clarion Ledger*, June 27, 2015, https://www.clarionledger.com/story/opinion/columnists/

2015/06/27/weber-sometimes-heritage-harm/29392617/; and Eric Thomas Weber, "Mr. Bryant, Take Down This Flag," *Clarion Ledger*, September 18, 2015, https://www.clarionledger.com/story/opinion/columnists/2015/09/18/weber-mr-bryant-take-down-flag/72413896/.

76. Emily Wagster Pettus, "KKK Plans to Protest at Ole Miss Over Song, Chant," BET, November 23, 2009, https://www.bet.com/article/sowav2/kkk-plans-to-protest-at-ole-miss-over-song-chant.

77. Judson Berger, "Arizonans Rally to Prevent Westboro Church Disruption of Shooting Victims' Funerals," Fox News, November 11, 2010, https://www.foxnews.com/politics/arizonans-rally-to-prevent-westboro-church-disruption-of-shooting-victims-funerals.

78. Ibid.

79. Paul P. Murphy, "White Nationalists Use Tiki Torches to Light Up Charlottesville March," CNN, August 14, 2017, https://www.cnn.com/2017/08/12/us/white-nationalists-tiki-torch-march-trnd/index.html.

80. Scott Neuman, "Boston Right-Wing 'Free Speech' Rally Dwarfed by Counterprotestors," NPR News, August 19, 2017, https://www.npr.org/sections/the-two-way/2017/08/19/544684355/bostons-free-speech-rally-organizers-deny-links-to-white-nationalists?t=1648596601730.

81. Robbie Brown, "Anti-Obama Protest at Ole Miss Turns Unruly," *New York Times*, November 7, 2012, https://www.nytimes.com/2012/11/08/us/anti-obama-protest-at-university-of-mississippi-turns-unruly.html.

82. Michele Reese, "Ole Miss Students Walk in Unity after Campus Protest," WREG Memphis Channel 3 News, November 7, 2012, https://wreg.com/news/ole-miss-students-walk-in-unity-after-campus-protest/.

83. I am grateful to a blind reviewer for deeply thoughtful suggestions for lines of concern that must be factored into a defense of my argument.

84. Mari J. Matsuda, Charles R. Lawrence, III, Richard Delgado, and Kimberlé Williams Crenshaw, eds., *Words That Wound: Critical Race Theory, Assaultive Speech, and the First Amendment* (Boulder, CO: Perseus Press, 1993).

85. Liam Stack, "Attack on Alt-Right Leader Has Internet Asking: Is It O.K. to Punch a Nazi?," *New York Times*, January 21, 2017, https://www.nytimes.com/2017/01/21/us/politics/richard-spencer-punched-attack.html.

86. Rachel A. Feinstein, *When Rape Was Legal: The Untold History of Sexual Violence During Slavery* (New York: Routledge, 2018).

87. Shelby Steele, *White Guilt: How Blacks and White Together Destroyed the Promise of the Civil Rights Era* (New York: Harper, 2006).

88. Hildebrand, "Does Every Theory Deserve a Hearing?"

89. Editorial Board, "America Has a Free Speech Problem," *New York Times*, March 18, 2022, https://www.nytimes.com/2022/03/18/opinion/cancel-culture-free-speech-poll.html.

Chapter 8

1. Robby Soave, "Bernie Sanders: Donald Trump Won Because People Are Tired of Political Correctness," *Reason*, December 13, 2016, https://reason.com/2016/12/13/bernie-sanders-donald-trump-won-because/.

2. Nick Gass, "Trump: I'm So Tired of This Politically Correct Crap," *Politico*, September 23, 2015, https://www.politico.com/story/2015/09/donald-trump-politically-correct-crap-213988.

3. Dana Milbank, "The GOP Turns 'Political Correctness' Into the Mother of All Straw Men," *Washington Post*, December 21, 2015, https://www.washingtonpost.com/opinions/the-gop-turns-political-correctness-into-the-mother-of-all-straw-men/2015/12/21/90ab5398-a816-11e5-bff5-905b92f5f94b_story.html.

4. See staff writer, "More People Tired of Political Correctness but Research Reveals Big Political Divide," *Christian Today*, December 22, 2018, https://www.christiantoday.com/article/more-people-are-tired-of-political-correctness-but-research-reveals-big-political-divide/131302.htm; and NPR/PBS News Hour/Marist Poll, "PDTCIVGAL1," November 28–December 4, 2018, http://maristpoll.marist.edu/wp-content/uploads/2018/12/NPR_PBS-NewsHour_Marist-Poll_USA-NOS-and-Tables_Civility_1812051719.pdf#page=3.

5. James Hibberd, "Steve Harvey Slams 'Cancel Culture': 'Political Correctness Has Killed Comedy,'" *Hollywood Reporter*, January 11, 2022, https://www.hollywoodreporter.com/tv/tv-news/steve-harvey-cancel-culture-1235073289/.

6. Rebecca Shaw, "Political Correctness Isn't Killing Comedy. Scared Old Stagnant Comedians Are," *Guardian*, May 27, 2018, https://www.theguardian.com/culture/2018/may/28/political-correctness-isnt-killing-comedy-scared-old-stagnant-comedians-are.

7. Katie Lobosco, "Ben Carson: Political Correctness Is Going to 'Destroy Our Nation,'" CNN Politics, October 22, 2019, https://www.cnn.com/2019/10/22/politics/ben-carson-transgender-political-correctness/index.html.

8. Tania Ahsan, "Don't Call Me Babe," *Guardian*, June 5, 2006, https://www.theguardian.com/money/2006/jun/05/careers.theguardian5.

9. Joanna Allhands, "Are We Finally Ready to Stop Fighting the War on Christmas?," *Republic*, December 20, 2017, https://www.azcentral.com/story/opinion/op-ed/joannaallhands/2017/12/20/stop-fighting-war-christmas/949183001/.

10. Axel Honneth, *The Struggle for Recognition: The Moral Grammar of Social Conflicts* (Cambridge, MA: MIT Press, 1995).

11. Oxford English Dictionary, "Definition of politically correct," OED Online, June 2022, Oxford University Press, https://www-oed-com.ezproxy.uky.edu/view/Entry/146889?redirectedFrom=%22politically+correct%22.

12. William James, *Pragmatism and Other Writings* (New York: Penguin Classics, 2000), 24.

13. For several examples, see Jonathan Zimmerman, "The Two Kinds of PC," InsideHigherEd.com, June 16, 2016, https://www.insidehighered.com/views/2016/06/16/examination-two-kinds-political-correctness-essay; Kat Chow, " 'Politically Correct': The Phrase Has Gone from Wisdom to Weapon," NPR.org, December 14, 2016, https://www.npr.org/sections/codeswitch/2016/12/14/505324427/politically-correct-the-phrase-has-gone-from-wisdom-to-weapon; Matthew Hutson, "Why Liberals Aren't as Tolerant as They Think," *Politico*, May 9, 2017, https://www.politico.com/magazine/story/2017/05/09/why-liberals-arent-as-tolerant-as-they-think-215114/; John Wilson, "Myths and Facts: How Real Is Political Correctness?," *William Mitchell Law Review* 22, no. 2 (1996): 517–43, https://open.mitchellhamline.edu/cgi/viewcontent.cgi?article=2045&context=wmlr; Melanie Tannenbaum, "Decoding Trump-Mania: The Psychological Allure of Hating Political Correctness, Part 3," *Scientific American*, September 8, 2015, https://blogs.scientificamerican.com/psysociety/decoding-trump-mania-the-psychological-allure-of-hating-political-correctness-part-3/; and Manuel Doria, "The Unreasonable Destructiveness of Political Correctness in Philosophy," *Philosophies* 2, no. 17 (2017): 1–56.

14. Kyle Balluck, "Carson: 'Political Correctness Will Destroy Us If We Don't Wake Up,' " *The Hill*, January 3, 2016, https://thehill.com/blogs/ballot-box/presidential-races/264607-carson-political-correctness-will-destroy-us-if-we-dont.

15. Stephen Hawkinds, Daniel Yudkin, Miriam Juan-Torres, and Tim Dixon, "Hidden Tribes: A Study of America's Polarized Landscape," [Report] More in Common, New York, NY, 2018, https://hiddentribes.us/media/qfpekz4g/hidden_tribes_report.pdf.

16. Ibid., 12.

17. Ibid., 14.

18. Yascha Mounk, "Americans Strongly Dislike PC Culture," *Atlantic*, October 10, 2018, https://www.theatlantic.com/ideas/archive/2018/10/large-majorities-dislike-political-correctness/572581/.

19. Justin Victory, "Pro-Confederate Groups, Fed Up with 'Political Correctness BS,' to Rally at Ole Miss," *Clarion Ledger*, February 19, 2019, https://www.clarionledger.com/story/news/2019/02/19/pro-confederate-flag-group-rally-ole-miss-liberal-conservative-colonel-reb/2916686002/. The "groove" was likely referring to the nine-acre grove at the heart of the University of Mississippi's campus.

20. Staff, "Hospital Employee Fired After Photo of Him Wearing 'Mississippi Justice' T-Shirt While Voting Goes Viral," ActionNews5.com, November 9, 2018, https://www.actionnews5.com/2018/11/08/hospital-employee-fired-after-photo-him-wearing-mississippi-justice-t-shirt-while-voting-goes-viral/.

21. "The Declaration of Causes of Seceding States," American Battlefield Trust, sponsored by the History Channel, https://www.battlefields.org/learn/primary-sources/declaration-causes-seceding-states.

22. State of Mississippi, "A Declaration of the Immediate Causes which Induce and Justify the Secession of the State of Mississippi from the Federal Union," in *An Address Setting Forth the Declaration of the Immediate Causes Which Induce and Justify the Secession of Mississippi from the Federal Union and the Ordinance of Secession* (Jackson: Mississippian Book and Job Printing Office, 1861), 3, https://ia600202.us.archive.org/26/items/addresssettingfo01miss/address settingfo01miss.pdf.

23. Janelle Ross, "The Story Behind the University of New Hampshire's 'Bias-Free Language Guide,'" *Washington Post*, July 30, 2015, https://www.washington post.com/news/the-fix/wp/2015/07/30/the-story-behind-the-university-of-new-hampshires-bias-free-language-guide/?utm_term=.d154c4136193.

24. Audrey Elisa Kerr, "The Paper Bag Principle: Of the Myth and Motion of Colorism," *Journal of American Folklore* 118, no. 469 (2005): 271–89.

25. Ibid. On "passing as white," see also Emery Petchauer, "Passing as White: Race, Shame, and Success in Teacher Licensure Testing Events for Black Preservice Teachers," *Race, Ethnicity, and Education* 18, no. 6 (2015): 834–87.

26. Henry Louis Gates Jr., and Cornel West, *The Future of the Race* (New York: Vintage Press, 1997), 18.

27. Amanda Taselaar, "Don't Call It a Brown Bag Lunch," *Time*, August 6, 2013, http://newsfeed.time.com/2013/08/06/dont-call-it-a-brown-bag-lunch-seattle-frowns-on-popular-term/.

28. See Rebecca Nicholson, " 'Poor Little Snowflake'—The Defining Insult of 2016," *Guardian*, November 28, 2016, https://www.theguardian.com/science/2016/nov/28/snowflake-insult-disdain-young-people; and Ross K. Baker, "My University Doesn't Graduate Politically Correct Snowflakes, That's Fake News," *USA Today*, May 14, 2018, https://www.usatoday.com/story/opinion/2018/05/14/universities-fake-news-our-graduates-not-pc-snowflakes-column/605916002/.

29. Kristine Phillips, "A School District Drops 'To Kill a Mockingbird' and 'Huckleberry Finn' Over Use of the N-Word," *Washington Post*, February 7, 2018, https://www.washingtonpost.com/news/education/wp/2018/02/07/a-school-district-drops-to-kill-a-mockingbird-and-huckleberry-finn-over-use-of-the-n-word/.

30. Darby Williams, "The Shrew's Dilemma," *Michigan Daily*, August 5, 2021, https://www.michigandaily.com/arts/campus-culture/the-shrews-dilemma/.

31. Suzanne Ito, "Confederate Flag at Louisiana Courthouse Taints Death Penalty System with Racial Bias," ACLU Speak Freely, May 10, 2011, https://www.aclu.org/blog/smart-justice/mass-incarceration/confederate-flag-louisiana-courthouse-taints-death-penalty.

32. Bill Chappell, "The Slants Win Supreme Court Battle Over Band's Name in Trademark Dispute," NPR, June 19, 2017, https://www.npr.org/sections/thetwo-way/2017/06/19/533514196/the-slants-win-supreme-court-battle-over-bands-name-in-trademark-dispute.

33. Sydney Page, "Once the 'World's Only Klan Museum,' It Is Becoming a Center for History and Healing," *Washington Post*, January 8, 2021, https://www.washingtonpost.com/lifestyle/2021/01/08/kkk-museum-redneck-race-healing/.

34. Corey Brettschneider, *When the State Speaks, What Should It Say? How Democracies Can Protect and Promote Equality* (Princeton, NJ: Princeton University Press, 2012).

35. A friend, colleague, and editor, Tibor Solymosi, wondered what to think about the name "Oklahoma," whose etymology translates as "red people." The word was "coined by Choctaw scholar and Presbyterian minister Allen Wright (1826–1885), later principal chief of the Choctaw Nation, and first used in the Choctaw-Chickasaw treaty of April 28, 1866." I would not speak for others about whether the word is problematic, but it is a matter of culture to consider and for which it is important that people listen to those who would speak to what such a word means for their culture and identities. "Oklahoma," Online Etymology Dictionary, https://www.etymonline.com/search?q=oklahoma.

36. Of course, the same root is found in police and politesse.

37. Henry Samuel, "France's Académie Française Battles to Protect Language from English," *Telegraph*, October 11, 2011, https://www.telegraph.co.uk/news/worldnews/europe/france/8820304/Frances-Academie-francaise-battles-to-protect-language-from-English.html.

38. Harmeet Kaur, "FYI: English Isn't the Official Language of the United States," CNN, June 15, 2018, https://www.cnn.com/2018/05/20/us/english-us-official-language-trnd/index.html.

39. National Endowment for the Arts, "Quick Facts," Arts.gov, https://www.arts.gov/sites/default/files/Quick_Facts_February2020.pdf.

40. Janima Nam, "The Art of Funding," *Metropole*, Spring 2021, 88, https://michael-wimmer.at/wp-content/uploads/2021/03/88_MET_Spring_21_CityLife.pdf.

41. Kaur, "FYI: English Isn't the Official Language of the United States."

42. Joshua Q. Nelson, "North Dakota Parents Furious after School Board Nixes Pledge of Allegiance: 'Bunch of Crap,'" FoxNews.com, August 12, 2022, https://www.foxnews.com/media/north-dakota-parents-furious-school-board-nixes-pledge-allegiance-bunch-crap.

43. Herbert Jack Rotfeld, "Can You Really Say That?," *Journal of Consumer Affairs* 42, no. 3 (2008): 484–87.

44. Allana Akhtar, "Brits Are Calling Out the 'Dystopian' and 'Post-Apocalyptic' American Pharma Ads That Aired During Oprah's Interview with Meghan Markle and Prince Harry," *Business Insider*, March 8, 2021, https://www.businessinsider.com/brits-call-american-pharmaceutical-ads-post-apocalyptic-2021-3.

45. Dan Mangan, "Americans Oppose Fast Approvals, Want Drug Ads Off TV: Survey," NBCNews.com, May 11, 2016, https://www.nbcnews.com/health/health-care/americans-oppose-fast-approvals-want-drug-ads-tv-survey-n572301.

46. When I mention conventional thinking here, the point is in distinction from Larry A. Hickman's observation that when you add one drop of water to another, you do not get two drops of water, but one larger drop. See Larry A. Hickman, *Philosophical Tools for Technological Culture* (Bloomington: Indiana University Press, 2001), 50.

47. Aristotle, *Nichomachean Ethics* (New York: Oxford World Classics, 1998), Book I.3, 3.

48. Lia Sestric, "30 U.S. Cities Where Million-Dollar Homes Are Practically the Norm," BusinessInsider.com, December 13, 2017, https://www.businessinsider. com/30-us-cities-where-million-dollar-homes-are-practically-the-norm-2017-12.

49. Associated Press, "Annual Cost to Attend Duke University Approaches $75,000," *Winston-Salem Journal*, February 23, 2019, https://journalnow.com/annual-cost-to-attend-duke-university-approaches-75-000/article_0040438a-483e-5395-b9a0-b772ab6ddeb3.html.

50. See Office of Minority Health, "Profile: Black/African Americans," US Department of Health and Human Services, https://www.minorityhealth.hhs.gov/omh/browse.aspx?lvl=3&lvlid=61.

51. James E. Murray Jr., "Making Distinctions: An Ethical Argument for Increasing American Descendants of Slavery (ADOS) Presence In Universities Through Disaggregating "Black" Racial Data/Categorization" (paper presented at Mid-Western Educational Research Association [MWERA] 43rd Annual Meeting, October 13–15, 2021, Cincinnati, OH).

52. Honneth, *The Struggle for Recognition*.

53. Victoria Moll-Ramirez, Cecily Cruz, Penelope Lopez, and Kiara Alfonseca, "Latinx? Latino? Hispanic? A Linguistics Expert Explains the Confusion," ABCNews.com, January 15, 2022, https://abcnews.go.com/US/latinx-latino-hispanic-linguistics-expert-explains-confusion/story?id=82273936.

54. Garrett Epps, "Clarence Thomas Takes on a Symbol of White Supremacy," *Atlantic*, June 18, 2015, https://www.theatlantic.com/politics/archive/2015/06/clarence-thomas-confederate-flag/396281/.

55. Howard A. Ohline, "Republicanism and Slavery: Origins of the Three-Fifths Clause in the United States Constitution," *William and Mary Quarterly* 28, no. 4 (October 1971): 563–84.

56. Samuel Issacharoff and Pamela S. Karlan, "Groups, Politics, and the Equal Protection Clause," *University of Miami Law Review* 58, no. 1 (2003): 35–50.

57. Jennifer K. Walter and Eran P. Klein, eds., *The Story of Bioethics: From Seminal Works to Contemporary Explorations* (Washington, DC: Georgetown University Press, 2003).

58. Honneth, *The Struggle for Recognition*, 92–130.

59. Honneth, *The Struggle for Recognition*, 131–39.

60. Honneth, 129.

61. Nicola Slawson, "First Thing: Joe Biden Says 'White Supremacy Is a Poison,'" *Guardian*, May 18, 2022, https://www.theguardian.com/us-news/2022/may/18/first-thing-joe-biden-says-white-supremacy-is-a-poison.

62. Larry McShane, "Interracial Marriage Should Be Illegal, Say 46% of Mississippi Republicans in New Poll," *New York Daily News*, April 8, 2011, https://www.nydailynews.com/news/national/interracial-marriage-illegal-46-mississippi-republicans-new-poll-article-1.111449.

63. Hawkinds, "Hidden Tribes," 12.

64. Tanya Titchkosky, "Disability: A Rose by Any Other Name? 'People-First' Language in Canadian Society," *Canadian Review of Sociology* 38, no. 2 (2001): 125–40.

65. Jim Sinclair, "Why I Dislike "Person First" Language," *Autonomy: The Critical Journal of Interdisciplinary Autism Studies* 1, no. 2 (2013), http://www.larry-arnold.net/Autonomy/index.php/autonomy/article/view/OP1.

66. Madeleine Mendelow, "Beyond the Binary," *Psychiatric Times*, April 4, 2022, https://www.psychiatrictimes.com/view/beyond-the-binary.

67. Ryan T. Anderson, "Transgender Ideology Is Riddled with Contradictions. Here Are the Big Ones." Heritage Foundation, Commentary, February 9, 2018, https://www.heritage.org/gender/commentary/transgender-ideology-riddled-contradictions-here-are-the-big-ones.

68. See Tinbete Ermyas and Kira Wakeam, "Wave of Bills to Block Trans Athletes Has No Basis in Science, Research Says," NPR.org, March 18, 2021, https://www.npr.org/2021/03/18/978716732/wave-of-new-bills-say-trans-athletes-have-an-unfair-edge-what-does-the-science-s; and David W. Chen, "Transgender Athletes Face Bans From Girls' Sports in 10 U.S. States," *New York Times*, October 28, 2021, https://www.nytimes.com/article/transgender-athlete-ban.html.

69. Nicholas Confessore and Karen Yourish, "A Fringe Conspiracy Theory, Fostered Online, Is Refashioned by the G.O.P.," *New York Times*, May 15, 2022, https://www.nytimes.com/2022/05/15/us/replacement-theory-shooting-tucker--carlson.html.

70. Daniel Arkin, "Fox News' Tucker Carlson Under Fresh Scrutiny After Buffalo Mass Shooting," NBC News, May 16, 2022, https://www.nbcnews.com/news/us-news/fox-news-tucker-carlson-fresh-scrutiny-buffalo-mass-shooting-rcna29084.

71. Michelle Boorstein, "Matthew Shepard, Whose 1998 Murder Became a Symbol for the Gay Rights Movement, Will Be Interred at Washington National Cathedral," *Washington Post*, October 11, 2018, https://www.washingtonpost.com/religion/2018/10/11/matthew-shepard-whose-murder-became-symbol-gay-rights-movement-will-be-interred-washington-national-cathedral/.

72. Jason Silverstein, "The Global Impact of George Floyd: How Black Lives Matter Protests Shaped Movements Around the World," CBS News, June 4, 2021, https://www.cbsnews.com/news/george-floyd-black-lives-matter-impact/.

73. Madeleine Carlisle, "Anti-Trans Violence and Rhetoric Reached Record Highs Across America in 2021," *Time*, December 30, 2021, https://time.com/6131444/2021-anti-trans-violence/.

Bibliography

"About." McNairScholars.com. https://mcnairscholars.com/about/.

ABS Contributor. "8 Disturbingly Racist Children's Books Designed to Devalue Black People." *Atlanta Black Star*, February 21, 2014. http://atlantablackstar. com/2014/02/21/8-disturbingly-racist-childrens-books-designed-to-devalue-black-people/.

ACLU. "Confederate Flag to Be Removed from Outside Louisiana Courthouse." News release, November 4, 2011. https://www.aclu.org/press-releases/confederate-flag-be-removed-outside-louisiana-courthouse.

Ackerman, Daniel. "Before Face Masks, Americans Went to War Against Seat Belts." *Business Insider*, May 26, 2020. https://www.businessinsider.com/when-americans-went-to-war-against-seat-belts-2020-5.

Ahmed, Saeed. "It's 19 Weeks Into the Year and America Has Already Seen 198 Mass Shootings." NPR, May 15, 2022. https://www.npr.org/2022/05/15/1099008586/mass-shootings-us-2022-tally-number.

Ahsan, Tania. "Don't Call Me Babe." *Guardian*, June 5, 2006. https://www.theguardian.com/money/2006/jun/05/careers.theguardian5.

Akhtar, Allana. "Brits Are Calling Out the 'Dystopian' and 'Post-Apocalyptic' American Pharma Ads That Aired During Oprah's Interview with Meghan Markle and Prince Harry." *Business Insider*, March 8, 2021. https://www.business insider.com/brits-call-american-pharmaceutical-ads-post-apocalyptic-2021-3.

Alexander, Harriet, and Fiona Govan. "Beware Greeks Who Will Not Pay Their Income Tax." *Sunday Telegraph*, June 26, 2011, 28–29.

Alexander, Michelle. *The New Jim Crow*. New York: The New Press, 2012.

Allhands, Joanna. "Are We Finally Ready to Stop Fighting the War on Christmas?" *Republic*, December 20, 2017. https://www.azcentral.com/story/opinion/op-ed/joannaallhands/2017/12/20/stop-fighting-war-christmas/949183001/.

Anderson, Elizabeth. *The Imperative of Integration*. Princeton, NJ: Princeton University Press, 2010.

Anderson, Elizabeth. *Private Government: How Employers Rule Our Lives (and Why We Don't Talk About It)*. Princeton, NJ: Princeton University Press, 2019.

Anderson, Nick, and Susan Svrluga. "From Slavery to Jim Crow to George Floyd: Virginia Universities Face a Long Racial Reckoning." *Washington Post*, November 26, 2021. https://www.washingtonpost.com/education/2021/11/26/virginia-universities-slavery-race-reckoning/.

Anderson, Ryan T. "Transgender Ideology Is Riddled with Contradictions. Here Are the Big Ones." The Heritage Foundation, Commentary, February 9, 2018. https://www.heritage.org/gender/commentary/transgender-ideology-riddled-contradictions-here-are-the-big-ones.

Anderson, Theresa, Amelia Coffey, Hannah Daly, Heather Hahn, Elaine Maag, and Kevin Werner. "Balancing at the Edge of the Cliff: Experiences and Calculations of Benefits Cliffs, Plateaus, and Trade-Offs." Urban Institute, 2022. https://www.urban.org/sites/default/files/publication/105321/balancing-at-the-edge-of-the-cliff.pdf.

Andrews, Kenneth T. "Movement-Counter Movement Dynamics and the Emergence of New Institutions: The Case of 'White Flight' Schools in Mississippi." *Social Forces* 80, no. 3 (2002): 911–36.

Apel, Therese. "Deryl Dedmon, Two Others Sentenced from 7-50 Years in Hate Crime." *Clarion Ledger*, February 10, 2015. https://www.clarionledger.com/story/news/2015/02/10/deryl-dedmon-two-others-to-be-sentenced-in-hate-crime-tuesday/23166397/.

Appiah, Kwame Anthony. *The Honor Code: How Moral Revolutions Happen*. New York: W.W. Norton, 2011.

Aristotle. *Nichomachean Ethics*. Translated by David Ross. New York: Oxford University Press, 2009.

Arkin, Daniel. "Fox News' Tucker Carlson Under Fresh Scrutiny After Buffalo Mass Shooting." NBC News, May 16, 2022. https://www.nbcnews.com/news/us-news/fox-news-tucker-carlson-fresh-scrutiny-buffalo-mass-shooting-rcna29084.

Armoudian, Maria. "Where the Bucks Don't Stop." *Australasian Journal of American Studies* 37, no. 1 (2018): 25–62.

Armstrong, April C. "African Americans and Princeton University." Mudd Manuscript Library Blog, Princeton University Archives and Public Policy Papers Collection, May 27, 2015. https://blogs.princeton.edu/mudd/2015/05/african-americans-and-princeton-university/.

Arneson, Krystin. "Why Doesn't the U.S. Have Mandated Paid Maternity Leave?" BBC, June 28, 2021. https://www.bbc.com/worklife/article/20210624-why-doesnt-the-us-have-mandated-paid-maternity-leave.

Ashtari, Shadee. "KKK Leader Disputes Hate Group Label: 'We're a Christian Organization.'" *Huffington Post*, March 21, 2014. http://www.huffingtonpost.com/2014/03/21/virginia-kkk-fliers_n_5008647.html.

Asser, Seth M., and Rita Swan. "Child Fatalities from Religion-Motivated Medical Neglect." *Pediatrics* 101, no. 4 (1998): 625–29.

Associated Press. "Annual Cost to Attend Duke University Approaches $75,000." *Winston-Salem Journal*, February 23, 2019. https://journalnow.com/annual-cost-to-attend-duke-university-approaches-75-000/article_0040438a-483e-5395-b9a0-b772ab6ddeb3.html.

Associated Press. "Jefferson Davis School in Mississippi Renamed in Honor of Barack Obama." *Birmingham News*, October 18, 2017. https://www.al.com/news/2017/10/mississippi_renames_jefferson.html.

Associated Press. "Supreme Court Won't Hear Case Involving Transgender Rights." *U.S. News and World Report*, November 1, 2021. https://www.usnews.com/news/health-news/articles/2021-11-01/supreme-court-wont-hear-case-involving-transgender-rights.

Associated Press. "Timeline of the Nationwide Protest Movement that Began at Columbia University." APNews.com, May 6, 2024. https://apnews.com/article/israel-palestinian-campus-protests-timeline-f7cd3abe635f8afa4532b7bed9212b56.

Avery, Alison, Justin Chase, Linda Johansson, Samantha Litvak, Darrel Montero, and Michael Wydra. "America's Changing Attitudes toward Homosexuality, Civil Unions, and Same-Gender Marriage: 1977–2004." *Social Work* 52, no. 1 (2007): 71–79.

Baker, Liz. "A Jury Finds Ahmaud Arbery's 3 Killers Guilty of Federal Hate Crimes." NPR, February 22, 2022. https://www.npr.org/2022/02/22/1082225480/ahmaud-arbery-hate-crimes.

Baker, Ross K. "My University Doesn't Graduate Politically Correct Snowflakes, That's Fake News." *USA Today*, May 14, 2018. https://www.usatoday.com/story/opinion/2018/05/14/universities-fake-news-our-graduates-not-pc-snowflakes-column/605916002/.

Balfantz, Robert, and Johns Hopkins Researchers. "More Information on the Methodology, Data and Terms Used in the AP Dropout Factory Story." Center for Social Organization of Schools, 2007. http://web.jhu.edu/CSOS/images/AP.html.

Balluck, Kyle. "Carson: 'Political Correctness Will Destroy Us If We Don't Wake Up.'" *The Hill*, January 3, 2016. https://thehill.com/blogs/ballot-box/presidential-races/264607-carson-political-correctness-will-destroy-us-if-we-dont.

Balter, Michael. "Human Altruism Traces Back to the Origins of Humanity." *Science*, August 27, 2014. https://www.science.org/content/article/human-altruism-traces-back-origins-humanity.

Barnes, Robert. "Supreme Court: Texas Doesn't Have to Allow Confederate Flag License Plates." *Washington Post*, June 18, 2015. http://www.washingtonpost.com/politics/courts_law/supreme-court-texas-doesnt-have-to-allow-confederate-flag-license-plates/2015/06/18/d328b824-15c6-11e5-89f3-61410da94eb1_story.html.

Barnum, Matt, and Kalyn Belsha. "Protests, Donations, Lesson Plans: How the Education World Is Responding to George Floyd's Killing." Chalkbeat, June 2, 2020. https://www.chalkbeat.org/2020/6/2/21278591/education-schools-george-floyd-racism.

Baron, Dennis. "A Brief History of the Singular 'They.'" *Oxford English Dictionary*, September 4, 2018. https://public.oed.com/blog/a-brief-history-of-singular-they/.

Barrabi, Thomas. "Walmart, McDonald's Among Largest Employers of SNAP, Medicaid Recipients: Report." Fox Business, November 18, 2020. https://www.foxbusiness.com/markets/walmart-mcdonalds-largest-employers-snap-medicaid-recipients.

Barragán, James. "In Roe Decision, Justice Clarence Thomas Invites New Legal Challenges to Contraception and Same Sex Marriage Rights." *Texas Tribune*, June 24, 2022. https://www.texastribune.org/2022/06/24/roe-wade-clarence-thomas-contraception-same-sex-marriage/.

Barthold, Lauren Swayne. "Rorty, Religion, and the Public-Private Distinction." *Philosophy and Social Criticism* 38, no. 8 (2012): 861–78.

Bassuk, Ellen L., Carmela J. DeCandia, Corey Anne Beach, and Fred Berman. "America's Youngest Outcasts: A Report on Child Homelessness." American Institutes for Research, National Center on Family Homelessness. Waltham, MA, November 2014. https://www.air.org/sites/default/files/downloads/report/Americas-Youngest-Outcasts-Child-Homelessness-Nov2014.pdf.

Bauer, Lauren. "Does Head Start Work? The Debate Over the Head Start Impact Study, Explained." Brookings, June 14, 2019. https://www.brookings.edu/blog/brown-center-chalkboard/2019/06/14/does-head-start-work-the-debate-over-the-head-start-impact-study-explained/.

Beiner, Camila. "Homeless Youth and Children Are Wildly Undercounted, Advocates Say." NPR.org, February 15 2022. https://www.npr.org/2022/02/15/1073791409/homeless-youth-and-children-are-wildly-undercounted-advocates-say.

Bell, Derrick. "Brown v. Board of Education and the Interest-Convergence Dilemma." *Harvard Law Review* 93, no. 3 (1980): 518–33.

Bell, Derrick. *Faces at the Bottom of the Well: The Permanence of Racism*. New York: Basic Books, 1993.

Bell, Derrick. *Silent Covenants: Brown v. Board of Education and the Unfulfilled Hopes for Racial Reform*. New York: Oxford University Press, 2005.

Benedict, Ruth. *Patterns of Culture*. 1934; reprint, New York: Mariner Books, 2005.

Bentley, Rosalind. "After Dylann Roof, What's the Fate of the Confederate Flag?" *Atlanta Journal-Constitution*, January 9, 2017. https://www.ajc.com/news/crime--law/after-dylann-roof-what-the-fate-the-confederate-flag/HaCtiPvplkXOdQbn6jAhAN/.

Berger, Judson. "Arizonans Rally to Prevent Westboro Church Disruption of Shooting Victims' Funerals." Fox News, November 11, 2010. https://www.foxnews.com/politics/arizonans-rally-to-prevent-westboro-church-disruption-of-shooting-victims-funerals.

"Biography: James K. Vardaman." *American Experience*, PBS. 2008. http://www.pbs.org/wgbh/americanexperience/features/biography/flood-vardaman/.

Blake, John. "Why Sunday Morning Remains America's Most Segregated Hour." CNN Belief Blog, October 6, 2010. http://religion.blogs.cnn.com/2010/10/06/why-sunday-morning-remains-americas-most-segregated-hour/.

Blinder, Alan. "NASCAR's Confederate Flag Ban Faces a Test in Alabama." *New York Times*, June 20, 2020. https://www.nytimes.com/2020/06/20/sports/autoracing/nascar-confederate-flag-ban-talladega.html.

Bloom, Ester. "The Self-Made Man Is a Myth, Arnold Schwarzenegger Tells Students." CNBC.com, May 15, 2017. https://www.cnbc.com/2017/05/15/arnold-schwarzenegger-channels-elizabeth-warren-in-u-of-houston-speech.html.

Blow, Charles M. "Talking Down and Stepping Up." *New York Times*, July 12, 2008. http://www.nytimes.com/2008/07/12/opinion/12blow.html.

Boatright, John R. "Executive Compensation: Unjust or Just Right?" In *Oxford Handbook of Business Ethics*, edited by George G. Brenkert, 161–200. New York: Oxford University Press, 2010.

Bobic, Igor. "Both Mississippi Senators Urge State to Change Its Flag in Wake of Charleston Shooting." *Huffington Post*, June 24, 2015. http://www.huffingtonpost.com/2015/06/24/mississippi-senators-confederate-flag_n_7656660.html.

Bologna, Giacomo. "Mississippi Voted to Keep Its State Flag in 2001. A Lot Has Changed Since Then." *Clarion Ledger*, June 8, 2020. https://www.clarionledger.com/story/news/politics/2020/06/08/mississippi-flag-confederate-emblem-time-reconsider-protests-george-floyd/5318216002/.

Bonesteel, Matt. "NCAA Bans Championship Events in Mississippi Because of Its Flag." *Washington Post*, June 19, 2020. https://www.washingtonpost.com/sports/2020/06/19/sec-issues-ultimatum-mississippi-over-state-flag-that-features-confederate-symbol/.

Boorstein, Michelle. "Matthew Shepard, Whose 1998 Murder Became a Symbol for the Gay Rights Movement, Will Be Interred at Washington National Cathedral." *Washington Post*, October 11, 2018. https://www.washingtonpost.com/religion/2018/10/11/matthew-shepard-whose-murder-became-symbol-gay-rights-movement-will-be-interred-washington-national-cathedral/.

Boren, Zachary Davies. "The US Is an Oligarchy, Study Concludes." *Telegraph*, April 16, 2014. http://www.telegraph.co.uk/news/worldnews/northamerica/usa/10769041/The-US-is-an-oligarchy-study-concludes.html.

Boxill, Bernard. "The Responsibility of the Oppressed to Resist Their Own Oppression." *Journal of Social Philosophy* 41 (2010): 1–12.

Boxill, Bernard. "Self-Respect and Protest." *Philosophy and Public Affairs* 6, no. 1 (1976): 58–69.

Brandenburg v. Ohio. 395 U.S. 444 (1969). Justia. US Supreme Court. https://supreme.justia.com/cases/federal/us/395/444/.

Brennan, Karen. "Evidence of Infanticide and Exposure in Antiquity: Tolerated Social Practice, Uncontrolled Phenomenon or Regulated Custom?" *University College Dublin Law Review* 2 (2002): 92–119.

Brent, Joseph. *Charles Sanders Peirce: A Life.* Bloomington: Indiana University Press, 1998.

Brettschneider, Corey. *When the State Speaks, What Should It Say? How Democracies Can Protect Expression and Promote Equality.* Princeton, NJ: Princeton University Press, 2012.

Brodsky, Richard. "Moochers, Makers, Boehner, Rand, and Obama: Getting to a Real Debate with the Tea Party." *Huffington Post,* January 23, 2014. http:// www.huffingtonpost.com/richard-brodsky/moochers-makers-boehner-r_b_4077188.html.

Brown, Robbie. "Anti-Obama Protest at Ole Miss Turns Unruly." *New York Times,* November 7, 2012. https://www.nytimes.com/2012/11/08/us/anti-obama-protest-at-university-of-mississippi-turns-unruly.html.

Bruenig, Matt. "White High School Dropouts Have More Wealth than Black and Hispanic College Graduates." *Huffington Post,* December 6, 2017. https:// www.huffpost.com/entry/white-high-school-dropout_b_5881838.

Bruno, Robert. "When Did the U.S. Stop Seeing Teachers as Professionals?" *Harvard Business Review,* June 20, 2018. https://hbr.org/2018/06/when-did-the-u-s-stop-seeing-teachers-as-professionals.

Burch, Robert. "Charles Sanders Peirce." *Stanford Encyclopedia of Philosophy,* 2010. http://plato.stanford.edu/entries/peirce/.

Bushman, Brad. "Do Violent Video Games Play a Role in Shootings?" CNN.com, September 18, 2013. http://www.cnn.com/2013/09/18/opinion/bushman-video-games/.

Calamur, Krishnadev. "Alabama Governor Orders Removal of Confederate Flags from Capitol." NPR, June 24, 2015. http://www.npr.org/sections/thetwo-way/2015/06/24/417162233/alabama-governor-orders-removal-of-confederate-flags-from-capitol.

Cameron, Chris. "These Are the People Who Died in Connection with the Capitol Riot." *New York Times,* January 5, 2022. https://www.nytimes.com/2022/01/05/us/politics/jan-6-capitol-deaths.html.

Carbado, Devon W., and Mitu Gulati. *Acting White? Rethinking Race in "Post-Racial" America.* New York: Oxford University Press, 2015.

"Careers in Pharmacy." University of Mississippi. https://pharmacy.olemiss.edu/careers-in-pharmacy/.

Carlisle, Madeleine. "Anti-Trans Violence and Rhetoric Reached Record Highs Across America in 2021." *Time,* December 30, 2021. https://time.com/6131444/2021-anti-trans-violence/.

Caron, Christina. "In 19 States, It's Still Legal to Spank Children in Public Schools." *New York Times,* December 13, 2018. https://www.nytimes.com/2018/12/13/us/corporal-punishment-school-tennessee.html.

Carr, Sarah. "In Southern Towns, 'Segregation Academies' Are Still Going Strong." *Atlantic,* December 13, 2012. www.theatlantic.com/national/

archive/2012/12/ in-southern-towns-segregation-academies-are-still-going-strong/266207/.

Carson, Clayborn, senior ed. *The Papers of Martin Luther King, Jr., Volume 3: Birth of a New Age*. Los Angeles: University of California Press, 1997.

Cashin, Sheryll D. "Democracy, Race, and Multiculturalism in the Twenty-First Century: Will the Voting Rights Act Ever Be Obsolete?" *Washington University Journal of Law and Policy* 22 (2006): 71–105.

Cavanaugh, Ray. "Max Yasgur Rented Out His Farm for Woodstock. His Neighbors Sued Him." *Time*, August 14, 2019. https://time.com/5645555/woodstock-max-yasgur/.

CBS. "CBS Poll: Ready for a Black President?" CBS News, June 4, 2008. https://www.cbsnews.com/news/cbs-poll-ready-for-a-black-president/.

Chandler, Clay. "Gunn: Confederate Part of Mississippi Flag 'Needs to Be Removed.'" *Clarion Ledger*, June 22, 2015. http://www.clarionledger.com/story/news/2015/06/22/petition-mississippi-confederate-flag/29113157/.

Chandler, Eliza. "Interactions of Disability Pride and Shame." In *The Female Face of Shame*, edited by Erica L. Johnson and Patricia Moran, 74–86. Bloomington: Indiana University Press, 2013.

Chappell, Bill. "In Final Vote, South Carolina Senate Moves to Take Down Confederate Flag." NPR, July 7, 2015. http://www.npr.org/sections/thetwo-way/2015/07/07/420825226/in-final-vote-south-carolina-senate-moves-to-take-down-confederate-flag.

Chappell, Bill. "Should Young Americans Be Required to Do Public Service? Federal Panel Says Maybe." NPR, January 23, 2019. https://www.npr.org/2019/01/23/687715869/should-young-americans-be-required-to-do-public-service-federal-panel-says-maybe.

Chappell, Bill. "The Slants Win Supreme Court Battle Over Band's Name in Trademark Dispute." NPR, June 19, 2017. https://www.npr.org/sections/thetwo-way/2017/06/19/533514196/the-slants-win-supreme-court-battle-over-bands-name-in-trademark-dispute.

"Charles Sanders Peirce—Biography." European Graduate School, Library, Biography. http://www.egs.edu/library/charles-sanders-peirce/biography/.

Chen, David W. "Transgender Athletes Face Bans From Girls' Sports in 10 U.S. States." *New York Times*, October 28, 2021. https://www.nytimes.com/article/transgender-athlete-ban.html.

Choi, Jung Hyun, and Laurie Goodman. "Why Do Black College Graduates Have a Lower Homeownership Rate than White People Who Dropped Out of High School." Urban Wire, The Urban Institute, February 27, 2020. https://www.urban.org/urban-wire/why-do-black-college-graduates-have-lower-homeownership-rate-white-people-who-dropped-out-high-school.

Chokshi, Niraj. "That Wasn't Mark Twain: How a Misquotation Is Born." *New York Times*. April 26, 2017, https://www.nytimes.com/2017/04/26/books/famous-misquotations.html.

Chotiner, Isaac. "Why the Marriage-Equality Movement Succeeded." *New Yorker*, June 10, 2021. https://www.newyorker.com/news/q-and-a/sasha-issenberg-on-the-fight-for-marriage-equality.

Chow, Kat. " 'Politically Correct': The Phrase Has Gone from Wisdom to Weapon." NPR, December 14, 2016. https://www.npr.org/sections/codeswitch/2016/12/14/505324427/politically-correct-the-phrase-has-gone-from-wisdom-to-weapon.

Chua, Amy. "How America's Identity Politics Went from Inclusion to Division." *Guardian*, March 1, 2018. https://www.theguardian.com/society/2018/mar/01/how-americas-identity-politics-went-from-inclusion-to-division.

Clear, Todd R. "A Private-Sector, Incentives-Based Model for Justice Reinvestment." *Criminology & Public Policy* 10, no. 3 (2011): 585–608.

Coates, Ta-Nehisi. "The Case for Reparations." *Atlantic*, June 2014. http://www.theatlantic.com/features/archive/2014/05/the-case-for-reparations/361631/.

Cole, Devan. "Justice Thomas Renews Attacks on Landmark First Amendment Decision in Fiery Dissent." CNN, June 27, 2023. https://www.cnn.com/2023/06/27/politics/clarence-thomas-first-amendment-libel-new-york-times-supreme-court/index.html.

Coleman, Alistair. " 'Hundreds Dead' Because of COVID-19 Misinformation." BBC News, August 12, 2020. https://www.bbc.com/news/world-53755067.

Confessore, Nicholas, and Karen Yourish. "A Fringe Conspiracy Theory, Fostered Online, Is Refashioned by the G.O.P." *New York Times*, May 15, 2022. https://www.nytimes.com/2022/05/15/us/replacement-theory-shooting-tucker-carlson.html.

Confessore, Nicholas. "Koch Brothers' Budget of $889 Million for 2016 Is on Par with Both Parties' Spending." *New York Times*, January 27, 2015, A1.

Convention of the Mississippi Legislature. "An Address Setting Forth the Declaration of the Immediate Causes Which Induce and Justify the Secession of Mississippi from the Federal Union and the Ordinance of Secession." Jackson: Mississippi Book and Job Printing Office, 1861. https://archive.org/details/addresssettingfo01miss.

Coppola, Frances. "Everything You've Been Told About Government Debt Is Wrong." *Forbes*, April 17, 2018. https://www.forbes.com/sites/francescoppola/2018/04/17/everything-youve-been-told-about-government-debt-is-wrong/?sh=5e36b34314f4.

Corngold, Josh. "John Dewey, Public School Reform, and the Narrowing of Educational Aims." *Philosophy of Education* (2010): 237–40.

Costa, M. Victoria. "Rawlsian Civic Education: Political Not Minimal." *Journal of Applied Philosophy* 21 (2004): 1–14.

Coy, Peter. "The 'Benefits Cliff' Discourages People from Making More Money." *New York Times*, November 10, 2021. https://www.nytimes.com/2021/11/10/opinion/benefits-cliff-welfare.html.

Croucher, Shane. "China, Russia, and Iran Chide U.S. Over Racism While Persecuting Minorities in Their Own Countries." *Newsweek*, June 8, 2020. https://www.newsweek.com/china-russia-iran-us-protests-racism-persecution-minorities-1509341.

Cruse, Craig, and David Powers. "Estimating School District Poverty with Free and Reduced-Priced Lunch Data." US Census Bureau, Small Area Estimates Branch, 2006. https://www.census.gov/library/working-papers/2006/demo/cruse-01.html.

Cullen, Jim. "Problems and Promises of the Self-Made Myth." *Hedgehog Review* 15, no. 2 (2013): 8+. https://hedgehogreview.com/issues/the-american-dream/articles/problems-and-promises-of-the-self-made-myth.

Cunha, Darlena. "Why Drug Testing Welfare Recipients Is a Waste of Taxpayer Money." *Time*, August 15, 2014. https://time.com/3117361/welfare-recipients-drug-testing/.

Curran, Charlotte. "The Ethics of Fat Shaming." *Philosophy Now* 144 (July 2021): 10–12.

Curry, Tommy J. "George Floyd Jr as a Philosophical Problem: Why Disaggregated Data Should Guide How Philosophers Theorize Black Male Death." *Harvard Review of Philosophy* XXVIII (2021): 171–91.

Darolia, Rajeev, Peter Mueser, and Jacob Cronin. "Labor Market Returns to a Prison GED." *Economics of Education Review* 82 (2021): 1–27.

Darwall, Stephen. "Respect and the Second-Person Standpoint." *Proceedings and Addresses of the American Philosophical Association* 78, no. 2 (November 2004): 43–59.

Darwin, Charles. *The Descent of Man*. New York: Penguin Classics, 2004.

Dean, Charles J. "Alabama Gov. Bentley Removes Confederate Flags from Capitol Grounds." *Birmingham News*, June 24, 2015. https://www.al.com/news/2015/06/confederate_flag_removed_from.html.

Debnam, Dean. "MS GOP: Bryant for Gov., Barbour or Huckabee for Pres." Public Policy Polling, April 7, 2011, 1–17. https://www.publicpollingpolling.com/wp-content/uploads/2017/09/PPP_Release_MS_0407915.pdf.

"The Declaration of Causes of Seceding States." *American Battlefield Trust*. Sponsored by the History Channel. https://www.battlefields.org/learn/primary-sources/declaration-causes-seceding-states.

Deloache, Judy S., Cynthia Chiong, Kathleen Sherman, Nadia Islam, Mieke Vanderborgth, Georgene L. Troseth, Gabrielle A Strouse, and Katherine O'Doherty. "Do Babies Learn from Baby Media?" *Psychological Science* 21, no. 11 (2010): 1570–74.

Demby, Gene. "Sagging Pants and the Long History of 'Dangerous' Street Fashion." NPR.org, September 11, 2014. http://www.npr.org/sections/codeswitch/2014/09/11/347143588/.

Desilver, Drew. "The Polarization in Today's Congress Has Roots that Go Back Decades." Pew Research Center, March 10, 2022. https://www.pewresearch.org/fact-tank/2022/03/10/the-polarization-in-todays-congress-has-roots-that-go-back-decades/.

Desilver, Drew. "U.S. Students' Academic Achievement Still Lags That of Their Peers in Many Other Countries." Pew Research Center, STEM Education and Workforce, February 15, 2017. https://www.pewresearch.org/fact-tank/2017/02/15/u-s-students-internationally-math-science/.

Dewberry, David R., Ann Burnette, Rebekah Fox, and Pat Arneson. "Teaching Free Speech Across the Communication Studies Curriculum." *First Amendment Studies* 52, no. 1–2 (July 2018): 80–95.

Dewey, John. *America's Public Philosopher: Essays on Social Justice, Economics, Education, and the Future of Democracy*, edited by Eric Thomas Weber. New York: Columbia University Press, 2021.

Dewey, John. "The Basic Values and Loyalties of Democracy." In *America's Public Philosopher: Essays on Social Justice, Economics, Education, and the Future of Democracy*, edited by Eric Thomas Weber, 55–58. New York: Columbia University Press, 2021.

Dewey, John. *A Common Faith*. 1933; reprint, New Haven, CT: Yale University Press, 2013.

Dewey, John. "Creative Democracy—The Task Before Us." In *America's Public Philosopher*, edited by Eric Thomas Weber, 59–65. New York: Columbia University Press, 2021.

Dewey, John. *Democracy and Education*. In *The Middle Works of John Dewey, 1899–1924: 1916*, edited by Jo Ann Boydston, vol. 9. Carbondale: Southern Illinois University Press, 2008.

Dewey, John. "Democracy and Educational Administration." In *The Later Works of John Dewey*, edited by Jo Ann Boydston, vol. 11, 218–19. Carbondale: Southern Illinois University Press, 1987.

Dewey, John. "Democracy Is Radical." In *The Later Works of John Dewey*, edited by Jo Ann Boydston, vol. 11, 296–99. 1937; reprint, Carbondale: Southern Illinois University Press, 1987.

Dewey, John. "Dewey Outlines Utopian Schools." *New York Times*, Sunday, April 23, 1933. Education, 7.

Dewey, John, and James Tufts. *Ethics (1908)*. In *The Collected Works of John Dewey, The Middle Works*, edited by Jo Ann Boydston, vol. 5. Carbondale: Southern Illinois University Carbondale, 1978.

Dewey, John. "Ethics and International Relations." *Foreign Affairs* 1 (1923): 85–95. Republished in MW.15.53–65.

Dewey, John. "The Ethics of Democracy." In *The Early Works of John Dewey*, edited by Jo Ann Boydston, vol. 1, 227–49. Carbondale: Southern Illinois University Press, 2008.

Dewey, John. *Experience and Nature*. In *The Collected Works of John Dewey, The Later Works*, edited by Jo Ann Boydston, vol. 1. 1925; reprint, Carbondale: Southern Illinois University Press, 2008.

Dewey, John. *Freedom and Culture*. In *The Collected Works of John Dewey, The Later Works*, edited by Jo Ann Boydston, vol. 13. Carbondale: Southern Illinois University Press, 2008.

Dewey, John. "The Future of Philosophy." In *The Later Works of John Dewey*, edited by Jo Ann Boydston, vol. 17, 466–70. Carbondale: Southern Illinois University Press, 2008.

Dewey, John. *How We Think*. In *The Later Works of John Dewey, 1925–1953: 1933*, edited by Jo Ann Boydston, vol. 8. Carbondale: Southern Illinois University Press, 2008.

Dewey, John. "The Influence of Darwin on Philosophy." In *The Middle Works of John Dewey*, edited by Jo Ann Boydston, vol. 4, 3–15. Carbondale: Southern Illinois University Press, 2008.

Dewey, John. *Logic: The Theory of Inquiry*. In *The Collected Works of John Dewey, The Later Works*, edited by Jo Ann Boydston, vol. 12. 1938; reprint, Carbondale: Southern Illinois University Press, 1986.

Dewey, John. "Philosophy and Democracy." In *The Middle Works of John Dewey*, edited by Jo Ann Boydston, vol. 11, 41–53. Carbondale: Southern Illinois University Press, 1982.

Dewey, John. "Politics and Culture." *Modern Thinker* 1 (1932): 168–74. Republished in LW 6.40–48.

Dewey, John. *Reconstruction in Philosophy*. In *The Collected Works of John Dewey, The Middle Works, 1899–1924: 1920*, edited by Jo Ann Boydston, vol. 12. Carbondale: Southern Illinois University Press, 1988.

Dewey, John. "The Reflex Arc Concept in Psychology." *Psychological Review* 3, no. 4 (1896): 357–70.

Dewey, John. "Search for the Great Community." Chapter 4 of *The Public and Its Problems*. In *The Collected Works of John Dewey*, edited by Jo Ann Boydston, vol. 5, 325–50. Carbondale: Southern Illinois University Press, 1988.

Dewey, John. "Social Absolutism." In *The Collected Works of John Dewey: The Middle Works*, edited by Jo Ann Boydston, vol. 13, 315–16. Carbondale: Southern Illinois University Press, 1983.

Dewey, John. "The Supreme Intellectual Obligation." *Science Education* 18 (February 1934): 1–4.

Dillon, Robin S., ed. *Dignity, Character, and Self-Respect*. New York: Routledge, 1995.

Disability and Health Branch of the CDC. "Disability Impacts All of Us." Centers for Disease Control and Prevention, September 16, 2020. http://cdc.gov/ncbddd/disabilityandhealth/infographic-disability-impacts-all.html.

Donovan, Josephine. "Attention to Suffering: Sympathy as a Basis for Ethical Treatment of Animals." Chapter 6 in *The Feminist Care Tradition in Animal Ethics*, edited by Carol J. Adams and Josephine Donovan, 174–97. New York: Columbia University Press, 2007.

Donne, John. "No Man Is an Island." In "Preface" to *Devotions Upon Emergent Occasions and Death's Duel*. New York: Vintage Press, 1999.

Doria, Manuel. "The Unreasonable Destructiveness of Political Correctness in Philosophy." *Philosophies* 2, no. 17 (2017): 1–56.

Douglas, John. *The Anatomy of Motive*. New York: Simon and Schuster, 2012.

Douglas-Gabriel, Danielle. "Tuition-Free College Movement Gains Momentum, Despite Biden's Stalled Plan." *Washington Post*, March 5, 2022. https://www.washingtonpost.com/education/2022/03/05/tuition-free-college-states/.

Dovidio, John F., Brenda Major, and Jennifer Crocker. "Stigma: Introduction and Overview." In *The Social Psychology of Stigma*, edited by Todd F. Heatherton, Robert E. Kleck, Michelle R. Hebl, and Jay G. Hull, 1–28. New York: The Guilford Press, 2003.

Doyle, William. *An American Insurrection: James Meredith and the Battle of Oxford, Mississippi, 1962*. New York: Anchor Books, 2003.

Edelman, Marian Wright. "The Cradle to Prison Pipeline: America's New Apartheid." *Harvard Journal of African American Public Policy* XV, Summer Issue (2009): 67–68.

Editorial Board. "America Has a Free Speech Problem." *New York Times*, March 18, 2022. https://www.nytimes.com/2022/03/18/opinion/cancel-culture-free-speech-poll.html.

Editors. "The 2014 Race Card: Democratic Appeals to Racial Division Are Worse than Ever." *Wall Street Journal*, October 26, 2014. http://www.wsj.com/articles/the-2014-race-card-1414192776.

Editors. "Hungry Heroes: 25 Percent of Military Families Seek Food Aid." NBC News, August 17, 2014. https://www.nbcnews.com/feature/in-plain-sight/hungry-heroes-25-percent-military-families-seek-food-aid-n180236.

Editors. "Paul Ryan." Biography.com, April 2, 2014. https://www.biography.com/political-figure/paul-ryan.

Edmonson, Henry T., III. *John Dewey and the Decline of American Education*. Wilmington, DE: ISI Books, 2006.

Edsall, Thomas B. "America Has Split, and It's Now in 'Very Dangerous Territory.'" *New York Times*, January 26, 2022. https://www.nytimes.com/2022/01/26/opinion/covid-biden-trump-polarization.html.

Edwards, Peter. "White Clergy Offer Their Photos for Target Practice; Twitter Campaign a Response to Miami Police Snipers Using Black Men's Mug Shots." *Toronto Star*, January 27, 2015, A10.

Ehrenreich, Barbara. *Bright-Sided*. New York: Metropolitan Books, 2009.

Eisen, Norman, and Fred Wertheimer. "Finally, a Road Map to Hold Trump Accountable." CNN.com, March 30, 2022. https://www.cnn.com/2022/03/30/opinions/trump-road-map-accountability-january-6-eisen-wertheimer/index.html.

Elassar, Alaa. "Why the Noose Is Such a Potent Symbol of Hate." CNN, June 23, 2020. https://www.cnn.com/2020/06/23/us/noose-hate-symbol-racism-trnd/index.html.

Ellis, Atiba R. "*Citizens United* and Tiered Personhood." *John Marshall Law Review* 44, no. 3 (2011): 717–49.

Empson, Liz, and Matthew Yarnell. "Enough Is Enough: PA. Needs to Protect Seniors, Respect Caregivers." *Pennsylvania Capital-Star*, June 6, 2021. https://www.penncapital-star.com/commentary/enough-is-enough-pa-needs-to-protect-seniors-respect-caregivers-opinion/.

Epps, Garrett. "Clarence Thomas Takes on a Symbol of White Supremacy." *Atlantic*, June 18, 2015. https://www.theatlantic.com/politics/archive/2015/06/clarence-thomas-confederate-flag/396281/.

Ermyas, Tinbete, and Kira Wakeam. "Wave of Bills to Block Trans Athletes Has No Basis in Science, Research Says." NPR, March 18, 2021. https://www.npr.org/2021/03/18/978716732/wave-of-new-bills-say-trans-athletes-have-an-unfair-edge-what-does-the-science-s.

Erzurum, Serpil. "How Much of the Population Will Need to Be Vaccinated Until the Pandemic Is Over?" Cleveland Clinic, May 5, 2021. https://health.clevelandclinic.org/how-much-of-the-population-will-need-to-be-vaccinated-until-the-pandemic-is-over/.

Esposito, Lisa. "The Countless Ways Poverty Affects People's Health." *U.S. News and World Report*, April 20, 2016. https://health.usnews.com/health-news/patient-advice/articles/2016-04-20/the-countless-ways-poverty-affects-peoples-health.

Equal Justice Initiative. "Lynching in America: Confronting the Legacy of Racial Terror, Third Edition." Report. Montgomery, Alabama, 2017. https://eji.org/wp-content/uploads/2005/11/lynching-in-america-3d-ed-110121.pdf.

Equal Justice Initiative. "Reconstruction in America: Racial Violence after the Civil War, 1865–1876." Report. Montgomery, Alabama, 2020. https://eji.org/wp-content/uploads/2020/07/reconstruction-in-america-report.pdf.

Farrington, Robert. "These States Offer Tuition-Free Community College." *Forbes*, March 25, 2020. https://www.forbes.com/sites/robertfarrington/2020/03/25/these-states-offer-tuition-free-community-college/.

Feinblatt, John. "A Bad Week for the NRA." *Huffington Post*, October 3, 2014. http://www.huffingtonpost.com/john-feinblatt/a-bad-week-for-the-nra_b_5929188.html.

Feinstein, Rachel A. *When Rape Was Legal: The Untold History of Sexual Violence During Slavery*. New York: Routledge, 2018.

Ferrell, Jeff. "Confederate Flag Comes Down Friday." KSLA News 12, November 3, 2011. https://www.ksla.com/story/15955226/caddo-parish-commission-votes-to-remove-confederate-flag/.

Fielding-Singh, Priya. "Free School Meal Programs Don't Just Feed Hungry Kids—They're a Major Win for Moms." *Washington Post*, August 13, 2021. https://www.washingtonpost.com/opinions/2021/08/13/universal-free-school-meals-moms-california-maine/.

Finseth, Ian. "David Walker, Nature's Nation, and Early African-American Separatism." *Mississippi Quarterly* 54, no. 3 (2001): 337–62.

Firestone, David. "Mississippi Votes by Wide Margin to Keep State Flag That Includes Confederate Emblem." *New York Times*, April 18, 2001. https://www.nytimes.com/2001/04/18/us/mississippi-votes-wide-margin-keep-state-flag-that-includes-confederate-emblem.html.

"Flag of Mississippi." Wikipedia. https://en.wikipedia.org/wiki/Flag_of_Mississippi.

Fletcher, Helen Jill, and Janet P. D'Amato. *10 Little Indians: A Counting Song and Counting Book Record*. A Peter Pan Book and Record, 1960.

Flexner, Abraham. *The Usefulness of Useless Knowledge*. Princeton, NJ: Princeton University Press, 2017.

Forstenzer, Joshua. "Deweyan Democracy, Robert Talisse, and the Fact of Reasonable Pluralism." *Transactions of the Charles S. Peirce Society* 53, no. 4 (2017): 553–78.

Foster, Dawn. "How Being Poor Can Lead to a Negative Spiral of Fear and Self-Loathing." *Guardian*, June 30, 2015. https://www.theguardian.com/society/2015/jun/30/poverty-negative-spiral-fear-self-loathing.

Fox, Alex. "Nearly 2,000 Black Americans Were Lynched During Reconstruction." *Smithsonian Magazine*, June 18, 2020. https://www.smithsonianmag.com/smart-news/nearly-2000-black-americans-were-lynched-during-reconstruction-180975120/.

Frank, Anne. *The Diary of a Young Girl*. Garden City, NY: Doubleday, 1952.

Frieden, Terry. "Mississippi Town Sued Over 'School-to-Prison Pipeline.'" CNN, October 26, 2012. https://www.cnn.com/2012/10/24/justice/mississippi-civil-rights-lawsuit/index.html.

Friere, Paolo. *Teachers as Cultural Workers*. Boulder, CO: Westview Press, 1998.

Fryer, Roland, and Paul Torelli. "An Empirical Analysis of 'Acting White.'" *Journal of Public Economics* 94 (2010): 380–96.

Frost, Amanda. "Keeping Up Appearances: A Process-Oriented Approach to Judicial Recusal." *University of Kansas Law Review* 53 (2004): 531–94.

Gabbatt, Adam. "Women in Combat: Pentagon to Overturn Military Ban." *Guardian*, January 24, 2013. https://www.theguardian.com/world/2013/jan/23/pentagon-overturn-ban-women-combat.

Gallagher, David M. "Thomas Aquinas on Self-Love as the Basis for Love of Others." *Acta Philosophica* 8 (1999): 23–44.

Gass, Nick. "Trump: I'm So Tired of This Politically Correct Crap." *Politico*, September 23, 2015. https://www.politico.com/story/2015/09/donald-trump-politically-correct-crap-213988.

Gates, Henry Louis, Jr., and Cornel West. *The Future of the Race*. New York: Vintage Press, 1997.

Gatti, Roberta. "Yes, Culture Matters for Economic Development." World Bank, March 28, 2016. https://www.worldbank.org/en/news/feature/2016/03/28/yes-culture-matters-for-economic-development.

Gaus, Gerald. "Should Philosophers 'Apply Ethics'? By 'Applying Ethics,' Do Philosophers Actually Succeed in Corrupting Philosophy?" *Think* (Spring 2005): 63–67.

Gibbons, Amy. "The Countries Offering Students Free (or Somewhat Affordable) University Education." *Independent*, December 5, 2016. https://www.independent.co.uk/student/study-abroad/free-university-education-courses-study-abroad-brexit-erasmus-students-germany-copenhagen-france-a7457576.html.

Gilbert, Daylyn. "Racial Reckoning withing the Classroom." *Harvard Political Review*, January 6, 2021. https://harvardpolitics.com/racial-reckoning-classroom/.

Gilens, Martin, and Benjamin I. Page. "Testing Theories of American Politics: Elites, Interest Groups, and Average Citizens." *Perspectives on Politics* 12, no. 3 (September 2014): 564–81.

Gillespie, Patrick. "Growing Up Poor Makes It Harder to Succeed: Janet Yellen." CNN Business, March 23, 2017. https://money.cnn.com/2017/03/23/news/economy/fed-yellen-income-inequality-poor-success-study/.

Gittens, Cheryl Bailey. "The McNair Program as a Socializing Influence on Doctoral Degree Attainment." *Peabody Journal of Education* 89 (2014): 368–79.

Goodman, Nelson. *Fact, Fiction, and Forecast*. Cambridge, MA: Harvard University Press, 1955.

Golden, Andrew. "The Commanders Name Lands 'With a Thud' for Some Washington Fans." *Washington Post*, February 2, 2022. https://www.washingtonpost.com/sports/2022/02/02/washington-commanders-fan-reaction/.

Gopnik, Alison. "How Humans Evolved to Care for Others." *Wall Street Journal*, April 16, 2020. https://www.wsj.com/articles/how-humans-evolved-to-care-for-others-11587045511.

Graham, Patricia Albjerg. *Schooling America: How the Public Schools Meet the Nation's Changing Needs*. New York: Oxford University Press, 2005.

Granato, Jim, Ronald Inglehart, and David Leblang. "The Effect of Cultural Values on Economic Development: Theory, Hypotheses, and Some Empirical Tests." *American Journal of Political Science* 40, no. 3 (1996): 607–31.

Green, Rep. Mark. "Every Military Family Deserves Our Gratitude." *The Hill*, November 27, 2020. https://thehill.com/blogs/congress-blog/politics/527737-every-military-family-deserves-our-gratitude/.

Guiso, Luigi, Paola Sapienza, and Luigi Zingales. "Does Culture Affect Economic Outcomes?" *Journal of Economic Perspectives* 20, no. 2 (2006): 23–48.

Halsey, Ashley, III. "Bad Highway Design, Conditions Contribute to Half of Fatal Auto Accidents in U.S." *Washington Post*, July 2, 2009. https://www.washington post.com/wp-dyn/content/article/2009/07/01/AR2009070101700.html.

Hamby, Alyson R. "You Are Not Cordially Invited: How Universities Maintain First Amendment Rights and Safety in the Midst of Controversial On-Campus Speakers." *Cornell Law Review* 104, no. 1 (November 2018): 287–316.

Harlow, Caroline Wolf. "Education and Correctional Populations. Special Report." NCJ 195670. Washington, DC: United States Department of Justice, Bureau of Justice Statistics, 2003.

Harris, Bracey. "Ex-Ole Miss Student Sentenced for Noose on Statue." *USA Today*, September 17, 2015. http://www.usatoday.com/story/news/nation/2015/09/17/ex-ole-miss-student-sentenced-noose-statue/72376068/.

Harris, Bracey. "KKK Protests 'Take Down the Flag' Rally at Ole Miss." *Clarion Ledger*, October 15, 2015. https://www.clarionledger.com/story/news/2015/10/16/ole-miss-students-rally-remove-state-flag-campus/74046586/.

Harris, Elizabeth A. "In Backlash to Racial Reckoning, Conservative Publishers See Gold." *New York Times*, August 15, 2021. https://www.nytimes.com/2021/08/15/books/race-antiracism-publishing.html.

Harris, Leonard. "Rendering the Text: Introduction." In *The Philosophy of Alain Locke: Harlem Renaissance and Beyond*, edited by Leonard Harris, 3–27. Philadelphia: Temple University Press, 1989.

Haslett, Tobi. "The Man Who Led the Harlem Renaissance—And His Hidden Hungers." *New Yorker*, May 14, 2018. https://www.newyorker.com/magazine/2018/05/21/the-man-who-led-the-harlem-renaissance-and-his-hidden-hungers.

Hattenstone, Simone. "Angela Davis on the Power of Protest: 'We Can't Do Anything without Optimism.'" *Guardian*, March 5, 2022. https://www.theguardian.com/us-news/2022/mar/05/angela-davis-on-the-power-of-protest-we-cant-do-anything-without-optimism.

Hawkinds, Stephen, Daniel Yudkin, Miriam Juan-Torres, and Tim Dixon. "Hidden Tribes: A Study of America's Polarized Landscape." More in Common. New York, NY, 2018. https://hiddentribes.us/media/qfpekz4g/hidden_tribes_report.pdf.

Hay, Carol. "A Feminist Kant." *New York Times: The Stone*, December 8, 2013. http://opinionator.blogs.nytimes.com/2013/12/08/a-feminist-kant/.

Hay, Carol. *Kantianism, Liberalism, and Feminism: Resisting Oppression.* New York: Palgrave MacMillan, 2013.

Hayden, Erik. "Poll: 46 Percent of Mississippi GOP Want to Ban Interracial Marriage." Atlantic Newswire, April 7, 2011. http://www.thewire.com/national/2011/04/mississippi-republicans/36455/.

Heggeness, Misty L., Jason Fields, Yazmin A García Trejo, and Anthony Schulzetenberg. "Tracking Job Losses for Mothers of School-Age Children During a Health Crisis." Census.gov, March 3, 2021. https://www.census.gov/library/stories/2021/03/moms-work-and-the-pandemic.html.

"Heights and Views." National Capital Planning Commission. https://www.ncpc.gov/topics/heights/.

Hibberd, James. "Steve Harvey Slams 'Cancel Culture': 'Political Correctness Has Killed Comedy.'" *Hollywood Reporter*, January 11, 2022. https://www.hollywoodreporter.com/tv/tv-news/steve-harvey-cancel-culture-1235073289/.

Hickman, Larry A. "Foreword." In *John Dewey and Chinese Education*, edited by ZHANG Huajun and Jim GARRISON, ix–xi. Boston, MA: Brill, 2022.

Hickman, Larry A. *Philosophical Tools for Technological Culture*. Bloomington: Indiana University Press, 2001.

Hickman, Larry A. *John Dewey's Pragmatic Technology*. Bloomington: Indiana University Press, 1990.

Hildebrand, David. "Does Every Theory Deserve a Hearing?" *Southern Journal of Philosophy* 44, no. 2 (2006): 217–36.

Hill, Thomas. "Servility and Self-Respect." *Monist* 57, no. 1 (1973): 87–104.

Hitson, Hadley. "Unanimous: ASB Senate Votes to Move the Monument." *Daily Mississippian*, March 6, 2019. https://thedmonline.com/unanimous-asb-senate-votes-to-move-the-monument/.

Hodenfield, Jan. "After Woodstock: Money and Smiles—The Aftermath of the Party of the Year." *Rolling Stone*, October 4, 1969. https://www.rollingstone.com/music/music-news/after-woodstock-money-and-smiles-182998/.

Hodgson, Geoffrey M. "The Evolution of Morality and the End of Economic Man." *Journal of Evolutionary Economics* 24 (2014): 83–106.

Holmes, John Haynes. "Salute to Montgomery." *Liberation* 1, no. 10 (1956): 5.

Homler, Ryan. "A Timeline of the Washington Football Team's Name Change Saga." NBCSports.com, July 3, 2021. https://www.nbcsports.com/washington/football-team/timeline-washington-football-teams-name-change-saga.

Honneth, Axel. *The Struggle for Recognition: The Moral Grammar of Social Conflicts*. Cambridge, MA: MIT Press, 1995.

Hooper, Molly K. "GOP Rep.: Obamas Part of 'Uppity' Class." *USA Today*, September 4, 2008. http://usatoday30.usatoday.com/news/politics/election2008/2008-09-04-westmoreland_N.htm.

Hutson, Matthew. "Why Liberals Aren't as Tolerant as They Think." *Politico*, May 9, 2017. https://www.politico.com/magazine/story/2017/05/09/why-liberals-arent-as-tolerant-as-they-think-215114/.

Iasevoli, Brenda. "Building Respect for Teachers: What Can Be Done?" HMHco.com, November 4, 2021. https://www.hmhco.com/blog/building-respect-for-teachers-what-can-be-done.

Ikuenobe, Polycarp. "Culture of Racism, Self-Respect, and Blameworthiness." *Public Affairs Quarterly* 18, no. 1 (2004): 27–55.

Ingber, Stanley. "The Marketplace of Ideas: A Legitimizing Myth." *Duke Law Journal* 1 (1984): 1–91.

Ingraham, Christopher. "How the Confederacy Lives on in the Flags of Seven Southern States." *Washington Post*, June 21, 2015. https://www.washington post.com/news/wonk/wp/2015/06/21/how-the-confederacy-lives-on-in-the-flags-of-seven-southern-states/.

Institute for Constitutional Advocacy and Protection (ICAP). "Fact Sheet: Protecting Against Voter Intimidation." Georgetown University Law Center, 2020. https://www.law.georgetown.edu/icap/wp-content/uploads/sites/32/2020/10/Voter-Intimidation-Fact-Sheet.pdf.

Issacharoff, Samuel, and Pamela S. Karlan. "Groups, Politics, and the Equal Protection Clause." *Issues in Legal Scholarship* 2, no. 1 (2003): i–17.

Ito, Suzanne. "Confederate Flag at Louisiana Courthouse Taints Death Penalty System with Racial Bias." ACLU Speak Freely, May 10, 2011. https://www.aclu.org/blog/smart-justice/mass-incarceration/confederate-flag-louisiana-courthouse-taints-death-penalty.

Jacobs, James B., and Kimberly A. Potter. "Hate Crimes: A Critical Perspective." *Crime and Justice: A Review of Research* 22 (1997): 1–50.

Jacobs, Karrie. "Why Libraries May Never Stop Being People Places." *New York Times*, April 21, 2022. https://www.nytimes.com/2022/04/21/style/libraries-outdoor-public-space.html.

James, William. *Pragmatism and Other Writings*. New York: Penguin Classics, 2000.

James, William. *The Principles of Psychology*, vols. 1 and 2. 1890; reprint, New York: Dover Publications, 1950.

Jeong, Sarah. "Should We Be Able to Reclaim a Racist Insult—as a Registered Trademark?" *New York Times*, January 17, 2017. https://www.nytimes.com/2017/01/17/magazine/should-we-be-able-to-reclaim-a-racist-insult-as-a-registered-trademark.html.

Johns Hopkins Researchers. "Dropout Factories: Take a Closer Look at Failing Schools Across the Country." Associated Press, 2007. http://hosted.ap.org/specials/ interactives/wdc/dropout/.

Johnson, Matt. "The Psychology of the Self-Made Man: Can a Person Be Solely Responsible for Creating Their Own Fortune?" *Psychology Today*, March 27, 2021. https://www.psychologytoday.com/us/blog/mind-brain-and-value/202103/the-psychology-and-mythology-the-self-made-man.

Johnston, J. S. "Rawls's Kantian Educational Theory." *Educational Theory* 55 (2005): 200–18.

Jones, James H. *Bad Blood: The Tuskegee Syphilis Experiment, New and Expanded Edition*. New York: The Free Press, 1993.

Jones, Ja'han. "The MAGA Movement is a KKK Re-up. The Latest Jan. 6 Hearing Proves It." MSNBC, July 13, 2022. https://www.msnbc.com/the-reidout/reidout-blog/summary-jan-6-hearing-kkk-rcna37960.

Jones, Nate. "Want to Be Class President in Mississippi? You Need to Be White." *Time*, August 27, 2010. http://newsfeed.time.com/2010/08/27/want-to-be-class-president-in-mississippi-you-need-to-be-white/.

Jonsson, Patrik. "A Bid to Buff Mississippi's Image." *Christian Science Monitor*, December 12, 2006, 2.

Joseph, Pamela Bolotin, Nancy Stewart Green, Edward R. Mikel, and Mark A Windschitl. "Narrowing the Curriculum." Chapter 2 in *Cultures of Curriculum*, edited by Pamela Bolotin Joseph, 2nd ed., 36–54. 2000; reprint, New York: Routledge, 2011.

Kajitani, Alex. "Fixing the Teacher Shortage Begins with Stopping the Bleeding." *Ed Week*, December 2, 2015. https://www.edweek.org/leadership/opinion-fixing-the-teacher-shortage-begins-with-stopping-the-bleeding/2015/12.

Karageorge, Eleni X. "Growing Up in High-Poverty Areas Can Affect Your Employment." US Bureau of Labor Statistics, March 2016. https://www.bls.gov/opub/mlr/2016/beyond-bls/growing-up-in-high-poverty-areas-can-affect-your-employment.htm.

Kaur, Harmeet. "FYI: English Isn't the Official Language of the United States." CNN, June 15, 2018. https://www.cnn.com/2018/05/20/us/english-us-official-language-trnd/index.html.

Kautzer, Chad. "Notes for a Critical Theory of Community Self-Defense." In *Setting Sights: Histories and Reflections on Community Armed Self-Defense*, edited by scott crow, 35–48. Oakland, CA: PM Press, 2018.

Kelly, Morgan. "Poor Concentration: Poverty Reduces Brainpower Needed for Navigating Other Areas of Life." News, Princeton.edu, August 29, 2013. https://www.princeton.edu/news/2013/08/29/poor-concentration-poverty-reduces-brainpower-needed-navigating-other-areas-life.

Kernohan, Andrew. *Liberalism, Equality, and Cultural Oppression*. New York: Cambridge University Press, 1998.

Kerr, Audrey Elisa. "The Paper Bag Principle: Of the Myth and Motion of Colorism." *Journal of American Folklore* 118, no. 469 (2005): 271–89.

Kessler, Sharon E., Tyler R. Bonnell, Joanna M. Setchell, and Colin A. Chapman. "Social Structure Facilitated the Evolution of Care-Giving as a Strategy for Disease Control in the Human Lineage." *Nature* 8 (2018): 1–14. https://www.nature.com/articles/s41598-018-31568-2.pdf.

Kim, Catherine Y., Daniel J. Losen, and Damon T. Hewitt. *The School-to-Prison Pipeline: Structuring Legal Reform*. New York: New York University Press, 2010.

King, Kelly V., and Sasha Zucker. "Curriculum Narrowing: Policy Report." San Antonio, TX: Harcourt Assessment, 2005. http://images.pearsonclinical.com/images/PDF/assessmentReports/CurriculumNarrowing.pdf.

King, Martin Luther, Jr. "Letter from a Birmingham Jail." In *Why We Can't Wait*, 77–100. New York: Signet Classics, 1963.

King, Martin Luther, Jr. "Love, Law, and Civil Disobedience." In *The Essential Writings and Speeches of Martin Luther King, Jr.*, edited by James M. Washington, 43–53. New York: Harper Collins, 1986.

King, Martin Luther, Jr. *Stride Toward Freedom: The Montgomery Story*. 1958; reprint, New York: Beacon Press, 1986.

King, Martin Luther, Jr. *A Testament of Hope: The Essential Writings and Speeches*, edited by James M. Washington. New York: Harper One, 2003.

Klibanoff, Eleanor. "U.S. Supreme Court Rules There's No Right to Abortion, Setting Up Texas Ban." *Texas Tribune*, June 24, 2022. https://www.texastribune.org/2022/06/22/supreme-court-abortion-texas/.

Korsgaard, Christine M. "Realism and Constructivism in Twentieth-Century Moral Philosophy." *Philosophy in America at the Turn of the Century*, edited by Robert Audi, 99–122. APA Centennial Supplement "Journal of Philosophical Research," 2003.

Kozol, Jonathan. *Savage Inequalities: Children in America's Schools*. New York: Broadway Books, 2012.

Kuhse, Helga, and Peter Singer. "Debate: Severely Handicapped Newborns." *Law, Medicine, and Healthcare* 14, no. 3–4 (1986): 149–53.

Lachs, John. *The Cost of Comfort*. Bloomington: Indiana University Press, 2019.

Lachs, John. *Freedom and Limits*. New York: Fordham University Press, 2014.

Lachs, John. "Human Natures." *Proceedings and Addresses of the American Philosophical Association* 63, no. 7 (1990): 29–39.

Lachs, John. *Intermediate Man*. Indianapolis, IN: Hackett, 1981.

Lachs, John. "Leaving Others Alone." *Journal of Speculative Philosophy* 18, no. 4 (2004): 261–72.

Lachs, John. *Meddling: On the Virtue of Leaving Others Alone*. Bloomington: Indiana University Press, 2014.

Lachs, John. *The Relevance of Philosophy to Life*. Nashville, TN: Vanderbilt University Press, 1995.

Lachs, John. *Stoic Pragmatism*. Bloomington: Indiana University Press, 2012.

Lanford, Michael. "The Political History of the Georgia HOPE Scholarship Program: A Critical Analysis." *Policy Reviews in Higher Education* 1, no. 2 (2017): 187–208.

Laplace, Pierre Simon. *Théorie Analytique des Probabilités*. Paris: Imprimerie Royale, 1847.

Larson, Carlton F. W. "Should 'Fire' in a Theater: The Life and Times of Constitutional Law's Most Enduring Analogy." *William and Mary Bill of Rights Journal* 24 (2015): 181–212.

Laughlin, Meg. "Polishing Mississippi." *St. Petersburg Times*. December 17, 2006, 1D.

Lee, Harper. *To Kill a Mockingbird*. New York: Harper Perennial, 2002.

Lehrman, Lewis E. *Lincoln at Peoria, The Turning Point: Getting Right with the Declaration of Independence*. Mechanicsburg, PA: Stackpole Books, 2008.

Leifheit, Kathryn M., Gabriel L. Schwartz, Craig E. Pollack, Kathryn J. Edin, Maureen M. Black, Jacky M. Jennings, and Keri N. Althoff. "Severe Housing Insecurity During Pregnancy: Association with Adverse Birth and Infant Outcomes." *International Journal of Environmental Research and Public Health* 17, no. 8659 (2020): 1–12.

Lemon, Jason. "Trump Indictment in Georgia Expected Before DOJ Charges." *Newsweek*, July 21, 2022. https://www.newsweek.com/donald-trump-georgia-indictment-prediction-laurence-tribe-1726833.

Lerner, Sharon. "A School District that Was Never Desegregated." *Atlantic*, February 5, 2015. http://www.theatlantic.com/education/archive/2015/02/a-school-district-that-was-never-desegregated/385184/.

Lester, David. "Measuring Maslow's Hierarchy of Needs." *Psychological Reports: Mental and Physical Health* 113, no. 1 (2013): 15–17.

Levin, Michael. "Why Homosexuality Is Abnormal." *Monist* 67 (1984): 251–83.

Levy, Leil. "No-Platforming and Higher-Order Evidence, or Anti-Anti-No-Platforming." *Journal of the American Philosophical Association* 5, no. 4 (2019): 487–502.

Liptak, Adam. "Justice Clarence Thomas Calls for Reconsideration of Landmark Libel Ruling." *New York Times*, February 19, 2019. https://www.nytimes.com/2019/02/19/us/politics/clarence-thomas-first-amendment-libel.html.

Livingston, Gretchen, and Deja Thomas. "Among 41 Countries, Only U.S. Lacks Paid Parental Leave." Pew Research Center, December 16, 2019. https://www.pewresearch.org/fact-tank/2019/12/16/u-s-lacks-mandated-paid-parental-leave/.

Lobosco, Katie. "Americans Are Moving to Europe for Free College Degrees." CNNMoney.com, February 23, 2016. https://money.cnn.com/2016/02/23/pf/college/free-college-europe/.

Lobosco, Katie. "Ben Carson: Political Correctness Is Going to 'Destroy Our Nation.'" CNN Politics, October 22, 2019. https://www.cnn.com/2019/10/22/politics/ben-carson-transgender-political-correctness/index.html.

Locke, Alain. "The Ethics of Culture." In *The Philosophy of Alain Locke: Harlem Renaissance and Beyond*, edited by Leonard Harris, 435–41. Philadelphia: Temple University Press, 1989.

Locke, Alain. "Frontiers of Culture." In *The Philosophy of Alain Locke: Harlem Renaissance and Beyond*, edited by Leonard Harris, 229–36. Philadelphia: Temple University Press, 1989.

Lombardo, Clare. "Why White School Districts Have So Much More Money." NPR, February 26, 2019. https://www.npr.org/2019/02/26/696794821/why-white-school-districts-have-so-much-more-money.

Losen, Daniel J., and Kevin G. Welner. "Disabling Discrimination in Our Public Schools: Comprehensive Legal Challenges to Inappropriate and Inadequate Special Education Services for Minority Children." *Harvard Civil Rights-Civil Liberties Law Review* 36 (2001): 407–60.

Love, David A. "MLK Disobeyed Unjust Laws. The State of America Today Requires that We Not Forget That." NBC News, January 17, 2022. https://www.nbcnews.com/think/opinion/mlk-disobeyed-unjust-laws-state-america-today-requires-we-not-ncna1287569.

Lynch, Michael P. *Know-It-All Society*. New York: Liveright, 2020.

Lynch, Michael P. *On Truth in Politics: Why Democracy Demands It*. Princeton, NJ: Princeton University Press, 2025.

Lyon, Chris. "Caddo Parish Commission Votes to Remove Confederate Monument at Courthouse." *Heliopolis: Shreveport News and Culture*, October 19, 2017. https://heliopolis.la/caddo-parish-commission-votes-remove-confederate-monument-courthouse/.

Mangan, Dan. "Americans Oppose Fast Approvals, Want Drug Ads Off TV: Survey." NBC News, May 11, 2016. https://www.nbcnews.com/health/health-care/americans-oppose-fast-approvals-want-drug-ads-tv-survey-n572301.

Mani, Anandi, Sendhil Mullainathan, Eldar Shafir, and Jiaying Zhao. "Poverty Impedes Cognitive Function." *Science* 341 (August 2013): 976–80.

Manicas, Peter. "*Charles Sanders Peirce: A Life* (Review)." *Biography* 17, no. 1 (1994): 63–66.

Manson, Neil C., and Onora O'Neill. *Rethinking Informed Consent in Bioethics*. New York: Cambridge University Press, 2007.

Martin, Roland. "A Remarkable Night for the Country: Analysts React to Obama's Victory." CNN.com, November 5, 2008. https://edition.cnn.com/2008/POLITICS/11/05/analysts.react/.

Masket, Seth. "Texas' College Tenure Decision Undermines One of America's Proudest Accomplishments." NBCNews.com, March 9, 2022. https://www.nbcnews.com/think/opinion/texas-tenure-attack-america-s-colleges-embarrassing-ncna1291314.

Maslow, Abraham H. *Motivation and Personality*. New York: Harper and Row, 1954.

Matsuda, Mari J. "Public Response to Racist Speech: Considering the Victim's Story." In *Words That Wound: Critical Race Theory, Assaultive Speech, and the First Amendment*, edited by Mari J. Matsuda, Charles R Lawrence, III, Richard Delgado, and Kimberlé Williams Crenshaw, 17–51. Boulder, CO: Perseus Press, 1993.

Matsuda, Mari J., Charles R. Lawrence III, Richard Delgado, and Kimberlé Williams Crenshaw, Editors. *Words That Wound: Critical Race Theory, Assaultive Speech, and the First Amendment*. Boulder, CO: Perseus Press, 1993.

McCann, Bill. "Will 'Teflon Don' Ever Be Held Accountable." *Austin-American Statesman*, April 7, 2022. https://www.statesman.com/story/news/2022/04/07/opinion-donald-trump-ever-held-accountable/9472134002/.

McCann, Meghan, and Josephine Hauer. "Moving on Up: Helping Families Climb the Economic Ladder by Addressing Benefits Cliffs." National Conference of State Legislatures, August 20, 2019. https://www.ncsl.org/Portals/1/Documents/cyf/Benefits-Cliffs_v03_web.pdf.

McCormack, Simon. "Dylann Roof Charged with 9 Counts of Murder." *Huffington Post*, June 19, 2015. http://www.huffingtonpost.com/2015/06/19/dylan-roof-confesses_n_7620314.html.

McCulloch, Derek. "TEN LITTLE NIGGER BOYS." YouTube video. Posted by "EMGColonel," September 18, 2017. https://www.youtube.com/watch?v=vioBurOEefo&t=83s.

McIntyre, Lee. *Post-Truth*. Cambridge, MA: MIT Press, 2018.

McKeon, Denise. "Research Talking Points on Dropout Statistics: High School Attendance, Graduation, Completion, & Dropout Statistics." National Education Association, February, 2006. http://www.nea.org/home/i3579.htm.

McShane, Larry. "Interracial Marriage Should Be Illegal, Say 46% of Mississippi Republicans in New Poll." *New York Daily News*, April 8, 2011. https://www.nydailynews.com/news/national/interracial-marriage-illegal-46-mississippi-republicans-new-poll-article-1.111449.

Meckler, Laura. "Study Finds Black and Latino Students Face Significant 'Funding Gap.'" *Washington Post*, July 22, 2020. https://www.washingtonpost.com/education/study-finds-black-and-latino-students-face-significant-funding-gap/2020/07/21/712f376a-caca-11ea-b0e3-d55bda07d66a_story.html.

Menand, Louis. *The Metaphysical Club: A Story of Ideas in America*. New York: Farrar, Straus, and Giroux, 2001.

Mendelow, Madeleine. "Beyond the Binary." *Psychiatric Times*, April 4, 2022. https://www.psychiatrictimes.com/view/beyond-the-binary.

Michaels, Ralf. "Legal Culture." In *Oxford Handbook of European Private Law*, edited by Basedow, Hopt, and Zimmermann. London: Oxford University Press, 2012. https://scholarship.law.duke.edu/cgi/viewcontent.cgi?article=3012&context=faculty_scholarship.

Milbank, Dana. "Doctor of Divisiveness." *Washington Post*, May 29, 2014, A2.

Milbank, Dana. "The GOP Turns 'Political Correctness' Into the Mother of All Straw Men." *Washington Post*, December 21, 2015. https://www.washingtonpost.com/opinions/the-gop-turns-political-correctness-into-the-mother-of-all-straw-men/2015/12/21/90ab5398-a816-11e5-bff5-905b92f5f94b_story.html.

Mill, John Stuart. *On Liberty*. 1859; reprint, Indianapolis, IN: Hackett, 1978.

Miller, Brian, and Mike Lapham. *The Self-Made Myth: And the Truth about How Government Helps Individuals and Business Succeed*. San Francisco: Berrett-Koehler, 2012.

Mills, Charles W. "Retrieving Rawls for Racial Justice? A Critique of Tommie Shelby." *Critical Philosophy of Race* 1, no. 1 (2013): 1–27.

Minersville School District v. Gobitis, 310 U.S. 586 (1940).

Mississippi Convention. *An Address Setting Forth the Declaration of the Immediate Causes Which Induce and Justify the Secession of Mississippi from the Federal Union and the Ordinance of Secession.* Jackson: Mississippi Book and Job Printing Office, 1861. https://archive.org/details/addresssettingfo01miss.

Mitchell, Jerry. "Ole Miss Student Charged for Defacing Meredith Statue." *Clarion Ledger*, March 27, 2015. https://www.usatoday.com/story/news/nation/2015/03/27/ole-miss-meredith-statue-vandalism/70562446/.

Moll-Ramirez, Victoria, Cecily Cruz, Penelope Lopez, and Kiara Alfonseca. "Latinx? Latino? Hispanic? A Linguistics Expert Explains the Confusion." ABC News, January 15, 2022. https://abcnews.go.com/US/latinx-latino-hispanic-linguistics-expert-explains-confusion/story?id=82273936.

Morris, Monique, Mankappr Conteh, and Melissa Harris-Perry. *Pushout: The Criminalization of Black Girls in Schools.* New York: The New Press, 2018.

Morrison, Toni. *The Bluest Eye.* New York: Random House, 2007.

Moses, Joy. "The Facts About Americans Who Receive Public Benefits: Misperceptions About Poverty in Our Country Complicate Effective Policymaking." Center for American Progress, December 2011. https://cdn.americanprogress.org/wp-content/uploads/issues/2011/12/pdf/public_benefits_pdf.pdf?_ga=2.33085566.179903058.1647009053-54787874.1646749890.

Mounk, Yascha. "Americans Strongly Dislike PC Culture." *Atlantic*, October 10, 2018. https://www.theatlantic.com/ideas/archive/2018/10/large-majorities-dislike-political-correctness/572581/.

Mount Vernon Ladies' Association. "Ten Facts about Washington and Slavery." http://www.mountvernon.org/george-washington/slavery/ten-facts-about-washington-slavery/.

Murdock, Sebastian. "KKK Plans Pro-Confederate Flag Rally in South Carolina." *Huffington Post*, June 30, 2015. http://www.huffingtonpost.com/2015/06/30/kkk-south-carolina-confederate_n_7695738.html.

Murphy, Eddie and Bruce Gowers. *Eddie Murphy "Delirious."* Beverly Hills, CA: Entertainment Studios, 1983.

Murphy, Paul P. "White Nationalists Use Tiki Torches to Light Up Charlottesville March." CNN, August 14, 2017. https://www.cnn.com/2017/08/12/us/white-nationalists-tiki-torch-march-trnd/index.html.

Murray, James E., Jr., "Making Distinctions: An Ethical Argument for Increasing American Descendants of Slavery (ADOS) Presence In Universities Through Disaggregating "Black" Racial Data/Categorization." Mid-western Educational Research Association (MWERA) 43rd Annual Meeting, October 13–15, 2021, Cincinnati, OH.

Murray, Justin. "Why It's So Hard to Escape America's Anti-Poverty Programs." Foundation for Economic Education (Fee.org), March 30, 2020. https://fee.org/articles/why-its-so-hard-to-escape-americas-anti-poverty-programs/.

Myatt, Mike. "Self-Made Man—No Such Thing." *Forbes*, November 15, 2011. https://www.forbes.com/sites/mikemyatt/2011/11/15/self-made-man-no-such-thing/.

Nam, Janima. "The Art of Funding." *Metropole*, Spring 2021. https://michael-wimmer.at/wp-content/uploads/2021/03/88_MET_Spring_21_CityLife.pdf.

National Endowment for the Arts. "Quick Facts." Arts.gov. https://www.arts.gov/sites/default/files/Quick_Facts_February2020.pdf.

Neidig, Harper, and Rebecca Beitsch. "DOJ Has Multiple Possible Paths to Trump Indictment." *The Hill*, July 27, 2022. https://thehill.com/homenews/house/3576858-doj-has-multiple-possible-paths-to-trump-indictment-heres-what-it-could-look-like/.

Nellis, Ashley. "The Color of Justice: Racial and Ethnic Disparity in State Prisons." The Sentencing Project. Washington, DC, October 2021. https://www.sentencingproject.org/publications/color-of-justice-racial-and-ethnic-disparity-in-state-prisons/.

Nelson, Joshua Q. "North Dakota Parents Furious After School Board Nixes Pledge of Allegiance: 'Bunch of Crap.'" Fox News, August 12, 2022. https://www.foxnews.com/media/north-dakota-parents-furious-school-board-nixes-pledge-allegiance-bunch-crap.

Neuman, Scott. "Boston Right-Wing 'Free Speech' Rally Dwarfed by Counter-protestors." NPR News, August 19, 2017. https://www.npr.org/sections/thetwo-way/2017/08/19/544684355/bostons-free-speech-rally-organizers-deny-links-to-white-nationalists?t=1648596601730.

Neville, Robert C. *The Highroad Around Modernism*. Albany: State University of New York Press, 1992.

Newdow v. Cong., 383 F. Supp. 2d 1229 (E.D. Cal. 2005), *sub nom.* Newdow v. Rio Linda, No. 05-17257 (9 Cir. 2007).

Ngo, Madeleine. "After Dropping Free Community College Plan, Democrats Explore Options." *New York Times*, October, 22, 2021. https://www.nytimes.com/2021/10/22/us/politics/free-community-college-democrats.html.

Nicholson, Rebecca. "'Poor Little Snowflake'—The Defining Insult of 2016." *Guardian*, November 28, 2016. https://www.theguardian.com/science/2016/nov/28/snowflake-insult-disdain-young-people.

Nozick, Robert. *Anarchy, State, and Utopia*. 1974; reprint, New York: Basic Books, 2013.

NPR/PBS News Hour/Marist Poll. "PDTCIVGAL1." November 28–December 4, 2018. http://maristpoll.marist.edu/wp-content/uploads/2018/12/NPR_PBS-NewsHour_Marist-Poll_USA-NOS-and-Tables_Civility_1812051719.pdf#page=3.

Nussbaum, Martha. *Frontiers of Justice: Disability, Nationality, Species Membership*. Cambridge, MA: The Belknap Press of Harvard University Press, 2006.

O'Brien, Matthew. "Why the U.S. Government Never, Ever Has to Pay Back All Its Debt." *Atlantic*, February 1, 2013. https://www.theatlantic.com/business/archive/2013/02/why-the-us-government-never-ever-has-to-pay-back-all-its-debt/272747/.

Office of Minority Health. "Profile: Black/African Americans." US Department of Health and Human Services. https://www.minorityhealth.hhs.gov/omh/browse.aspx?lvl=3&lvlid=61.

Ohline, Howard A. "Republicanism and Slavery: Origins of the Three-Fifths Clause in the United States Constitution." *William and Mary Quarterly* 28, no. 4 (October 1971): 563–84.

"Oklahoma." Online Etymology Dictionary. https://www.etymonline.com/search?q=oklahoma.

Oxford English Dictionary. "Definition of politically correct." OED Online, June 2022. Oxford University Press. https://www-oed-com.ezproxy.uky.edu/view/Entry/146889?redirectedFrom=%22politically+correct%22.

Page, Sydney. "Once the 'World's Only Klan Museum,' It Is Becoming a Center for History and Healing." *Washington Post*, January 8, 2021. https://www.washingtonpost.com/lifestyle/2021/01/08/kkk-museum-redneck-race-healing/.

Paul, Heike. "Expressive Individualism and the Myth of the Self-Made Man." In *The Myths That Made America: An Introduction to American Studies*. Bielefeld, German: Transcript Verlag, 2014.

Peralta, Eyder. "PA Judge Sentenced to 28 Years in Massive Juvenile Justice Bribery Scandal." NPR.org, August 11, 2011. http://www.npr.org/sections/thetwo-way/2011/08/11/139536686/pa-judge-sentenced-to-28-years-in-massive-juvenile-justice-bribery-scandal.

Perlman, Merrill. "AP Tackles Language About Race in This Year's Style Guide." *Columbia Journalism Review*, April 1, 2019. https://www.cjr.org/language_corner/ap-style-guide-race-black-vs-african-american.php

Peirce, Charles Sanders. "The Fixation of Belief." In *The Essential Peirce: Selected Philosophical Writings*, edited by Nathan Houser and Christian Kloesel, 109–23 (1877; repr., Indianapolis: Indiana University Press, 1992).

Peirce, Charles Sanders. "How to Make Our Ideas Clear." *Popular Science Monthly* 12 (January 1878): 286–302.

Peirce, Charles Sanders. "Some Consequences of Four Incapacities." In *The Collected Papers of Charles Sanders Peirce*, edited by Charles Hartshorne and Paul Weiss, vol. 5, 1932–35. Cambridge, MA: Harvard University Press,

Peirce, Charles Sanders. "Truth." Chapter 4 in *The Collected Papers, Volume 5, Pragmatism and Pragmaticism, Book 3, Unpublished Papers*, edited by Charles Hartshorne and Paul Weiss. Cambridge, MA: Harvard University Press, 1934.

Perez, Juan. "Governors Want to Boost Teacher Pay." *Politico*, January 24, 2022. https://www.politico.com/newsletters/weekly-education/2022/01/24/governors-want-to-boost-teacher-pay-00001091.

Petchauer, Emery. "Passing as White: Race, Shame, and Success in Teacher Licensure Testing Events for Black Preservice Teachers." *Race, Ethnicity, and Education* 18, no. 6 (2015): 834–57.

Pettus, Emily Wagster. "KKK Plans to Protest at Ole Miss Over Song, Chant." BET, November 23, 2009. https://www.bet.com/article/sowav2/kkk-plans-to-protest-at-ole-miss-over-song-chant.

Pew Research Center. "Beyond Red vs. Blue: The Political Typology," June 2014. https://www.pewresearch.org/politics/wp-content/uploads/sites/4/2014/06/6-26-14-Political-Typology-release1.pdf.

Phillips, Kristine. "A School District Drops 'To Kill a Mockingbird' and 'Huckleberry Finn' Over Use of the N-Word." *Washington Post*, February 7, 2018. https://www.washingtonpost.com/news/education/wp/2018/02/07/a-school-district-drops-to-kill-a-mockingbird-and-huckleberry-finn-over-use-of-the-n-word/.

Picchi, Aimee. "Almost Half of All Americans Work in Low-Wage Jobs." NBC News, December 2, 2019. https://www.cbsnews.com/news/minimum-wage-2019-almost-half-of-all-americans-work-in-low-wage-jobs/.

Pick, Hella. "KKK Men Charged with Murder." *Guardian*, August 8, 1964. https://www.theguardian.com/world/1964/aug/08/usa.hellapick.

Pilkington, ed. "Mississippi Church Bans African American Wedding After Complaints." *Guardian*, July 29, 2012. https://www.theguardian.com/world/2012/jul/29/mississippi-church-african-american-wedding.

The Place. "Does Poor Car Maintenance Lead to Accidents? Yes and These May be the Top 2 Culprits!" Fox 13 Salt Lake City, April 29, 2021. https://www.fox13now.com/the-place/does-poor-car-maintenance-lead-to-accidents-yes-and-these-may-be-the-top-2-culprits.

Plato. *Republic*. Translated by G. M. A. Grube. Indianapolis, IN: Hackett, 1992.

Pojman, Louis, and Robert Westmoreland, eds. *Equality: Selected Readings*. New York: Oxford University Press, 1997.

Politi, Daniel. "Donald Trump Vows to Curb Press Freedom Through Harsher Libel Laws." *Slate*, February 27, 2016. https://slate.com/news-and-politics/2016/02/donald-trump-vows-to-curb-press-freedom-through-libel-laws.html.

Politi, Daniel. "Dylann Roof Burns U.S. Flag, Details White Supremacist Worldview in Shocking Online Manifest." *Slate*, June 20, 2015. https://slate.com/news-and-politics/2015/06/dylann-roof-details-white-supremacist-worldview-in-shocking-online-manifesto.html.

Popper, Karl. *The Open Society and Its Enemies*. Princeton, NJ: Princeton University Press, 2013.

Przybyla, Heidi, and Adam Edelman. "States Weigh a Raft of Proposed Laws to Limit Race, Sexuality Lessons in Schools." NBC News, January 28, 2022. https://www.nbcnews.com/politics/politics-news/states-weigh-raft-proposed-laws-limit-race-sexuality-lessons-schools-n1288108.

Pulrang, Andrew. "It's Time to Stop Even Casually Misusing Disability Words." *Forbes*, February 20, 2021. https://www.forbes.com/sites/andrewpulrang/2021/02/20/its-time-to-stop-even-casually-misusing-disability-words/?sh=404de22c7d4e.

Purnell, Deborah. "U.S. Marshals Share Recollections of Ole Miss Integration at Program." *University of Mississippi News*, October 2, 2012. https://news.olemiss.edu/u-s-marshals-share-recollections-of-ole-miss-integration-at-program/.

Putnam, Ruth Anna. "Democracy as a Way of Life." In *Pragmatism as a Way of Life: The Lasting Legacy of Willian James and John Dewey*, by Hilary Putnam and Ruth Anna Putnam, edited by David MacArthur, 439–52. Cambridge, MA: The Belknap Press of Harvard University Press, 2017.

"Putting on Weight; Government Debt—Governments Can Borrow More than Was Once Believed." *Economist*, September 12, 2020, 58.

Quine, Willard Van Orman. *Word and Object*. Cambridge, MA: MIT Press, 1960.

Ralston, Shane. "Can Pragmatists Be Institutionalists? John Dewey Joins the Non-ideal/Ideal Theory Debate." *Human Studies* 33, no. 1 (2010): 65–84.

Ralston, Shane. "A Deweyan Justification for Homeschooling." Chapter 5 in *John Dewey's Great Debates—Reconstructed*, 73–86. Charlotte, NC: Information Age Publishing, 2011.

Rampersad, Arnold. "The Book That Launched the Harlem Renaissance." *Journal of Blacks in Higher Education* 38 (Winter 2002–2003): 87–91.

Ramseth, Luke. "Mississippi Flag: Where Do Governor, Lieutenant Governor Stand on Confederate Emblem?" *Clarion Ledger*, April 11, 2019. https://www.clarionledger.com/story/news/politics/2019/04/11/mississippi-flag-candidates-stances-removing-confederate-symbol/3415376002/.

Rao, Nirupama. "Mahatma Gandhi's 'Light' Guided Martin Luther King, Jr." *Politico*, March 7, 2013. http://www.politico.com/story/2013/03/mahatma-gandhis-lightguided-martin-luther-king-jr-88581.html.

Ravitch, Diane. *The Death and Life of the Great American School System: How Testing and Choice Are Undermining Education*. New York: Basic Books, 1994.

Ravitch, Diane. *The Language Police: How Pressure Groups Restrict What Students Learn*. New York: Vintage Books, 2003.

Ravitch, Diane. *Reign of Error: The Hoax of the Privatization Movement and the Danger to America's Public Schools*. New York: Vintage Press, 2014.

Ravitch, Diane. *Slaying Goliath: The Passionate Resistance to Privatization and the Fight to Save America's Public Schools*. New York: Vintage Press, 2020.

Rawls, John. "The Idea of Public Reason Revisited." In *John Rawls: Collected Papers*, edited by Samuel Freeman, 573–615. 1997; reprint, Cambridge, MA: Harvard University Press, 1999.

Rawls, John. *Justice as Fairness: A Restatement*. Cambridge, MA: Harvard University Press, 2001.

Rawls, John. "Kantian Constructivism in Moral Theory." *Journal of Philosophy* 77, no. 9 (1980): 515–72.

Rawls, John. *The Law of Peoples*. Cambridge, MA: Harvard University Press, 2001.

Rawls, John. "The Law of Peoples." *Critical Inquiry* 20, no. 1 (1993): 36–68.

Rawls, John. *Political Liberalism*. New York: Columbia University Press, 1996.

Rawls, John. *A Theory of Justice*. 1971; reprint, Cambridge, MA: Harvard University Press, 1999.

Rawls, John. "Two Concepts of Rules." *Philosophical Review* 64, no. 1 (1955): 3–32.

Reese, Michele. "Ole Miss Students Walk in Unity after Campus Protest." WREG Memphis Channel 3 News, November 7, 2012. https://wreg.com/news/ole-miss-students-walk-in-unity-after-campus-protest/.

Remnick, David. "Charleston and the Age of Obama." *New Yorker*, June 19, 2015. http://www.newyorker.com/news/daily-comment/charleston-and-the-age-of-obama.

"Retire American Indian Team Nicknames? #TellUSAToday." Editorial collection of Twitter responses, *USA Today*, May 6, 2014. http://www.usatoday.com/story/opinion/2014/05/06/native-american-nicknames-redskins-tellusatoday-your-say/8785465/.

Reyes, Emily Alpert. "Survey Finds Dads Defy Stereotypes about Black Fatherhood." *Los Angeles Times*, December 20, 2013. http://articles.latimes.com/2013/dec/20/local/la-me-black-dads-20131221.

Richmond, Emily. "Schools Are More Segregated Today than During the Late 1960s." *Atlantic*, June 11, 2012. http://www.theatlantic.com/national/archive/2012/06/schools-are-more-segregated-today-than-during-the-late-1960s/258348/.

Rix, Kate. "Schools Need Teachers of Color. This Is How to Retain Them, Educators Say." NBC News, December 20, 2021. https://www.nbcnews.com/news/education/schools-need-teachers-color-retain-educators-say-rcna7732.

Robbins, Alexandra. "Teachers Deserve More Respect." *New York Times*, March 20, 2020. https://www.nytimes.com/2020/03/20/opinion/sunday/teachers-coronavirus.html.

Rojas, Rick. "Mississippi Voters Approve Flag with Magnolia Instead of Confederate Symbol." *New York Times*, November 4, 2020. https://www.nytimes.com/2020/11/03/us/politics/mississippi-voters-approve-flag-with-magnolia-instead-of-confederate-symbol.html.

Roman, Rebecca. "When Free Speech Isn't Free: The Rising Costs of Hosting Controversial Speakers at Public Universities." *University of Chicago Legal Forum 2020* (2020): 451–76.

Romero, Dennis, and Anthony Cusumano. "Death Sentence Upheld for Dylann Roof, Who Killed 9 in South Carolina Church Shooting." NBC News, August 25, 2021. https://www.nbcnews.com/news/us-news/death-sentence-upheld-man-who-killed-9-south-carolina-church-n1277667.

Rorty, Richard. *Contingency, Irony, and Solidarity*. New York: Cambridge University Press, 1989.

Rorty, Richard. "Human Rights, Rationality, and Sentimentality." In *Truth and Progress: Philosophical Papers*, vol. 3, 167–85. New York: Cambridge University Press, 1998.

Rorty, Richard. *Philosophy and Social Hope.* New York: Penguin Books, 1999.

Rorty, Richard. *Philosophy as Cultural Politics: Philosophical Papers*, vol. 4. New York: Cambridge University Press, 2007.

Rorty, Richard. "The Priority of Democracy to Philosophy." In *Objectivity, Relativism, and Truth: Philosophical Papers,* vol. 1, 175–96. 1991; reprint, New York: Cambridge University Press, 2008.

Rorty, Richard. "Rationality and Cultural Difference." In *Truth and Progress: Philosophical Papers*, vol. 3, 186–201. New York: Cambridge University Press, 1998.

Rose, Mike. *The Mind at Work: Valuing the Intelligence of the American Worker.* New York: Penguin Books, 2014.

Rosenfeld, Michael J. "Moving a Mountain: The Extraordinary Trajectory of Same-Sex Marriage Approval in the United States." *Socius* 3 (2017): 1–22.

Ross, Janelle. "The Story Behind the University of New Hampshire's 'Bias-Free Language Guide.'" *Washington Post*, July 30, 2015. https://www.washington post.com/news/the-fix/wp/2015/07/30/the-story-behind-the-university-of-new-hampshires-bias-free-language-guide/?utm_term=.d154c4136193.

Rotfeld, Herbert Jack. "Can You Really Say That?" *Journal of Consumer Affairs* 42, no. 3 (2008): 484–87.

Rovner, Julie. "Kill Grandma? Debunking a Health Bill Scare Tactic." NPR, August 12, 2009. https://www.npr.org/2009/08/12/111729363/kill-grandma-debunking-a-health-bill-scare-tactic.

Ryan, Paul. "The War on Poverty: 50 Years Later: A House Budget Committee Report." Washington, DC: House Budget Committee, 2014.

Ryan, William. *Blaming the Victim.* New York: Vintage Press, 1976.

Sachs, David. "How to Distinguish Self-Respect from Self-Esteem." *Philosophy and Public Affairs* 10, no. 4 (1981): 346–60.

Said, Edward W., and Christopher Hitchens, eds. *Blaming the Victims: Spurious Scholarship and the Palestinian Question.* 1988; reprint, New York: Verso Press, 2001.

Salter, Sid. "Charter Schools Offer Alternative to Mediocre/Failing Schools." *Desoto Times Tribune*, February 22, 2012. http://www.desototimes.com/articles/2012/02/23/opinion/editorials/doc4f453f741ac69454084633.txt.

Samuel, Henry. "France's Académie Française Battles to Protect Language from English." *Telegraph*, October 11, 2011. https://www.telegraph.co.uk/news/worldnews/europe/france/8820304/Frances-Academie-francaise-battles-to-protect-language-from-English.html.

Samuels, Alex. "Dan Patrick Says 'There Are More Important Things than Living and That's Saving This Country.'" *Texas Tribune*, April 21, 2020. https://www.texastribune.org/2020/04/21/texas-dan-patrick-economy-coronavirus/.

Samuelson, Scott. "Why I Teach Plato to Plumbers." *Atlantic*, April 29, 2014. https://www.theatlantic.com/education/archive/2014/04/plato-to-plumbers/361373/.

Sanchez, Ray, and Ed Payne. "Charleston Church Shooting: Who Is Dylann Roof?" CNN.com, June 19, 2015. http://www.cnn.com/2015/06/19/us/charleston-church-shooting-suspect/.

Santiago, Anna Maria. "Fifty Years Later: From a War on Poverty to a War on the Poor." *Social Problems* 62 (2015): 2–14.

Satel, Sally. *P.C., M.D.: How Political Correctness Is Corrupting Medicine.* New York: Basic Books, 2002.

Sauer, Pjotr. "Cosmopolitan No More: Russians Feel Sting of Cultural and Economic Shift." *Guardian*, May 20, 2022. https://www.theguardian.com/world/2022/may/20/russians-feel-sting-of-cultural-and-economic-rift-sanctions-ukraine.

Schafer, Matthew L., and Jeff Kosseff. "Protecting Free Speech in a Post-*Sullivan* World." *Federal Communications Law Journal* 75, no. 1 (2022): 1–52.

Schechter, Anna R., and Jon Schuppe. "Confederate Flag Rally Tests a Diminished Ku Klux Klan." MSNBC.com, July 18, 2015. http://www.msnbc.com/msnbc/confederate-flag-rally-tests-diminished-ku-klux-klan

Schnugg, Alyssa. "Federal Prison for Harris." *Oxford Eagle*, September 18, 2015. https://www.oxfordeagle.com/2015/09/18/federal-prison-for-harris/.

Schuppe, Jon. "South Carolina Gov. Nikki Haley Signs Bill Removing Confederate Flag." NBC News, July 9, 2015. https://www.nbcnews.com/storyline/confederate-flag-furor/gov-haley-sign-bill-removing-confederate-flag-n389231.

Schwartz, Amy Ellen, and Michah W. Robart. "Let Them Eat Lunch: The Impact of Universal Free Meals on Student Performance." Syracuse University Center for Policy Research 235, December 2017. https://surface.syr.edu/cpr/235.

Sege, Robert D., Benjamin S. Siegel, Council on Child Abuse and Neglect; Committee on Psychosocial Aspects of Child and Family Health. "Effective Discipline to Raise Healthy Children." *Pediatrics* 142, no. 6 (2018): 1–10. https://pediatrics.aappublications.org/content/pediatrics/142/6/e20183112.full.pdf.

Sentencing Project. "Report of the Sentencing Project to the United Nations Human Rights Committee: Regarding Racial Disparities in the United States Criminal Justice System." Washington, DC: Sentencing Project Research and Advocacy for Reform, August 2013. https://www.sentencingproject.org/wp-content/uploads/2015/12/Race-and-Justice-Shadow-Report-ICCPR.pdf.

Sentencing Project. "New Report Finds Imprisonment Rate of Black Men Has Fallen by Nearly 50% Since 2000, but Pushback Threatens Continued Progress." News release, October 11, 2023. https://www.sentencingproject.org/press-releases/new-report-finds-imprisonment-rate-of-black-men-has-fallen-by-nearly-50-since-2000-but-pushback-threatens-continued-progress/.

Sestric, Lia. "30 U.S. Cities Where Million-Dollar Homes Are Practically the Norm." *Business Insider*, December 13, 2017. https://www.businessinsider.com/30-us-cities-where-million-dollar-homes-are-practically-the-norm-2017-12.

Shafer-Landau, Russ. *Moral Realism: A Defense*. New York: Oxford University Press, 2003.

Sharlet, Jeff. " 'F--k Your Feelings': In Trump's America, the Partisan Battle Flag Is the New Stars and Stripes." *Vanity Fair*, September 8, 2020. https://www.vanityfair.com/news/2020/09/trump-partisan-battle-flag-is-the-new-stars-and-stripes.

Shaw, Rebecca. "Political Correctness Isn't Killing Comedy. Scared Old Stagnant Comedians Are." *Guardian*, May 27, 2018. https://www.theguardian.com/culture/2018/may/28/political-correctness-isnt-killing-comedy-scared-old-stagnant-comedians-are.

Shelley, Percy Bysshe. "A Defence of Poetry." In *English Essays: Sidney to Macaulay*. In *The Harvard Classics*, edited by Charles W. Eliot, vol. 27, 345–77. New York: P.F. Collier & Son, 1909–1914.

Shourd, Sarah. "Tortured by Solitude." *New York Times*, November 6, 2011, SR4.

Silverstein, Jason. "The Global Impact of George Floyd: How Black Lives Matter Protests Shaped Movements Around the World." CBS News, June 4, 2021. https://www.cbsnews.com/news/george-floyd-black-lives-matter-impact/.

Sims, Patsy. *The Klan*. Lexington: University Press of Kentucky, 1996.

Simmons, Kami Chavis. "Subverting Symbolism: The Matthew Shepard and James Byrd, Jr. Hate Crimes Prevention Act and Cooperative Federalism." *American Criminal Law Review* 49 (2012): 1863–1912.

Sinclair, Jim. "Why I Dislike "Person First" Language." *Autonomy: The Critical Journal of Interdisciplinary Autism Studies* 1, no. 2 (2013). http://www.larry-arnold.net/Autonomy/index.php/autonomy/article/view/OP1.

Singer, Peter. "Famine, Affluence, and Morality." *Philosophy and Public Affairs* 1, no. 3 (1972): 229–43.

"Singular 'They.'" *APA Publication Manual*. 7th ed. 2019. Section 4.18.

"Singular 'They.'" Merriam-Webster.com. September 2019. https://www.merriam-webster.com/words-at-play/singular-nonbinary-they.

Slawson, Nicola. "First Thing: Joe Biden Says 'White Supremacy Is a Poison.'" *Guardian*, May 18, 2022. https://www.theguardian.com/us-news/2022/may/18/first-thing-joe-biden-says-white-supremacy-is-a-poison.

Smith, Robin M., and Mara Sapon-Shevin. "Disability Humor, Insults, and Inclusive Practice." *Social Advocacy and Systems Change* 1, no. 2 (2008–2009): 1–18.

Smith, Savannah. "Why Mississippi Voted to Change Its Flag after Decades of Debate." NBC News, June 30, 2020. https://www.nbcnews.com/news/us-news/why-mississippi-voted-change-its-flag-after-decades-debate-n1232607.

Soave, Robby. "Bernie Sanders: Donald Trump Won Because People Are Tired of Political Correctness." *Reason*, December 13, 2016. https://reason.com/2016/12/13/bernie-sanders-donald-trump-won-because/.

Sonnenfeld, Jeffrey, and Steven Tlan. "Actually, the Russian Economy Is Imploding." *Foreign Policy*, July 22, 2022. https://foreignpolicy.com/2022/07/22/russia-economy-sanctions-myths-ruble-business/.

Sorial, Sarah. "Can Saying Something Make It So? The Nature of Seditious Harm." *Law and Philosophy* 29, no. 3 (2010): 273–305.

South Carolina Convention (1860–1862). *Declaration of the Immediate Causes Which Induce and Justify the Secession of South Carolina from the Federal Union and the Ordinance of Secession.* Charleston, SC: Evans and Cogswell, Printers to the Convention, 1860. https://archive.org/details/declarationofimm00sout.

Spalding, Matthew. "Why the U.S. Has a Culture of Dependency." Heritage Foundation. Commentary: Poverty and Inequality, September 21, 2012. https://www.heritage.org/poverty-and-inequality/commentary/why-the-us-has-culture-dependency.

Stack, Liam. "Attack on Alt-Right Leader Has Internet Asking: Is It O.K. to Punch a Nazi?" *New York Times*, January 21, 2017. https://www.nytimes.com/2017/01/21/us/politics/richard-spencer-punched-attack.html.

Staff. "Hospital Employee Fired After Photo of Him Wearing 'Mississippi Justice' T-Shirt While Voting Goes Viral." *Action News 5*, November 9, 2018. https://www.actionnews5.com/2018/11/08/hospital-employee-fired-after-photo-him-wearing-mississippi-justice-t-shirt-while-voting-goes-viral/.

Staff Writer. "More People Tired of Political Correctness but Research Reveals Big Political Divide." *Christian Today*, December 22, 2018. https://www.christiantoday.com/article/more-people-are-tired-of-political-correctness-but-research-reveals-big-political-divide/131302.htm.

Stanglin, Douglas. "Arizona Puts State Buildings on Sale to Plug Deficit." *USA Today*, January 12, 2010. http://content.usatoday.com/communities/ondeadline/post/2010/01/arizona-puts-state-buildings-on-sale-today-to-fill-empty-coffers/1#.U5ezOPldUnX.

Staples, Brent. "Barack Obama, John McCain, and the Language of Race." *New York Times*, September 22, 2008, A22.

Starr, Alexandra. "University of Mississippi Orders State Flag Removed." NPR, October 26, 2015. https://www.npr.org/sections/thetwo-way/2015/10/26/451955764/university-of-mississippi-orders-state-flag-removed.

Steele, Eli. "Rooftop Revelations: Can a Government that Helped Create a Culture of Dependency Reverse the Damage?" FoxNews.com, February 10, 2022. https://www.foxnews.com/opinion/rooftop-revelations-can-a-government-that-helped-create-a-culture-of-dependency-reverse-the-damage.

Steele, Shelby. *White Guilt: How Blacks and White Together Destroyed the Promise of the Civil Rights Era.* New York: Harper, 2006.

Steinhauer, Jennifer. "California, Nearly Broke, Edges Nearer Brink." *New York Times*, February 17, 2009, A14.

Stokes, Melvyn. *D. W. Griffith's The Birth of a Nation.* New York: Oxford University Press, 2007.

Stone, Geoffrey R. *Perilous Times: Free Speech in Wartime—From the Sedition Act of 1798 to the War on Terrorism.* New York: W. W. Norton, 2004.

Stone, Geoffrey R. "The Noose, Ole Miss, and Free Speech." *Huffington Post*, February 19, 2014. https://www.huffpost.com/entry/the-noose-ole-miss-and-fr_b_4820588.

Stone, Lisa. "UM Releases Enrollment for Fall 2020." *University of Mississippi News*, November 3, 2020. https://news.olemiss.edu/um-releases-enrollment-for-fall-2020/.

Stout, David. "Supreme Court Upholds Child Pornography Law." *New York Times*, May 20, 2008. http://www.nytimes.com/2008/05/20/washington/19cnd-scotus.html.

Stracqualursi, Veronica. "Mississippi Ratifies and Raises Its New State Flag Over the State Capitol for the First Time." CNN, January 13, 2021. https://www.cnn.com/2021/01/12/politics/mississippi-new-state-flag-flown/index.html.

Strauss, Steven. "Shouldn't We Drug Test CEOs of Banks Receiving Federal Aid?" *Huffington Post*, April 7, 2013. https://www.huffpost.com/entry/drug-test-ceos_b_3034127.

Student Government Assembly. "AR 35: In Support of Removing the Jefferson Davis Statue at UT." University of Texas at Austin, March 24, 2015. https://repositories.lib.utexas.edu/bitstream/handle/2152/42815/9AR%2035.pdf?sequence=1.

Sutter, John D. "Malala Is the New Symbol of Hope." CNN.com, October 13, 2014. http://www.cnn.com/2014/10/10/opinion/sutter-nobel-prize-malala/.

Svrluga, Susan. "Former Ole Miss Student Pleads Guilty to Hanging Noose Around Statue Honoring the First Black Student." *Washington Post*, March 24, 2016. https://www.washingtonpost.com/news/grade-point/wp/2016/03/24/former-ole-miss-student-pleads-guilty-to-hanging-noose-around-statue-honoring-the-first-black-student/.

Swansburg, John. "The Self-Made Man: The Story of America's Most Pliable, Pernicious, and Irrepressible Myth." Slate.com, September 29, 2014. http://www.slate.com/articles/news_and_politics/history/2014/09/the_self_made_man_history_of_a_myth_from_ben_franklin_to_andrew_carnegie.html.

Swerdlick, David. "Biden Said Black Trump Voters 'Ain't Black.' That's a Double Standard." *Washington Post*, May 22, 2020. https://www.washingtonpost.com/outlook/2020/05/22/biden-charlamagne-trump-black/.

Syed, Nabiha. "Real Talk about Fake News: Towards a Better Theory for Platform Governance." *Yale Law Journal Forum* 127 (2017–18): 337–57.

Talamo, Lex. "Caddo Confederate Monument Vote Close, Leaning for Removal." *Shreveport Times*, October 17, 2017. https://www.shreveporttimes.com/story/news/2017/10/17/caddo-confederate-monument-vote-close-leaning-removal/772654001/.

Tam, Luisa. "Why Privacy Is an Alien Concept in Chinese Culture." *South China Morning Post*, April 2, 2018. https://www.scmp.com/news/hong-kong/article/2139946/why-privacy-alien-concept-chinese-culture.

Tannenbaum, Melanie. "Decoding Trump-Mania: The Psychological Allure of Hating Political Correctness, Part 3." *Scientific American*, September 8, 2015. https://blogs.scientificamerican.com/psysociety/decoding-trump-mania-the-psychological-allure-of-hating-political-correctness-part-3/.

Tapper, Jake, Sara Sidner, Omar Jimenez, W. Kamau Bell, Anthony Barksdale, and Elie Honig. "Derek Chauvin Sentenced to 22-1/2 Years for George Floyd's Murder. Aired 4-5p ET." *CNN The Lead with Jake Tapper*, June 25, 2021.

Taranto, James. "Durham, We Have a Problem." *Wall Street Journal*, July 30, 2015. https://www.wsj.com/articles/durham-we-have-a-problem-1438279548.

Taselaar, Amanda. "Don't Call It a Brown Bag Lunch." *Time*, August 6, 2013. http://newsfeed.time.com/2013/08/06/dont-call-it-a-brown-bag-lunch-seattle-frowns-on-popular-term/.

Taylor, Robert S. *Reconstructing Rawls: The Kantian Foundations of Justice as Fairness*. University Park: Pennsylvania State University Press, 2011.

Teeman, Tim. "Why Did Matt Damon Think Calling Gay Men 'F*ggots' Was Ok?" *Daily Beast*, August 2, 2021. https://www.thedailybeast.com/why-did-it-take-matt-damons-daughter-to-stop-him-calling-gay-men-the-f-slur.

Tennessee Board of Regents. "Tennessee Promise." College System of Tennessee. https://www.tbr.edu/initiatives/tn-promise.

Thaler, Richard H., and Cass R. Sunstein. *Nudge: Improving Decisions About Health, Wealth, and Happiness*. New Haven: Yale University Press, 2008.

Titchkosky, Tanya. "Disability: A Rose by Any Other Name? 'People-First' Language in Canadian Society." *Canadian Review of Sociology* 38, no. 2 (2001): 125–40.

Totenberg, Nina, and Sarah McCammon. "Supreme Court Overturns Roe v. Wade, Ending Right to Abortion Upheld for Decades." NPR.org, June 24, 2022. https://www.npr.org/2022/06/24/1102305878/supreme-court-abortion-roe-v-wade-decision-overturn.

Tovey, Craig A. "In Defense of Basic Research." *Science* 355, no. 6327 (2017): 804.

Trau, Morgan. "As the School Year Begins, Calls for Book Bans Begin to Accelerate in Ohio." *Ohio Capital Journal*, August 9, 2022. https://ohiocapitaljournal.com/2022/08/09/as-the-school-year-begins-calls-for-book-bans-begin-to-accelerate-in-ohio/.

Travis, Clay. "On the Confederate Flag." Fox Sports, June 24, 2015. https://www.foxsports.com/stories/other/on-the-confederate-flag.

Treisman, Rachel. "Nearly 100 Confederate Monuments Removed in 2020, Report Says; More than 700 Remain." NPR, February 23, 2021. https://www.npr.org/2021/02/23/970610428/nearly-100-confederate-monuments-removed-in-2020-report-says-more-than-700-remai.

Triplett, Timm. "Rorty's Critique of Foundationalism." *Philosophical Studies* 52, no. 1 (1987): 115–29.

Trotter, M. "Australian Trees and Algerian Deserts." *Pall Mall Gazette*. London, 1868.

Tumulty, Karen. "How George Floyd Speaks to the Shame of Our History and the Promise of Our Future." *Washington Post*, June 9, 2020. https://www.washingtonpost.com/opinions/how-george-floyd-speaks-to-the-shame-of-our-history-and-the-promise-of-our-future/2020/06/09/8ff43956-aa6e-11ea-94d2-d7bc43b26bf9_story.html.

Turley, Jonathan. "No, the U.S. Does Not Need European-Style Hate Speech Laws." *USA Today*, November 8, 2019. https://www.usatoday.com/story/opinion/2019/11/08/no-us-not-need-european-style-hate-speech-laws-column/4157833002/.

Tyson, Karolyn, William Darity, and Domini R. Castellino. "It's Not 'a Black Thing': Understanding the Burden of Acting White and Other Dilemmas of High Achievement." *American Sociological Review* 70, no. 4 (2005): 582–605.

United Nations Human Rights Office of the High Commissioner. "One-Pager on 'Incitement to Hatred': The Rabat Threshold Test." United Nations, OHCHR.org, April 20, 2020. https://www.ohchr.org/en/documents/one-pager-incitement-hatred-rabat-threshold-test.

US Census Bureau. "National Poverty in America Awareness Month: January 2022." Census.gov, January 2022. Release Number CB22-SFS.013. https://www.census.gov/newsroom/stories/poverty-awareness-month.html.

US Department of Justice. "Hate Crime Laws: About Hate Crimes." Justice.gov, n.d. https://www.justice.gov/crt/hate-crime-laws.

United States v. *Williams*, 553 U. S. 285 (2008).

University of Kentucky Office of Student Conduct. University of Kentucky Creed. https://www.uky.edu/studentconduct/university-kentucky-creed.

University of Mississippi. UM Creed. https://olemiss.edu/info/creed.html.

Uusitalo, Susanne, and Barbara Broers. "Rethinking Informed Consent in Research on Heroin-Assisted Treatment." *Bioethics* 29, no. 7 (2015): 462–69.

Vargas, Theresa. "U.S. Patent Office Cancels Redskins Trademark Registration, Says Name Is Disparaging." *Washington Post*, June 18, 2014. https://www.washingtonpost.com/local/us-patent-office-cancels-redskins-trademark-registration-says-name-is-disparaging/2014/06/18/e7737bb8-f6ee-11e3-8aa9-dad2ec039789_story.html.

Vesslère, Samuel Paul. "Caring for Others Is What Made Our Species Unique." *Psychology Today*, October 28, 2015. https://www.psychologytoday.com/us/blog/culture-mind-and-brain/201510/caring-others-is-what-made-our-species-unique.

Victory, Justin. "Pro-Confederate Groups, Fed Up with 'Political Correctness BS,' to Rally at Ole Miss." *Clarion Ledger*, February 19, 2019. https://www.clarionledger.com/story/news/2019/02/19/pro-confederate-flag-group-rally-ole-miss-liberal-conservative-colonel-reb/2916686002/.

Walker, David. *Appeal to the Coloured Citizens of the World*. 1830; reprint, Baltimore: Black Classic Press, 1993.

Walker, Marlon A. "Despite Pay Hikes, School Districts Still Hemorrhaging Teachers." *Atlanta Journal-Constitution*, July 19, 2019. https://www.ajc.com/news/local-education/despite-pay-hikes-school-districts-still-hemorrhaging-teachers/wj3I0VLffX9JJCDiBZtMSI/.

Walker, Robert. *The Shame of Poverty*. New York: Oxford University Press, 2014.

Walter, Jennifer K., and Eran P. Klein, eds. *The Story of Bioethics: From Seminal Works to Contemporary Explorations*. Washington, DC: Georgetown University Press, 2003.

Walters, Anne. "Inequities in Access to Education: Lessons from the COVID-19 Pandemic." *CABL: The Brown University Child and Adolescent Behavior Letter* 36, no. 8 (2020): 8.

Wamsley, Laurel. "The U.S. Is Uniquely Terrible at Protecting Children from Gun Violence." NPR, May 28, 2022. https://www.npr.org/2022/05/28/1101307932/texas-shooting-uvalde-gun-violence-children-teenagers.

Waterhouse, Carlton. "Avoiding Another Step in a Series of Unfortunate Legal Events." *Boston College Third World Law Journal* 26, no. 2 (2006): 207–65.

Watkins, Billy. "Rural, Poor, Successful: Every Arkansas KIPP Delta Grad Accepted into College." *Clarion Ledger*, March 7, 2013. http://www.clarionledger.com/article/20130217/OPINION03/302170002/.

Waxman, Chaim I. *The Stigma of Poverty: A Critique of Poverty Theories and Policies*. New York: Pergamon Press, 1977.

Weber, Eric Thomas. "Converging on Culture: Rawls, Rorty, and Dewey on Culture's Role in Justice." *Essays in the Philosophy of Humanism* 22, no. 2 (2014): 231–61.

Weber, Eric Thomas. "Correcting Political Correctness." *Philosophers Magazine* 1 (2016): 113–14.

Weber, Eric Thomas. *Democracy and Leadership: On Pragmatism and Virtue*. Lanham, MD: Lexington Books, 2013.

Weber, Eric Thomas. "Justice as an Evolving, Regulative Ideal." *Pragmatism Today* 6, no. 2 (2015): 105–16. http://www.pragmatismtoday.eu/winter2015/10%20Weber.pdf.

Weber, Eric Thomas. "Lessons from America's Public Philosopher." *Journal of Speculative Philosophy* 29, no. 1 (2015): 118–35.

Weber, Eric Thomas. "Mr. Bryant, Take Down the Flag." *Clarion Ledger*, September 20, 2015, 2C. https://www.clarionledger.com/story/opinion/columnists/2015/09/18/weber-mr-bryant-take-down-flag/72413896/.

Weber, Eric Thomas. "Rawls, Dewey, and Education." *Human Studies* 31 (2008): 361–82.

Weber, Eric Thomas. *Rawls, Dewey, and Constructivism: On the Epistemology of Justice*. London: Continuum, 2010.

Weber, Eric Thomas. "Reciprocal Goodwill Is Answer to Flag Issue." *USA Today*, December 7, 2015. https://www.usatoday.com/story/opinion/columnists/2015/12/07/weber-reciprocal-goodwill-answer-flag-issue/76628426/.

Weber, Eric Thomas. "Self-Respect, Positive Power, and Stoic Pragmatism: Rawls, Dewey, and Lachs on Justice and Happiness." In *John Lachs's Practical Philosophy: Critical Essays on His Thought with Replies and Bibliography* (Netherlands: Brill Publishers, 2018), 182–96.

Weber, Eric Thomas. "Self-Respect and a Sense of Positive Power: On Protection, Self-Affirmation, and Harm in the Charge of 'Acting White.'" *Journal of Speculative Philosophy* 30, no. 1 (2016): 45–63.

Weber, Eric Thomas. "Sometimes Heritage Does Harm." *Clarion Ledger*, June 27, 2015. https://www.academia.edu/attachments/38038257/download_file?s=work_strip.

Weber, Eric Thomas. "Stoic Pragmatism for Parenting a Child with Disabilities: An Essay Addressing Philosophers, Parents, Teachers, and Educational Policymakers." In *Disability and American Philosophies*, edited by Nate Whelan-Jackson and Daniel J. Brunson, 182–98. London: Routledge Press, 2022.

Weber, Eric Thomas. "Students' Flag Request Was 'Emotional' but Courageous." *Clarion Ledger*, October 30, 2015, 2C. https://www.clarionledger.com/story/opinion/columnists/2015/10/30/students-flag-request-emotional-but-courageous/74885008/.

Weber, Eric Thomas. *Uniting Mississippi: Democracy and Leadership in the South*. Jackson: University Press of Mississippi, 2015.

Weber, Eric Thomas. "What a Flag Has to Do with Justice." *Prindle Post*, July 8, 2015. https://www.prindleinstitute.org/2015/07/what-a-flag-has-to-do-with-justice/.

Weissman, Jordan. "This State College President Earned $6 Million Last Year. Should You Be Mad?" *Slate*, May 20, 2014. https://slate.com/business/2014/05/college-president-pay-is-it-too-high.html.

Wermund, Benjamin. "The Red State That Loves Free College: How Tennessee Is Making Bernie Sanders' Favorite Education Idea a Reality." *Politico*, January 16, 2019. https://www.politico.com/agenda/story/2019/01/16/tennessee-free-college-000867/.

Westheimer, Joel. *What Kind of Citizen? Educating Our Children for the Common Good*. New York: Teachers College Press, 2015.

White, Morton. *A Philosophy of Culture: The Scope of Holistic Pragmatism*. Princeton, NJ: Princeton University Press, 2002.

Williams, Bailey. "Sen. Bernie Sanders Calls U.S. Politics 'Oligarchy'; Considers Run in 2016." Medill News Service—United Press International, March 9, 2015. http://www.upi.com/Top_News/US/2015/03/09/Sen-Bernie-Sanders-calls-US-politics-oligarchy-considers-run-in-2016/8711425927237/.

Williams, Darby. "The Shrew's Dilemma." *Michigan Daily*, August 5, 2021. https://www.michigandaily.com/arts/campus-culture/the-shrews-dilemma/.

Williams, Tanya Young. "I'm Tired of Talking about Racism and a Judge's Bid to Abolish the Grand Jury." *Huffington Post*, December 12, 2014. http://

www.huffingtonpost.com/tanya-young-williams/im-tired-of-talking-about_
b_6304140.html.

Williams, Violet M. *Ten Little Nigger Boys*. London: Raphael Tuck and Sons, 1956.

Willoughby, Brian. "Speak Up at School: How to Respond to Everyday Prejudice, Bias and Stereotypes—A Guide for Teachers." Teaching Tolerance, a Project of the Southern Poverty Law Center. Montgomery, Alabama, 2012. http:// www.tolerance. org/sites/default/files/general/Speak_Up_at_School.pdf.

Wilson, James Q. "Convincing Black Students that Studying Hard Is Not 'Acting White.'" *Journal of Blacks in Higher Education* 39 (2003): 85–88.

Wilson, John. "Myths and Facts: How Real Is Political Correctness?" *William Mitchell Law Review* 22, no. 2 (1996): 517–43. https://open.mitchellhamline. edu/cgi/viewcontent.cgi?article=2045&context=wmlr.

Winthrop, Rebecca. "Universal Education Is an Investment for America." Brookings, September 24, 2009. https://www.brookings.edu/blog/up-front/2009/09/24/ universal-education-is-an-investment-for-america/.

Wolfgang, Ben. "Scores Show Students Aren't Ready for College." *Washington Times*, August 17, 2011. https://www.washingtontimes.com/news/2011/aug/ 17/scores-show-students-not-ready-college/.

Woods, John. "*Argumentum ad Baculum*." *Argumentation* 12 (1998): 493–504.

Wright, Robin. "Fury at America and Its Values Spreads Globally." *New Yorker*, June 1, 2020. https://www.newyorker.com/news/our-columnists/after-the- killing-of-george-floyd-fury-at-america-and-its-values-spreads-globally.

Wright, Susan E. "Blaming the Victim, Blaming Society, or Blaming the Discipline: Fixing Responsibility for Poverty and Homelessness." *Sociological Quarterly* 34, no. 1 (1993): 1–16.

Wyllie, Irvin G. *The Self-Made Man in America: The Myth of Rags to Riches*. New Brunswick, NJ: Rutgers University Press, 1954.

Yaffe, Gideon. "More on 'Ought' Implies 'Can' and the Principle of Alternate Possibilities." *Midwest Studies in Philosophy* 29 (2005): 307–12.

Yancy, George, and Charles Mills. "Lost in Rawlsland." *New York Times—The Stone*, November 16, 2014. https://opinionator.blogs.nytimes.com/2014/11/16/ lost-in-rawlsland.

Young, Steven M. "Beyond Neutrality." *University of Toronto Law Journal* 49 (1999): 151–65.

Zakaria, Fareed. "The Downward Path of Upward Mobility." *Washington Post*, November 9, 2011. https://www.washingtonpost.com/opinions/the-downward- path-of-upward-mobility/2011/11/09/gIQAegpS6M_story.html.

Zapotosky, Matt. "Ex-Ole Miss Student Admits Helping Put Noose on Statue of Civil Rights Figure." *Washington Post*, March 24, 2016. https://www. washingtonpost.com/news/post-nation/wp/2016/03/24/ex-ole-miss-student- admits-helping-put-noose-on-statue-of-civil-rights-figure/.

Zimmer, Carl. "CRISPR, 10 Years On: Learning to Rewrite the Code of Life." *New York Times*, June 27, 2022. https://www.nytimes.com/2022/06/27/science/crispr-gene-editing-10-years.html.

Zimmerman, Jonathan. "The Two Kinds of PC." *Inside Higher Ed*, June 16, 2016, https://www.insidehighered.com/views/2016/06/16/examination-two-kinds-political-correctness-essay.

Index